macOS® Sequoia™

by Guy Hart-Davis

for dummies®

A Wiley Brand

macOS® Sequoia™ For Dummies®

Published by: John Wiley & Sons, Inc., 111 River Street, Hoboken, NJ 07030-5774, www.wiley.com

For general information on our other products and services, please contact our Customer Care Department within the U.S. at 877-762-2974, outside the U.S. at 317-572-3993, or fax 317-572-4002. For technical support, please visit https://hub.wiley.com/community/support/dummies.

Wiley publishes in a variety of print and electronic formats and by print-on-demand. Some material included with standard print versions of this book may not be included in e-books or in print-on-demand. If this book refers to media that is not included in the version you purchased, you may download this material at http://booksupport.wiley.com. For more information about Wiley products, visit www.wiley.com.

Library of Congress Control Number: 2024946904

ISBN 978-1-394-28676-8 (pbk); ISBN 978-1-394-28677-5 (ebk); ISBN 978-1-394-28678-2 (ebk)

SKY10090585_111124

Contents at a Glance

Contents at a Glance

Table of Contents

Introduction

ooks like you've made three good choices: You have a Mac, macOS Sequoia (aka macOS version 15), and this book. If you're brand-new to the Mac, you're all set to start enjoying computing with the finest operating system on the planet. If you've been using your Mac and macOS for a while, you're ready to start enjoying using them even more. Sure, this book is a computer book, but it's not one of those dull books best suited to serve as a doorstop; it's one that makes discovering the ins and outs of macOS Sequoia easy and even fun!

About This Book

macOS Sequoia For Dummies is the latest revision of the best-selling book by legendary Mac maven Bob "Dr. Mac" LeVitus, technology columnist at the *Houston Chronicle*. The book has been completely updated for macOS Sequoia to cover all the latest features — such as Apple Intelligence, Writing Tools, and iPhone Mirroring — and everything else that has changed. This edition combines all the old, familiar features of dozens of previous editions with the very latest information on Macs and macOS Sequoia.

Why write a *For Dummies* book about macOS Sequoia? Well, Sequoia is a big, somewhat complicated, personal-computer operating system. So *macOS Sequoia For Dummies*, a not-so-big, not-too-complicated book, shows you what Sequoia is all about without boring you to tears or poking you with sharp objects.

This book is chock-full of information and advice, explaining everything you need to know about macOS Sequoia in easy-to-understand language — along with time-saving tips, tricks, techniques, and step-by-step instructions. I feel confident that you'll find what you need to know about using macOS Sequoia in this book.

Still, a book this size can't explain everything you might want to know about an operating system the size of macOS Sequoia and the apps that run on it. If you're looking for information on topics such as Microsoft Office, Apple's lifestyle and productivity apps (such as iMovie, GarageBand, Numbers, and Pages), or programming, I recommend you look at other books published by Wiley. The Wiley website (https://www.wiley.com/) is the best place to start.

Within this book, you may note that some web addresses break across two lines of text. If you're reading this book in print and want to visit one of these webpages, simply key in the web address exactly as it's noted in the text, as though the line break doesn't exist. If you're reading it as an ebook, you've got it easy: Just click or tap the web address to be taken directly to the webpage.

Foolish Assumptions

Although I know what happens when you assume, I've made a few assumptions anyway. I assume that you, gentle reader, know nothing about using macOS — beyond knowing what a Mac is, that you want to use macOS, that you want to understand macOS without having to digest an incomprehensible technical manual, and that you made the right choice by selecting this particular book. So I do my best to explain each new concept fully.

Icons Used in This Book

Little pictures (icons) appear to the side of text throughout this book. Consider these icons to be miniature road signs, telling you a little something extra about the topic at hand. Here's what the icons look like and what they mean.

TIP

Look for Tip icons to find the juiciest morsels: shortcuts, tips, and undocumented secrets about Sequoia. Try them all; impress your friends!

REMEMBER

When you see this icon, it means that this particular morsel is something you may want to memorize (or at least write on your shirt cuff).

TECHNICAL STUFF

Put on your propeller-beanie hat and pocket protector; these tidbits include the truly geeky stuff. They're certainly not required reading, but they'll help you grasp the background, get the bigger picture, or both.

WARNING

Read these notes very carefully. Warning icons flag important cautionary information that could save you any amount of grief.

This icon highlights things new and different in macOS Sequoia.

NEW

App icons (such as the Launchpad icon shown here) and interface icons show you key items that you'll be clicking, dragging, and otherwise interacting with.

Beyond the Book

In addition to what you're reading right now, this book comes with a free access-anywhere cheat sheet that provides handy shortcuts for use with macOS Sequoia, offers recommendations for backing up your Mac to avoid losing data, and more. To get this cheat sheet, simply go to www.dummies.com and type **macOS Sequoia For Dummies Cheat Sheet** in the Search box.

Where to Go from Here

The first few chapters of this book explain the basic things you need to understand to operate your Mac effectively. If you're new to Macs and macOS Sequoia, start there.

Although macOS Sequoia looks slightly different from previous versions, it largely works the same as always. The first part of the book presents concepts so basic that if you've been using a Mac for long, you may think you know it all — and okay, you might know some (or most) of it. But remember that not-so-old-timers need a solid foundation, too. So skim the stuff you already know, and you'll get to the better stuff soon enough.

Enough of the introduction. Turn the page, and let's get started!

1
Getting Started with macOS

Chapter **1**

macOS Sequoia 101 (Prerequisites: None)

S o you're the proud owner of a Mac running macOS Sequoia? Great choice! Your Mac gives you powerful hardware in a sleek package, and Sequoia — macOS version 15, if you're feeling formal — puts an intuitive and easy-to-use interface on Unix, the best industrial-strength operating system in the world.

In this chapter, we'll make sure you're set up to put your Mac and macOS to good use. We'll start by taking a quick look at what macOS actually does. We'll then move along to getting started by the numbers: turning on your Mac, going through the setup routine if it's a new Mac or a new install, logging in, and meeting the desktop. We'll review how to use your mouse or trackpad. We'll go through a few essentials of treating your Mac well and avoiding avoidable damage, then look at how to get help on Macs, macOS, and apps. Finally, we'll talk about Apple's new feature group, Apple Intelligence, and where to find it on your Mac.

If your Mac is all set up and you're comfortable with start-up, login, navigation, and shutdown, feel free to skip this chapter and move ahead to whichever chapter will most benefit you immediately.

Before we start, a quick word about macOS version numbers and version names . . .

TECHNICAL STUFF

Each version of macOS has both a version number and a version name. This book covers macOS version 15, whose version name is Sequoia. Most people prefer the version names because they're easier to remember.

What about previous versions? Okay (deep breath): macOS version 14 was Sonoma, version 13 was Ventura, version 12 was Monterey, version 11 was Big Sur, version 10.15 was Catalina, 10.14 was Mojave, 10.13 was High Sierra, and 10.12 was Sierra. Before that, Apple called the operating system "OS X" (with the X pronounced "ten") rather than "macOS." OS X version 10.11 was El Capitan, 10.10 was Yosemite, 10.9 was Mavericks, 10.8 was Mountain Lion, 10.7 was Lion, 10.6 was Snow Leopard, 10.5 was Leopard, 10.4 was Tiger, 10.3 was Panther, 10.2 was Jaguar, 10.1 was Puma, and 10.0 was Cheetah.

Okay, What Does macOS Do?

The operating system (that is, the *OS* part of *macOS*) controls the basic and most important functions of your computer. In the case of macOS and your Mac, the operating system

>> Manages memory

>> Controls how windows, icons, and menus work

>> Keeps track of files

>> Manages networking and security

>> Does housekeeping (but only its own — not yours)

Other forms of software, such as word processors and web browsers, rely on the OS to create and maintain the environment in which they work. When you create a memo, for example, the word processor provides the tools for you to type and format the information and save it in a file. In the background, the OS is the muscle for the word processor, performing the following crucial functions:

>> Providing the mechanism for drawing and moving the on-screen window in which you write the memo

>> Keeping track of the file when you save it

>> Helping the word processor create drop-down menus and dialogs for you to interact with

>> Communicating with other programs

There's much, much more — but you get the idea.

Turning On Your Mac

No great surprises here: You turn on your Mac by pressing the power button — once you find it. Here's where to look:

>> **MacBook:** At the upper-right corner of the keyboard

>> **iMac:** At the back of the screen, lower-left corner or lower-right corner

>> **Mac mini, Mac Studio:** At the back of the enclosure

>> **Mac Pro:** On the front panel

 The power button usually looks like the little circle icon you see in the margin — but on some Mac models, the power button doubles as the Touch ID button for authenticating you via your fingerprint and doesn't show the icon.

What you should see on start-up

 When you turn on your Mac, the Mac powers up, checks the hardware, and then loads macOS. While loading macOS, the Mac displays a white Apple logo in the middle of the screen, as shown in the margin here.

If you need to set up macOS Sequoia, the setup routine begins automatically. See the following section, "Setting Up macOS Sequoia." Otherwise (assuming Sequoia has already been set up), the login screen appears, and you can log in. See the section "Logging In," later in this chapter.

What you may see if things go wrong

If something is wrong with your Mac, you may see any of the following on start-up:

>> **Blue/black/gray screen of death:** If any of your hardware fails when it's tested, you may see a blue, black, or gray screen. See Chapter 22 for moves to try to get your Mac well again. Failing those, it may need repairs. If your computer is under warranty, set up a Genius Bar appointment at your nearest Apple Store or dial 1-800-SOS-APPL (or the equivalent number in your country or region), and a customer-service person can tell you what to do.

>> **Prohibitory sign or flashing question mark in a folder:** These icons mean that your Mac can't find a start-up disk, hard drive, USB drive, or network server containing a valid Mac operating system. See Chapter 22 for ways to ease your Mac's ills.

>> **Kernel panic:** You may occasionally see a block of text in several languages, including English, as shown in Figure 1-1. This means that your Mac has experienced a *kernel panic*, the most severe type of system crash. Restart your Mac (there's no other choice). If either of these messages recurs, see Chapter 22 for advice.

FIGURE 1-1:
If you're seeing something like this, consult Chapter 22 for suggestions.

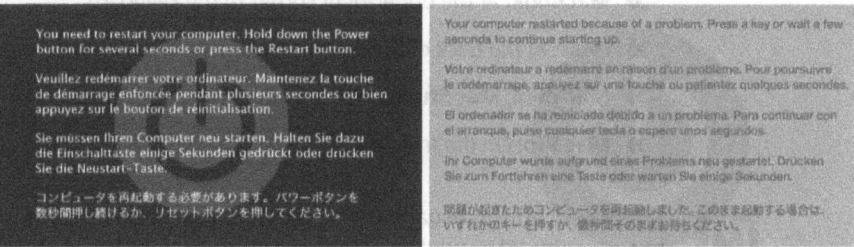

Okay, assuming you're not seeing any of the above nasties, let's return to our scheduled programming: first, setup (if your Mac needs it), and then login.

Setting Up macOS Sequoia

If your Mac is new, or if you've just installed Sequoia from scratch rather than upgrading it from an earlier version of macOS, you'll need to run through a setup routine. The following list explains the main steps:

>> **Specify your country or region.** On the Select Your Country or Region screen, click your country, and then click the Continue button.

» **Choose Accessibility features.** On the Accessibility screen, set up any accessibility features you need by clicking the Vision button, the Motor button, the Hearing button, or the Cognitive button, and then working through the resulting screens. You can set up most accessibility features at this point if you know that you or other users of the Mac will need them. However, you may find it better to set up only those features that you need now to help you complete the setup routine, and then configure other accessibility features after setup. If you don't need to set up any accessibility features now, click the Not Now button to move right along.

» **Connect to a Wi-Fi network.** On the Select Your Wi-Fi Network screen, click the network you want your Mac to use, and then type the network password in the Password box. Once the connection is established, click the Continue button.

TIP

If your Mac has an Ethernet port that is connected to your wired network via a cable, you won't need to connect to a Wi-Fi network.

» **Read about data and privacy.** On the Data & Privacy screen, read the information, and click the Learn More link if you want to learn more. Click the Continue button when you're ready to move along.

» **Choose whether to transfer your data to this Mac.** On the Migration Assistant screen, select the From a Mac, Time Machine Backup, or Startup Disk option button if you want to transfer data from one of these Mac-based sources; or select the From a Windows PC option button if you want to transfer data from a PC; and then click the Continue button and follow the prompts to specify the data. If you don't want to transfer data at all, or you want to transfer it later, click the Not Now button.

» **Sign in using your Apple ID.** On the Sign In with Your Apple ID screen, type the email address associated with your Apple ID. Enter the password, and then click the Continue button.

» **Accept the Terms and Conditions.** On the Terms and Conditions screen, read the terms and conditions. If you want to proceed, click the Agree button, and then click the Agree button again in the confirmation dialog.

» **Read the Find My information.** On the Find My screen, read how the Find My feature helps you retrieve your Mac when it goes missing and protects your Mac with Activation Lock. Click the Continue button to proceed.

» **Choose whether to enable Location Services.** On the Enable Location Services screen, select the Enable Location Services on This Mac check box if you want to turn on Location Services, which tell apps like Maps and services like Spotlight Suggestions where your Mac is located. Once more, click the Continue button to proceed.

>> **Choose whether to share your Analytics information.** On the Analytics screen, choose whether to share your analytics data with Apple and with app developers. This is a public-spirited action that helps Apple and the developers improve their software, and Apple anonymizes the data so that it cannot come back to haunt you. Click the Continue button to move along.

>> **Choose whether to enable Screen Time.** On the Screen Time screen, read the details of the Screen Time feature, which enables you to set usage limits for the Mac for yourself and other users. Click the Continue button if you want to enable Screen Time now; if not, click the Set Up Later button.

TIP

The setup routine implies Screen Time is something you should want to use. Screen Time can certainly be useful, especially if you need a commitment device to limit your Mac usage in certain ways (such as setting time limits on social media) or you need to manage family members' usage. But if your Mac is yours alone and you don't need or want Screen Time, don't set it up. Screen Time is not a notorious resource hog, but it certainly doesn't make your Mac run faster. You can set up Screen Time later if needed.

>> **Choose whether to enable Ask Siri.** On the Siri screen, select or clear the Enable Ask Siri check box, as needed, and then click the Continue button. If you enable Ask Siri, choose a voice on the Select a Siri Voice screen. Click the Continue button to keep moving along.

>> **Choose whether to set up Touch ID.** If your MacBook or your Mac's keyboard includes a Touch ID fingerprint reader, set up Touch ID fingerprint recognition by clicking the Continue button on the Touch ID screen, and then following the prompts. If you prefer to set up Touch ID later, click the Set Up Touch ID Later link.

>> **Choose Light Mode, Dark Mode, or Auto Mode.** On the Choose Your Look screen, click the Light button, the Dark button, or the Auto button, as needed. Auto Mode switches between light and dark to match the time of day in your current location. Click the Continue button one final time.

The setup routine finishes, and your desktop appears. Move on to the section "Meeting the macOS Desktop," later in this chapter.

Logging In

After starting up successfully, macOS displays the login screen. Figure 1-2 shows an example of the login screen with four user accounts set up on the Mac. As you can see, the user accounts appear at the bottom of the screen.

Input language

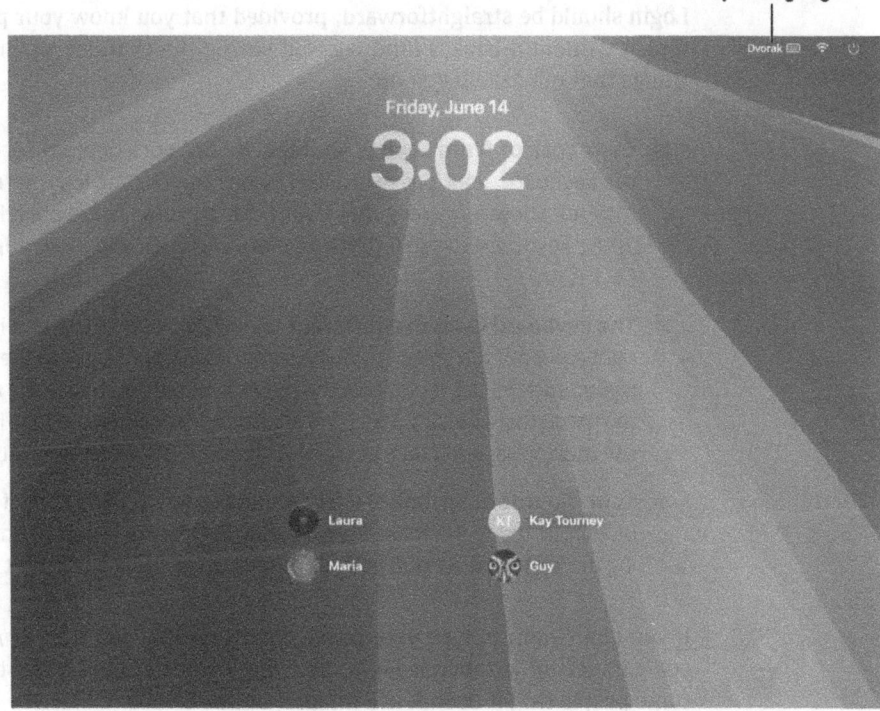

FIGURE 1-2:
On the login
screen, click your
username.
You may
sometimes
need to
change the
input language.

Friday, June 14

3:02

Laura   Kay Tourney

Maria   Guy

Click your username to display the Enter Password field (see the left screen in Figure 1-3), type your password, and then press Return or click the little right-arrow-in-a-circle to the right of the password (see the right screen in Figure 1-3). The arrow appears once you've typed something in the Enter Password field.

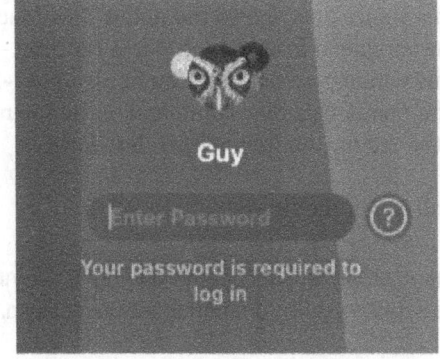

FIGURE 1-3:
Type your
password (left),
and then press
Return or click
the arrow (right).

Guy

Enter Password

Your password is required to log in

Guy

••••••••••••••••

Your password is required to log in

Login should be straightforward, provided that you know your password and can type it without mistakes (and without seeing the characters). But there are three things that might trip you up:

>> **Caps Lock or Num Lock is enabled.** If Caps Lock or Num Lock is enabled on the keyboard, your password likely won't match. The login screen may or may not show a warning that Caps Lock or Num Lock is on. If in doubt, look at the keyboard to see if there's a status light showing that Caps Lock or Num Lock is on.

>> **The keyboard is set to a different layout.** Look at the readout in the upper-right corner of the screen to make sure the keyboard is set to the appropriate layout, such as U.S. If not, click the readout, and then choose the right layout on the menu that appears. This problem occurs only when the Mac is configured to use multiple layouts, such as the U.S. layout and the Dvorak layout.

>> **Your Bluetooth keyboard isn't connected or isn't working.** If you're using a Bluetooth keyboard, make sure it's showing its usual lights. If not, try connecting the keyboard via USB (if it supports that) or using a different keyboard.

TIP

If you don't want to type your password every time you start or restart your Mac, you can set up automatic login. Full disclosure: This is almost never wise, but some people find it useful. See Chapter 20 for details.

Meeting the macOS Desktop

Once you've logged in, the macOS desktop appears. Figure 1-4 shows how the desktop looks before you customize it. The desktop is mostly empty space at first, so for visual interest, this figure also shows the About This Mac window, whose macOS readout shows the version of macOS your Mac is running — Sequoia 14.0 in this example. To open this window, click the icon in the upper-left corner of the screen, and then click the About This Mac command on the menu that opens. To close the window, click the red button in its upper-left corner.

Here are the elements you see in the figure:

>> **Apple menu:** This menu always appears at the left end of the menu bar. It gives you access to essential system commands, including Sleep, Restart, Shut Down, and Log Out.

>> **Menu bar:** This bar appears across the top of the screen and displays the menus for the active app. In Figure 1-4, the active app is Finder, the macOS file-management app. Chapters 4 and 5 dig into Finder in depth.

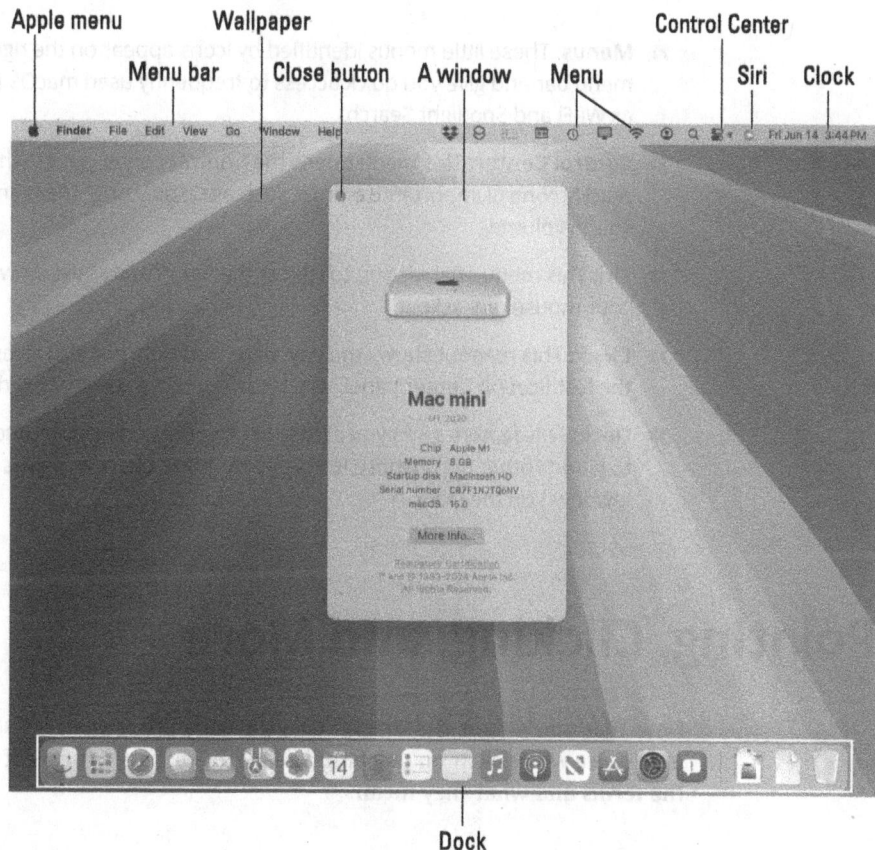

Apple menu Wallpaper Control Center

Menu bar Close button A window Menu Siri Clock

FIGURE 1-4:
The default
desktop with the
About This Mac
window open.

Dock

>> **Wallpaper:** This is the background that appears on the desktop. macOS includes a wide range of wallpapers, but you can also use your own pictures. Each major release of macOS includes a new wallpaper designed to suit that release's character.

TIP

Wallpaper — on the desktop? If the term seems strange — yes, it is. OS X and earlier versions of macOS used to call the wallpaper the "desktop background," but Apple switched to "wallpaper" a few years ago to make macOS more like iOS and iPadOS, which use the term "wallpaper" for the background on the iPhone and iPad.

>> **Close button:** You click this button to close the window on which it appears.

>> **A window:** Most apps and features appear in separate windows on the desktop. You can reposition windows as needed. Chapter 2 tells you what you need to know about windows.

>> **Menus:** These little menus identified by icons appear on the right side of the menu bar and give you quick access to frequently used macOS features, such as Wi-Fi and Spotlight Search.

>> **Control Center:** This menu opens the Control Center panel, which lets you quickly control important settings, such as display brightness and sound volume.

>> **Siri:** This menu enables you to trigger the Siri virtual assistant with a click of your mouse or trackpad.

>> **Clock:** This readout shows the day, date, and time but also gives you access to the Notification Center panel, which can contain a variety of widgets.

>> **Dock:** This feature gives you access to all your running apps and enables you to launch other apps whose icons appear here. Chapter 3 gives you the lowdown on the Dock.

Pointing, Clicking, and More

Now that you've got the macOS desktop on your screen, let's take a minute to make sure we're clear on pointing and all the different forms of clicking. Here are the terms and what they mean:

>> **Point:** Before you can click or press anything, *point* to it. Place your hand on your mouse, and move it so that the pointer arrow is over the object, such as an icon or a button.

If you're using a trackpad, slide your finger lightly across the pad until the pointer arrow is over the object.

>> **Click:** Also called *single click.* Use your index finger to push the mouse button (or the left mouse button if your mouse has more than one) down and then let it come back up. Usually the button will make a clicking sound. Use a single click to select an icon, press a button, or activate a check box or window.

In other words, first you point and then you click — *point and click,* in computer lingo.

If you're using a trackpad, press down on it to click. You can also configure the trackpad so that you can tap to click; see Chapter 6.

>> **Double-click:** *Click twice* in rapid succession. You double-click to open a folder or to launch a file or app.

Trackpad users: Press down on the pad two times in rapid succession. If you've enabled Tap to Click, you can double-tap to double-click. Again, see Chapter 6.

>> **Control-click or right-click:** Also called *secondary click*, this click displays the *contextual menu* or *shortcut menu* for the object you click — a menu that contains commands related to that object. Early Mac mice had only a single button, so to issue the secondary click, you would hold down the Control key on the keyboard while clicking. You can still use this method if you like, even if your mouse bristles with buttons; but usually it's easier to click with the secondary mouse button. Usually, this is the right button — hence the term *right-click*.

On the trackpad, either hold down the Control key while you press down on the trackpad with one finger, or tap the trackpad with two fingers without holding down the Control key.

If tapping your trackpad with two fingers didn't bring up a little menu, check your Trackpad pane in System Settings (see Chapter 6).

>> **Drag:** *Dragging* something usually means you have to click it first and hold down the mouse or trackpad button to keep hold of the object. Then you move the mouse (or your finger on the trackpad) so that the pointer and the selected object move across the screen to the object's destination, at which point you release the mouse button or trackpad button to drop the object. This technique is often called *drag-and-drop*.

>> **Wiggle (or jiggle):** If you lose the pointer on your screen, just wiggle your mouse back and forth (or jiggle your finger back and forth on the trackpad) for a few seconds. The pointer magically gets much bigger, making it easier to see. When you stop wiggling or jiggling, the pointer returns to its normal size.

>> **Choose an item from a menu:** To get to macOS menu commands, you open a menu and then choose the option you want. Click the menu name to open the menu, and then click the command you want. When the menu is open, you can also type the first letter or letters of the item to select it, and then press the spacebar or Return to execute the command.

TIP

You can also use the menus a different way. Move the pointer over the menu's name, and then click to open the menu. Keep holding down the button and drag downward until you select the command you want. When the command is high-lighted, let go of the button to execute the command. Some people find this method preferable, but even if you don't, it can come in handy. For example, you may realize mid-click that the pointer is pointing at the wrong menu item. To fix that, keep holding the click down, move the pointer to the right menu item, and then release the click.

REMEMBER

The terms given in the preceding list apply to all Macs — both MacBooks and Mac desktop systems. If you use a trackpad with your Mac, you'll want to add a few more terms — such as *tap*, *swipe*, *rotate*, *pinch*, and *spread* — to your lexicon. You can read all about them in chapters 2 and 11.

Putting Your Mac to Sleep and Shutting It Down

When you've finished using your Mac for now, you can put it to sleep or shut it down. If you're planning to use your Mac again in the near future, as will usually be the case, put it to sleep. But if you're not intending to use your Mac for several days, shutting down is the better choice.

WARNING

If you have a MacBook, and it will be enclosed in a bag or briefcase for more than a few hours, turn it off. Otherwise, it could overheat — even in Sleep mode.

Putting your Mac to sleep

When you put your Mac to sleep, it goes into a state in which it consumes only minimal amounts of electricity but from which it can usually be ready to use in a few seconds when you wake it.

To put your Mac to sleep, choose ⇨ Sleep. To wake it, press any key on the keyboard or click the mouse or trackpad.

TIP

You can put a MacBook to sleep by closing its lid and wake it (you've guessed!) by opening the lid.

TIP

You can configure macOS to put your Mac to sleep after a specified period of inactivity. See Chapter 20 to learn how to do this.

Shutting down your Mac

Always shut down your Mac via macOS rather than just switching off the power or unplugging it. Choose ⇨ Shut Down, and then click the Shut Down button in the Are You Sure You Want to Shut Down Your Computer Now? dialog (see Figure 1-5).

TIP

When the Shut Down button is highlighted, you can activate it by pressing the Return key rather than clicking it. The same goes for any highlighted button.

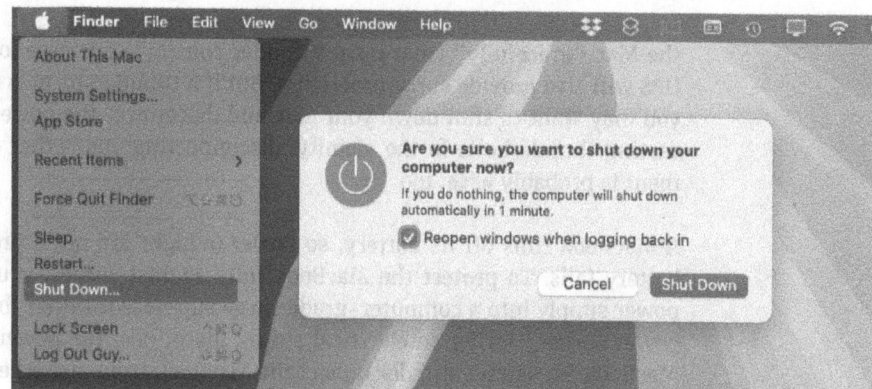

FIGURE 1-5:
Always shut down
your Mac by
choosing
⌘ ⇨ Shut Down
and then clicking
Shut Down in the
confirmation
dialog.

The Are You Sure You Want to Shut Down Your Computer Now? dialog includes the Reopen Windows When Logging Back In check box. If you select this check box, your Mac will start back up with the same windows (and apps) that were open when you shut down (or restarted). This can be a real time-saver, but you can clear the check box if you don't want those windows and apps reopened.

WARNING

Turning off the power without shutting down macOS can corrupt your files. At start-up, macOS checks the Mac's filesystem and attempts to fix any problems that it detects, so usually macOS is able to recover from the Mac being shut down improperly. Even so, make sure you shut down your Mac properly unless you absolutely cannot. Really, the only time you should turn off your Mac without shutting down properly is when your screen is completely frozen or when the Mac has crashed due to a kernel panic and you've already tried all the potential fixes explained in Chapter 22.

Care and Feeding of Your Mac

To keep your Mac happy and fully functional, you should feed it consistently, treat it gently, and back up your data regularly.

Feed your Mac

Your Mac's preferred diet is clean electricity, and it will get cranky if denied this sustenance.

To protect a desktop Mac against power outages or surges, power it via an uninterruptible power supply (UPS) rather than directly from a power socket. The UPS will enable the Mac to ride out brief outages and will give you time to shut down the Mac "gracefully" (that means "under control") during a longer outage. The UPS will also provide surge protection. But if a thunderstorm is rumbling nearby, you may want to shut down your Mac and disconnect the power cable. If Zeus is casting thunderbolts in the vicinity, disconnecting your other electronic equipment is probably wise, too.

A MacBook runs off its battery, so power outages are not a problem unless the battery fails. To protect the MacBook fully against surges, you should plug the power supply into a computer-grade surge suppressor rather than directly into a power socket. During an electrical storm, disconnect the power supply from the MacBook for safety; also disconnect the MacBook from any other devices that are connected to power sockets, such as external drives that have their own power supplies. You can then continue using the MacBook if you like.

Treat your Mac gently

Apple's design esthetic prioritizes style over substance. As a result, Apple's hardware products look great but are less tough than they might be. That means you should treat your Mac as gently as possible. Even if the Mac has a solid-state drive rather than a more fragile hard disk with spinning platters, the Mac is chock-full of sensitive components that you can damage with minimal effort.

WARNING

Definitely do not use household window cleaners or paper towels on your Mac's screen. Either one can harm it. Instead, use a soft clean cloth (preferably microfiber), and if you're going to use a liquid or spray, make sure it's specifically designed not to harm computer displays. Finally, only spray the cleaner onto a *cloth*; never spray anything directly onto the screen.

Back up your data

If the files on your Mac mean anything to you, you must back them up. Even if your most important file is your last saved game of Disco Elysium, you still need to back up your files. Fortunately, macOS includes a powerful but easy-to-use backup utility called Time Machine that can back up your data to an external hard drive. See Chapter 21 to learn how to use Time Machine. If you use Apple's iCloud service, you can use its online synchronization as another means of backing up your files.

Getting Help

macOS Sequoia includes excellent built-in help. Click the Help menu to reveal the Search field, the Tips for Your Mac item, and the macOS Help item. Click the macOS Help item to open the window shown in Figure 1-6.

Show Sidebar icon

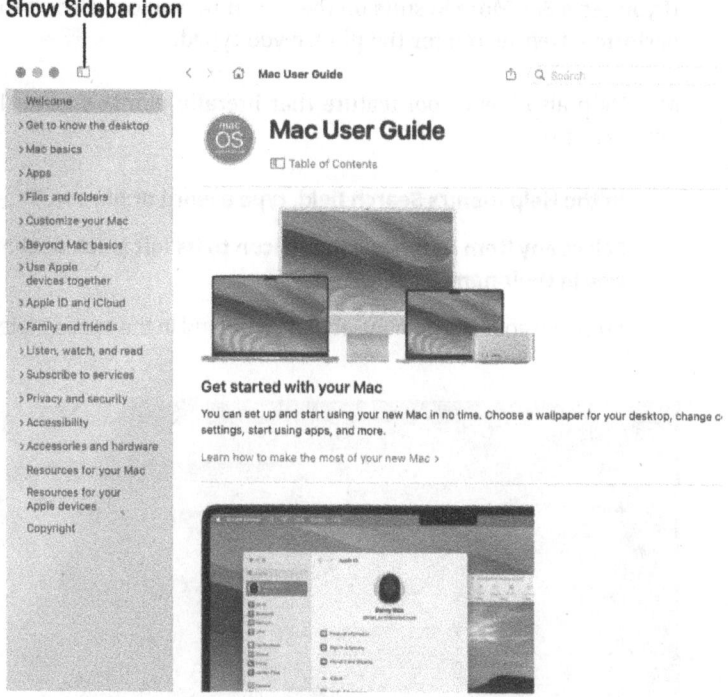

FIGURE 1-6:
Mac Help stands
ready to help you
figure out your
Mac and macOS.

TIP

Press Shift+⌘+? to open Help for the current app.

You can browse Help by clicking a topic in the table of contents and then clicking a subtopic. If you don't see the table of contents, click the Show Sidebar icon, labeled in Figure 1-6.

To search Mac Help, simply type a word or phrase in either Search field — the one in the Help menu itself or the one near the top of the Help window on the right side — and then press Return. In a few seconds, your Mac provides one or more articles to read, which (theoretically) are related to your question. As long as your Mac is connected to the Internet, search results include articles from the Apple online support database.

REMEMBER

Although you don't have to be connected to the Internet to use Mac Help, you do need an Internet connection to get the most out of it. (Chapter 13 can help you set up an Internet connection, if you don't have one.) That's because macOS installs only certain help articles on your hard drive and downloads others as needed from the Apple website, giving you the most up-to-date information. What it downloads, it leaves on your hard drive for future reference.

If you see a See More Results on the Web link, you can click it to launch Safari and perform a web search for the phrase you typed.

TIP

Mac Help also has a cool feature that literally points you to the commands you need. Try this:

1. **In the Help menu's Search field, type a word or phrase.**

2. **Select any item that has a menu icon to its left (such as the items with *side* in their names in Figure 1-7).**

   An arrow appears, pointing at that command in the appropriate menu.

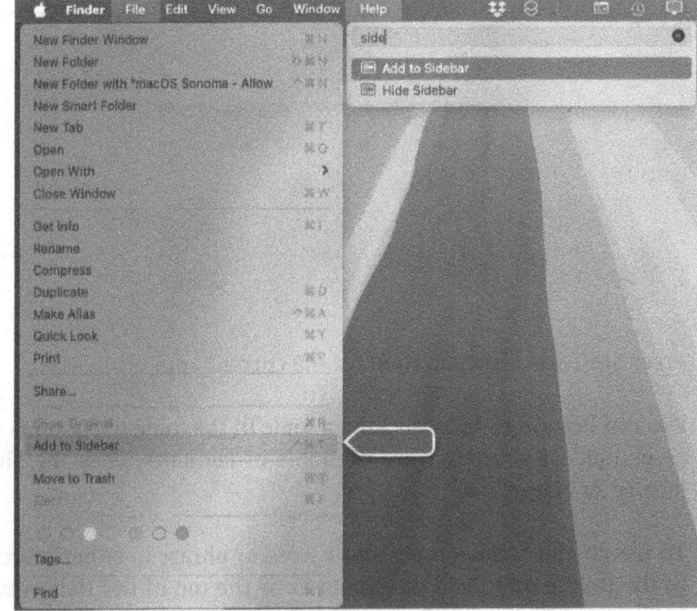

FIGURE 1-7:
Highlight a command in the Help menu to display an arrow showing where to find the command.

Finally, don't forget that most apps have their own Help systems, so if you want general help with your Mac, you need to first click the Finder icon on the Dock, click the desktop, or press the app-switching shortcut, ⌘+Tab, to activate Finder. Once Finder is active, you can choose Mac Help from Finder's Help menu.

Getting the Lowdown on Apple Intelligence

Unless you've been living in a lead-lined room, you've probably heard of Apple Intelligence, the suite of artificial intelligence (AI) features that Apple has added to macOS, iOS (the iPhone's operating system), and iPadOS (three guesses). Apple Intelligence aims to use AI tools to make your Apple devices and their apps more useful to you while protecting your privacy.

Here are seven quick examples of ways Apple Intelligence can help you with tasks on your Mac:

» **Proofread and rewrite text.** When you write an email message, you can have Apple Intelligence proofread it for you to identify errors and suggest fixes. Better yet, you can get Apple Intelligence to rewrite the message to change its tone — for example, changing from a casual tone to a more formal, professional tone. We'll look at how to use these features in the Mail app in Chapter 15, but you can use them elsewhere as well.

» **Summarize content.** Apple Intelligence can condense a long message, document, or report into a summary that you can read quickly. This feature can be a great time-saver.

» **Make Siri more helpful.** Siri, Apple's virtual assistant, has been helping out on the Mac since Apple released macOS Sierra in 2016, but Apple Intelligence boosts Siri to impressive new levels. One change that sounds minor but makes a huge difference is that Siri retains the content of your requests rather than treating each subsequent request as a blank slate, so you don't have to keep repeating yourself. Another improvement is that you can interact with Siri either by speaking or by typing, and you can switch easily between the two. Chapter 9 covers Siri.

» **Search for photos and videos.** Even if you diligently apply keywords to your photos and videos in the Photos app, searching for particular items can still be a slow and unwieldy process. But with Apple Intelligence, you can describe what you want in natural language — for example, you might say "black-and-white cat sprawled on my laptop" — and have Photos round up the matching items for you.

» **Create Memory movies to order.** If you've used the Photos app on the Mac, the iPhone, or the iPad, you know how Photos creates short movies called Memories from related photos. Up until now, Photos has just gone ahead and created Memories on its own initiative. Now, however, you can get Apple Intelligence to create a specific Memory movie for you.

>> **Create and edit images.** Apple Intelligence's Image Playground feature enables you to create images by supplying a text description of what you want an image to contain. As of this writing, Apple has announced Image Playground, but it is not yet available.

>> **Create custom emoji.** If you like emoji, those small but expressive icons, you'll likely love being able to create custom ones using Apple Intelligence. Apple calls these custom emoji "Genmoji," and you can create them in various apps, such as the Messages app (see Chapter 15).

When you use Apple Intelligence features, the device you're using — your Mac, iPhone, or iPad — performs the processing if it can. When the Apple Intelligence feature needs more complex computation than your device can provide, Apple Intelligence transfers the required data across the Internet to Apple's servers, which crunch the numbers and return the result. When transferring data across the Internet, Apple uses an approach called Private Cloud Compute that uses various technologies, including anonymization and encryption, to keep your data secure and private.

When your Apple Intelligence tasks require input from ChatGPT or other tools provided by OpenAI, a market-leading AI company, Apple Intelligence notifies you of the planned data transfer and gets your approval before performing it.

IN THIS CHAPTER

» **Understanding Finder**

» **Checking out the parts of a window**

» **Opening a dialog with your Mac**

» **Resizing, moving, and closing windows**

» **Working with menus**

Chapter 2

Desktop and Windows and Menus (Oh My!)

This chapter introduces important features of macOS, starting with the first things you see when you log in: Finder and its desktop. After a quick look around the desktop, you dig into two of its most useful features: windows and menus.

Windows are (and have always been) an integral part of using your Mac — in fact, Macs had windows before Microsoft Windows was invented. Windows in Finder show you the contents of different storage containers, such as the SSD (solid-state drive), a flash (thumb) drive, a network drive, a disk image, or a folder. Windows in apps do many things, such as displaying a spreadsheet or an email message.

Menus are another integral part of macOS. The latter part of this chapter starts you out with a few menu basics so that you're ready to learn more advanced moves later in the book.

Touring Finder and the macOS Desktop

Finder is the app that creates the desktop, keeps track of your files and folders, and is always running. Just about everything you do on your Mac begins and ends with Finder. It's where you manage files, store documents, launch apps, and much more. Mastering Finder and the desktop is the first step in mastering your Mac.

Finder has the following key features:

>> **Desktop:** The *desktop* is the area behind the windows and the Dock. In macOS Sequoia, the default desktop background is a colorful abstract graphic. Apple calls the desktop background the *wallpaper*.

The desktop also may contain an icon for your Mac's start-up disk.

TIP

If you don't see a disk icon on the desktop, never fear — you learn how to enable this behavior in Chapter 4.

The desktop isn't a window, yet it acts like one. Like a folder or disk window, the desktop can contain icons. But unlike most windows, the desktop is always there behind any open windows. You may find the desktop a handy place to keep folders or documents you use frequently.

TECHNICAL STUFF

Some folks use the terms *desktop* and *Finder* interchangeably to refer to the total Mac environment you see after you log in — the icons, windows, menus, and all that other cool stuff. This book refers to the app you use when the desktop is showing as *Finder*, whereas *desktop* means the area behind your windows and the Dock.

>> **Dock:** The Dock is Finder's main navigation shortcut tool. It makes getting to frequently used items easy, even when you have a screen full of windows. Plus it's extremely customizable, as you find out in Chapter 3.

>> **Icons:** Icons are the little pictures you see in folder and disk windows and on your desktop. Icons represent the things you work with on your Mac, such as apps, documents, folders, utilities, and more.

>> **Windows:** Opening most items (by double-clicking their icons) makes a window appear. Windows in Finder show you the contents of disk drives and folders; windows in apps usually show the contents of documents. In the sections that follow, you learn the full scoop on macOS windows.

>> **Menus:** Menus let you choose to do things, such as create new folders; duplicate files; and cut, copy, or paste text. You learn menu basics later in this chapter in the "Sampling the Menus" section; you find details about working with menus for specific tasks throughout this book.

In this chapter, you get comfortable with Finder and the desktop. In Chapter 8, you learn how to navigate and manage your files in Finder. But before you start using Finder, you need to know the basics of working with windows and menus.

Dissecting a Window

Windows appear everywhere in macOS. When you open a folder, Finder displays its contents in a window. When you write a letter, the document that you're working on appears in a window. When you browse the Internet, webpages appear in a window . . . and so on.

Most windows look largely the same from one app to another, but some apps add features around the edges of the document window and on toolbars. For example, Microsoft Word packs extra features, such as Quick Access Toolbar and the Search field, into the title bar of its window to save space.

Many windows are divided into separate sections, which are called *panes* to maintain the window metaphor. Each pane typically displays a different kind of information. For example, many windows use the sidebar, a pane at the side of the window, to provide navigation.

When you finish this chapter, which focuses exclusively on Finder windows, you'll know how to use most windows in most apps.

The following list shows you the main features of a typical Finder window (see Figure 2-1). Later sections of this chapter discuss these features in greater detail.

TIP

If your windows don't look exactly like Figure 2-1, don't worry. You can make your windows look and feel any way you like. As the upcoming "Working with Windows" section explains, you can easily move and resize windows.

Meanwhile, here's what you see in the Finder window:

>> **Close, Minimize, and Zoom buttons:** Click the Close button to close the window, click the Minimize button to minimize it, or click the Zoom button to enlarge it. See the next section for more details.

>> **Back icon:** Click this icon to go back to the previous folder or location displayed in this window.

>> **Forward icon:** Click this icon to go forward again to a folder from which you've gone back (by clicking the Back icon).

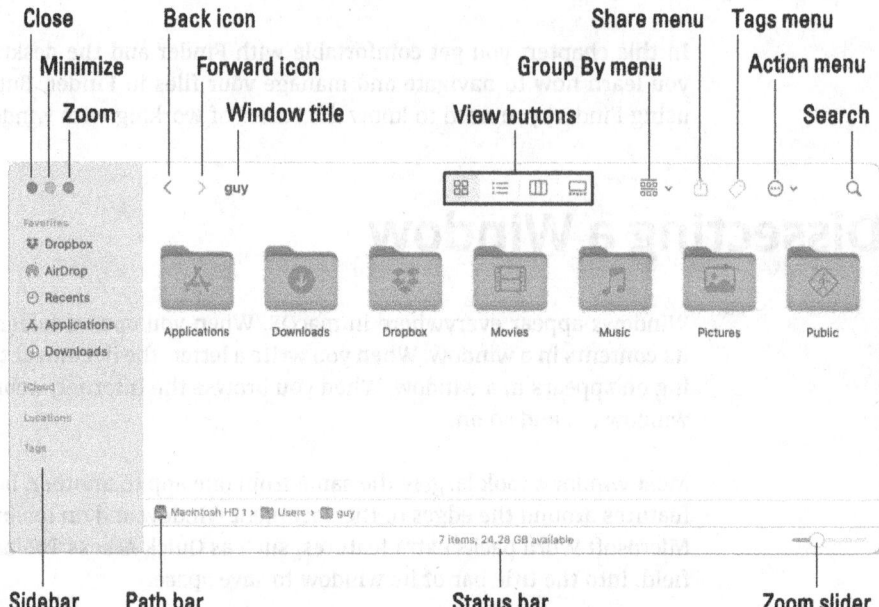

Close
Minimize
Zoom
Back icon
Forward icon
Window title
View buttons
Share menu
Group By menu
Tags menu
Action menu
Search

FIGURE 2-1:
A typical Finder
window in
macOS Sequoia.

Sidebar   Path bar   Status bar   Zoom slider

REMEMBER

As you navigate from folder to folder, Finder remembers your breadcrumb trail separately for each window and each tab, enabling you to quickly traverse backward or forward. You can also navigate backward or forward from the keyboard by using the shortcuts ⌘ +[for Back and ⌘ +] for Forward.

WARNING

The Forward and Back icons remember only the other folders you've visited in the active window or tab. If you've set the Finder to make folders always open in a new window, or if you've forced a folder to open in a new window, which we'll get to shortly — the Forward and Back icons won't work.

>> **Window title:** Shows the name of the window (*guy* in Figure 2-1).

TIP

>> ⌘ -click (or Control-click) the window title to see a pop-up menu with the complete path to this folder. (Go on, try it now.) This tip applies to most windows you'll encounter, not just Finder windows. So ⌘ - or Control-click a window's title (a right-click or two-fingered tap on a trackpad will work, too), and you'll (usually) see the path to its enclosing folder on your disk, though some third-party apps don't follow this convention.

>> **View buttons:** Choose among four views of your window: Icon, List, Column, and Gallery. Find out more about views in Chapter 4.

>> **Group By menu:** Click this menu button to group this window's icons by Name, Kind, Application, Date Last Opened, Date Added, Date Modified, Date Created, Size, or Tags; or by None, which is the default.

- >> **Share menu:** Another icon that opens a menu. Click it to share selected files or folders via means such as Mail, Messages, AirDrop, or Notes. Or click Edit Actions to add other commands to your Share menu, such as Add (the selected item) to Photos.

- >> **Tags menu:** Yet another menu; click it to assign a tag to the selected files or folders.

- >> **Action menu:** This icon opens a pop-up menu of commands you can apply to currently selected items in the Finder window or on the desktop. It's nearly the same list of commands you'll find in the contextual (shortcut) menu when you right-click or Control-click that item or items.

  Some menu icons and items in these menus aren't available (that is, they appear dimmed) until you select one or more icons in the Finder window. If nothing happens when you click a toolbar icon, click a file or folder icon to select it and try again.

TIP

- >> **Search:** Click the magnifying-glass icon and then type a string of characters in the field that appears. The Spotlight search feature digs into your system to find items that match by filename or document contents (yes, it will find words within most documents).

- >> **Sidebar:** Frequently used items live here, giving you quick access to them. You can customize the sidebar with the items you need.

- >> **Path bar:** This bar near the bottom of the window shows the path from the drive, such as your Mac's SSD, to the folder. You can toggle the display of the path bar by choosing View ⇨ Show Path Bar and View ⇨ Hide Path Bar.

- >> **Status bar:** This bar across the bottom of the window shows the status of the selected object. For example, in Figure 2-1, the status bar shows *7 items, 24.28 GB available.* You can toggle the display of the status bar by choosing View ⇨ Show Status Bar and View ⇨ Hide Status Bar.

- >> **Zoom slider.** This slider at the right end of the status bar enables you to change the size of icons in Icon View. This slider does not appear in List view, Columns view, or Gallery view.

Zooming, splitting, and minimizing windows

In the upper-left corner of a standard window are three round buttons for controlling the window. These three buttons (sometimes called *gumdrop buttons* because they look like gumdrops) are officially known as Close, Minimize, and Zoom, and their colors (red, yellow, and green, respectively) are designed to pop off the screen.

Here's what they do:

>> **Close (red):** Click this button to close the window. Depending on the app, closing its last open window may or may not quit the app.

>> **Minimize (yellow):** Click this button to minimize the window. Clicking Minimize shrinks the window to an icon on the right side of the Dock.

TIP

See the section "Global Dock settings" in Chapter 3 if a window icon doesn't appear on your Dock when you minimize the window.

To view the window again, click the Dock icon for the window that you minimized. If the window happens to be a QuickTime movie, the movie audio continues to play, and a tiny still image from the video appears as its icon on the Dock. (You learn about the Dock in Chapter 3.)

>> **Zoom (green):** Click this button and the window expands to cover the whole screen, including the menu bar.

TIP

You can also zoom a window to the largest size it will go without covering the menu bar. To do this, hold down the Option key when you click the Zoom button.

To shrink the window back to its previous dimensions, slide the pointer up to the very top of the screen, wait for the menu bar to appear, and then click the green Zoom button.

Another way to escape from a full-screen window is to press the Esc key. This move works in Finder and in many other apps, but not all apps.

Split view is partially hidden beneath the green Zoom button. To reach the Split View commands, either click and hold the green button for a moment or *hover* the pointer over the Zoom button for a moment — that is, hold it over the button without clicking.

Either way, a pop-up menu appears with commands for moving, resizing, and arranging the window (see Figure 2-2). You can then:

● In the Move & Resize section, click Left, Right, Up, or Down to make the window take up half the screen but leave the menu bar displayed. To make the window take up one of the four quadrants, hold down 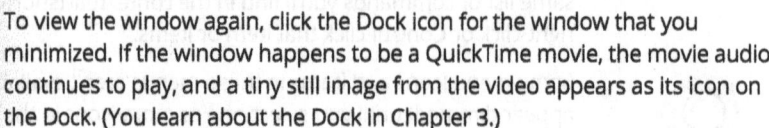, and then click the appropriate icon.

● In the Fill & Arrange section, click Fill Screen to make the window fill the screen area but leave the menu bar displayed. Click one of the three Split icons — Left and Right; Left Half, Right Quarters; or Four Quarters — to implement that kind of split. To center the window on the display, hold down 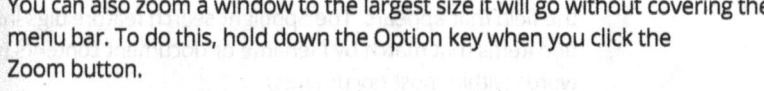, and then click the Center icon, which replaces the Fill Screen icon.

- Click Full Screen to display the submenu, and then click Entire Screen, Left of Screen, or Right of Screen, as needed.

- If your Mac has multiple displays connected or has iPad available to act as extra displays, click the appropriate Move To command. In the example, the snappily named DP2VGA 11487 is a second display connected to the Mac.

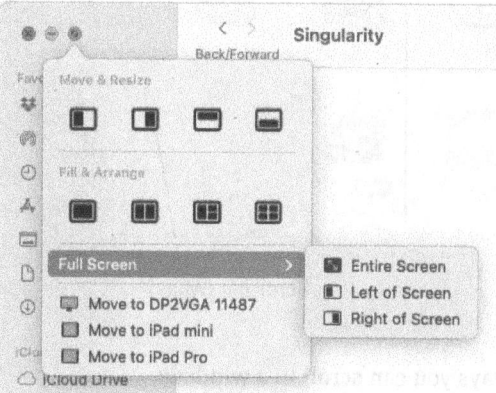

FIGURE 2-2:
Hold the pointer over the green gumdrop button to display the menu for moving, sizing, and arranging the window.

TIP

You can also resize and reposition windows with the mouse or trackpad. Drag a window to the left edge or right edge of the screen to make the window take up the left half of the screen. Drag a window to one of the corners of the screen to make the window take up that quadrant.

Scrolling

Another way to see more of what's in a window or pane is to scroll through it. Scroll bars appear at the bottom and right sides of any window or pane that contains more stuff — icons, text, pixels, or whatever — than you can see in the window. In Figure 2-3, for example, dragging the scroll box, also called the "thumb," on the right side of the smaller window would reveal the icons below the icons that are currently visible. Dragging the scroll box on the bottom of the smaller window would reveal items to the right of the currently visible icons.

Simply drag a scroll box to move it up or down or from side to side.

If your scroll bars don't look exactly like the ones in Figure 2-3 or work as described in the following list, don't worry. These are System Settings you can configure to your heart's desire, as you discover in Chapter 6.

Scroll box (gray)

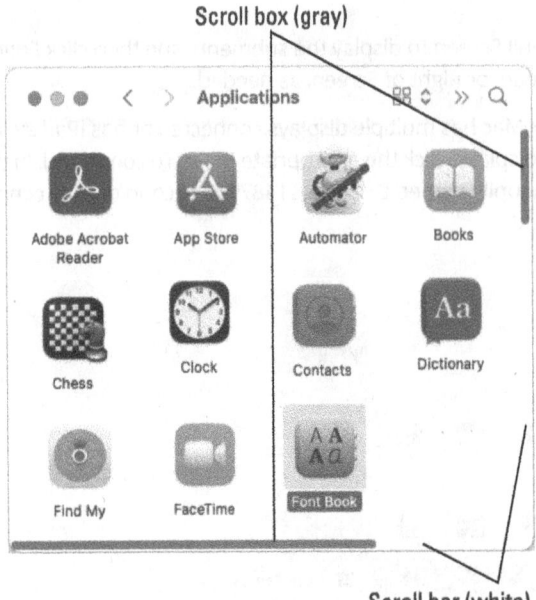

FIGURE 2-3:
Use the scroll
bars to scroll to
view other
parts of the
active window.

Scroll bar (white)

Here are some ways you can scroll in a window:

>> **Click a scroll box and drag.** The content of the window scrolls proportionally to how far you drag the scroll box.

>> **Click in the scroll bar but don't click the scroll box.** The window scrolls either one page up (if you click above the scroll box) or down (if you click below the scroll box). You can change a setting in the Appearance pane in System Settings to cause the window to scroll proportionally to where you click.

The Page Up and Page Down keys on your keyboard function the same way as clicking the vertical scroll bar in Finder and many apps. These keys don't work in every app, though, so don't become too dependent on them. Also, if you have a mouse, a trackball, or another pointing device that includes a scroll wheel, you can scroll vertically in the active (front) window with the scroll wheel or press and hold down the Shift key to scroll horizontally. This move, too, works only in some apps, including Finder and TextEdit.

>> **Use the keyboard.** In Finder, first click an icon in the window and then use the arrow keys to move up, down, left, or right. Using an arrow key selects the next icon in the direction it indicates — and automatically scrolls the window, if necessary. In other apps, you might or might not be able to use the keyboard to scroll. To find out, try it.

TIP

>> **Use a two-finger swipe (on a trackpad).** If you have a MacBook, or you use a Magic Trackpad or Magic Mouse with your desktop Mac, just move the arrow pointer over the window and then swipe the trackpad or Magic Mouse with two fingers to scroll.

Active and inactive windows

To work within a window, you must make the window active. The *active* window is always the front-most window, and *inactive* windows always appear behind the active window. You might not see an inactive window if it's behind a bigger window, active or not. If a window is minimized, you'll see it only as a button on the Dock.

Only one window can be active at a time. To make a window active, click it anywhere — in the middle, on the title bar, or on a scroll bar.

TIP

The exceptions are the Close, Minimize, and Zoom buttons on inactive windows, which always do what they do, regardless of whether a window is active or inactive.

Look at Figure 2-4 for an example of an active window in front of an inactive window (the Applications window and the Utilities window, respectively).

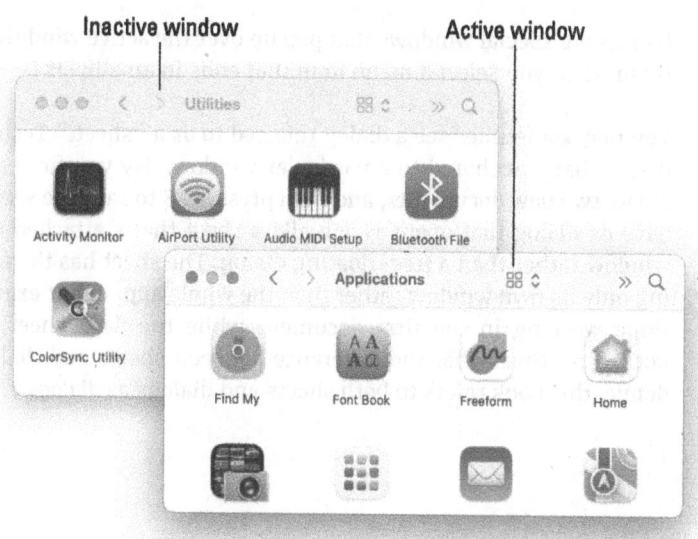

Inactive window   Active window

FIGURE 2-4:
An active window in front of an inactive window.

The following major visual cues distinguish active from inactive windows:

TIP

>> **The active window's title bar:** By default, the Close, Minimize, and Zoom buttons are bright red, yellow, and green, respectively, and the inactive windows' buttons are light gray.

If you move your mouse pointer over an inactive window's gumdrop buttons, they light up in their usual colors so you can close, minimize, or zoom the window without first making it active.

>> **The active window's toolbar:** Toolbar icons are darker and more distinctive; the inactive window's toolbar icons are light gray and more subdued.

>> **The active window's drop shadow:** The active window has a more prominent shadow, as you can see in Figure 2-4.

To resize a window, hold the pointer over a window's edge or corner or over the dividing line between two panes in the same window (such as the sidebar and the main area of Finder windows). When the pointer changes to a double-headed arrow, drag the edge, corner, or dividing line to resize the window or pane.

Opening a Dialog with Your Mac

Dialogs are special windows that pop up over the active window. You generally see them when you select a menu item that ends in an ellipsis (. . .).

TECHNICAL
STUFF

You may sometimes see a dialog referred to as a "sheet." Technically, a *sheet* is a dialog that's anchored to a particular window. Say you fire up the TextEdit app, create two new documents, and then press ⌘+S to save the second document. The Save As dialog that opens is actually a sheet that's attached to that document's window rather than a free-floating dialog. The sheet has the advantage of blocking only its own window rather than the whole app; in our example, you can continue working in the first document while the Save sheet blocks the second document. Given that the difference between sheets and dialogs is largely academic, this book refers to both sheets and dialogs as *dialogs*.

Dialogs can contain a number of standard Mac controls, such as radio buttons, pop-up menus, tabs, text-entry fields, and check boxes. You see these features again and again in dialogs. Take a moment to look at each of these controls in Figure 2-5, which shows the Settings window from the TextEdit app.

>> **Radio buttons:** *Radio buttons* are so named because, like the buttons on an old-style radio, only one at a time can be active. (When a radio button is active, it appears to be pushed in, just like the old radio buttons.) Radio buttons always appear in a group of two or more; when you select one, any radio button previously selected is automatically deselected. To select a radio button, click either the button part or the button's name.

>> **Tabs:** When a dialog contains more information than can fit in a single window, the info may be divided among panes denoted by tabs. In Figure 2-5, the New Document tab is selected on the left, and the Open and Save tab is selected on the right.

>> **Pop-up menus:** These menus pop up when you click them, enabling you to make your selection by clicking an item on the menu. In Figure 2-5, right, all five pop-up menus (Opening Files, Saving Files, Document Type, Styling, and Encoding) are unclicked and unpopped.

You can always recognize a pop-up menu because it appears in a slightly rounded rectangle and has a double-ended arrow symbol (or a pair of arrows, if you like) on the right.

>> **Text-entry fields:** In text-entry fields, you type text (including numbers) from the keyboard. In Figure 2-5, left, the Width, Height, Author, Organization, and Copyright settings are text-entry fields.

>> **Check boxes:** The last type of control that you see frequently is the check box. In a group of check boxes, you can select as many options as you like. Check boxes are selected when they contain a check mark and deselected when they're empty, as shown in Figure 2-5.

There's one other control you should become familiar with, the disclosure triangle. If you see a triangle in a dialog, try clicking it. If it's a disclosure triangle, it will reveal additional options (or its contents if it's a folder in Finder's List view, as you see in Chapter 8).

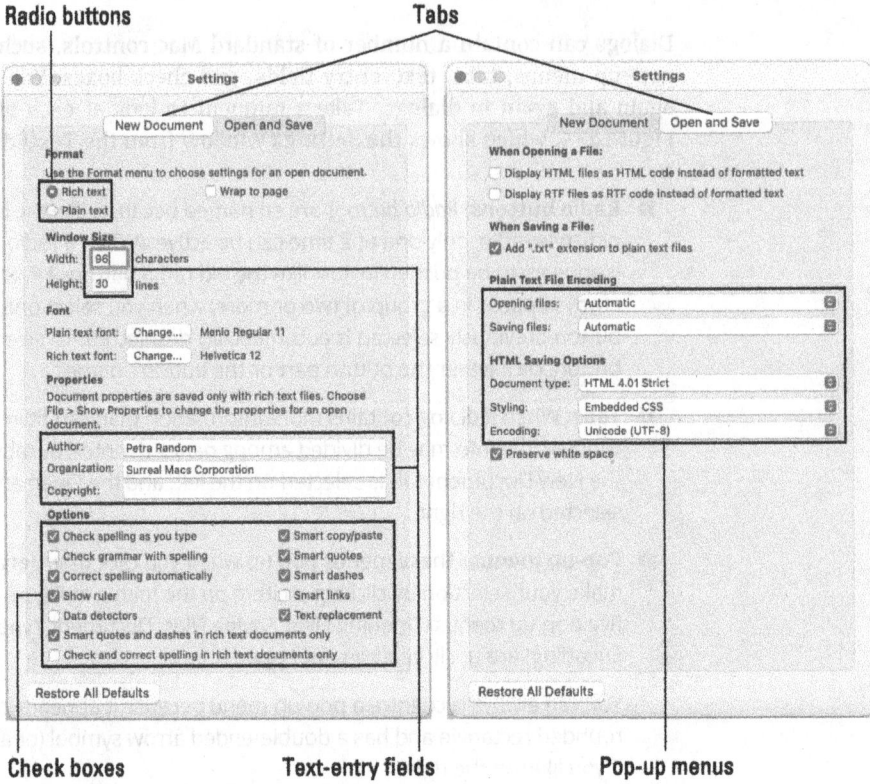

Radio buttons   Tabs

FIGURE 2-5:
This Settings
window offers
most of the
dialog controls
you're likely to
encounter.

Check boxes   Text-entry fields   Pop-up menus

Working with Windows

In the following sections, you learn to move, resize, and use windows.

Opening and closing windows

Here are the essentials of opening and closing windows, including keyboard
shortcuts that can save you time:

>> **New Finder Window (⌘ +N):** Opens a new Finder window. In other apps, ⌘ +N
might open a new document, project, or whatever that app helps you create.

>> **Open (⌘ +O):** Opens the selected item, be it a file, a window, or a folder.

>> **Close Window (⌘ +W):** Closes the active window. If no windows are open or if
no window is selected, the Close Window command appears dimmed and
can't be chosen. You can also close a window by clicking the red Close button
in the top-left corner.

If you need to close all your open Finder windows, open the File menu, hold down the Option key, and then click the Close All command that replaces the Close Window command. Alternatively, press ⌘+Option+W.

When you open the File menu and press the Option key, you'll see several commands change. Try pressing the Option key for the various Finder menus, and you'll find at least a dozen useful commands that are normally hidden.

Resizing windows and window panes

If you want to see more (or less) of what's in a window, just hover the pointer over any edge or corner. When the pointer turns into a little double-headed arrow, drag to resize the window.

Display windows, like those in Finder, frequently consist of multiple panes. In a Finder window, hold the pointer over the thin line that divides the sidebar pane on the left from the contents pane on the right. The pointer changes to a vertical bar with arrows pointing out of both sides, as shown in the margin. If you hover the pointer over the dividing line for a horizontal pane, the pointer changes to a horizontal bar with arrows pointing up and down.

When you see this pointer, you can click and drag anywhere in the dividing line that separates the sidebar from the rest of the window. Doing so resizes the two panes relative to each other; one gets larger, and one gets smaller.

Moving windows

To move a window, click anywhere in a window's title bar or toolbar (except on a button, an icon, a menu, or a search field), drag the window to wherever you want it, and then release it.

If you can't see the pointer on the screen, wiggle your finger on the trackpad or jiggle the mouse. These movements magnify the pointer to make it easier to spot.

Shuffling windows

When you need to manage your open windows, use these commands on the Window menu:

>> **Minimize (⌘+M):** Minimizes the active Finder window to the Dock, just like clicking the yellow gumdrop button.

>> **Zoom:** Zooms the window to fill the screen, just like clicking the green gumdrop button.

>> **Fill (F):** Enlarges the window to fill the screen, leaving the menu bar displayed.

>> **Center (C):** Centers the window on the screen horizontally and vertically.

>> **Move and Resize:** On this submenu, click the appropriate item in the Halves section, the Quarters section, or the Arrange section. Click the Return to Previous Size item (or press R) to return the window to its previous size.

>> **Full Screen Tile:** On this submenu, click the Left of Screen item or the Right of Screen item, as needed.

  You may see additional commands, such as moving the window to another monitor (if your Mac is using multiple monitors) or moving it to a different device (such as an iPad) via Sidecar when a suitable device is close enough to your Mac (see Chapter 23).

>> **Cycle through Windows (⌘ + ` [the back-tick character on the keyboard]):** Each time you choose this command or use the keyboard shortcut for it, a different window becomes active. So if you have three windows open — Window 1, Window 2, and Window 3 — and you're using Window 1, this command activates Window 2, making Window 1 inactive. If you choose it again, the command activates Window 3, making Window 2 inactive. Choose it one more time to complete the cycle and make Window 1 active again.

The next four commands on the Window menu help you manage tabs in Finder windows. Tabs let you view multiple folders, locations, or disks in a single window, with each item in its own tab, as shown in Figure 2-6. Tabbed windows help cram a lot of information into a little space.

Utilities tab   Applications tab   Downloads tab

FIGURE 2-6:
Finder tabs let you view the contents of several folders merely by clicking the appropriate tab.

The remaining commands on the Window menu are as follows:

>> **Show Previous Tab (Control+Shift+Tab):** Each time you choose this command or use its keyboard shortcut, the previous tab becomes active.

The previous tab is the one to the left of the active tab, unless the active tab is the left-most tab, in which case the previous tab is the right-most tab. In Figure 2-6, Utilities is the active tab. Use this command, and Downloads becomes the active tab. Use it again, and Applications becomes active.

>> **Show Next Tab (Control+Tab):** Same as Show Previous Tab, except in reverse. Instead of showing the previous tab (the one to the left), this command shows the next tab (the one to the right).

>> **Move Tab to New Window (no keyboard shortcut):** Moves the active tab into a new window of its own.

>> **Merge All Windows (no keyboard shortcut):** Combines all open windows and tabs in one window.

TIP

Drag a tab left or right to change the order. You can also drag a tab from one Finder window and drop it on the tab bar in another window. If you miss the tab bar, the tab will be displayed in a new window.

One more thing: In Sequoia, all these commands and keyboard shortcuts appear in most apps that display windows.

>> **Bring All to Front (no keyboard shortcut):** Windows from different apps can interleave. You can have (from front to back) a Finder window, a Microsoft Word window, an Adobe Photoshop window, another Microsoft Word window, and another Finder window. In this example, choosing Bring All to Front while Finder is the active app enables you to have both Finder windows move in front of those belonging to Word and Photoshop.

TIP

If you want to bring all the windows belonging to Finder (or any other app, for that matter) to the front at the same time, you can also click the appropriate Dock icon (Finder, in this case).

If you hold down the Option key when you click the Window menu, Minimize Window changes to Minimize All, and the Zoom command changes to Zoom All.

>> **Other items:** The remaining items on the Window menu — if any — are the names of all currently open Finder windows. Click a window's name to bring it to the front.

Sampling the Menus
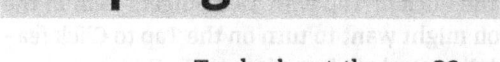

To check out the macOS menus, click the Finder button on the Dock to activate Finder and then look at the top of your screen. From left to right, you see the Apple menu, the Finder menu, and six other menus. To use a menu, click its name to make the menu appear, and then click to select a menu item.

After you click a menu's name, the menu stays open until you select an item, click outside the menu, or press Esc.

Using the ever-changing menu bar

The Apple menu (🍎) always appears at the left end of the menu bar, but the next section of the menu bar displays the menus for the active app — so every time you make a different app active, the menu bar changes. You can see this in Figure 2-7, which shows the menu bars with Finder active (top), Preview active (middle), and TextEdit active (bottom).

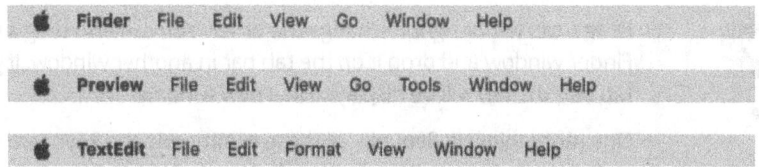

An easy way to tell which app is active is to look at the application menu — the left-most menu with a name, just to the right of the Apple menu.

The commands on the menus change to suit the active app and its features. Most apps include a File menu, which includes commands such as New, Open, Save, and Print; and many apps have an Edit menu, which typically includes the Cut, Copy, and Paste commands. Beyond that, there's a lot of variation.

Using the contextual (shortcut) menus

Contextual menus (also called *shortcut menus*) list commands that apply only to the item that is currently selected. Contextual menus might be available in windows, on objects (such as files), and in most places on the desktop.

To see whether a contextual menu is available for an object, Control-click or right-click that object. If you're using a trackpad, click with two fingers.

TIP

If clicking with two fingers on the trackpad doesn't work for you, launch System Settings, and click the Trackpad icon in the sidebar. On the Point & Click tab, go to the Secondary Click line and select the Click or Tap with Two Fingers item in the pop-up menu. While you're here, you might want to turn on the Tap to Click feature, too; if so, go to the Tap to Click line, and set its switch to On (blue).

Figure 2-8, left, shows the contextual menu that appears when you Control-click (or right-click) a document icon. Figure 2-8, right, shows the contextual menu you see when you Control-click the desktop.

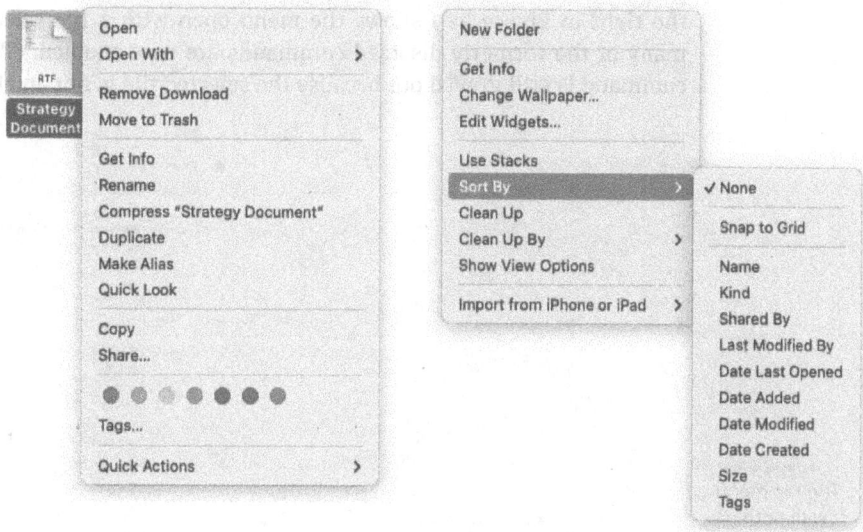

FIGURE 2-8:
Only relevant
items appear
on a contextual
menu.

Contextual menus are also available in most apps. Open your favorite app and try Control-clicking to find out whether those menus are there. In most cases, using a contextual menu is a quick way to avoid going to the menu bar to choose a command. In some apps — such as iMovie and Music — contextual menus are the *only* way to access some commands.

In Finder, you can access most of the commands on the contextual menus by using the Action menu instead. Select the object, click Action (shown in the margin), and you'll be in business.

To take actions quickly, get in the habit of Control-clicking (or right-clicking or two-finger clicking) items on your screen.

REMEMBER

Recognizing disabled commands

Menu items that appear in black on a menu are currently available. Menu items that aren't currently available are grayed out, which indicates that they're currently disabled. You can't select a disabled menu item.

In Figure 2-9, the File menu on the left is pulled down while nothing is selected in Finder; this is why many of the menu items are disabled (in gray). These items are disabled because an item (such as a window or an icon) must be selected for you to use one of these menu items. For example, the Show Original command is grayed out because it works only if the selected item is an alias. The File menu on the right in Figure 2-9 shows the menu open with a file selected; you can see many of the formerly disabled commands are now enabled. (The Show Original command is still grayed out because the selected file is not an alias.)

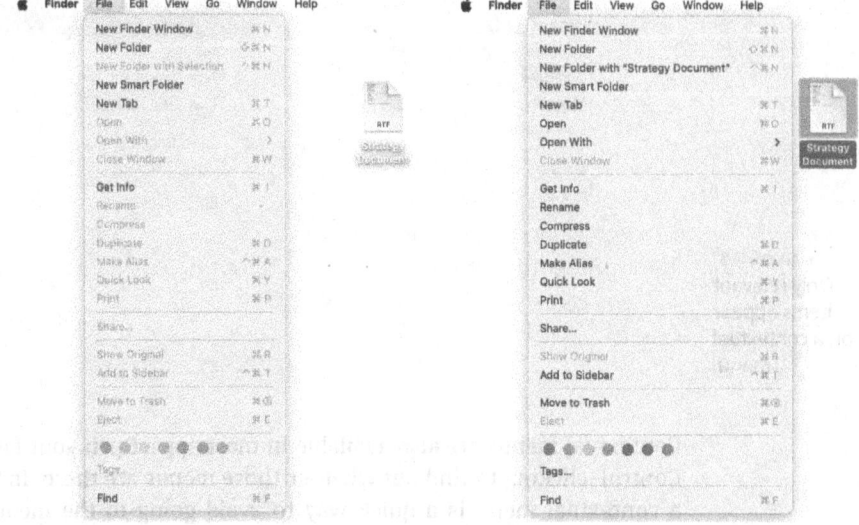

FIGURE 2-9:
The File menu
with nothing
selected (left) and
with a file
selected (right);
the disabled
items appear
grayed out.

Items that end in an ellipsis (. . .), such as the Tags command in Figure 2-9, open a dialog with additional options.

Navigating submenus

Some menu items have more menus attached to them, and these are called *submenus*, which are menus that are subordinate to a menu item. If a menu has a > arrow to the right of its name, it has a submenu. Submenus are sometimes called *continuation menus*.

To use a submenu, click a menu name once (to open the menu) and then slide the pointer down to any item with a > arrow. When the item is highlighted, the submenu pops out, as shown in Figure 2-10.

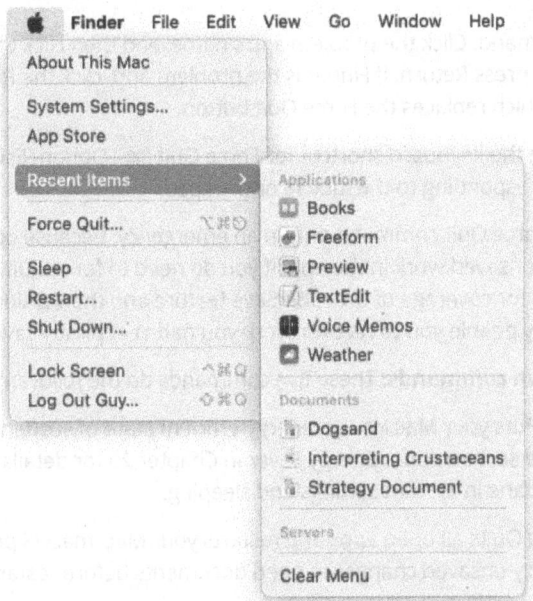

| <img src="apple"> | Finder | File | Edit | View | Go | Window | Help |

About This Mac

System Settings...
App Store

Recent Items   >   Applications
                                             📖 Books
Force Quit...   ⌥⌘⎋   🎨 Freeform
                                             🖼 Preview
Sleep   / TextEdit
Restart...   🎙 Voice Memos
Shut Down...   ☁ Weather

                                            Documents
Lock Screen   ⌃⌘Q   📄 Dogsand
Log Out Guy...   ⇧⌘Q   ↔ Interpreting Crustaceans
                                             📄 Strategy Document

                                            Servers

                                            Clear Menu

FIGURE 2-10:
The Apple menu's
Recent Items
command, with
its submenu
displayed.

Under the Apple menu tree

On the far-left side of the menu bar sits a little <img src="apple">, which displays a menu when clicked. No matter what app is active, the <img src="apple"> menu is always available in the top-left corner of your menu bar.

TIP

The menu bar is always available, even with apps that hide it in full-screen mode. To make it reappear, move the pointer to the top of the screen and wait a second or two.

From top to bottom, the <img src="apple"> menu gives you a number of commands, including the following:

>> **About This Mac:** Displays a window showing what version of macOS you're running, what kind of Mac and processor (chip) you're using, how much memory your Mac has, and the Mac's serial number.

>> **System Settings:** Opens the System Settings app (see Chapter 6).

>> **App Store:** Launches the Mac App Store app.

>> **Recent Items:** Displays a menu that lets you quickly access apps, documents, and servers you've used recently, as shown previously in Figure 2-10.

>> **Force Quit:** Opens the Force Quit Applications window, which enables you to forcibly close an app that has stopped responding or that refuses to obey a

Quit command. Click the problem app's name, and then click the Force Quit button or press Return. If Finder is the problem app, click the Relaunch button, which replaces the Force Quit button.

TIP

Memorize the keyboard shortcut for Force Quit (⌘ +Option+Esc) in case your Mac isn't responding to the mouse or trackpad.

WARNING

Use the Force Quit command only in an emergency, because otherwise you may lose unsaved work in the app. If you do need to force-quit an app, see Chapter 7 for coverage of the Auto Save feature and the Versions feature, which may enable you to recover work you hadn't explicitly saved.

» **Shut Down commands:** These five commands do the following:

- *Sleep:* Puts your Mac into an energy-efficient state of suspended animation. See the section about Energy Saver in Chapter 20 for details on the Energy Saver pane in System Settings and sleeping.

- *Restart:* Quits all open apps and restarts your Mac. macOS prompts you to save any unsaved changes in open documents before restarting the Mac.

- *Shut Down:* Turns off your Mac. Refer to Chapter 1 for details.

- *Lock Screen (⌘ +Control+Q):* Locks your screen instantly, and then requires your account password or your fingerprint to unlock it.

- *Log Out <your account name> (⌘ +Shift+Q):* Quits all open apps and logs you out. Again, your Mac will prompt you to save unsaved changes in open documents before complying. When it's done, the login screen appears.

Giving commands via keyboard shortcuts

Most menu items, or at least the most common ones, have *keyboard shortcuts* to help you quickly navigate your Mac. Using these key combinations gives menu commands without you opening the menus. Instead, you simply hold down the modifier key or keys, such as the Command (⌘) key or the Command key and the Control key, while you press another key. Memorize the shortcuts that you use often.

Learn how to change keyboard shortcuts and even how to create ones of your own in Chapter 6.

REMEMBER

Some people refer to the Command key as the *Apple key*. That's because on many keyboards that key has both the pretzel-like Command-key symbol (⌘) and an Apple logo (🍎) on it. To avoid confusion, this book always refers to ⌘ as the Command key.

Chapter **3**

What's Up, Dock?

The Dock appears at the bottom of your screen by default, providing quick access to your apps, documents, and folders. It's a great place to put files, folders, and apps you use a lot so that they're always just one click away.

TIP

Some people prefer to have the Dock located on the left or right side of the screen instead of at the bottom. You see how to relocate your Dock (and more) in the coming pages.

Folder icons on the Dock are called *stacks*, which display their contents as your choice of a fan, a grid, or a list when clicked. Other icons on the Dock open an app or document with one click.

REMEMBER

A Dock icon is merely a pointer (also known as an *alias* or a *shortcut*) to an app, document, or folder stored on your Mac's drive. So, you can add and remove icons from your Dock without affecting the actual apps, documents, and folders.

Meeting Your Dock

The Dock is the bar that runs across the bottom of your macOS desktop and contains a range of icons. Figure 3-1 shows the Dock split into two pieces, with the left half above and the right half below, so that you can more easily see what's what.

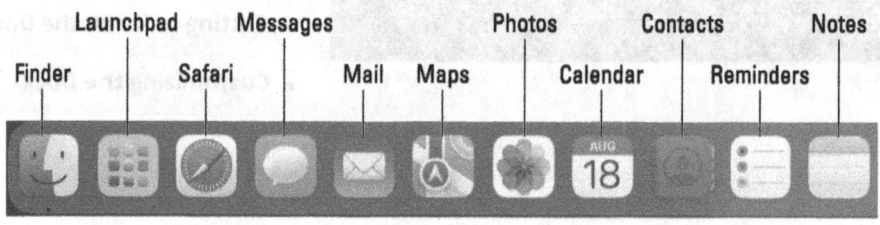

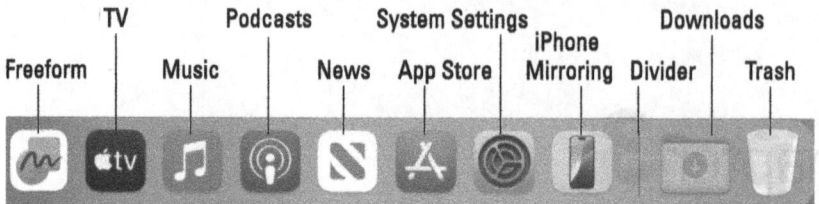

FIGURE 3-1:
The Dock with a
typical selection
of icons.

REMEMBER

Icons on the Dock and Launchpad (see Chapter 10) are unusual in that you activate them with a single click. Most everywhere else in Finder, you click an icon to select it and double-click it to open the item it represents.

Here's what happens when you click Dock icons:

>> **App icon:** The app opens and becomes active; or if the app is already open, it becomes active. The app's menus appear on the menu bar.

>> **Document icon:** The document opens in its default app, which becomes the active app.

REMEMBER

If the item is an app or document and is already open when you click its Dock icon, the app or document becomes active.

>> **Folder icon or disk icon:** A stack, fan, or grid with its contents appears so you can choose an item. If you choose Show in Finder from this menu, a Finder window opens, showing the contents of the folder or disk.

Identifying the Dock's default icons

The Dock typically starts you off with icons for a number of commonly used macOS apps, and you can add icons for your own apps, files, or folders there. (The "Adding Dock icons" section later in this chapter shows you how to do that.)

The following list explains the items you'll usually find, pointing to where in the book you'll find more coverage of each:

>> **Finder:** The always-running app that manages the desktop, files, folders, disks, and more (this chapter and chapters 4–8)

» **Launchpad:** A display of all your apps (Chapter 9)

» **Safari:** A web browser (Chapter 13)

» **Messages:** An app for sending and receiving text and multimedia messages, transferring files, and remotely controlling other Macs (Chapter 15)

» **Mail:** An email app (Chapter 15)

» **Maps:** An app that serves up maps and driving directions (Chapter 11)

» **Photos:** An app for managing and editing photographs (Chapter 18)

» **FaceTime:** An app for making and receiving audio and video calls (Chapter 14)

» **Calendar:** A calendar app for managing appointments and events (Chapter 10)

» **Contacts:** A contact-manager app (Chapter 14)

» **Reminders:** A to-do list and reminder app (Chapter 10)

» **Notes:** An app for making and sharing notes (Chapter 10)

» **Freeform:** An app for whiteboarding and brainstorming (not covered)

» **TV:** A video player and store (Chapter 18)

» **Music:** An audio player and store (Chapter 17)

» **Podcasts:** A player for video podcasts and audio-only podcasts (Chapter 17)

» **News:** A news reader (Chapter 12)

» **App Store:** An app for accessing paid or free Mac apps (Chapter 20)

» **System Settings:** An app for configuring your Mac (chapters 6, 16, and 20)

» **iPhone Mirroring:** An app for controlling your iPhone from your Mac (Chapter 20)

» **Divider:** The line that separates apps on the left and documents or folders on the right (this chapter)

» **Downloads folder:** A folder that contains files you've downloaded (Chapter 4)

» **Trash:** Where you drag files and folders to delete them, or drag removable media to eject it (this chapter)

Hold the pointer over a Dock icon to display a bubble showing the icon's name.

If you see a question mark instead of an icon on the Dock, it means that the file (app, document, or folder) it represents has been deleted. Drag the question-mark icon up off the Dock until a Remove bubble appears, and then release it.

Trash talkin'

The *Trash* is a special container where you put the items you no longer want to hang around on your Mac's drive. Tired of tripping over old PDF and DMG files you've downloaded but no longer need? Drag them to the Trash.

To put something in the Trash, just drag its icon onto the Trash icon on the Dock; when the Trash icon becomes highlighted, drop the icon. macOS moves the file from its current location to the Trash folder.

If you find dragging files to the Trash to be awkward, try these other methods:

>> **File menu:** Select your victims, and then choose File ⇨ Move to Trash.

>> **Contextual menu:** Control-click or right-click the file you want to deep-six, and then click Move to Trash on the contextual menu. Trashing multiple files? Select them, and then Control-click or right-click the selection.

>> **Action menu:** Select the file or files, click the Action menu, and then click Move to Trash.

>> **Keyboard:** Select the file or files, and then press ⌘ +Delete (⌘ +Backspace on some non-Apple keyboards).

TIP

If you accidentally move something to the Trash and want it back right now, you can put it back where it came from in two ways.

Way #1

Choose Edit ⇨ Undo or press ⌘ +Z.

Finder usually remembers more than one action for Undo and can often undo the last several things you did in Finder. If you've performed multiple other file-related activities in Finder since moving the file to the Trash, you'll have to undo all those actions before you can undo your accidental Move to Trash. Incidentally, if you open the Edit menu, the trashing is listed as a Move — such as Undo Move of "Bar Ratings" — with no explicit mention of the Trash.

Don't worry if you can't use Undo to recover the file from the Trash — files you drag to the Trash aren't deleted immediately. You know how the garbage in the can on the street curb sits there until the sanitation engineers come by and pick it up each Thursday? Your Mac's Trash works the same way, but without the smell. Items sit in the Trash, waiting for a sanitation engineer (you) to come along and empty it.

Way #2

So if you miss the window of opportunity to use the Undo command, retrieve the file from the Trash like this:

>> **Open the Trash.** Click the Trash icon on the Dock. A Finder window called Trash opens, showing you its contents — all the files and folders put in the Trash since the last time it was emptied.

>> **Restore a file to its previous folder.** Control-click or right-click the file, and then click Put Back on the contextual menu. If the Put Back command is dimmed, the previous folder isn't available. Perhaps you trashed it? Have a quick rummage through the Trash. If you find the folder there, Control-click or right-click it, and then click Put Back to put the folder back; you can then put the file back inside it. If you don't find the folder in the Trash, go on to the next option.

>> **Restore a file to a different folder.** Drag the file from the Trash to the desktop or the folder in which you want to put it.

TIP

You can also use the ⌘ +Delete keyboard shortcut to put a trashed file back in its folder — as long as the folder exists. If the folder is no longer there, macOS displays a warning saying that the file could not be put back and the folder "doesn't exist anymore."

Emptying the Trash

You can empty the Trash in three ways:

>> **Open the Trash, make sure it contains nothing valuable, and then click the Empty button in the upper-right corner.** Depending on how you use the Trash, you may find it wise to look quickly through what you're about to jettison.

>> **Choose Finder ⇨ Empty Trash, and then click the Empty Trash button in the confirmation dialog.**

>> **With the Finder active, press ⌘ +Shift+Delete, and then click the Empty Trash button in the confirmation dialog.**

WARNING

After you empty the Trash, the files that it contained are pretty much gone forever, or at least gone from your Mac's drive. There is no Undo for Empty Trash. To protect against accidental loss, read Chapter 21, and back up your Mac's drive at least once so that you can recover files from backup if necessary.

The Trash icon shows you when it has files waiting for you there; as in real life, Trash that contains files or folders looks like it's full of crumpled paper. Conversely, when your Trash is empty, the Trash icon looks empty.

Finally, although you can't open a file that's in the Trash, you can select it and use Quick Look (press the spacebar or ⌘+Y) to see its contents before you decide to use Empty Trash and permanently delete it.

Opening app menus on the Dock

Clicking an app icon on the Dock launches that app — or, if the app is already open, make that app active. But some app icons on the Dock — such as Calendar, Safari, and Music — also hide menus containing some handy commands. (Folder icons on the Dock have a different but no less handy menu, as you'll see in a moment.)

You can make menus for apps on the Dock appear in two ways:

» Press and continue to hold down the mouse button.

» Control-click or right-click; on a trackpad, tap with two fingers.

Take either of those actions, and you'll see a menu for that Dock icon, as shown in Figure 3-2 for the News icon.

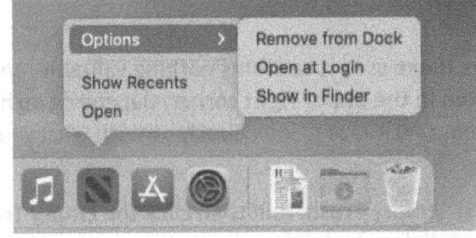

FIGURE 3-2:
The Options
submenu for an
app icon (News)
on the Dock.

The Options submenu offers three choices:

» **Keep in (or Remove from) Dock:** Adds the app's icon to the Dock (or removes it from the Dock), waiting until after you quit the app if it's running. The little dot below the icon means the app is running.

» **Open at Login:** Launches this app automatically every time you log in to this user account. This is handy for apps you want to keep running all the time, such as Mail or Safari.

>> **Show in Finder:** Opens a Finder window showing the enclosing folder (in this instance, that would be the Applications folder) and selects the app's icon.

Apart from the Options submenu, the menu contains these commands:

>> **Show Recents:** Displays recently used windows for this app if there are any.

>> **Open/Quit:** Opens the app, or quits the app if it's already open.

When you Control-click or right-click the Dock icon for an app that's currently running, you may see different menus, like the ones shown in Figure 3-3 (clockwise from top left: Safari, Preview, System Settings, TextEdit, and Music).

FIGURE 3-3:
Press and hold down or Control-click or right-click an open app's Dock icon, and menus such as these appear.

As you can see, some open apps provide useful app-specific commands or options.

TIP

Music has one of the best Dock menus, letting you control your music from the Dock with options such as Play/Pause, Next or Previous Track, Repeat, and Shuffle.

Other apps, including Preview and Safari in Figure 3-3, offer you a list of open windows with a check mark to indicate the active window or diamonds to indicate windows minimized to the Dock.

Finally, the items above the list of open windows for TextEdit are recently used documents.

Reading Dock icon body language

As you use the Dock or when you're just doing regular stuff on your Mac, the Dock icons use movement and symbols to communicate their status to you. Table 3-1 tells you what you need to know.

TABLE 3-1   ## What Dock Icons Tell You

Icon Movement or Symbol	What It Means
The icon moves up and out of its place on the Dock for a moment.	You clicked a Dock icon, and it's letting you know that you activated it.
The icon bounces while that app is open but isn't active.	The app needs your attention. Click its icon to find out what it wants.
A dot appears below its Dock icon.	The app is open.
An icon that isn't ordinarily on the Dock appears there.	A temporary Dock icon appears for every app that's currently open until you quit that app. The icon appears because you've opened something or something has opened itself automatically. When you quit the app, its icon disappears.

Opening files from the Dock

REMEMBER

The Dock enables you to open apps quickly and easily using these moves:

>> **Drag a document icon on an app's Dock icon.** If the app knows how to handle that type of document, its Dock icon is highlighted, and the document opens in that app. If the app can't handle that particular type of document, the Dock icon isn't highlighted, and you can't drop the document on it.

TIP

If the app can't handle a document, select the document icon, choose File ⇨ Open With, and then click the app to use. You can also Control-click or right-click the document icon, click Open With, and then click the app on the Open With submenu. To change the default app for this document type, hold down the Option key to replace the Open With command with the Always Open With command, and then click the app you want.

>> **Choose Show in Finder on the Dock menu to find the file linked to a Dock icon.** macOS opens a Finder window to the folder that contains the file and selects the file's icon.

Customizing Your Dock

You can customize the Dock to contain exactly the items you find most useful. You can also resize the Dock and configure settings for it.

Adding Dock icons

TIP

Put things on the Dock that you need quick access to and that you use often, or add items that aren't quickly available from menus or a Finder window's sidebar. If you like using the Dock better than the Finder window's sidebar (for example), add your Documents, Movies, Pictures, Music, or even your Home folder or your Mac's drive to the Dock.

Adding an app, file, or folder to the Dock is as easy as 1-2-3:

TIP

1. **Open a Finder window that contains the app, file, or folder you want to add.**

   You can also drag an item from the desktop or any Finder window.

2. **Click the item you want to add to the Dock.**

   Figure 3-4 illustrates adding the TextEdit app. (It's highlighted.)

3. **Drag the icon out of the Finder window and onto the Dock.**

   The icons to the left and right of the new icon part to make room for it. Note that the Dock icon isn't the actual item. That item remains wherever it was — in a window or on the desktop. The icon you see on the Dock is a *shortcut*, or in macOS terms, an *alias*, that opens the item.

   Furthermore, when you remove an icon from the Dock, as you find out how to do in a moment, you aren't removing the actual app, document, or folder. You're removing *only its shortcut* from the Dock.

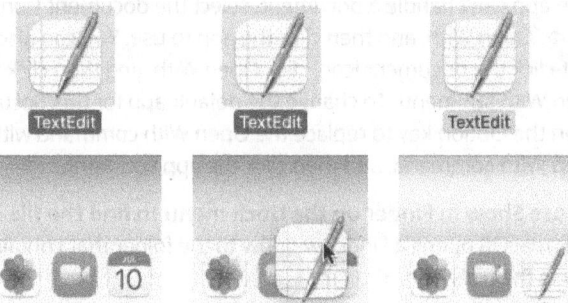

FIGURE 3-4:
Adding an icon to
the Dock is as
easy as 1-2-3. Just
drag the icon
onto the Dock.

Folder, disk, document, and URL icons must sit on the right side of the divider line on the Dock; app icons must sit on the left side of it.

TIP

As long as you follow the rule, you can add several items to one or the other side of the divider line at the same time by selecting them all and dragging the group to that side of the Dock. You can delete only one icon at a time from the Dock, however.

Adding a URL to the Dock works slightly differently. Follow these steps:

1. **Open Safari, and go to the page you want to add to the Dock.**

2. **Click in the address bar to display the full URL, together with a small icon to its left.**

   The default icon looks like a wireframe globe, but many sites use custom icons.

3. **Drag that icon to the right side of the dividing line on the Dock.**

4. **Release the icon when it appears where you want it on the Dock.**

   The icons on the Dock make room, and the URL appears as a Dock icon that looks like Earth. Click that URL icon to open that page in Safari.

TIP

If you want quick access to many URLs, put the URLs in a folder, and then put that folder on the Dock. Then you can just Control-click or right-click the folder to pop up a menu with all your URLs, and click the URL you want.

TIP

If you open an item whose icon normally doesn't appear on the Dock, and you want to keep its temporary icon on the Dock permanently, you have two ways to tell it to stick around after you quit the app:

» Control-click (or click and hold down) and choose Options ⇨ Keep in Dock from the menu that pops up.

>> Drag the icon (for an app that's currently open) off and then back to the Dock (or to a different position on the Dock) in a single move.

Removing an icon from the Dock

TIP

After you figure out which apps you use and don't use, remove the apps you never (or rarely) use from the Dock. You can run them from Launchpad easily enough — it just takes two clicks instead of one.

Removing an item from the Dock takes just a couple of seconds:

1. **Drag its icon off the Dock and a good distance on the desktop, away from the Dock.**

2. **When the Remove bubble appears, release the icon.**

You can also choose Remove from Dock from the item's Dock menu to get it off your Dock, but this way is more fun.

REMEMBER

You can't remove the icon of an app that's currently running from the Dock by dragging it. Either wait until you quit the app or Control-click (or click and hold down) and deselect Options ⇨ Keep in Dock.

When you remove an icon from the Dock, you're just removing the alias. The item remains unchanged.

Resizing the Dock

To shrink or enlarge the Dock (and its icons) quickly, follow these steps:

1. **Move the pointer over the divider line between apps and documents near the right side of the Dock so that the Sizer appears.**

2. **Drag the Sizer down to make the Dock smaller or up to make it larger.**
    You can enlarge the Dock until it fills your screen from side to side. You can also resize the Dock using the Size slider in the Desktop & Dock pane in System Settings.

Configuring your Dock settings

You can change a few things about the Dock to make it look and behave just the way you want it to. This section first covers global settings that apply to the Dock itself. After that, it explains some settings that apply only to folder and disk icons on the Dock.

Global Dock settings

To change global Dock settings, Control-click or right-click the Dock divider line, and then click Dock Preferences on the contextual menu. Alternatively, choose System Settings, and then click the Desktop & Dock icon in the left pane of the System Settings window. Either way, the Desktop & Dock pane appears (see Figure 3-5).

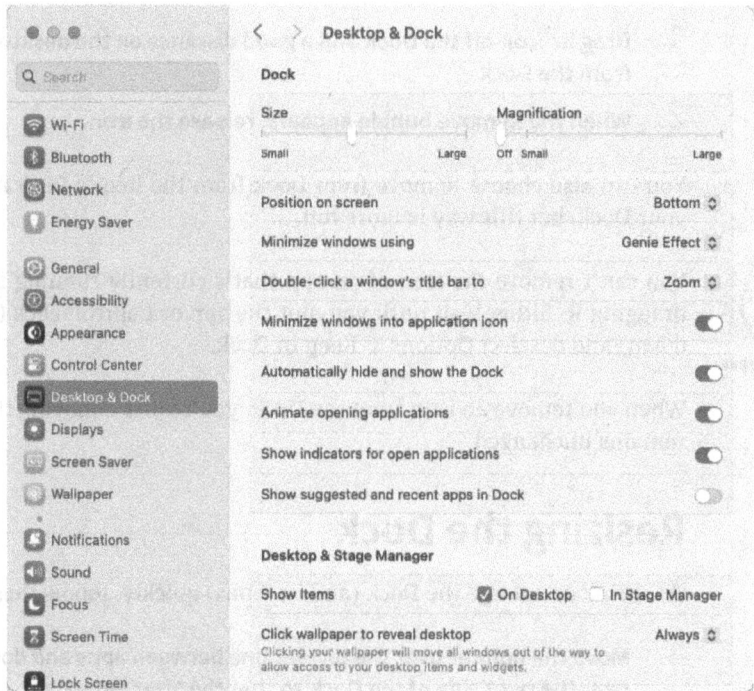

FIGURE 3-5:
The Desktop & Dock pane in System Settings.

Now you can adjust your Dock with the following settings:

REMEMBER

>> **Size:** Drag the slider to the right (larger) or left (smaller) to adjust the size of the Dock in your Finder. The Dock resizes as you drag.

As you add items to the Dock, the icons — and the Dock itself — shrink to accommodate the new ones.

>> **Magnification:** This slider controls how big icons grow when you pass the pointer over them — handy when you've stuffed the Dock with so many icons it's hard to tell which is which. Or you can drag this slider to the Off position to turn off magnification entirely.

>> **Position on Screen:** In this pop-up menu, choose Left, Bottom, or Right to control which side the Dock appears on. Bottom is the default, but you may find Left or Right works better for your Mac's screen size and the apps you use most.

>> **Minimize Windows Using:** In this pop-up menu, choose the animation to play when you click a window's Minimize (yellow by default) button. The Genie Effect is the default, but the Scale Effect seems a bit faster.

>> **Double-Click a Window's Title Bar to Minimize (or Zoom):** In this pop-up menu, choose Minimize to minimize the window, choose Zoom to zoom it, or choose Do Nothing to have nothing happen.

Double-clicking to minimize achieves the same result as clicking the (usually) yellow Minimize button in a window's upper-left corner. The difference is that the Minimize button is a tiny target and way over on the upper-left side of the window, whereas the title bar is a much easier target.

>> **Minimize Windows into Application Icon:** If you set this switch to On (blue), you won't see a separate Dock icon for each window you minimize; instead, the minimized window zips away to the app's icon on the Dock, and you restore it by Control-clicking or right-clicking the app's icon and then clicking the window name on the pop-up menu. If this switch is set to Off (white), each window you minimize gets its own icon on the right side of the Dock, and you need only click the icon to restore the window.

>> **Automatically Hide and Show the Dock:** You can free up some screen real estate by setting this switch to On (blue), making the Dock hide until you summon it by moving the pointer to the side of the screen where it's hiding. Set this switch to Off (white) to have the Dock appear normally.

Press ⌘+Option+D to quickly toggle Dock hiding on and off.

>> **Animate Opening Applications:** Set this switch to On (blue) to have Dock icons bounce when you click them to open an item. Set this switch to Off (white) if you prefer to suppress the bouncing.

>> **Show Indicators for Open Applications:** Set this switch to On (blue) if you want each open app to display a little black indicator dot below its icon on the Dock, like the Finder icon shown in the margin. If you set this switch to Off (white), none of your Dock icons will display an indicator dot.

» **Show Suggested and Recent Apps in Dock:** This setting automatically adds to the Dock icons for apps that you've used recently but that aren't kept on the Dock, plus icons for apps macOS suggests you use. These icons appear in a special Suggested and Recent Apps section of the Dock between your app icons on the left and the folder and Trash icons on the right, as shown in Figure 3-6.

Notice the dividing lines, which represent the left and right edges of the Suggested and Recent Apps section.

FIGURE 3-6:
The Suggested and Recent Apps section of the Dock shows the three recent and suggested apps for which the left side of the Dock doesn't contain icons.

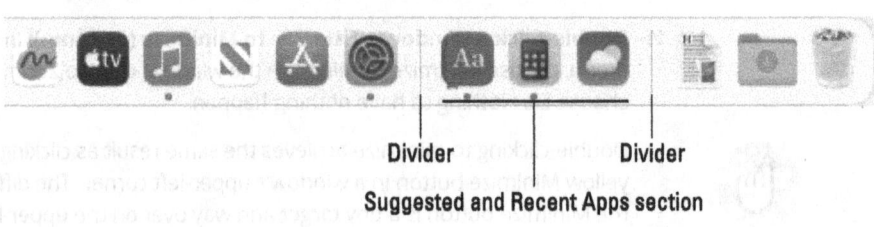

Divider Divider

Suggested and Recent Apps section

Folder and disk Dock icon menu preferences

If you click a folder or disk icon on the Dock, its contents are displayed in a fan (left), grid (middle), or list (right) menu, as shown in Figure 3-7.

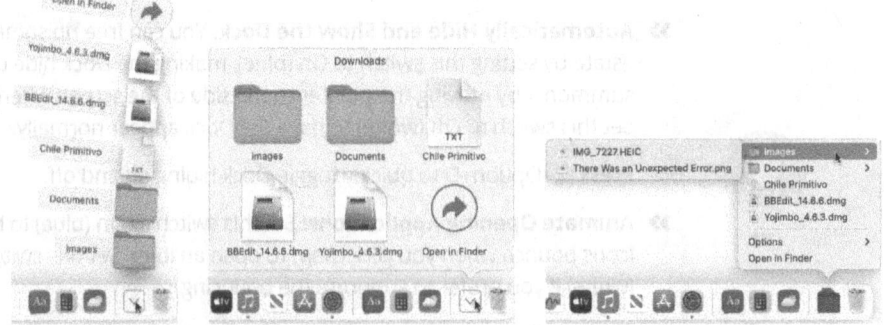

FIGURE 3-7:
My Documents folder's Dock menu as a fan, grid, and list.

If you Control-click or right-click a folder or disk icon on the Dock, its contextual menu appears, as shown in Figure 3-8.

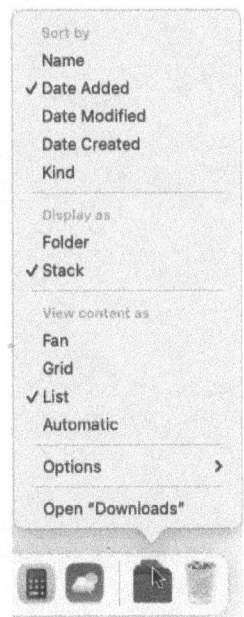

FIGURE 3-8:
The contextual
menu for my
Documents
folder.

Here are the choices on the contextual menu:

>> **Sort By** determines the order in which items in the folder or drive appear when you click its Dock icon.

>> **Display As** determines what the Dock icon for a folder or drive looks like. If you choose Stack, the icon takes on the appearance of the last item moved into the folder or drive. If you choose Folder, the Dock icon looks like a folder.

>> **View Content As** lets you choose Fan, Grid, or List as the menu type for the folder or drive.

TIP

The default is Automatic, which lets the Dock try to choose the menu type for you. You'll probably do better to choose the menu type that suits a particular folder or drive. The list menu is a good choice for folders, because it lets you see and access folders inside folders. For folders containing images, try the grid menu, which displays recognizable thumbnails of the images.

>> **The Options submenu** contains the following items:

- *Remove from Dock* removes the icon from the Dock.

- *Show in Finder* opens the window containing the item and selects the item. So, for example, in Figure 3-8, the Downloads folder would open.

The Dock is your friend. Now that you know what it can do, make it work the way you want it to. Put those apps and folders you use most on the Dock, and you'll save yourself a significant amount of time and effort.

IN THIS CHAPTER

» Getting to know Finder

» Using aliases for quick access to files

» Viewing windows four ways

» Navigating Finder

» Customizing Finder windows

» Getting information on files
and folders

Chapter 4

Getting to Know Finder and Its Desktop

I n macOS, Finder is the file-management app, which enables you to browse files, launch apps, and manage System Settings. Finder runs all the time and manages your desktop, which is technically a Finder window even though it doesn't look like one. In this chapter and the next, you learn how to get the most from Finder and the desktop. This chapter shows you the essentials of Finder, whereas the next chapter presents additional desktop and Finder features to save you time and effort.

Getting the Hang of Finder, the Desktop, and Icons

All apps are special in their own way, but Finder is more special than others. Finder launches automatically when you log in, stays running in the background all the time, and doesn't include a Quit command. You should make friends with Finder, because you will use it constantly on your Mac.

Introducing the desktop

The *desktop* is the backdrop for Finder — everything you see behind the Dock and any open windows. Figure 4-1 shows the macOS desktop with a Finder window open in front of it. Here's what you need to know:

>> **Your desktop is a special folder called Desktop.** This folder is special because it appears as the desktop rather than in a Finder window. You can access the contents of your desktop either directly or through a Finder window. For example, in Figure 4-1, you can access Sample file.jpeg either on the desktop or through the Finder window that shows the desktop's contents.

>> **You can store your Desktop folder and your Documents folder either on iCloud Drive or in your Home folder on your Mac.** Storing these folders on iCloud Drive lets you sync files easily across multiple devices and access the files no matter where you are, as long as your Mac has an Internet connection. It also provides a kind of automated backup of these folders.

In Figure 4-1, the Desktop folder and Documents folder are stored on iCloud Drive. You can see that these folders appear in the iCloud section of the sidebar. Normally, you would click the Desktop folder in the sidebar to display its contents, but in the figure, iCloud Drive is selected to make its contents, including the Desktop folder and Documents folder, appear in the first column in the main part of the window.

TIP

To control where macOS stores your Desktop folder and Documents folder, choose System Settings ➪ Apple ID ➪ iCloud ➪ Drive. In the iCloud Drive dialog, set the Sync This Mac switch and the Desktop & Documents Folders switch to On (blue) to move the folders to iCloud Drive. To move the folders back to your Mac, set these two switches to Off (white). Click the Done button to close the iCloud Drive dialog.

>> **Items on the desktop behave the same as items in a window.** You move and copy desktop items just as you would items in a window.

>> **Your Mac's start-up disk may appear in the upper-right corner of the desktop.** These days, this disk is usually a solid-state drive (SSD), but it can be a hard drive with spinner platters instead. Your Mac's start-up disk probably has the name Macintosh HD unless you've renamed it. To control whether the start-up disk appears on the desktop, choose Finder ➪ Settings, click the General tab, and then select the Hard Drives check box.

>> **Other disc or drive icons may appear on the desktop.** When you insert a CD or DVD in an optical drive, or connect an external hard drive or a thumb drive, the disc or drive icon may appear on the desktop near the top-right corner. To control whether these icons appear, open Finder Settings and select the External Disks check box and the CDs, DVDs, and iPods check box.

>> **You can move an item to the desktop to make it easier to find.** Simply drag any file or folder out of any window and onto the desktop. This action moves the file from wherever it was to the desktop. Now you can drag the file or folder elsewhere on the desktop if necessary.

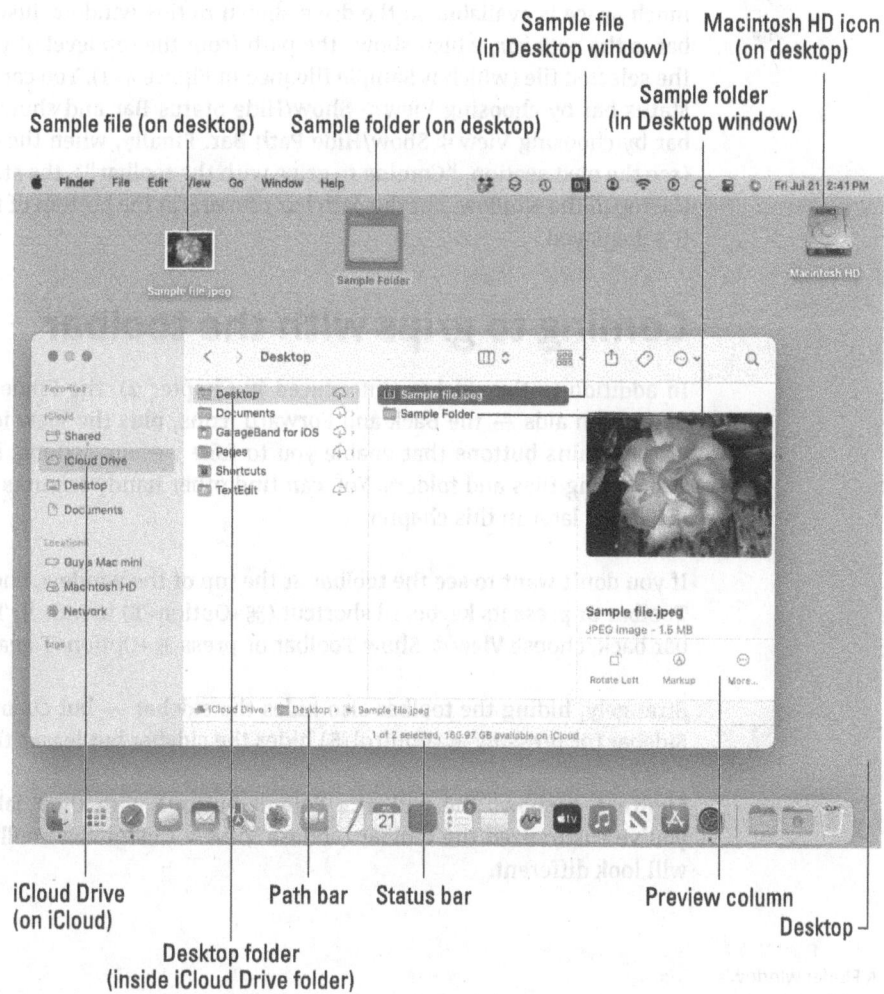

FIGURE 4-1:
A typical Finder
window
and desktop.

Sample file
(in Desktop window)

Macintosh HD icon
(on desktop)

Sample folder
(in Desktop window)

Sample file (on desktop)   Sample folder (on desktop)

iCloud Drive
(on iCloud)

Path bar   Status bar

Preview column

Desktop

Desktop folder
(inside iCloud Drive folder)

If you drag an item from an external volume to any location on your start-up disk (including the desktop), macOS copies the item rather than moving it. When you drag an item, macOS moves it if the source folder and destination folder are on the same disk or volume, but copies the item if the source folder and destination folder are on different disks or volumes.

TECHNICAL STUFF

TIP

Volume is the generic term for any storage container — a hard drive, SSD, CD, DVD, disk image, or remote disk — that appears in the sidebar's Locations section.

At the bottom of the Finder window in Figure 4-1 are two optional bars. The lower of the two is called the *status bar*; it tells you how many items are in each window and, if any are selected, how many of the total you've selected, as well as how much space is available on the drive shown in this window. Just above the status bar is the *path bar*, which shows the path from the top level of your hard drive to the selected file (which is Sample file.jpeg in Figure 4-1). You can show or hide the status bar by choosing View ⇨ Show/Hide Status Bar and show or hide the path bar by choosing View ⇨ Show/Hide Path Bar. Finally, when the toolbar is hidden (see the next section, "Coming to grips with the toolbar"), the status bar moves to the top of the window, but the path bar remains at the bottom of the window when it's displayed.

Coming to grips with the toolbar

In addition to the sidebar (introduced in Chapter 2), the Finder's toolbar offers navigation aids — the Back and Forward icons, plus the View icons. The toolbar also contains buttons that enable you to take various actions, such as grouping and sorting files and folders. You can find other handy features on the Go menu, discussed later in this chapter.

If you don't want to see the toolbar at the top of the window, choose View ⇨ Hide Toolbar or press its keyboard shortcut (⌘+Option+T) to hide it. To bring the toolbar back, choose View ⇨ Show Toolbar or press ⌘+Option+T again.

Strangely, hiding the toolbar also hides the sidebar — but choosing View ⇨ Hide Sidebar (or pressing ⌘+Control+S) hides the sidebar but leaves the toolbar visible.

Figure 4-2 shows the toolbar's default buttons with their labels displayed. If you've customized the toolbar (choose View ⇨ Customize Toolbar), your toolbar will look different.

FIGURE 4-2:
A Finder window's default toolbar.

TIP

To see text labels for your toolbar icons (as shown in Figure 4-2), Control-click or right-click the toolbar and then choose Icon and Text from the contextual menu.

Here's the lowdown on the toolbar's default icons, from left to right:

>> **Back icon and Forward icon:** Clicking the Back icon and Forward icon displays the folders that you've viewed in this window or this tab in sequential order. These icons work a lot like those in a web browser.

The Back icon and Forward icon are really handy, but you can press ⌘ +[for Back and ⌘ +] for Forward to zip along your folder paths.

>> **View icons:** The four View icons change the way that the window displays its contents.

You have four ways to view a window: Icon, List, Column, and Gallery. Play with the four Finder views to see which one works best for you. Icon view is great for images and other files you can identify by their thumbnails. Column view is best for navigating, whereas List view makes it simple to sort a folder's contents by creation date or size; List view also lets you view the contents of multiple folders at the same time. Gallery view is great for folders with documents because you can see the contents of many document types right in the window.

Press ⌘ +1 for Icon view, ⌘ +2 for List view, ⌘ +3 for Column view, and ⌘ +4 for Gallery view. See the section "Opening a Window and Enjoying the View," later in this chapter, for more on views.

>> **Group By/Sort By:** Click this icon to see a pop-up menu with options for grouping this window's contents. Hold down the Option key to change the sort order within the selected group. This menu works in all four views. Read more about it in the section "What's your view?" later in this chapter.

>> **Share:** Click here to share the selected items with others. A pop-up menu lets you choose to share via apps such as Mail, Messages, AirDrop, and Notes.

macOS lets you add other services (such as Vimeo or LinkedIn) and apps (such as Photos and Aperture) to your Share menu. To manage these extensions, click Share and then click Edit Actions. Alternatively, you can launch the System Settings app, click the General icon in the sidebar, click Login Items & Extensions on the General screen, and then click the *i* icon to the right of the Sharing button.

>> **Add Tags:** Click this icon to assign one or more named and colored tags to selected items. You find out more about tags and tagging in "Customizing Finder Windows" later in this chapter.

>> **Action:** Click this icon to see a pop-up menu of all the context-sensitive actions you can perform on selected icons, as shown in Figure 4-3.

TIP

If you see angle brackets (>>) at the right edge of the toolbar, as in Figure 4-3, at least one toolbar item isn't visible. Click the angle brackets, and a menu displays all hidden items (View, Group By, Share, Add Tags, and Action in Figure 4-3). Or expand the window so that it's wide enough to display all the items on the toolbar.

>> **Search:** Click the magnifying-glass icon, and the Search box appears, enabling you to search for files or folders quickly. Just type a word (or even a few letters), and in a few seconds, Finder displays a list of files that match. You can also start a search by choosing File ⇨ Find or pressing ⌘+F. You find out all about searching in Chapter 10.

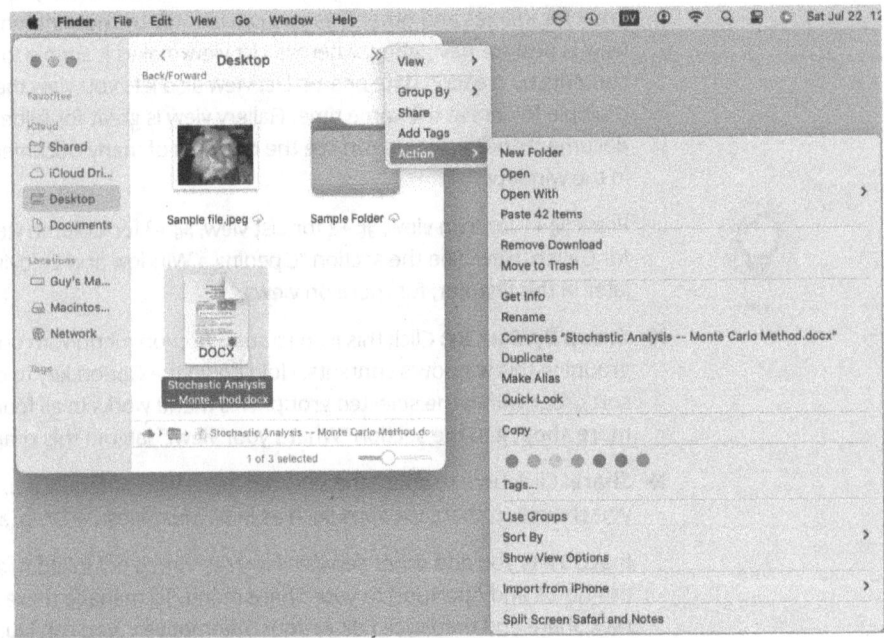

FIGURE 4-3:
Use the Action pop-up menu to perform common actions on selected items.

Grasping what an icon is

In Finder, an *icon* is a visual representation of an item or a container on your hard drive. A *container* can be an SSD, a hard drive, a USB thumb drive, a folder, a CD, a DVD, or a shared network volume. A container can contain a virtually unlimited number of app files, document files, and folders — and those folders can contain an unlimited number of app files, document files, and folders.

REMEMBER

Icons on the Dock and in the sidebar of Finder windows are different from the icons that represent files, folders, and so on. The difference is that the Dock and sidebar icons are aliases, small files that point to actual files and folders.

Working with icons is easy:

» Click to select.

» Double-click to open.

» Drag to move.

» Release the mouse button to drop.

Identifying your Finder icons in the wild

Although all icons work the same way, they come in different kinds, shapes, and sizes. Here are the major icon types:

» **App icons** represent apps, also known as *applications* or *programs* — the software you use to accomplish tasks on your Mac. Mail, Safari, and Calendar are apps. So are Microsoft Word and Adobe Photoshop.

App icons are usually squarish so that they can look more or less regular on the Dock and on the Launchpad screen. The first row of icons in Figure 4-4 displays an assortment of app icons.

» **Document icons** represent files created by apps. Letters created with TextEdit are documents. This chapter began life as a document created in Microsoft Word. Spreadsheet, PDF, video, image, and song files are all documents.

Document icons are often reminiscent of a piece of paper, as shown in the second row of icons in Figure 4-4.

TIP

If your document icons are generic (like the first three icons in the second row of Figure 4-4), but you prefer icons that reflect their contents (like the last three icons in the second row of Figure 4-4), open View Options or press the ⌘+J shortcut and then select the Show Icon Preview check box. (See Chapter 20 for additional details about View Options.)

» **Folder and disk icons** represent the Mac's organizational containers. You can put icons — and the apps or documents they stand for — in folders or disks. You can put folders in disks or in other folders, but you can't put a disk inside another disk.

Folders look like manila folders and can contain just about any other file. You use folders to organize your files and apps on your hard drive. You can have as many folders as you want. The third row of Figure 4-4 shows some typical folder icons.

Although disks behave pretty much like folders, their icons often look like disks, as shown in the last row of Figure 4-4.

>> **Alias icons** are wonderful organizational tools. See the next section, "Alias Files and Folders," to find out just how useful they are.

Font Book   Freeform   Home   Image Capture   Launchpad   Mail   Maps

Excel Spreadsheet.xlsx   Word Document.docx   Another Word Document.docx   Image File.jpg   Archive (Zip) File.zip   Music File.m4a

Applications   Downloads   Movies   Music   Pictures   Public

Macintosh HD   DVD   USB Disk   Network   Time Machine Disk

FIGURE 4-4: Icons come in many shapes and designs.

TIP

If you're looking for details about how to organize your icons in folders, move them around, delete them, and so on, skip ahead to Chapter 8.

Alias Files and Folders

An *alias* is a tiny file that automatically opens the file, folder, disk, or network volume that it represents. Aliases are great organizational tools that let you access a file from more than one place without creating multiple copies of the file.

An alias is very different from a duplicated file. The Preview app, for example, uses around 11 megabytes (MB) of disk space. If you *duplicate* Preview, you'll have two 11 MB files. But if you create an alias to Preview, it uses a mere 4 kilobytes (K) of disk space, yet it opens the Preview app when you double-click it. So try placing aliases of the apps and files you use most often in convenient places such as the desktop or a folder in your Home folder.

Understanding the advantages of aliases

An alias enables you to open any file, folder, or app on any drive from anywhere else on any drive. These are the main benefits of aliases:

TIP

>> **Convenience:** Aliases enable you to make items appear to be in more than one place. Say you're creating several crucial documents; you might place an alias of each document on the desktop so you can open the documents quickly from there rather than navigating to the folder that contains them.

The Dock is the king of shortcuts. Make sure that your Dock contains a shortcut for each app you want to be able to launch instantly; use Launchpad for apps you launch less frequently. Put aliases to essential documents on folders on the right side of the Dock.

>> **Flexibility and organization:** You can create aliases and store them anywhere on your Mac to represent the same document in several folders.

>> **Integrity:** Some apps must remain in the same folder as their supporting files and folders, such as dictionaries, thesauri, data files, and templates. But you can put aliases to such apps wherever you find helpful.

Creating aliases

The icon for an alias looks the same as the icon for the original file or folder it represents, but a tiny arrow (shown in the margin) appears in the lower-left corner of its icon. If you create the alias in the same folder as the original icon, Finder tacks *alias* onto the name for clarity. Figure 4-5 shows an alias and its *parent* icon — the icon for the item that opens when you double-click the alias.

Rose 42.png   Rose 42.png alias

FIGURE 4-5:
An alias (right)
and its parent.

To create an alias for an icon, do one of the following:

>> Click the parent icon and choose File ⇨ Make Alias or press ⌘+Control+A.

>> Click the parent icon, open the Action menu (on the toolbar of all Finder windows), and choose the Make Alias command.

>> Control-click or right-click the parent icon, and choose Make Alias from the contextual menu that appears.

>> Click the parent icon, press and hold down ⌘+Option, and then drag the icon to where you want the alias. An alias appears where you release the mouse button. If you drag to a different folder, the alias doesn't receive the *alias* suffix. (If you drag within a folder, the alias still gets the suffix.)

Deleting aliases

To delete an alias, drag it to the Trash icon on the Dock. You can also Control-click or right-click the alias and choose Move to Trash from the contextual menu that appears, or select the icon and press ⌘+Delete.

Deleting an alias does *not* delete the parent item. To delete the parent item, you have to hunt it down and kill it yourself. Read on . . .

Hunting down an alias's parent

You can track down an alias's parent by using the Show Original command:

>> Select the alias icon, and then choose File ⇨ Show Original or press ⌘+R.

>> Select the alias icon, open the Action menu on the toolbar, and then choose the Show Original command.

>> Control-click or right-click the alias icon, and then choose Show Original from the contextual menu.

Finder opens a window to the folder containing the parent and selects the parent.

Opening a Window and Enjoying the View

Finder offers four views, so you can select the best one for any occasion. Some people like one view so much that they rarely (or never) use others. Other people use keyboard shortcuts to switch views instantly without reaching for the mouse.

Moving through folders fast in Column view

Column view enables you to look through a lot of folders quickly and at the same time, and it's especially useful when those folders are filled with graphics files.

 To switch the current window to Column view, shown in Figure 4-6, click the Column view icon on the toolbar (shown in the margin), choose View ⇨ As Columns in Finder, or press ⌘+3.

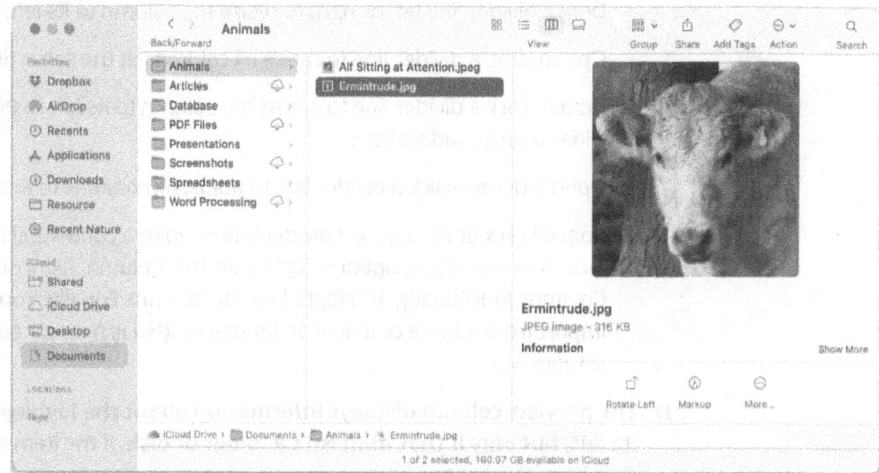

FIGURE 4-6:
A Finder window
in Column view.

Here's how you'd click in Column view to see the list of folders and files in Figure 4-6:

1. Click the Documents icon in the sidebar to display its contents in the first column.

2. Click the Animals folder in this column to display its contents in the second column.

3. Click Ermintrude.jpg in the second column to display the file's preview in the Preview pane, along with information about the file, such as its size (316 KB), and buttons for rotating the image, applying markup to it, and taking other actions.

TIP

To display the Preview pane in any view, choose View ⇨ Show Preview or press ⌘+Shift+P. You can modify the information you see in the preview by choosing View ⇨ Show Preview Options and enabling the items you want to display in the preview column.

Here's what you need to know to work effectively in Column view:

>> **You can have as many columns in a Column view window as your screen can handle.** Drag any edge or corner of the window to enlarge it so that new columns have room to open. You can also click the green Zoom button to make the window fill the screen, or Option-click the green Zoom button to maximize the window without hiding the menu bar.

>> **Drag the column divider lines to resize the column width:**

  • Drag a divider line left or right to resize the column to its left.

  • Option-drag a divider line to resize all columns at the same time.

  • Double-click a divider line to adjust the column to its left to Right Size, just wider than its widest item.

  • Option–double-click a divider line to adjust all columns to Right Size.

  • Control-click or right-click a divider line to open a contextual menu that includes three sizing options: Right Size This Column, Right Size All Columns Individually, and Right Size All Columns Equally. You'll also see Import from iPhone or iPad if an iPhone or iPad is near (or connected to) your Mac.

>> **The preview column displays information about the highlighted item to its left, but only if that item isn't a folder or disk.** If the item is a folder or a disk, its contents appear as another column.

For many items, the picture you see in the preview column is an enlarged view of the file's icon. You see a preview only (as in Figure 4-6) when the selected item is saved in a format that Quick Look (which you discover in Chapter 9) can interpret — most image file formats, including TIFF, JPEG, PNG, GIF, and PDF, plus many other file formats, including Microsoft Word and Pages.

TIP

If you don't want the preview in Column view but do want it in all other views, choose View ➪ Show View Options and deselect the Show Preview Column check box in the resulting dialog. You can do the same for any other view or turn the preview off in all views by choosing View ➪ Hide Preview.

Perusing in Icon view

Icon view is a free-form view that allows you to move your icons around freely within a window. Figure 4-4, earlier in this chapter, shows Icon view.

To display a window in Icon view, click the Icon view icon on the toolbar (shown in the margin), choose View ➪ As Icons from the menu bar, or press ⌘+1.

TIP

In Icon view, drag the Icon Size slider at the right end of the status bar to make the icons just the size you want. If you hide the window's sidebar and toolbar, the status bar and the Icon Size slider move to the top of the window.

Listless? Try viewing folders as a list

Next up is List view (shown in Figure 4-7), which displays little angle brackets to the left of each folder. These angle brackets, which were called *disclosure triangles* (and actually were triangles) in earlier macOS releases, let you see the contents of a folder without opening it. List view also allows you to select items from multiple folders at the same time and to move or copy items between folders in a single window. List view is the view in which macOS Sequoia presents Spotlight search results.

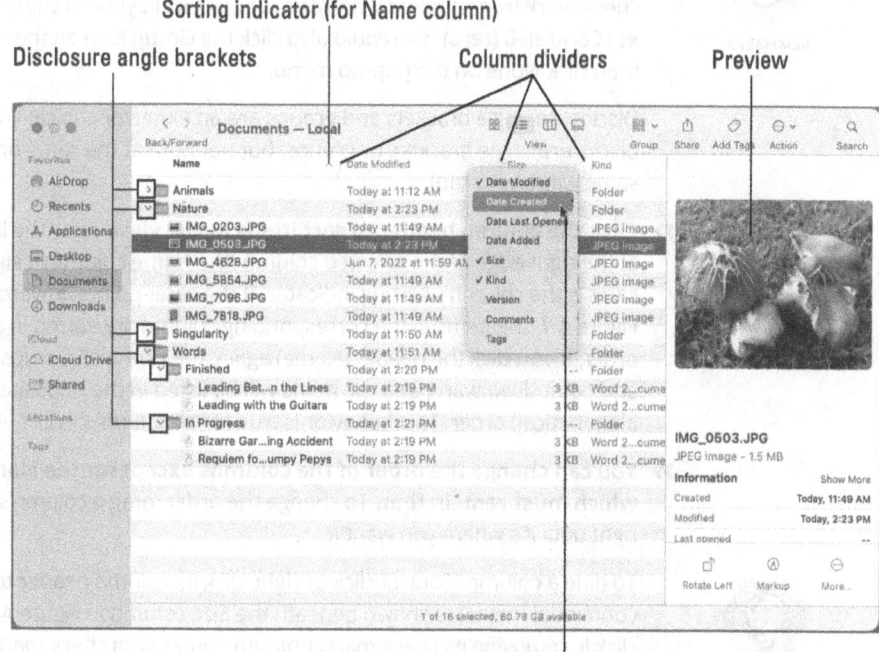

Sorting indicator (for Name column)

Disclosure angle brackets   Column dividers   Preview

Control-click or right-click in header to select which columns to display

FIGURE 4-7:
A window in
List view.

To display a window in List view, click the List view icon on the toolbar (shown in the margin), choose View ⇨ As List in Finder, or press ⌘+2.

Here's how to browse and find things in List view:

>> **To disclose a folder's contents, click the angle bracket to its left or, if the folder is selected, press → or Option+→.** Pressing → expands the folder only; pressing Option+→ expands all subfolders as well. Figure 4-7 shows the results of clicking the angle bracket to the left of the Words folder and selecting (highlighting) the Words folder and pressing Option+→, thus expanding the Words folder's subfolders (the Finished folder and the In Progress folder).

To close an open folder, click the angle bracket again or select the folder and press ←. To close all open folders in a List-view window, choose Edit ⇨ Select All (or press ⌘ +A) and then press Option+←.

The angle brackets don't appear if you're using groups. To see the angle brackets, turn groups off by choosing View ⇨ Use Groups (removing the check mark from the menu item) or pressing its keyboard shortcut, ⌘ +Control+0 (zero). You could also click the Group icon on the toolbar, and then click None on the pop-up menu.

Disclosure angle brackets and groups are an either/or choice: You have either disclosure angle brackets or groups, but not both at the same time (in the same window or tab).

>> **Click the column header to sort items in List view.** Note the little caret (^) at the right edge of the selected column (the Name column in Figure 4-7). That caret is the column's sorting indicator. If the caret points upward, as it does in Figure 4-7, the items in the corresponding column are sorted in alphabetical order; if you click the header (Name) again, the caret will flip upside down and point downward, and the items will be listed in the opposite (reverse alphabetical) order. This behavior is true for all columns in List-view windows.

>> **You can change the order of the columns except for the Name column, which must remain first.** To change the order, drag a column's name left or right until it's where you want it.

To hide a column, Control-click or right-click its column header to display the contextual menu (as shown beneath the Size column in Figure 4-7), and then click it, removing its check mark. Column names with check marks are displayed; column names that are unchecked are hidden.

You can fine-tune all four views and the desktop by using the View Options window, which you open by choosing View ⇨ Show View Options or pressing ⌘ +J. The options you see apply to the active window or to the desktop (when the desktop is active). Click the Use as Defaults button to apply these options to all windows in that view (that is, Icon, List, Column, or Gallery).

>> **To widen or shrink a column, hover the pointer over the dividing line between that column, and drag left or right.** When your pointer is over the dividing line in the header, it changes to a double-headed resizer, as shown in the margin.

Playing to the Gallery

Gallery view is good for scanning visually through your files. To display a window in Gallery view, click the Gallery view icon on the toolbar (shown in the margin), choose View ⇨ As Gallery in Finder, or press ⌘+4. Figure 4-8 shows Gallery view.

FIGURE 4-8:
A Finder window
in Gallery view.

Gallery view is primarily useful for folders containing images or documents. It has three noteworthy features:

>> The selected item (IMG_7096.JPG in Figure 4-8) appears in a preview at the top of the window.

>> The preview column displays additional information about the selected item.

>> You can flip through previews by clicking the images to the left or right of the current image or by pressing ← or →.

What's your view?

In addition to the four views, Finder's View menu offers several commands that might help you browse your files and folders more easily:

>> **Use Groups** (active window only): When this command is enabled, it subdivides the items in the active window into groups, as shown in Figure 4-9. In the figure, the items in the Recents folder are grouped by Kind, which gives groups such as Documents, Images, and PDF Documents.

>> **Sort By:** This submenu offers the following options for sorting items in the active window:

- None (⌘+Option+Control+0); Icon view only
- Snap to Grid (no shortcut)
- Name (⌘+Option+Control+1)
- Kind (⌘+Option+Control+2)
- Date Last Opened (⌘+Option+Control+3)
- Date Added (⌘+Option+Control+4)
- Date Modified (⌘+Option+Control+5)
- Date Created (no shortcut)
- Size (⌘+Option+Control+6)
- Tags (⌘+Option+Control+7)

TIP

The Sort By command becomes Group By when Groups are enabled.

>> **Clean Up:** Clean Up is available only in Icon view or on the desktop when no windows are active. Choose this command to align icons to an invisible grid; use it to keep your windows and desktop neat and tidy. (If you like this invisible grid, don't forget that you can turn it on or off for the desktop and individual windows by using View Options.) If no windows are active, the command cleans up your desktop instead. (To deactivate all open windows, click anywhere on the desktop or close all open windows.)

>> **Clean Up By:** This command combines the tidiness of the Clean Up command with the organizational rigor of the Sort By command. Clean Up By sorts the icons by your choice of criteria:

- Name (⌘+Option+1)
- Kind (⌘+Option+2)
- Date Modified (⌘+Option+5)

- Date Created (no shortcut)

- Size (⌘ +Option+6)

- Tags (⌘ +Option+7)

Clean Up By is similar to the Sort By command, but unlike Sort By, Clean Up By is a one-time action. After you've used Clean Up By, you can once again move icons around and reorganize them any way you like.

TIP

Unlike Clean Up By, Sort By is persistent and will continue to reorganize your icons automatically. After you tell macOS to sort the icons in a window, you can't move those icons around.

The Clean Up and Clean Up By commands are available only for windows viewed as icons. The Sort By command is available in all four views and remains in effect if you switch to a different view or close the window. To stop Finder from arranging icons in a window, choose View ⇨ Sort By ⇨ None, or Option-click the toolbar's Group pop-up menu and choose None.

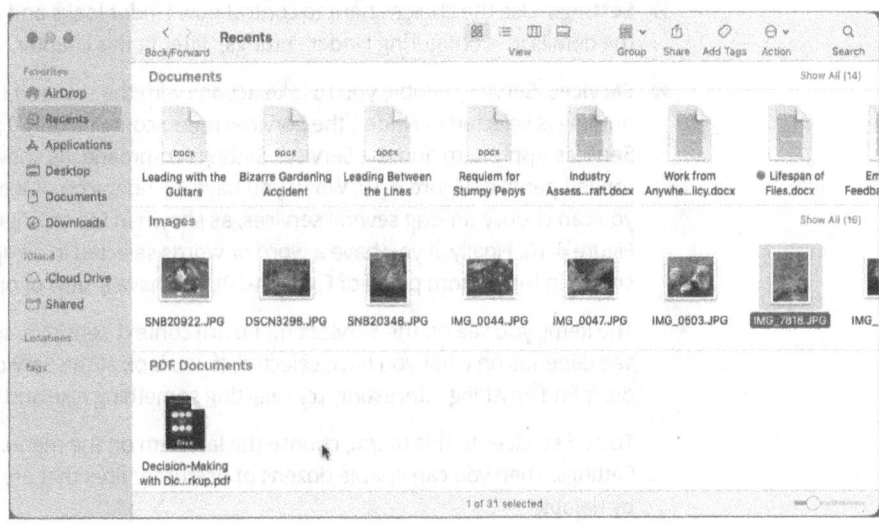

FIGURE 4-9:
The items in this window are grouped by Kind.

WARNING

If you place icons carefully in specific places on your desktop, beware of the Clean Up By and Sort By commands, because they'll wreck your arrangement. You can't undo either Clean Up By or Sort By.

Finder on the Menu

To get things done in Finder, you'll want to use the menus extensively. The following subsections explain what the key menu commands do.

The actual Finder menu

Here are a few of the main items you can find on the Finder menu:

>> **About Finder:** Choose this command to find out which version of Finder is running on your Mac.

TIP

For Finder, the About menu item isn't particularly useful, but you'll likely find it more helpful for other apps. The About dialog for other apps usually gives information about the app's version number, which you may need for troubleshooting esoteric problems, and — for a paid app — your license or subscription number, which you may need to commandeer tech support.

>> **Settings:** Use the choices here to control how Finder looks and acts. Find out the details in "Configuring Finder settings," later in this chapter.

>> **Services:** Services enable you to take actions with the selected file or folder. If nothing is selected in Finder, the Services menu contains only a grayed-out No Services Apply item and the Services Settings command, as shown in the top-left panel of Figure 4-10. When you have a Finder icon or icons selected, you can choose among several services, as shown in the top-right panel of Figure 4-10. Finally, if you have a word or words selected in an app (TextEdit is shown in the bottom panel of Figure 4-10), you have a slew of options.

The items you see on the Services menu are context-sensitive, so what you see depends on what you have selected. If you look at the Services menu and don't find anything interesting, try selecting something else and looking again.

To add services to this menu, choose the last item on the menu: Services Settings. Then you can enable dozens of useful services that aren't available by default.

>> **Hide Finder (⌘ +H):** Use this command when Finder windows are open and are distracting you. Issuing the Hide Finder command makes Finder inactive (another app becomes active) and hides any open Finder windows. To make Finder visible again, click the Finder icon on the Dock. To make Finder, and any other apps you've hidden, visible again, open the active app's menu and choose Show All. For example, if TextEdit is the active app, choose TextEdit ⇨ Show All.

TIP

The advantage of hiding Finder — rather than closing or minimizing all your windows to get a clean screen — is that you don't have to open all the windows again when you're ready to get them back. Instead, just choose Show All (to see all windows in all apps) or click the Finder icon on the Dock to see all Finder windows.

>> **Hide Others (Option+⌘ +H):** This command hides all windows of all running apps except the active app. It appears on most apps' self-named menus and is good for hiding distractions to help you focus on the active app.

TIP

You can give the Hide Others command by holding down ⌘ +Option and clicking the app's icon on the Dock. For example, ⌘ +Option-click Safari to display Safari and hide all other apps.

>> **Show All:** Use this command as the antidote to both of the Hide commands. Choose it, and nothing is hidden anymore.

These three commands require at least one app to be running and not hidden (in addition to Finder). When Finder is the only app running or not hidden, these three commands are unavailable.

TIP

See Chapter 9 for information on Mission Control and Stage Manager, two features that enable you to switch quickly among apps.

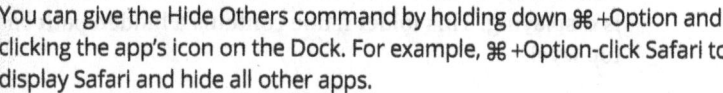

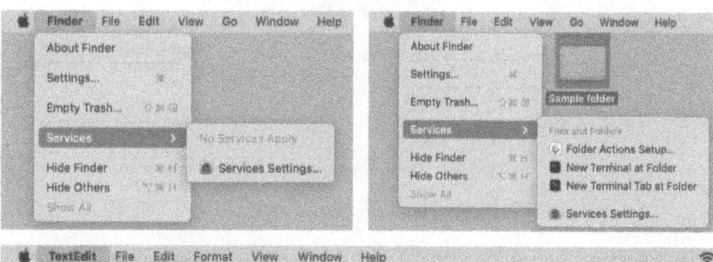

FIGURE 4-10:
Services available with nothing selected (top left), an icon selected (top right), and some text selected in a TextEdit document (bottom).

Finally, if you noticed that Finder menu's Empty Trash command isn't mentioned here, that's because it gets detailed coverage in Chapter 8.

Navigating with the current folder's pop-up menu

Each Finder window's title bar bears the name of the folder (or disk) the window is displaying. This folder name contains a hidden path back from the folder to the top level.

To display the path, ⌘-click, Control-click, or right-click the folder name. Figure 4-11 shows the pop-up menu that appears. Here, the current folder name is Process, so that appears at the top of the menu. Below it is the path of folders back to the Mac's drive (Macintosh HD) and the Mac itself (Guy's Mac mini). Click the folder you want to display.

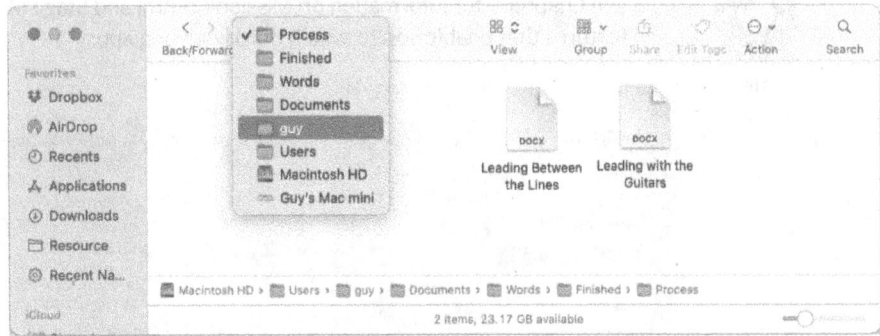

FIGURE 4-11:
Traverse folders swiftly from this convenient pop-up menu.

REMEMBER

You can display the path bar near the bottom of the window (as in Figure 4-11) by choosing View ➪ Show Path Bar. Then you can double-click any folder displayed on the path bar to open it. You can also Control-click or right-click a folder in the path bar to display a contextual menu packed with useful commands.

This pop-up-menu move works not only in Finder windows, but also on the title bar of most document windows (Word, Photoshop, and so on), showing you the path to the folder containing the document you're working on.

Go places with the Go menu

The Go menu is chock-full of shortcuts. The items on this menu take you to various places on your Mac — many of the same ones where you can go with the Finder window's toolbar — and a few other places. These are the menu items:

>> **Back (⌘ +[):** Returns you to the previous folder open in this Finder window or tab. It's equivalent to the Back button on the Finder toolbar, in case you have the toolbar hidden.

>> **Forward (⌘ +]):** Moves you forward again through the folders to which you've just gone back. For example, say you're in the Documents folder, and you open a subfolder called Words, then open a subfolder of Words called Archive. From the Archive folder, clicking Back once takes you back to the Words folder; clicking again takes you back to the Documents folder. You can then click Forward once to return to the Words folder, and click Forward again to return to the Archive folder.

>> **Enclosing Folder (⌘ +↑):** Displays the folder that contains (encloses) the currently selected item.

>> **Recents (Shift+⌘ +F):** Displays all your recent document files.

TIP

After choosing Recents, you might choose View ⇨ Sort By (or View ⇨ Group By) to put these files in your preferred order.

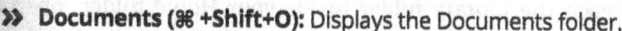

>> **Documents (⌘ +Shift+O):** Displays the Documents folder.

>> **Desktop (⌘ +Shift+D):** Displays the Desktop folder, viewing your desktop's files and folders in a window instead of directly.

>> **Downloads (⌘ +Option+L):** Displays the Downloads folder, which is where files you download in Safari, save as attachments in Mail, or receive via AirDrop (explained shortly) are saved by default.

>> **Home (⌘ +Shift+H):** Displays your Home folder (which is named with your short name).

>> **Computer (⌘ +Shift+C):** Displays the Computer folder, showing your Mac's disks and the network to which the Mac is connected.

>> **AirDrop (⌘ +Shift+R):** Displays the AirDrop folder. AirDrop lets you share files wirelessly with Macs, iPhones, and iPads around you. No setup or special settings are required. Just click the AirDrop icon in the Finder sidebar, choose this menu item, or press the keyboard shortcut, and your Mac automatically discovers nearby devices using AirDrop.

>> **Network (⌘ +Shift+K):** Displays whatever is accessible on your network.

>> **iCloud Drive (⌘ +Shift+I):** Displays the contents of your iCloud Drive (which you read more about in Chapter 8).

>> **Applications (⌘ +Shift+A):** Displays your Applications folder, which contains the apps that came with your Mac and apps you install.

>> **Utilities (⌘ +Shift+U):** Displays the Utilities folder inside the Applications folder. Chapter 24 introduces you to some of the most useful utilities.

>> **Recent Folders:** This submenu gives you quick access to folders you've visited recently. Every time you open a folder, macOS creates an alias to it and stores it in the Recent Folders folder. You can open any of these aliases by choosing Go ⇨ Recent Folders. If you've been using folders that have embarrassing names, and someone is about to look over your shoulder, click Clear Menu to wipe the list.

>> **Go to Folder (⌘ +Shift+G):** Displays the Go to the Folder window, which enables you to go quickly to a folder by typing its path. Start by typing a forward slash, **/**, and then begin typing the folder name. The Go To area lists matching folders; if the one you want appears, press the down-arrow key to select it, and then press Return. Otherwise, keep typing, separating folder names with forward slashes. If macOS completes the folder name you're typing with ghostly letters spelling out the right folder, press Tab to accept the suggestion.

>> **Connect to Server (⌘ +K):** Displays the Connect to Server dialog, which enables you to reach resources on a network or the Internet.

TIP

To reach the Library folder inside your Home folder, open the Go menu, press Option to display the Library item on the menu, and then click Library. macOS hides the command to discourage casual access to the Library folder.

Customizing Finder Windows

Finder not only enables you to open multiple windows, each containing as many tabs as needed, but also lets you customize what it displays and the way it works. The following subsections explain how to customize your Finder windows.

Adding files and folders to the sidebar

To give yourself quick access to a file or folder, add it to the sidebar. Select the file or folder, and then choose File ⇨ Add to Sidebar or press ⌘ +Control+T.

TIP

You can add folders (but not files) to the sidebar by dragging them to the sidebar. Finder displays a horizontal blue line with a loop at its left end to indicate where the folder will land; drag up or down, as needed, and then release the folder.

You can move either files or folders to folders in the sidebar by dragging them over the folder name. When the folder name becomes highlighted, drop the item.

After you've loaded up the sidebar with the items you want, you can drag them up and down into your preferred order.

To remove an item from the sidebar, right-click or Control-click the item, and then choose Remove from Sidebar from the contextual menu. Or drag the item off the sidebar and drop it when the little x-in-a-circle icon appears.

Configuring Finder settings

You can find Finder and Desktop settings by choosing Finder ➪ Settings. In the Finder Settings window that appears, click the icons on the toolbar to display one of the four Finder Settings panes: General, Tags, Sidebar, and Advanced.

General pane

The General pane of the Finder Settings window (shown on the left in Figure 4-12) gives you the following options:

>> **Show These Items on the Desktop check boxes:** Select or deselect these check boxes to choose whether icons for hard drives; external disks; CDs, DVDs, and iPods; and connected servers appear on the desktop. macOS Sequoia selects the External Disks check box and the CDs, DVDs, and iPods check box by default but leaves the Hard Disks check box and the Connected Servers check box deselected. If you don't want disk icons cluttering your beautiful desktop, deselect (clear) these check boxes. When they're deselected, you can still work with hard drives, CDs, DVDs, and other types of disks. You just have to open a Finder window and select the disk or disc you want in the sidebar.

>> **New Finder Windows Show:** Choose whether opening a new Finder window displays Recents, your Home folder, the Documents or Desktop folders, or any other disk or folder. Recents is the default. You may want to use your main project folder.

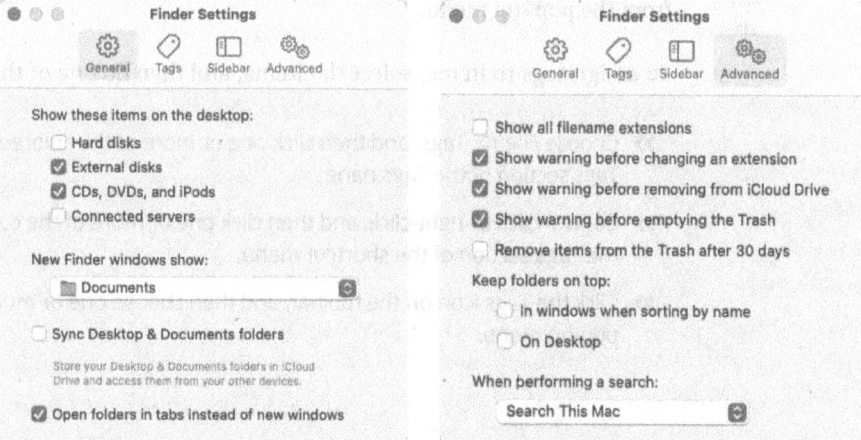

FIGURE 4-12:
The General pane (left) and Advanced pane (right) of the Finder Settings dialog.

>> **Sync Desktop & Documents Folders check box:** Select this check box to sync your Desktop folder and your Documents folder with iCloud Drive so that you can access them from your other devices.

>> **Open Folders in Tabs Instead of New Windows check box:** Selecting this check box spawns a new tab in the current window when you press ⌘ and then double-click a folder or disk. If you don't enable this option, ⌘+double-clicking a folder or disk icon opens it in a new window.

The default behavior is for folders to open in place when you double-click (open) them, which prevents window clutter. If you want a new window or tab instead, press ⌘ before you double-click. This action forces the folder to open in a new window or tab (depending on whether the box is selected).

Tags pane

The Tags pane of the Finder Settings window is where you manage your tags, which appear on Finder's File menu, contextual menus, the sidebar, and the toolbar. You can see a file or folder's tags in Finder windows, Get Info windows and inspectors, and apps' Open and Save dialogs, and you can use them as criteria for searches and smart folders.

>> To rename a tag, click its name and then type a new one.

>> To change a tag's color, click the colored circle to the left of its name and then choose a different color.

>> Select the boxes for tags that you want to appear in the sidebar and on the toolbar.

TIP

To see your deselected tags in the sidebar or on the toolbar, click All Tags in the Tags list in the sidebar, or click Add Tags on the toolbar and then choose Show All from the pop-up menu.

To assign tags to items, select the items, and then do one of the following:

>> Choose File ⇨ Tags, and then click one or more of the colored dots in the Tags section of the Tags pane.

>> Control-click or right-click, and then click one or more of the colored dots in the Tags section of the shortcut menu.

>> Click the Tags icon on the toolbar, and then choose one or more tags from the pop-up menu.

Here are three more essential moves with tags:

>> **To create a custom tag on the fly:** Control-click or right-click an item, choose Tags from the contextual menu, type a label for the new tag, and then press Return.

>> **To untag an item:** Control-click or right-click the item, choose Tags from the contextual menu, choose the tag you want to remove, and then press Delete.

>> **To remove every instance of a tag from every file and folder on your disk:** Control-click or right-click the tag in the Tags pane of Finder Settings, and choose Delete Tag from the contextual menu. Don't worry — deleting a tag won't delete the items. Deleting it just removes that tag from every item.

TIP

Click a tag in the sidebar to see every file on all connected drives with that tag.

Sidebar pane

The Sidebar pane of the Finder Settings window lets you choose which items are displayed in the sidebar. Select the check box to display the item; deselect the check box to not display it.

Advanced pane

The Advanced pane of the Finder Settings window (shown on the right in Figure 4-12) contains the following check boxes and a pop-up menu:

>> **Show All Filename Extensions check box:** Tells Finder to display the two-, three-, four-, or more-character file extensions (such as .docx in Summary. docx) that make your Mac's file lists look more like those in Linux or Windows. The Finder hides file extensions from you by default, but if you want to be able to see them in Finder when you open or save files, select this check box.

>> **Show Warning Before Changing an Extension check box:** Allows you to turn off the nagging dialog that appears if you attempt to change the file extension.

>> **Show Warning Before Removing from iCloud Drive:** Warns you when you go to remove a file or folder from your iCloud drive.

>> **Show Warning Before Emptying the Trash check box:** Allows you to turn off the dialog telling you how many items are in the Trash and asking whether you really want to delete them.

>> **Remove Items from the Trash After 30 Days check box:** Automatically deletes any item that has been in the Trash for more than 30 days.

» **Keep Folders on Top (two check boxes):** These two options sort folders first and then files:

- *In Windows When Sorting by Name:* Select this check box to sort folders before files in all windows sorted by name.

- *On Desktop:* Select this check box to sort folders before files on the desktop.

» **When Performing a Search pop-up menu:** Choose the default search location for searches you start. Your choices are Search This Mac (the default), Search the Current Folder, and Use the Previous Search Scope.

Digging for Data in the Info Window

When you need more information about an item than a Finder window shows, you can open an Info window that not only gives you all the details available, but also enables you to choose which other users (if any) you want to have the privilege of using this item. (See Chapter 16 for a full discussion of sharing files and privileges.) The Info window is also where you can lock an item so that it can't be renamed or dragged to the Trash.

To open the Info window for an item, click the item and choose File ⇨ Get Info (or press ⌘ +I). The Info window opens, showing several sections that you can expand or collapse by clicking their headings, such as General and More Info. Figure 4-13 shows the Info window for an image (a .jpeg file named Rainbow 97.jpeg) with its various sections expanded and collapsed.

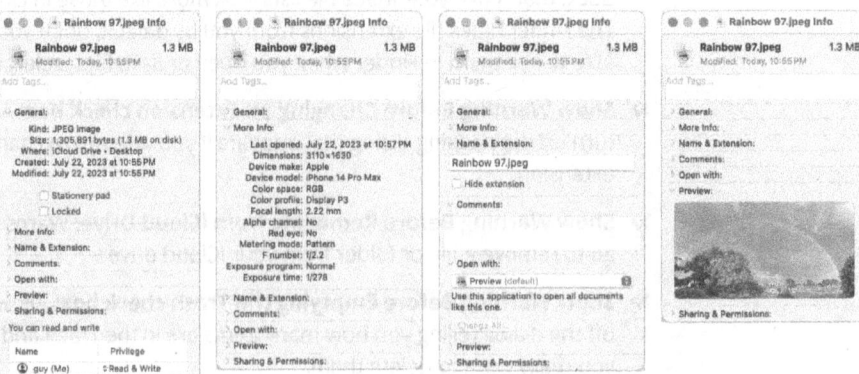

FIGURE 4-13:
A typical Info window for an image (Rainbow 97.jpeg).

The selection of information in the Info window varies depending on the item and its file format. The sections that you see for most items include the following:

» **Add Tags:** Click this field to add tags to this item.

» **General:** For information of the general kind, such as

- *Kind:* What kind of file this is (app, document, disk, folder, and so on)

- *Size:* How much hard drive space the file uses

- *Where:* The path to the folder that contains this file

- *Created:* The date and time when the file was created

- *Modified:* The date and time when the file was last modified (saved)

» Six other options may appear in the General section:

- *Version:* This section displays copyright information and the file's version number.

- *Shared Folder* (check box): This control designates the folder as Shared, so other users are allowed to see and use its contents. You find out all about sharing in Chapter 16.

- *Stationery Pad* (check box): This control appears only in the Info windows of document icons. If you select it, the file becomes a template. When you open a Stationery Pad document, a copy of its contents appears in a new Untitled document that you'd typically save with a descriptive name.

- *Locked* (check box): If this box is selected, you receive the following warning if you try to put the item in the Trash: *This Item Is Locked. Do You Want to Move It to the Trash Anyway?* Your options are Stop and Continue. If you choose Continue, the item goes into the Trash as usual. You can retrieve the item from the Trash like any other item by using the Put Back command or by dragging the item out of the Trash. When you empty the Trash, the item is deleted just as though it weren't locked.

- *Prevent App Nap* (check box): macOS can tell when an app is hidden behind other windows. If an app isn't doing something — playing music, downloading files, or checking your email, for example — App Nap conserves valuable battery runtime on MacBooks by slowing the app. As soon as you activate the app again, it shifts back to full speed instantly.

  Although App Nap can reduce CPU energy use by up to 23 percent, it may interfere with the operations of some apps. If it does, try selecting this check box.

- *Open Using Rosetta* (check box): Select this check box to use the Rosetta emulation software to run an app designed for Intel Macs on a Mac that has an Apple Silicon processor (such as an M1 or M2).

>> **More Info:** This section shows when the file was created, modified, and last opened (documents only). For a photo, you also see a lot of details including the camera, focal length, light-metering mode, f-stop, and exposure time.

>> **Name & Extension:** This section displays the file's full name, including its (possibly hidden) extension.

>> **Comments:** In this field, you can type your own comments for Spotlight to use in searches. Chapter 9 explains Spotlight in depth.

>> **Open With:** Open the pop-up menu, and then select the app you want to use as the default for opening this file. Click the Change All button to make the selected app the default for all files of this type.

>> **Preview:** When you select a document icon, the menu offers a Preview section that you can expand to see a glimpse of what's in that document. You can also see this preview in the right-most column when you select a document icon in Column view. If you select a QuickTime movie or sound, you can play your selection right there in the Preview pane without launching a separate app. And when you select most pictures, you see a preview of the actual picture.

>> **Sharing & Permissions:** This section shows which users have access to this item and how much access they're allowed. (See Chapter 16 for more about access privileges.)

TIP

If you press the Option key when you pull down Finder's File menu, the Get Info command changes to Show Inspector (alternatively, press ⌘+Option+I). The Get Info Inspector window looks and acts almost exactly like the Info window, with two exceptions:

>> **Inspector displays info for only the currently selected item.** If you click a different item, Inspector instantly displays the info for the item you clicked, so you can Get Info on lots of items in a row by using the arrow keys or by pressing Tab or Shift+Tab. This can be a great way to work on several files in sequence. By contrast, you may want to open separate Info windows for several files so that you can compare their details.

>> **Inspector displays cumulative information if you select multiple items.** For example, Inspector displays the total size of all the selected files.

IN THIS CHAPTER

» **Organizing your desktop with Stacks**

» **Adding widgets to your desktop**

» **Automating tasks with Quick Actions**

» **Editing image, video, and audio files without an application**

» **Capturing stills and movies of your screen**

Chapter **5**

Getting Fancy with the Desktop and Finder

I n this chapter, you first learn how to organize your desktop with Stacks and how to decorate it with widgets that display information you want to have available at a glance. You then move on to handling tasks swiftly using Quick Actions and capturing screenshots and screen recordings.

Cleaning Up Your Desktop Automatically with Stacks

Putting icons on the desktop can be a great way of giving yourself access to key files. The problem is that your desktop may end up looking like Figure 5-1 — or worse.

FIGURE 5-1:
A messy,
disorganized
desktop.

Good news: Your Mac's Stacks feature lets you streamline your desktop in moments. Click the desktop to make it active, and you can organize it with Stacks in three ways:

>> Choose View ➪ Use Stacks.

>> Press ⌘ +Control+0 (that's a zero).

>> Control-click or right-click anywhere on the desktop, and then choose Use Stacks from the contextual menu.

The Use Stacks command is available only when the desktop is active.

REMEMBER When you choose Use Stacks, your desktop transforms instantly from the mess shown in Figure 5-1 to the six nicely organized stacks shown in the left part of Figure 5-2. Folders on the desktop aren't affected by Stacks; all other icons on the desktop are organized automatically into stacks (Documents, Images, PDF Documents, Music, Presentations, and Spreadsheets in the example).

Click a stack to see its contents, as shown in the right part of Figure 5-2 for the Images stack.

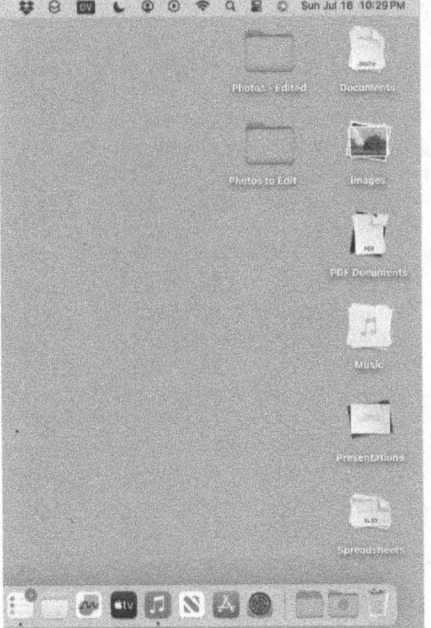

FIGURE 5-2:
Stacks (left)
create order out
of chaos. Click a
stack (Images,
right) to see
its contents.

The expanded stack (Images, directly below the Documents stack icon in the top-right corner) now displays a down-facing caret, indicating that the stack is expanded. Click the stack again to close it. Finally, note that stacks ignore your disk icons (if any).

Choosing Use Stacks is just the start of things. When you're using Stacks, you can group items by choosing View ⇨ Group Stacks By, which offers the following choices:

» None (no keyboard shortcut); disables Stacks view

» Kind (Control+⌘+2)

» Date Last Opened (Control+⌘+3)

» Date Added (Control+⌘+4)

» Date Modified (Control+⌘+5)

» Date Created (no keyboard shortcut)

» Tags (Control+⌘+7)

The stacks in Figure 5-2 are grouped by Kind, but it may be easier to find what you're looking for if you use one of the other options. If you know when you added, modified, or last opened the file, for example, you can choose one of the date-based options, such as Date Created, which is shown in Figure 5-3.

FIGURE 5-3:
Grouping stacks
by Date Created
gives you a
different
perspective from
grouping
them by Kind.

TIP

You can also Control-click or right-click and choose Group Stacks By. The contextual menu offers all the same commands except None.

Finally, if you're not already using tags (discussed in Chapter 4) to organize your files, Stacks may be just the incentive you need to start.

Adding Widgets to Your Desktop

A *widget* is a kind of mini-app that provides quick access to specific information. For example, the Stocks widget displays tickers for stocks you specify; the Weather widget suggests whether you'll get wet, baked, or frozen today; and the Reminders widget nags you about the tasks you're neglecting.

macOS has widgets of its own, but it also lets you use widgets from your iPhone (if you have one). You can place the widgets on the desktop, in Notification Center, or both — whichever you find most useful.

TIP

Widgets tend to be a polarizing feature: Many people love them, many others hate them, and only a few seem to be apathetic. If you find widgets a great way to track information and boost your productivity, use them freely. If you see widgets as useless clutter, simply don't use them.

To add widgets to the desktop, follow these steps:

1. **Control-click or right-click open space on the desktop, and then click Edit Widgets on the contextual menu to open the Widgets dialog (see Figure 5-4).**

2. **In the left pane, click the category of widgets, such as News.**

   You can also search for a widget by clicking the Search Widgets box in the upper-left corner of the Widgets dialog and then typing your search term.

3. **To see a widget's name, move the pointer over it.**

   The name appears in a ScreenTip, as for the Today – Large widget in Figure 5-4.

4. **Either click the widget you want to add, or drag it to where you want it on the desktop.**

   If you click, macOS puts the widget in a default position. You can then drag it elsewhere if you want.

5. **When you finish adding widgets, click Done to close the Widgets dialog.**

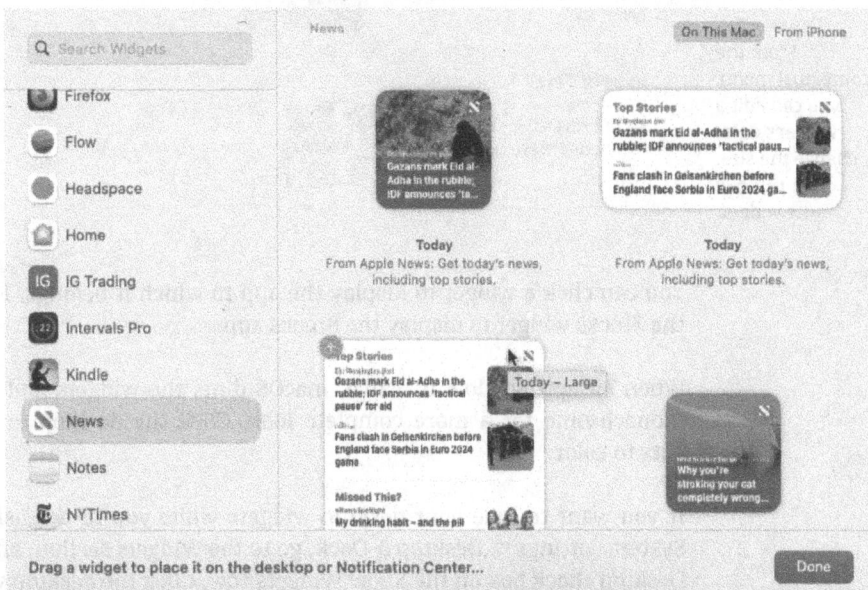

FIGURE 5-4:
In the Widgets dialog, select the category of widgets, and then click the widget to add to the desktop.

The widgets you've added appear on your desktop, and you can drag them to different positions if you want. For further customization, Control-click or right-click a widget, and then choose the appropriate command on the contextual menu (see Figure 5-5):

» **Edit *"Widget"*:** If this command appears, click it to open the widget for editing. Only some widgets have configurable settings. Make your choices, and then click Done.

» **Small, Medium, Large, Extra Large:** Click the size to use for the widget. Some widgets have only some of these sizes.

» **Remove Widget:** Click this command to remove the widget.

» **Edit Widgets:** Click this command to open the Widgets dialog again.

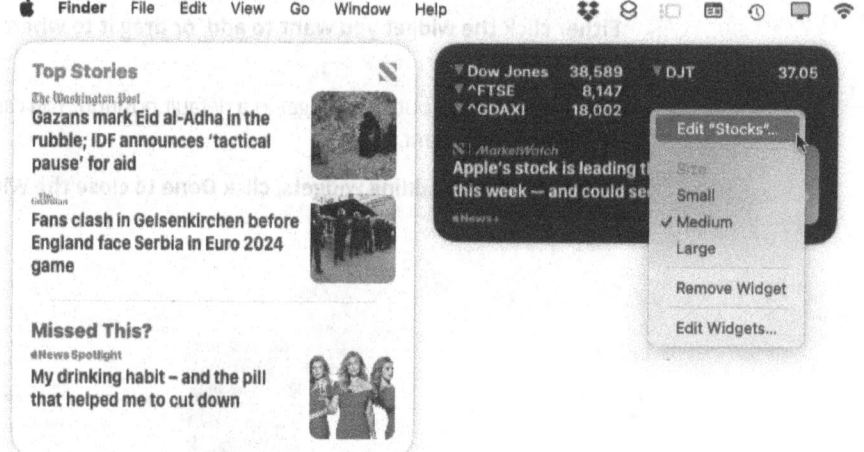

FIGURE 5-5:
From the contextual menu, you can edit a widget's data, change the size, or remove the widget.

You can click a widget to display the app to which it belongs. For example, click the Stocks widget to display the Stocks app.

When an app window is active, macOS dims the widgets and displays them in monochrome for a more complete look. Click the desktop to restore the widgets to color.

If you want to hide your desktop widgets while you're not using them, choose System Settings ⇨ Desktop & Dock, go to the Widgets section, and deselect the On Desktop check box on the Show Widgets row. Click the desktop when you want to display the widgets.

You can also drag a widget from Notification Center to the desktop, or vice versa.

TIP

Doing Things Faster with Quick Actions

Quick Actions are mini-apps that let you perform certain tasks without launching a full-scale application. You'll find them in the Preview panes of Finder windows, in Quick Look windows, and in contextual menus. They're super-useful and can save you the time and effort of opening a program to perform a simple task, such as adding circles and arrows to an image (and much more), trimming video, and rotating pictures.

Getting the most out of Markup

In macOS Sequoia, the Markup icon (shown in the margin) and the Rotate icon (see Figure 5-6) are available in Quick Look windows and the Preview panes of Finder windows, and the commands are on Finder's contextual menu (Control-click or right-click).

Show Markup Toolbar   Rotate

FIGURE 5-6:
Click the Show
Markup Toolbar
icon to see the
Markup toolbar;
click the Rotate
icon to rotate
your image in 90°
increments.

Click the Rotate icon to rotate your document counterclockwise by 90°. To rotate clockwise, hold down Option while you click.

TIP

When you have an image selected and you click the Markup icon in a Quick Look overlay, in a Preview panes in a Finder window, or on a Finder contextual menu, an overlay appears, displaying the image below the Markup toolbar, as shown in Figure 5-7.

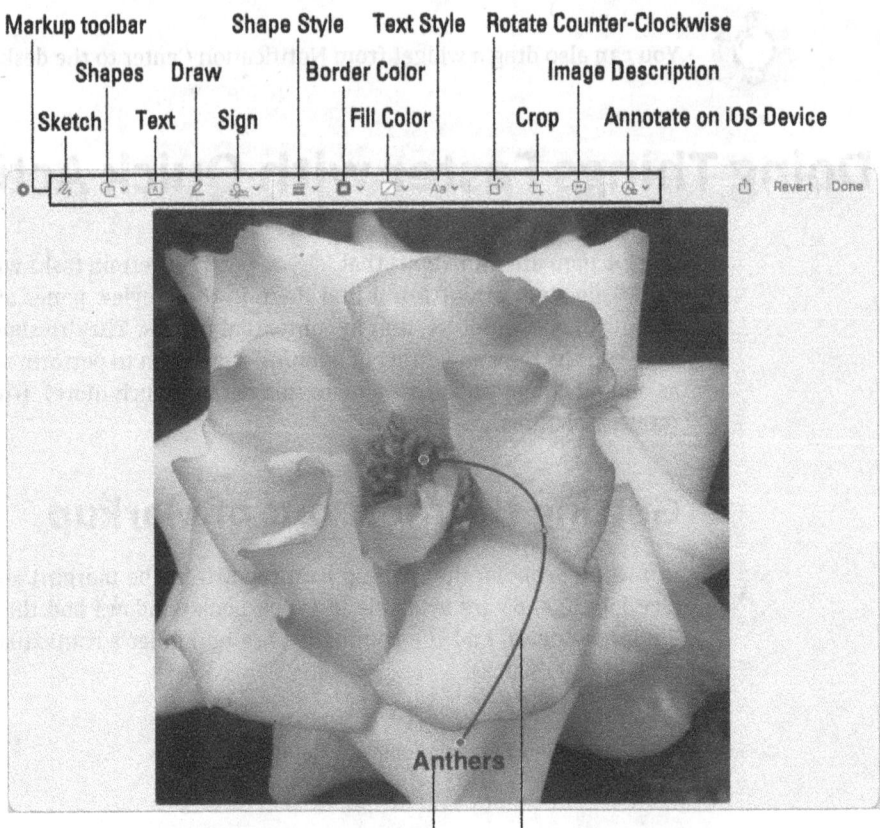

Markup toolbar — Shapes — Draw — Shape Style — Text Style — Border Color — Rotate Counter-Clockwise — Image Description — Sketch — Text — Sign — Fill Color — Crop — Annotate on iOS Device

Revert Done

Anthers

Text added using Markup   Arrow added using Markup

FIGURE 5-7:
The Markup
toolbar above an
image with text
and an arrow
added
using Markup.

Here's how the tools work:

>> **Sketch:** Sketch a shape with a single stroke. Here's the cool part: If your drawing is recognized as a standard shape, such as a circle, a rectangle, or an arrow, it's replaced by a perfectly drawn rendition of the shape. If you don't like it perfect, you can use what you drew instead by choosing it from the palette that appears after you use the tool.

>> **Shapes:** Click a shape to place it on the image and then drag the shape where you want. To resize a shape, use its blue handles. If the shape has green handles, you can use them to alter the shape.

>> You can also zoom in or out and highlight specific shapes by using the pair of tools at the bottom of the Shapes drop-down menu (and shown in Figure 5-8):

- *Highlight:* Click this button to display the highlight and then drag the highlight where you want. To resize it, use the blue handles.

- *Loupe:* Click this button to display the loupe and then drag the loupe over the area you want to magnify. To increase or decrease the magnification level, drag the green handle clockwise or counterclockwise; to increase or decrease the size of the loupe, drag the blue handle in or out. To magnify an area further, you can create additional loupes and stack them; use the yellow guides on the loupes to align them.

» **Text:** Type your text and then drag the text box where you want.

» **Draw:** Use your finger to draw a shape with a single stroke. Press more firmly on the trackpad to draw thicker, heavier lines. This tool is available only on Macs with a Force Touch trackpad.

» **Sign:** If signatures are listed, click one and drag it where you want. To resize it, use the blue handles.

» To create a signature:

- *Using your trackpad:* Click the Sign tool, click Create Signature (if shown), and then click Trackpad. Click the Click Here to Begin prompt, sign your name on the trackpad by using your finger, and then press any key to indicate that you've finished. If the signature is good, click Done; otherwise, click Clear, and try again. If your trackpad supports it, press your finger more firmly on the trackpad to sign with a heavier, darker line.

- *Using a camera:* Click the Sign tool, click Create Signature (if shown), and then click Camera (Mac camera) or iPhone or iPad (camera). Hold your signature (on white paper) facing the camera so that your signature is level with the blue line in the window. When your signature appears in the window, click Done. If you don't like the results, click Clear, and try again.

» **Shape Style:** Change the thickness and type of lines used in a shape or add a shadow to a shape.

» **Border Color:** Change the color of a shape's border.

» **Fill Color:** Change the color of a shape's fill.

» **Text Style:** Change the font type, style, and color.

» **Rotate Counter-Clockwise:** Rotate the item 90° counterclockwise.

» **Crop:** Click to display crop handles at the corners of the image, plus a textual Crop button at the right end of the toolbar. Drag the handles to select the area you want to keep, and then click the Crop button.

>> **Image Description:** Click this button to open the Image Description dialog, type a description of the image, and then click Done.

>> **Annotate on iOS Device (Quick Look only):** Click this button to open the image on your iPhone or iPad so that you can work on it there.

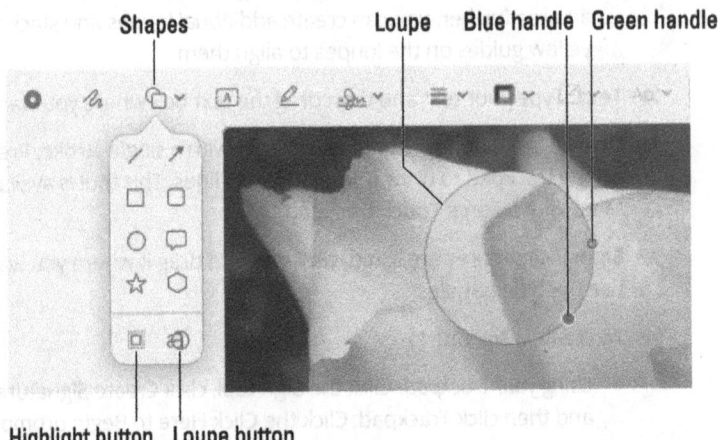

Shapes   Loupe   Blue handle   Green handle

FIGURE 5-8:
The Shapes
drop-down menu
(left) and the
loupe (right)
in action.

Highlight button   Loupe button

Trimming video without launching an app

Although QuickTime Player has allowed you to trim videos for years, you have to launch it and usually wait a few seconds for the video to appear. The Quick Actions feature includes a faster, easier way to trim your videos without launching Quick-Time Player (or another app).

When a video file is selected, you'll find the Trim icon (shown in the margin) available in Quick Look windows, in Finder Preview panes, and on the contextual menu (Control-click or right-click a video and choose Quick Actions ⇨ Trim).

Click the Trim icon, and a filmstrip appears below the video, with handles for setting the beginning and end of the video, as shown in Figure 5-9.

Drag the left handle to where you want the video to begin and then drag the right handle to where you want the video to end. Click Done, and you're done. You've trimmed excess footage from your video without launching an app.

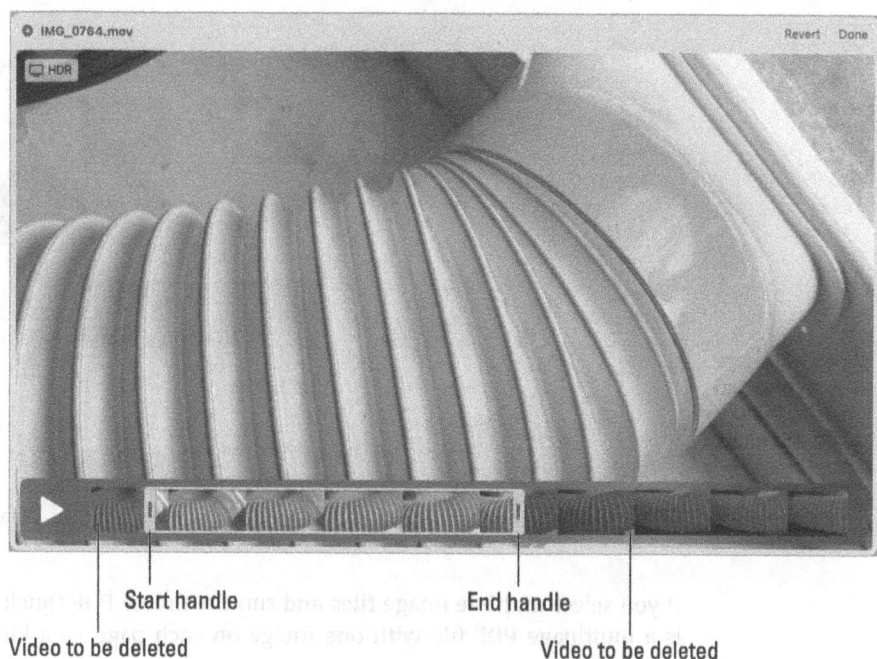

FIGURE 5-9:
Drag the handles
to set the start
and end points.

Start handle · End handle
Video to be deleted · Video to be deleted

Creating PDFs Without Launching an App

You've already seen three Quick Actions: Rotate, Markup, and Trim. This section shows you one more, the Create PDF Quick Action, which creates PDFs.

In most applications, you can create a PDF from the Print dialog (see Chapter 19). But wouldn't it be handy if you could create PDFs without launching an application and choosing Print?

In macOS Sequoia, you can do this, though only for image files (such as JPEG, TIFF, and PNG files), not for files such as Microsoft Word documents or Microsoft Excel workbooks. Just use the Create PDF Quick Action, which you'll find in Quick Look windows, in the Preview panes of Finder windows, and on the contextual menu (Control-click or right-click).

You can tell whether the file can be converted because the Create PDF command or icon appears only when suitable files are selected, as shown in Figure 5-10.

TIP

If the Create PDF Quick Action icon doesn't appear in the Preview panes when you select an image or images, try clicking the More icon (three dots in a circle) because the Create PDF Quick Action occasionally hides on the More menu.

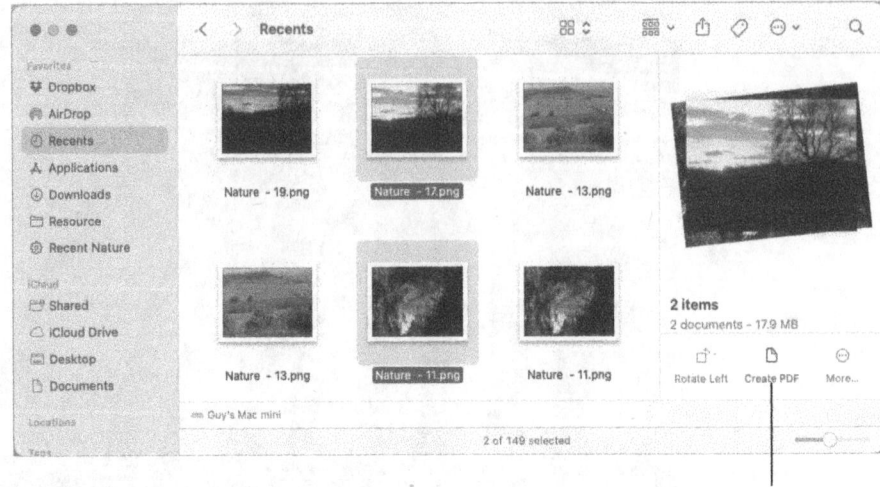

FIGURE 5-10:
When two image
files are selected
in a Finder
window, the
Create PDF
Quick Action
icon appears.

Create PDF Quick Action

If you select multiple image files and run the Create PDF Quick Action, the result is a multipage PDF file with one image on each page — a kind of virtual contact sheet.

TIP

If you find Quick Actions useful, consider creating some of your own. You can do this using Automator, a utility included with macOS.

Shooting Screen Stills and Movies

If you've used a Mac for long, you probably know that you can quickly grab a picture of what's on your screen by using the Screen Capture utility:

>> **Capture the whole screen.** Press ⌘+Shift+3.

>> **Capture part of the screen.** Press ⌘+Shift+4. The pointer changes to a crosshair icon. Move the crosshair where you want to start capturing, click, and then drag diagonally to the opposite corner. When you release the mouse button, Screen Capture grabs the selected area.

>> **Capture a window.** Press ⌘+Shift+4. The pointer changes to a crosshair icon. Press the spacebar, and the crosshair vanishes, replaced by a camera icon. Move this icon over the window you want to capture, so that macOS highlights the window, and then click. This method works for a menu too; just open the menu before you press ⌘+Shift+4.

These keyboard shortcuts still work in Sequoia. When you capture a screen or partial screen with them, a thumbnail of the screenshot appears in the bottom-right corner of the screen.

If you do nothing, the thumbnail disappears after about 5 seconds, and the screenshot is saved. To see additional options, Control-click or right-click the thumbnail and choose an option from the contextual menu, as shown in Figure 5-11. You can click Markup on the contextual menu to open the screenshot, for example, and start decorating it with Markup.

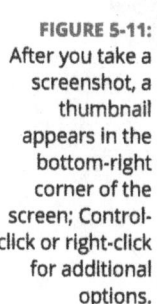

FIGURE 5-11:
After you take a screenshot, a thumbnail appears in the bottom-right corner of the screen; Control-click or right-click for additional options.

When you finish annotating, click Done to save the screenshot and annotations to the desktop, or click Revert to close the overlay without saving your annotations.

TIP

Screen Capture also lets you shoot a screen and put it straight on the Clipboard without saving it to a file. Then you can paste the screen from the Clipboard into a document. To use this trick, add the Control key to the keyboard shortcut, so you press ⌘+Shift+Control+3 for a full screen and ⌘+Shift+Control+4 for a partial screen or a window.

One more fabulous screen-shooting shortcut provides even more control over screenshots and adds the capability to record screen movies. This magical shortcut is ⌘+Shift+5, and it's the only shortcut you really have to memorize, because its floating toolbar, shown in Figure 5-12, includes all the functionality of the ⌘+Shift+3 and ⌘+Shift+4 shortcuts — and more.

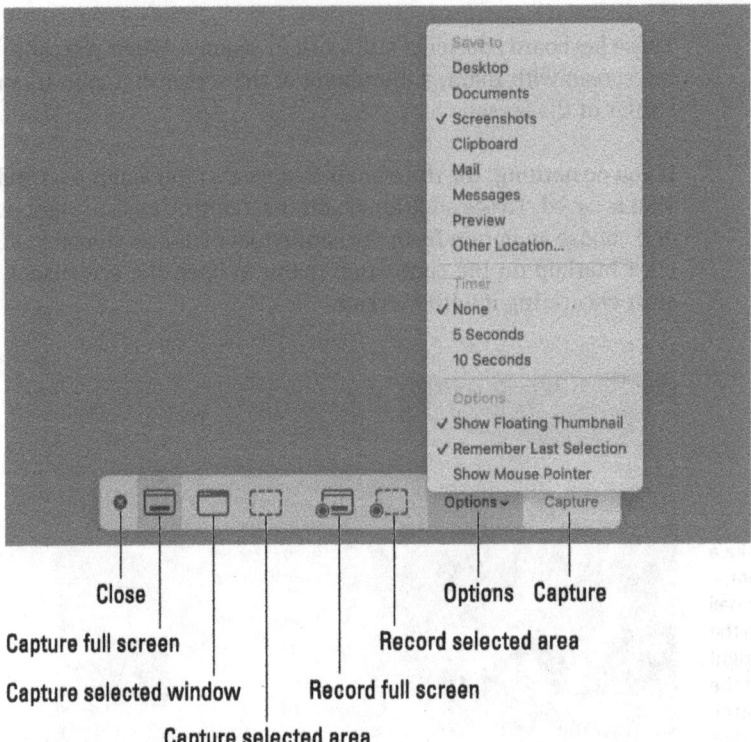

Save to
Desktop
Documents
✓ Screenshots
Clipboard
Mail
Messages
Preview
Other Location...

Timer
✓ None
5 Seconds
10 Seconds

Options
✓ Show Floating Thumbnail
✓ Remember Last Selection
Show Mouse Pointer

Options ⌄   Capture

Close   Options   Capture

Capture full screen   Record selected area

Capture selected window   Record full screen

Capture selected area

Notice the Options pop-up menu, which lets you do the following:

>> Change the destination for screenshots from the Desktop (the default) to the Documents folder, another folder, the Clipboard, the Mail app, the Messages app, the Preview app, or Other Location (you choose).

>> Set a 5- or 10-second timer for shots.

>> Turn the floating thumbnail on and off.

>> Remember the last selection you made (or not).

>> Show or hide the mouse pointer, including it in or excluding it from the screenshot.

 After configuring the options, you capture screenshots by clicking the Capture button. If you've chosen a movie option — Record Entire Screen or Record Selected Portion — the Capture button turns into the Record button; click it to begin recording. When you do, the Stop Recording icon (shown in the margin) appears on the menu; click it to end your recording.

Chapter **6**

Setting Your Mac Straight

E veryone works a bit differently, and everyone likes to use the Mac in their own way. In this chapter, you find out how to tweak various settings to make everything just the way you like it. The first things many people like to do are set their wallpaper and screen saver to provide visual interest. You can begin with that stuff, but keep in mind that you can do much more.

You can change the colors in windows, the standard font, and more if you like. macOS lets you choose how on-screen elements behave and how your keyboard, mouse, and trackpad work.

Introducing System Settings

System Settings is your main tool for configuring macOS and making it behave the way you prefer. Start by opening the System Settings window and getting the hang of navigating through its screens. Follow these steps:

1. **Open the System Settings window, shown in Figure 6-1.**

   You can open System Settings in at least four ways:

   • Choose ⇨ System Settings.

- Click the System Settings icon on your Dock. If System Settings isn't running, you can go straight to a settings category: Control-click or right-click the System Settings icon to display a contextual menu listing the settings categories, and then click the category you want.

- Open Launchpad, and then click the System Settings icon.

- Open your Applications folder, and then double-click the System Settings icon.

2. **Click any of the icons in the sidebar of the System Settings window.**

   As usual, the sidebar in the System Settings window enables you to navigate among the app's many categories of settings. The right pane displays the settings in the category you click in the sidebar. So, for example, when you click the General icon in the sidebar, the right pane displays the General category, which (for simplicity) we'll call the General pane.

   When you finish working in System Settings, quit the app by choosing System Settings ➪ Quit System Settings (or pressing ⌘ +Q) or by clicking the red gumdrop (Close) button.

REMEMBER

Although System Settings quits when you close its window, some apps *don't* quit when you close their last open window. Worse, there's no easy way to know whether an app will or won't quit when you close its last window — so if in doubt, give the Quit command rather than just clicking the red gum-drop button.

3. **If the pane you display contains a list of subcategories with angle brackets (>) to their right, click the subcategory you want to display.**

   Many of the categories have so many settings that they won't fit in a single pane, so instead they have a list of subcategories. You click the button for the appropriate subcategory to display its pane, which contains the settings. For example, click the Language & Region button in the General pane to display the Language & Region pane (see Figure 6-2).

When you've gone one screen deeper like this, you can click the Back arrow (<) to the left of the current pane's name to go back to the previous pane. In this case, clicking Back (<) would take you back to the General pane — and from there, you could click the Forward arrow (>) to display the Language & Region pane again. Even if you've navigated several panes deep, you can simply click another category in the sidebar to go straight to that category.

TIP

The sidebar shows the categories with the most frequently used categories at the top: iCloud and Apple Account, Wi-Fi, Bluetooth, Network, Energy Saver, and so on. If you prefer to navigate an alphabetical list, click the View menu, and then click the category you want. If you need to search for the setting you want, click the Search box at the top of the sidebar, and then type your search term.

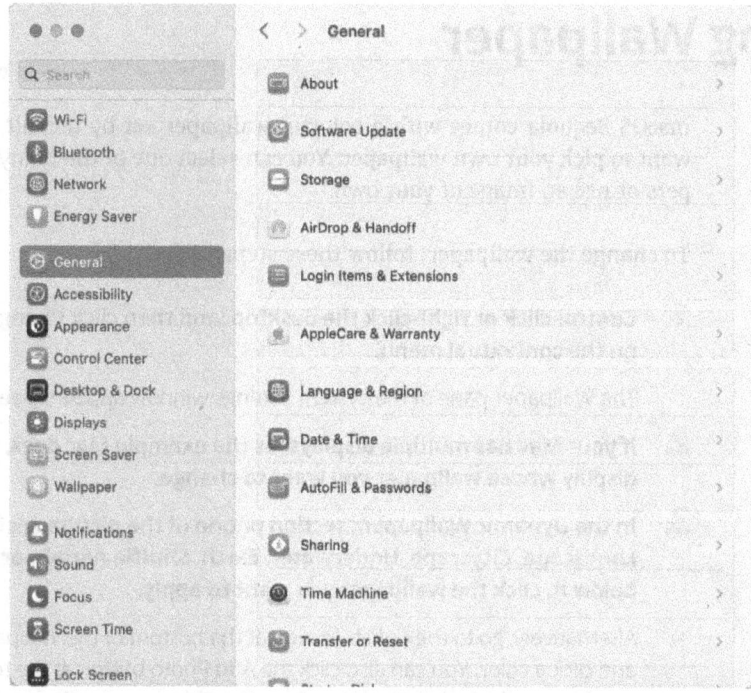

FIGURE 6-1:
The System
Settings app gives
you access to the
full range of
settings for
configuring
macOS to behave
the way
you prefer.

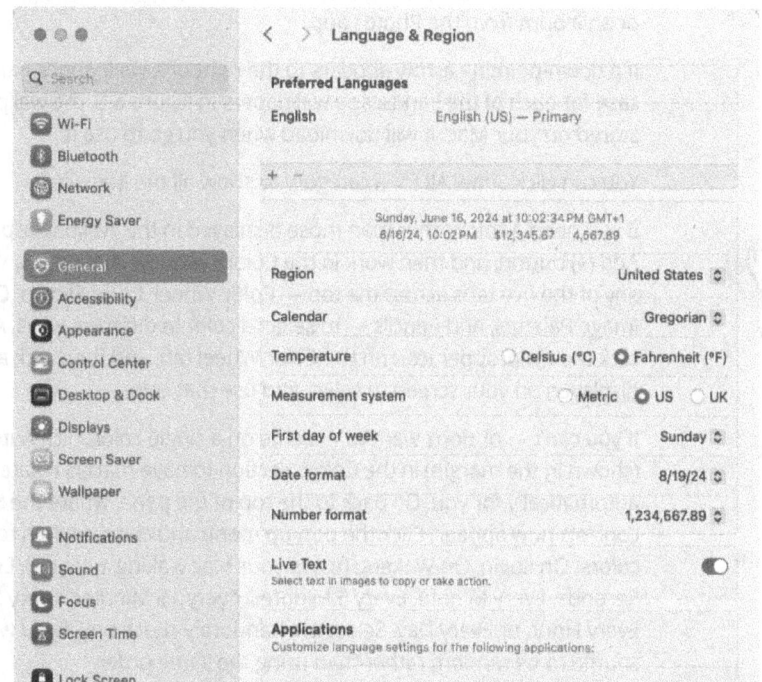

FIGURE 6-2:
When you
navigate to a
lower-level pane,
such as Language
& Region, click
the Back (<)
button to go back
to the previous
pane.

Setting Wallpaper

macOS Sequoia comes with a colorful wallpaper set by default, but you'll likely want to pick your own wallpaper. You can select one of the many built-in wallpapers or use an image of your own.

To change the wallpaper, follow these steps:

1. **Control-click or right-click the desktop, and then click Change Wallpaper on the contextual menu.**

   The Wallpaper pane of the System Settings window appears (see Figure 6-3).

2. **If your Mac has multiple displays, as the example Mac does, click the display whose wallpaper you want to change.**

3. **In the Dynamic Wallpapers section or one of the picture sections — Landscape, Cityscape, Underwater, Earth, Shuffle Aerials, or Pictures — below it, click the wallpaper you want to apply.**

   Alternatively, go to the Colors section at the bottom of the Wallpapers pane, and click a color. You can also click the Add Photo button at the top of the pane to add an individual photo either from the Photos app or from your Mac's file-system, or click the Add Folder or Album button to add a folder of images or an album from the Photos app.

   If a down-pointing arrow appears to the right of a wallpaper's name, as is the case for each of the Landscape wallpapers in Figure 6-3, the wallpaper is not stored on your Mac. It will download when you go to use it.

   You can click Show All for a category to show all the items in it.

TIP

   If you need a color other than those displayed in the Wallpaper pane, click the Add (+) button, and then work in the Colors window that opens. You can use any of the five tabs across the top — Color Wheel, Color Sliders, Color Palettes, Image Palettes, and Pencils — to select a color in different ways. Alternatively, click the eyedropper icon on the Color Wheel tab, and then click any color displayed on your screen to select and use that color.

   If you can't — or don't want to — settle on a single color, click Auto-Rotate (shown in the margin) in the Colors section to have macOS rotate the colors automatically for you. Go back to the top of the pane, where the Shuffle Colors controls now appear. Click the pop-up menu and choose when to change colors: On Login, On Wakeup (that's your Mac waking, not you), Every 5 Seconds, Every Minute, Every 5 Minutes, Every 15 Minutes, Every 30 Minutes, Every Hour, or Every Day. Select the Randomly check box if you want the shuffle to be random rather than using the same order.

4. **If you chose a wallpaper from the Dynamic Desktop category, go to the section at the top of the Wallpaper pane, click the pop-up menu, and choose an option.**

Your options are Automatic, Light, or Dark. Automatic switches from Light to Dark around sunset and switches back to Light around sunrise.

5. **If you chose a wallpaper from the Landscape section, the Cityscape section, the Underwater section, the Earth section, or the Shuffle Aerials section, go to the section at the top of the Wallpaper pane and choose options.**

For any of these wallpapers, set the Show as Screen Saver switch to On (blue) if you want to use the wallpaper as a screen saver when your Mac is idle. Set the Show on All Spaces switch to On (blue) if your Mac has multiple desktop spaces (either virtual spaces or multiple displays) and you want to use the wallpaper on all of them.

For the Shuffle Aerials wallpapers, click the Shuffle pop-up menu, and then specify the shuffle schedule by clicking Continuously, Every 12 Hours, Every Day, Every 2 Days, Every Week, or Every Month.

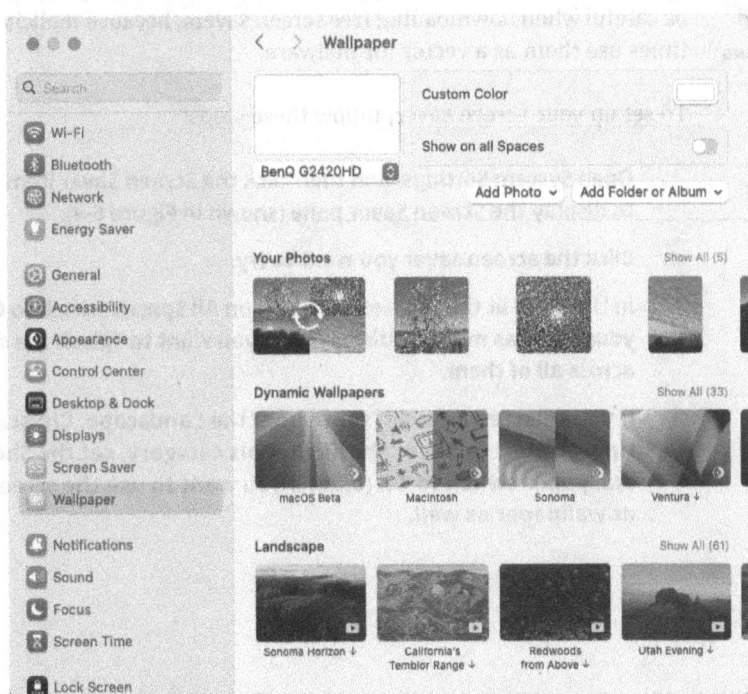

FIGURE 6-3:
From the Wallpaper pane, you can apply a different wallpaper to each display, if you like.

TIP

You can quickly set an image as your wallpaper from Finder or from the Photos app. In Finder, Control-click or right-click the image, and then click Set Desktop Picture on the contextual menu. In Photos, Control-click or right-click the image, click Share on the contextual menu, and then click Set Wallpaper on the Share submenu.

Configuring a Screen Saver or Just Turning Off the Display

If you like, you can set a screen saver to run on your Mac when you leave it unused for a while. A screen saver can be fun visually, but don't feel obliged to use one. Having the display simply put itself to sleep saves a little energy, and putting your Mac to sleep saves even more. Besides, do you spend time watching your Mac while you're not using it?

WARNING

macOS includes many screen savers, and the App Store offers various screensaver apps. If you want, you can supplement these with third-party screen savers — but be careful when downloading free screen savers, because malicious hackers sometimes use them as a vector for malware.

To set up your screen saver, follow these steps:

1. Open System Settings, and then click the Screen Saver item in the sidebar to display the Screen Saver pane (shown in Figure 6-4).

2. Click the screen saver you want to try.

3. In the pane at the top, set the Show on All Spaces switch to On (blue) if your Mac has multiple displays and you want to splash the screen saver across all of them.

4. If you selected a screen saver from the Landscape, Cityscape, Underwater, Earth, or Shuffle Aerials category, set the Show as Wallpaper switch to On (blue) if you want to use the screen saver as wallpaper as well.

5. **If you selected a screen saver from the Other category, see if the Options button appears in the area at the top of the Screen Saver pane.**

   If the Options button appears, click it to display the Options dialog, choose options for the screen saver, and then click the OK button. For example, if you select the Photos screen saver, the Options dialog enables you to select the source of the photos. If you select the Flurry screen saver, the Options dialog lets you choose the color cycle, specify the number of streams, and set their thickness and speed.

6. **Click the Lock Screen item in the sidebar of the System Settings app.**

   The Lock Screen pane appears (see Figure 6-5).

7. **Click the Start Screen Saver When Inactive pop-up menu, and then choose the delay.**

   Your choices run from For 1 Minute up to For 3 Hours, or Never. You'd select Never if you wanted to prevent the screen saver from running.

   TIP

   On a MacBook, you can choose separate Lock Screen settings for running on battery power and for running on the power adapter.

8. **Click the Turn Display Off When Inactive pop-up menu, and then specify the delay.**

   Your choices are the same as in the previous step. You'd select Never if you wanted to let the screen saver run forever.

   On a MacBook, configure both the Turn Display Off on Battery When Inactive setting and the Turn Display Off on Power Adapter When Inactive setting.

9. **Click the Require Password After Screen Saver Begins or Display Is Turned Off pop-up menu, and then choose the delay you want.**

   For security, choose the Immediately setting. If you find the screen saver triggers while you're using your Mac but are inactive, choose the After 5 Seconds setting. This will allow you to cancel the screen saver without having to enter your password. You can also choose longer settings ranging from After 1 Minute to After 8 Hours, but these settings might let someone else access your Mac without needing to authenticate themselves. The Never setting is seldom a good choice.

10. **When you've finished setting up the screen saver, close System Settings.**

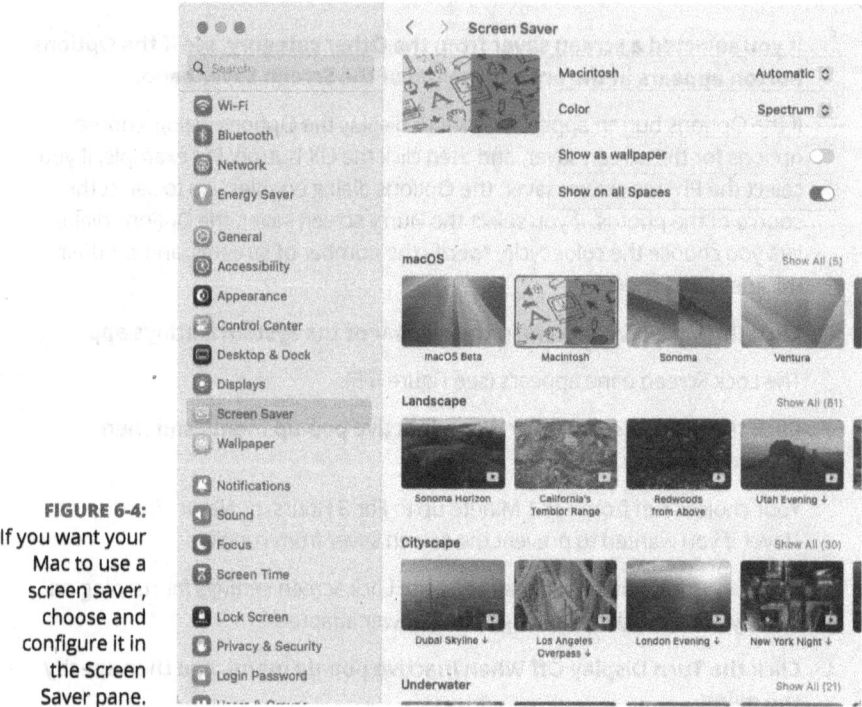

FIGURE 6-4:
If you want your
Mac to use a
screen saver,
choose and
configure it in
the Screen
Saver pane.

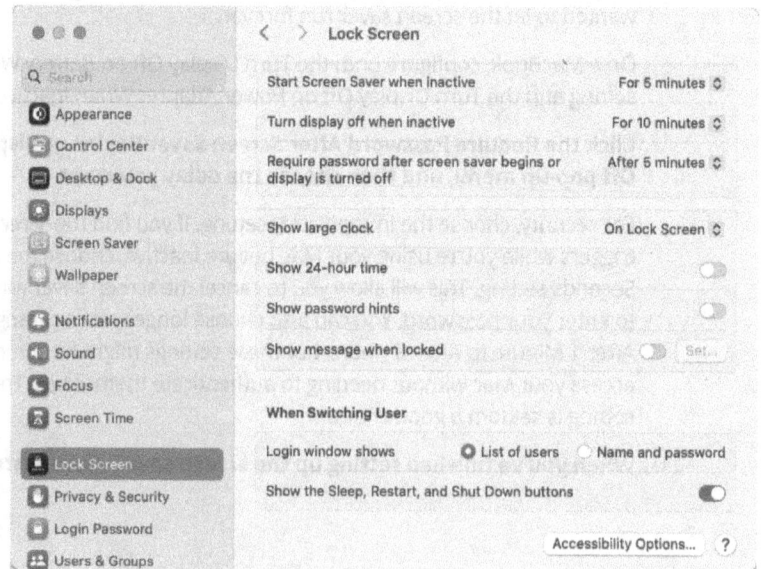

FIGURE 6-5:
In the Lock
Screen pane,
choose when to
start the screen
saver and when
to turn off
the display.

Configuring Appearance Settings

The Appearance pane in System Settings (see Figure 6-6) lets you choose between the Light and the Dark appearance, configure accent and highlight colors, adjust the size of sidebar icons, and choose how the scroll bars appear and behave. To get started, click the Appearance icon in the sidebar in System Settings.

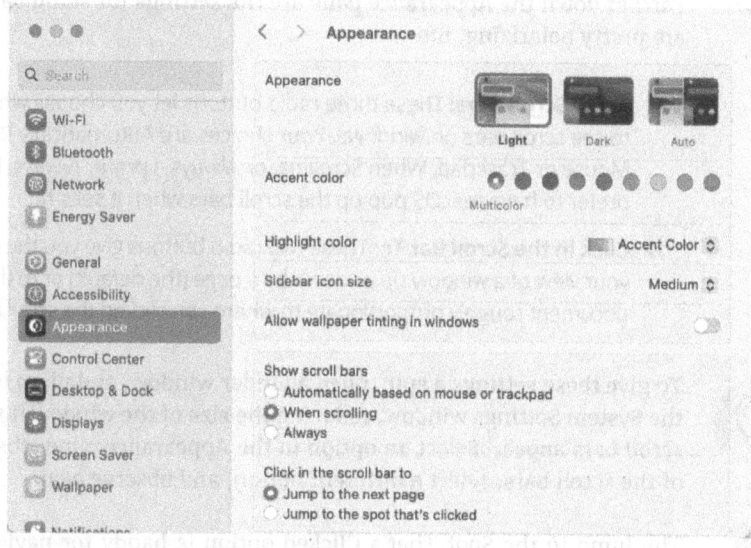

FIGURE 6-6:
Getting colorful in
the Appearance
pane in System
Settings.

Here's what you need to know about the color and sidebar-icon settings:

>> **Appearance:** This setting controls the overall look of macOS. Click Light to use the Light appearance all the time, click Dark to use the Dark appearance throughout, or click Auto to make macOS go Dark at sunset and Light at sunrise.

>> **Accent Color buttons:** Set the color of buttons and other interface elements to Multicolor (the first circle) or any of eight individual colors.

To preview an accent color, click it. The check boxes, drop-down menus, and radio buttons in the Appearance pane change to that accent color.

TIP

>> **Highlight Color pop-up menu:** From here, you can choose the color that text is surrounded by when you choose it in a document or select an icon. Choose Accent Color to go with the color you chose in the Accent Color buttons; choose a specific color, such as Blue or Graphite; or click Other to open the Colors window, in which you can choose exactly the shade of Mauvey Taupe or Cerulean Cinnamon you prefer.

- **Sidebar Icon Size pop-up menu:** Choose Small, Medium, or Large for icons in the Finder sidebar.

- **Allow Wallpaper Tinting in Windows switch:** Set this switch to On (blue) to let the wallpaper color bleed through slightly into windows in front of the wallpaper. This is one of those love-it-or-hate-it settings capable of starting a flame war in an empty chat room.

Farther down the Appearance pane are the settings for scroll bars. These settings are pretty polarizing, too:

- **Show Scroll Bars:** These three radio buttons let you choose when you want to see scroll bars on windows. Your choices are Automatically Based on Mouse or Trackpad, When Scrolling, or Always. I prefer Always, but you may prefer to have macOS pop up the scroll bars when it sees fit.

- **Click in the Scroll Bar To:** These two radio buttons give you the option of moving your view of a window up or down by a page (the default) or to the position in the document roughly proportionate to where you clicked the scroll bar.

TIP

To give these settings a spin, open a Finder window, and place it side by side with the System Settings window, reducing the size of the window if necessary to make scroll bars appear. Select an option in the Appearance pane, observe the behavior of the scroll bars, select a different option, and observe again.

TIP

The Jump to the Spot That's Clicked option is handy for navigating long documents. If you choose this option, remember that you can press Page Down to jump to the next page.

Choosing Desktop & Dock Settings

The Desktop & Dock pane in the Settings app enables you to tweak how the macOS desktop and Dock behave. You looked at the Dock settings in Chapter 3, so we'll skip lightly over them here and focus on the desktop settings. To get started, open the System Settings app, click the Desktop & Dock icon in the sidebar, and then scroll down the Desktop & Dock pane until you see the Desktop & Stage Manager heading.

At the top of this section, you can configure these three settings:

- **On Desktop:** Select this check box on the Show Items row to display items on your desktop any time you're not using the Stage Manager feature; clear this check box to hide desktop items.

>> **In Stage Manager:** Select this check box on the Show Items row to display items on your desktop when you are using Stage Manager; clear this check box to hide desktop items when you're using Stage Manager.

>> **Click Wallpaper to Show Desktop Items:** Open this pop-up menu and choose Always or Only in Stage Manager, as needed. If you clear the On Desktop check box, you'll likely want to choose Always in this pop-up menu. If you clear the In Stage Manager check box, you'll probably want to choose Only in Stage Manager in the pop-up menu.

Below the Desktop section is a box of controls for Stage Manager. We'll leave these until Chapter 9, which shows you how to use Stage Manager.

After that is the Widgets section, where you can adjust these five settings:

>> **On Desktop:** Select this check box on the Show Widgets row to display widgets on your desktop when you're not using Stage Manager; clear this check box to hide desktop widgets.

>> **In Stage Manager:** Select this check box on the Show Widgets row to display widgets on your desktop when you are using Stage Manager; clear this check box to hide desktop widgets when you're using Stage Manager.

>> **Widget Style:** Specify the style for your widgets by clicking this pop-up menu, and then clicking Automatic, Monochrome, or Full-Color.

>> **Use iPhone Widgets:** Set this switch to On (blue) if you want your Mac to use iPhone widgets as well as macOS widgets.

>> **Default Web Browser:** Open this pop-up menu and choose the browser you want to use as your default. Safari will be selected unless you've installed another browser, such as Google's Chrome or Mozilla Firefox.

In the Windows section of the Desktop & Dock pane, you can tweak these three settings:

>> **Prefer Tabs When Opening Documents:** Your choice in this pop-up menu controls when macOS uses tabbed windows. Try all the settings — Never, In Full Screen, or Always — and stick with the one you like best.

>> **Ask to Keep Changes When Closing Documents:** macOS can save versions of your documents automatically and without any action on your part. So when you quit an app or close a document, your changes can be saved automatically. If you want to be able to close documents without having to save your changes manually, set this switch to On (blue).

>> **Close Windows When Quitting an Application:** Your Mac's default behavior when you open an app you've used before is to reopen documents and windows that were open when you last quit that app. When you launch the app again, all the windows and documents magically reappear right where you left them. So set this switch to On (blue) to have your apps open to a clean slate, without reopening documents or windows from the previous session.

These last two items may not work as expected with older third-party apps. As a rule, the longer it's been since an app's last update, the more likely it is that the app will ignore these two settings.

WARNING

Right at the bottom of the Desktop & Dock pane is the Mission Control section. We'll look at these settings in Chapter 9, which covers Mission Control.

Adjusting the Keyboard, Mouse, Trackpad, and Other Hardware

The Keyboard, Mouse, and Trackpad panes in the System Settings app provide a slew of settings for adjusting the behavior of your keyboard, mouse, and trackpad so that these devices feel just right for you. To get started, open System Settings your preferred way, and click the Keyboard icon in the sidebar.

Choosing keyboard settings

In the Keyboard pane (see Figure 6-7), you can adjust the following settings:

>> **Key Repeat Rate:** Drag this slider to set how fast a key repeats when you hold it down. This feature comes into play when (for example) you hold down the hyphen (–) key to make a line or the asterisk (*) key to make a divider.

>> **Delay Until Repeat:** Drag this slider to set how long you have to hold down a key before it starts repeating.

>> **Press fn Key To** or **Press the Globe Key To:** The options on this pop-up menu are Show Emoji & Symbols, Change Input Source, Start Dictation (Press fn Twice or Press Globe Key Twice), and Do Nothing.

>> **Keyboard Navigation:** Set this switch to On (blue) to be able to move the focus (the part of the macOS user interface that's active) from one control to the next by pressing Tab. Press Shift+Tab to move to the previous control.

>> **Keyboard Shortcuts:** Click this button to display the Keyboard Shortcuts dialog, which you learn about in the next several sections.

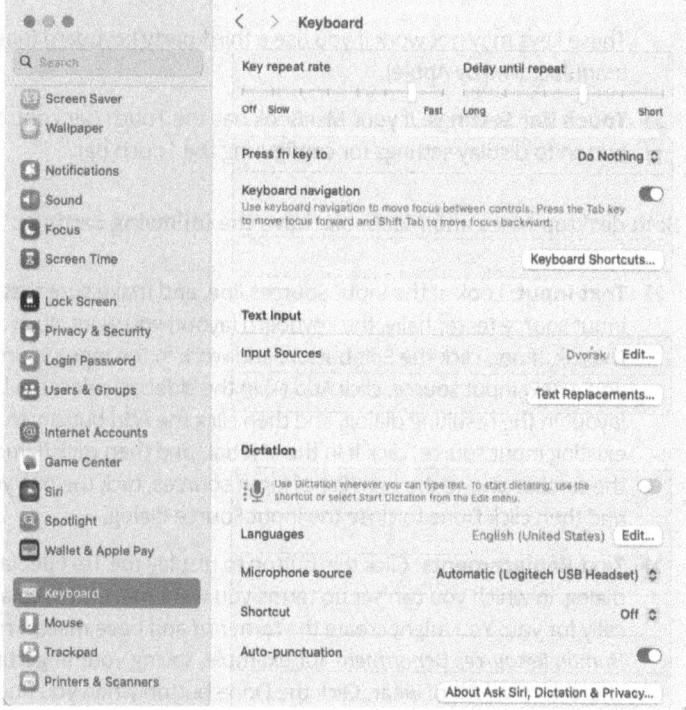

FIGURE 6-7:
Spend some time choosing settings in the Keyboard pane to get the most out of your Mac's keyboard.

If you have a MacBook, you also see one or more of these additional settings:

>> **Adjust Keyboard Brightness in Low Light:** Set this switch to On (blue) to let macOS turn your MacBook's ambient keyboard lighting on and off.

>> **Turn Keyboard Backlight Off After Inactivity:** This setting (choose 5, 10, or 30 seconds, or 1 or 5 minutes from the drop-down menu) lets you determine how long the keyboard backlighting remains on when your computer isn't in use.

Ambient keyboard lighting is a cool feature, but it reduces run time on the battery. Use it only when you really need it.

REMEMBER

>> **Use F1, F2, etc. Keys As Standard Function Keys:** Set this switch to On (blue) if you want to make the F keys at the top of your keyboard control the active software app.

To use the special hardware features printed on each F key (display brightness, screen mirroring, sound volume, mute, and so on), you have to press the Fn (Function) key before pressing the F key. If you set this switch to Off, you have to press the Fn key if you want to use the F keys with a software app.

These keys may not work if you use a third-party keyboard (one not manufactured by Apple).

>> **Touch Bar Settings:** If your MacBook has the Touch Bar control bar, click this button to display settings for configuring the Touch Bar.

Both desktop Macs and MacBooks have the following settings:

>> **Text Input:** Look at the Input Sources line, and make sure that it shows the input source (essentially, the keyboard layout) you want, such as U.S. or Dvorak. If not, click the Edit button, and work in the Input Source dialog. To add a new input source, click Add (+) in the sidebar, select the language and layout in the resulting dialog, and then click the Add button; to remove an existing input source, click it in the sidebar, and then click Remove (–). When the sidebar shows the right list of input sources, click the one you want to use, and then click Done to close the Input Source dialog.

>> **Text Replacements:** Click this button to display the Text Replacements dialog, in which you can set up terms you want macOS to replace automatically for you. You might create the term *hrd* and have macOS replace it with *Human Resources Department*, for example, saving your fingertips 20-odd characters' worth of wear. Click the Done button when you finish.

TIP

Text Replacements enables you to create multiline replacement items. Just hold down Option and press Return to start a new line of text. Even easier, paste multiple lines of text from another app into the With field.

Okay, what about those keyboard shortcuts? Go ahead and click the Keyboard Shortcuts button in the Keyboard pane. The Keyboard Shortcuts dialog pops open (see Figure 6-8), showing a list of categories in the sidebar pane on the left; click the category you want, and the details appear in the right pane, as for the Mission Control category in Figure 6-8. Double-click the shortcut you want to change, and press the keys you want to use for the shortcut. A warning triangle appears if the shortcut you've pressed is already in use elsewhere.

Here's what you can configure in the Keyboard Shortcuts dialog:

>> **Launchpad & Dock:** Enable, disable, or change the keyboard shortcuts for turning Dock hiding on or off and for showing Launchpad.

>> **Display:** Enable, disable, or change the shortcuts for increasing and decreasing display brightness.

>> **Mission Control:** Enable, disable, or change the shortcuts for the Mission Control feature, which you learn about in Chapter 9.

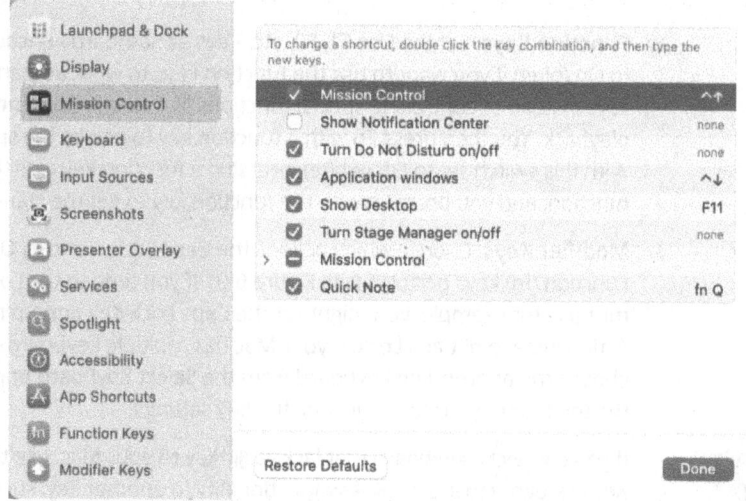

FIGURE 6-8:
The Keyboard
Shortcuts dialog
lets you play
around with
keyboard
shortcuts to your
heart's content.

» **Keyboard:** Enable, disable, or change the shortcuts for moving the focus by using the keyboard. Pressing ⌘ + ` (the back-tick character), for example, moves the focus to the next window in the same app.

» **Input Sources:** Enable, disable, or change the shortcuts for switching among the input sources you've set up on your Mac. If you've set up U.S., German, and Spanish input sources, for example, you can press a keyboard shortcut to select the next or previous input source.

» **Screenshots:** Enable, disable, or change the shortcuts for shooting screens, as discussed in Chapter 5.

» **Presenter Overlay:** Set up shortcuts for toggling the Presenter Overlay feature on and off in either its small size or its large size.

» **Services:** Enable, disable, or change the shortcuts for running the services you find on the Services submenu on an app's main menu (the menu that bears the app's name, such as the TextEdit menu for the TextEdit app).

» **Spotlight:** Enable, disable, or change the shortcuts for opening a Spotlight search overlay and for showing a Finder search window.

» **Accessibility:** Enable, disable, or change the shortcuts for Accessibility features, such as Zoom, VoiceOver, and Invert Colors.

» **App Shortcuts:** Enable, disable, or change the shortcuts for specific apps. There aren't many of these by default — in fact, you may find none at all — but you can add any you need by clicking the Add (+) button and working in the resulting dialog.

>> **Function Keys:** Set the Use F1, F2, etc. Keys as Standard Function Keys switch to On (blue) if you want to use the function keys to work as standard function keys instead of controlling special functions like screen brightness and media playback. You then press Fn with a function key to invoke the special function. With this switch set to Off (white), pressing a function key gets the special function, and you press Fn with the function key to get the standard function.

>> **Modifier Keys:** Choose which actions the Caps Lock, Control, Option, ⌘, and Function (fn) keys perform (see Figure 6-9). If you tend to turn on Caps Lock by mistake, for example, you might set the Caps Lock Key pop-up menu to No Action instead of Caps Lock. If your Mac has multiple keyboards connected, choose the appropriate keyboard from the Select Keyboard pop-up menu at the top before you start adjusting the key settings.

If you connect a keyboard that lacks a ⌘ key to your Mac, use the Modifier Keys category to assign ⌘-key functionality to another key, such as Caps Lock.

TIP

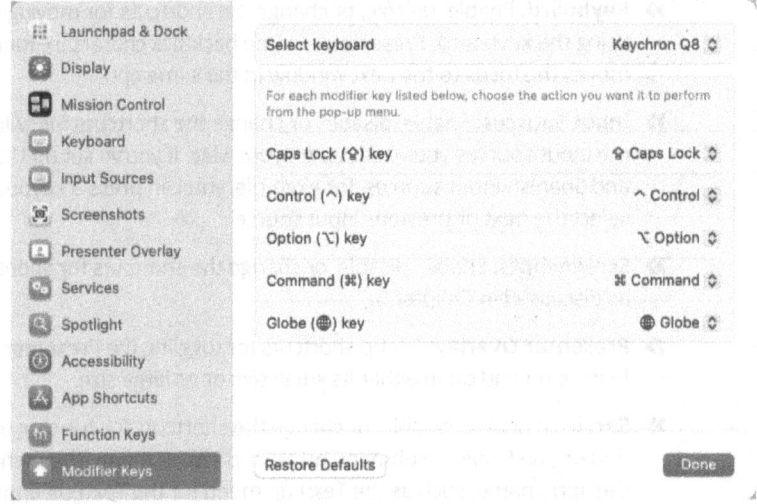

FIGURE 6-9:
The Modifier Keys category enables you to remap the modifier keys for a particular keyboard.

Tweaking your mouse

The Mouse pane of System Settings (see Figure 6-10) is where you set your mouse tracking speed, enable or disable the Natural Scrolling feature, choose how to issue secondary clicks, and set the double-click delay. Changes you make here take effect immediately, so you can see their effect easily.

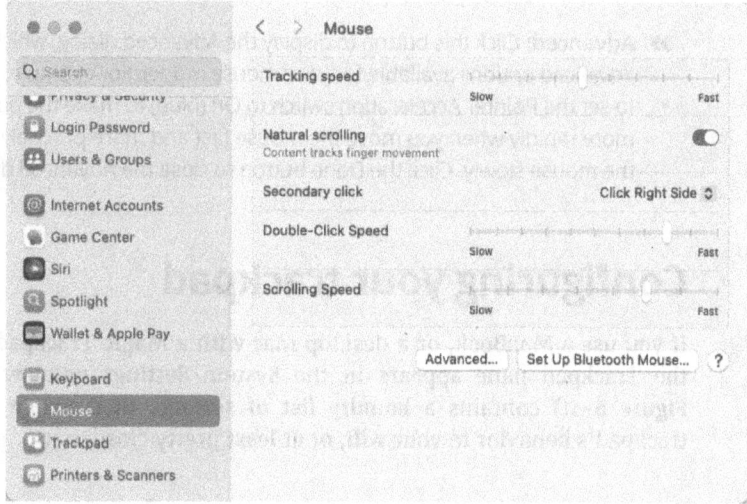

FIGURE 6-10:
The Mouse pane
in System
Settings.

If you have a MacBook or have connected an Apple Magic Trackpad to your Mac, use the Trackpad pane in System Settings to configure it. See the following sub-section "Configuring your trackpad" for details.

Here are the settings that appear in the Mouse pane when your Mac has a mouse attached:

>> **Tracking Speed:** Drag this slider left or right to adjust the speed at which the pointer moves on-screen as you move the mouse.

>> **Natural Scrolling:** Set this switch to On (blue) if you want content to scroll in the direction you move the scroll wheel rather than in the opposite direction (which is called *reverse scrolling*). Natural scrolling is like using an iPhone or iPad; you move your finger up the screen to scroll down, as though you're dragging the content up.

>> **Secondary Click:** Open this pop-up menu, and choose Click Right Side or Click Left Side, as needed. As you'd guess, the other side is your primary click side. So if you use the mouse with your right hand, you normally want to choose Click Right Side in the Secondary Click pop-up menu, leaving the left mouse button as the primary click.

>> **Double-Click Speed:** Drag this slider to specify how close together two clicks must be for the Mac to interpret them as a double-click, not as two separate clicks. The left end of the slider is Slow; the right end is Fast.

>> **Scrolling Speed:** This slider appears only if your mouse has a scroll ball or scroll wheel. Drag the slider to adjust the speed at which macOS scrolls the content of windows as you rotate the scroll ball or scroll wheel.

>> **Advanced:** Click this button to display the Advanced dialog, which contains any advanced options available for your mouse model. For example, you may be able to set the Pointer Acceleration switch to On (blue) to make the pointer move more rapidly when you move the mouse fast and more precisely when you move the mouse slowly. Click the Done button to close the Advanced dialog.

Configuring your trackpad

If you use a MacBook, or a desktop Mac with a Magic Trackpad (version 1 or 2), the Trackpad pane appears in the System Settings window. This pane (see Figure 6-11) contains a laundry list of settings that enable you to bend the trackpad's behavior to your will, or at least pretty close to it.

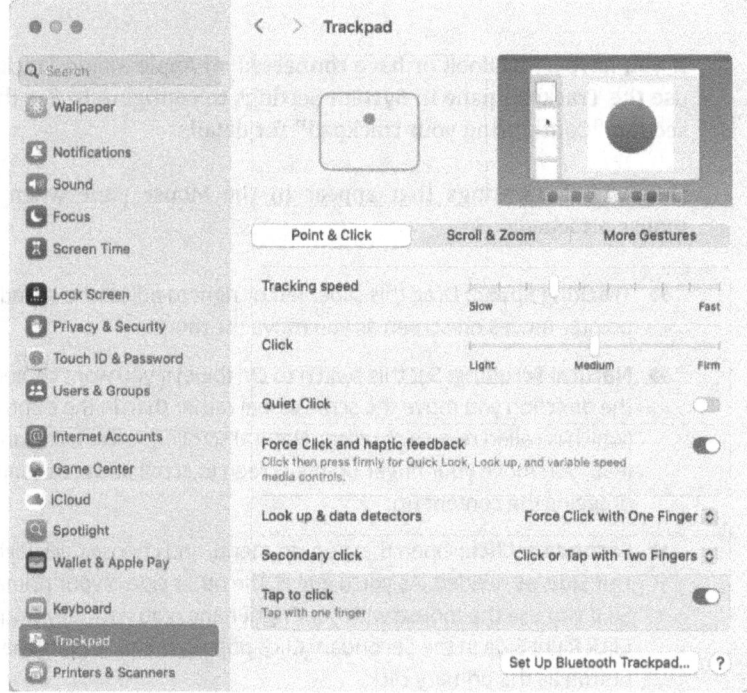

FIGURE 6-11: The Trackpad pane in System Settings offers controls for one-finger and multi-finger gestures.

The Trackpad pane contains three tabs: Point & Click, Scroll & Zoom, and More Gestures. These are the settings you'll typically find in the Point & Click tab:

>> **Tracking Speed:** Drag this slider along the Slow–Fast continuum to set the speed at which the pointer moves on-screen in response to your finger sliding across the trackpad.

>> **Click:** Select the click type you prefer: Light, Medium, or Firm. This setting appears for only some trackpads.

>> **Quiet Click:** Set this switch to On (blue) to suppress the click noise macOS plays to give you feedback when you click the trackpad.

>> **Force Click and Haptic Feedback:** Set this switch to On (blue) to use the Force Click feature, in which you click and then press the trackpad to use features such as Quick Look. Haptic Feedback is the visual and vibration feedback that lets you know you've pressed hard enough or long enough to get a response.

>> **Look Up & Data Detectors:** Set this switch to On (blue) to enable yourself to trigger the Look Up feature and data-detectors feature by tapping the trackpad with three fingers.

>> **Secondary Click:** From this pop-up menu, choose the gesture you want to use for secondary clicking (the equivalent of Control-clicking or right-clicking). Your choices are Click or Tap with Two Fingers, Click in Bottom Right Corner, Click in Bottom Left Corner, and Off.

>> **Tap to Click:** Set this switch to On (blue) to enable yourself to click by tapping the trackpad with one finger. I find using this gesture to be much easier than clicking the trackpad, but your mileage may vary.

These are the settings you'll find in the Scroll & Zoom tab in the Trackpad pane:

>> **Natural Scrolling:** Set this switch to On (blue) if you want content to scroll in the direction in which you move your finger on the trackpad rather than in the opposite direction (reverse scrolling).

>> **Zoom In or Out:** Set this switch to On (blue) if you want to be able to zoom in by placing your thumb and finger (or two fingers) close together on the trackpad, and then moving them apart, and zoom out by placing your thumb and finger (or two fingers) apart on the trackpad, and then moving them toward each other.

>> **Smart Zoom:** Set this switch to On (blue) to enable yourself to zoom in and out by double-tapping with two fingers.

>> **Rotate:** Set this switch to On (blue) to enable yourself to rotate an image or other rotatable item by placing two fingers on the trackpad and rotating them.

These are the settings you'll find in the More Gestures tab in the Trackpad pane:

>> **Swipe Between Pages:** From this pop-up menu, choose the gesture for swiping between pages. Your choices are Scroll Left or Right with Two Fingers, Swipe with Three Fingers, Swipe with Two or Three Fingers, and Off.

>> **Swipe Between Full Screen Applications:** From this pop-up menu, choose the gesture you want to use for navigating between full-screen apps. Your choices are Swipe Left or Right with Three Fingers, Swipe Left or Right with Four Fingers, and Off.

>> **Notification Center:** Set this switch to On (blue) if you want to be able to summon Notification Center by swiping left with two fingers from the right edge of the screen.

>> **Mission Control:** From this pop-up menu, choose the gesture you want to use to invoke the Mission Control feature, which you master in Chapter 9. Your choices are Swipe Up with Three Fingers, Swipe Up with Four Fingers, and Off.

>> **App Exposé:** From this pop-up menu, choose the gesture you want to use for App Exposé, which is part of Mission Control (again, see Chapter 9). Your choices are Swipe Down with Three Fingers, Swipe Down with Four Fingers, and Off.

>> **Launchpad:** Set this switch to On (blue) to enable yourself to display the Launchpad screen by placing your thumb and three fingers apart on the screen and pinching them together.

>> **Show Desktop:** Set this switch to On (blue) to enable yourself to display the desktop by placing your thumb and three fingers together on the screen, and then spreading them apart.

Configuring Sound Settings

Out of the box, macOS comes with a preset collection of beeps and controls. From the Sound pane in System Settings, however, you can change the way your Mac plays and records sound. As you can see in Figure 6-12, the Sound Effects section appears at the top of the Sound pane. Below it is the Output & Input section, which contains the Output tab and the Input tab.

In the Sound Effects section, you can configure the following settings:

>> **Alert Sound:** Click this pop-up menu, and then click the Alert sound you want. Click the Play button to the right of the pop-up menu to enjoy the sound again and again.

>> **Play Sound Effects Through:** Click this pop-up menu, and then click either Selected Sound Output Device (to use whichever speakers or headphone you're using for output) or a different device you want to use for sound effects.

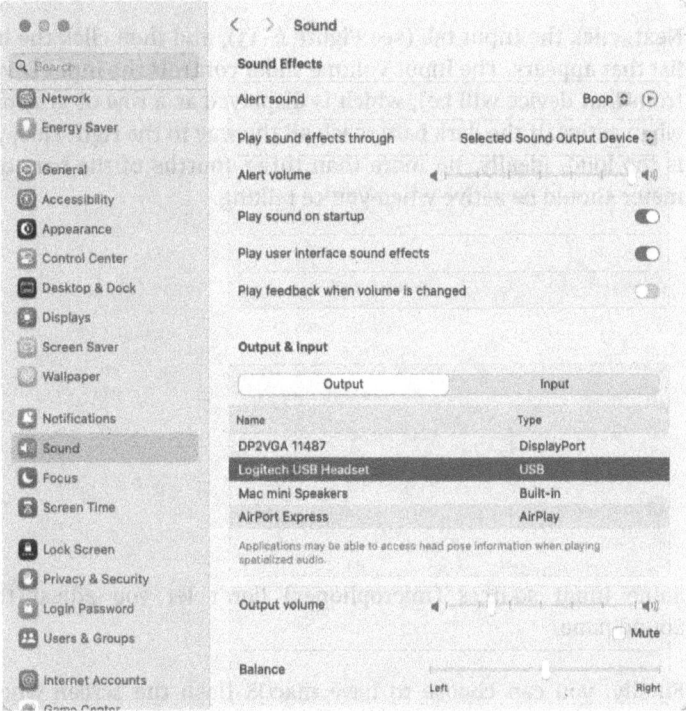

FIGURE 6-12:
Use the Sound
pane in System
Settings to adjust
sound effects,
sound output,
and sound input.

>> **Alert Volume:** Drag this slider to set the volume for the alert sounds.

>> **Play Sound on Startup:** Set this switch to On (blue) if you want your Mac to
play its start-up chime while it's booting. Usually, the start-up sound provides
early reassurance that your Mac is still alive and functional.

>> **Play User Interface Sound Effects:** Set this switch to On (blue) to have your
Mac play feedback sounds for actions such as dragging a file to the Trash.

>> **Play Feedback When Volume Is Changed:** Set this switch to On (blue) to
have your Mac beep once for each key press when you increase or decrease
volume. The beeps help you determine the volume you're setting.

In the Output & Input section, click the Output tab so that you can select the output device and set the volume:

>> **Output device:** In this (unnamed) list, click the output device for playing sounds.

>> **Output Volume:** Drag this slider to set the output volume.

>> **Mute:** Select this check box to mute sound output.

>> **Balance:** If this slider appears, drag it to adjust the left–right balance.

Next, click the Input tab (see Figure 6-13), and then click the input device in the list that appears. The Input Volume slider controls the Input Level (how loud input from that device will be), which is displayed as a row of gray bars that go darker when active. If the dark bars reach all the way to the right side, your input volume is too loud. Ideally, no more than three-fourths of the bars on the Input Level meter should be active when you're talking.

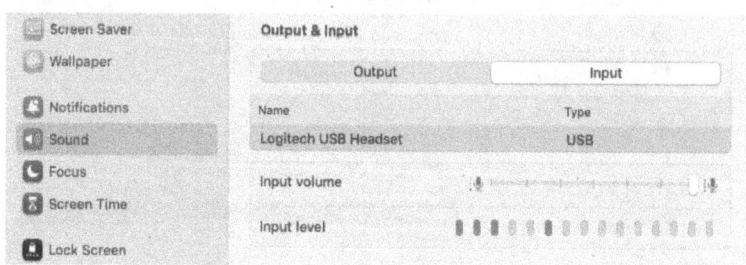

FIGURE 6-13: On the Input tab of the Sound pane, choose your input device and set the input volume.

TECHNICAL STUFF

Some input sources (microphones) don't let you adjust their level in the Sound pane.

Finally, you can choose to have macOS flash the screen when an alert sound occurs, have stereo audio play back in mono, or both. To reach these options, click Accessibility in the sidebar in System Settings, and then click Audio in the Accessibility pane. Set the Flash the Screen When an Alert Sound Occurs switch to On (blue) or Off (white), and then set the Play Stereo Audio as Mono switch to On (blue) or Off (white), as needed.

2

Getting Things Done

Open and save files. Heck, go wild and close them, too.

Get the secret to finding anything, anywhere, on any disk.

Master Mission Control and run the show with Stage Manager.

Save time and effort with Quick Look and Launchpad.

Stay organized with Calendar, Notes, and Screen Time.

Find yourself with Maps and take a topographic hike.

Come to grips with Stocks, News, Voice Memos, and Shortcuts.

Chapter **7**

Opening and Saving Files

This chapter shows you how to open and save files and how to use the file and folder system, vital knowledge for getting things done on macOS. The chapter starts by showing you how to find files and folders, then moves on to exploring the macOS folder structure. After that, you learn how to save files and how to open files, including how to search for files and folders within the Open dialog.

Where Did That File Go?

Given the number of files most of us create, it's all too easy to lose track of particular files if you don't keep your filesystem organized.

macOS provides two powerful tools that can help you track down files:

» **Spotlight:** This search feature maintains an index of files in your Mac's filesystem, enabling you to locate files by their names or contents. Such searching is handy unless you have files with the same name stored in different folders — in which case you'll need to work out which file is the one you want.

>> **Recents folder:** This smart folder displays aliases (shortcuts) to all the files you've used recently. To see Recents, open a Finder window and click the Recents item in the Favorites section of the sidebar. Recents is a good way to find files you've used recently, unless the sheer number of files in the Recents list overwhelms you.

TIP

If you're looking for a file you either created or worked on very recently, click Recents in the sidebar of a Finder window, and then switch to List view. Click the Date Last Opened column heading to sort by it, putting the most recently opened files at the top of the list. Even if you can't remember the file's name, you should be able to identify the file by looking at the timestamps. See Chapter 9 for further tips on finding files and folders you've misplaced.

Understanding the macOS Folder Structure

Let's start by looking at the folder structure of a typical macOS installation. Open a Finder window, and then click the icon for your Mac's hard drive (typically called Macintosh HD unless you've renamed it) in the sidebar. You'll see a window with the contents of your start-up disk: the Applications, Library, System, and Users folders (as shown in Figure 7-1).

TIP

If you don't see your start-up disk in the sidebar, choose Finder ⇨ Settings, click the Sidebar icon at the top of the window, go to the Locations section, and then select the Hard Disks check box.

FIGURE 7-1:
A bird's-eye view
of key folders
on your Mac.

In the Users folder, each user with an account on this Mac has their own set of folders containing documents, preferences, and other information that belongs to that user and account. See Chapter 16 for the lowdown on users and accounts.

TECHNICAL STUFF

If you're the sole person who accesses your Mac, it probably has only one user — you. However, the folder structure that macOS uses is the same whether your Mac has one user or dozens.

In the Users folder, you find your personal Home folder (which bears your account name), along with a Shared folder, where you can put files you want to share with other users. All these files are stored in a nested folder structure that you can see in Figure 7-1.

TIP

To help yourself understand the folder structure, choose View ➪ Show Path Bar to display the path bar at the bottom of the window, as shown in Figure 7-1.

Understanding nested folders

Folders within other folders are called *nested folders* or *subfolders*. To get a feel for the way nested folders work in macOS, check out the example of nested folders on the desktop in Figure 7-2.

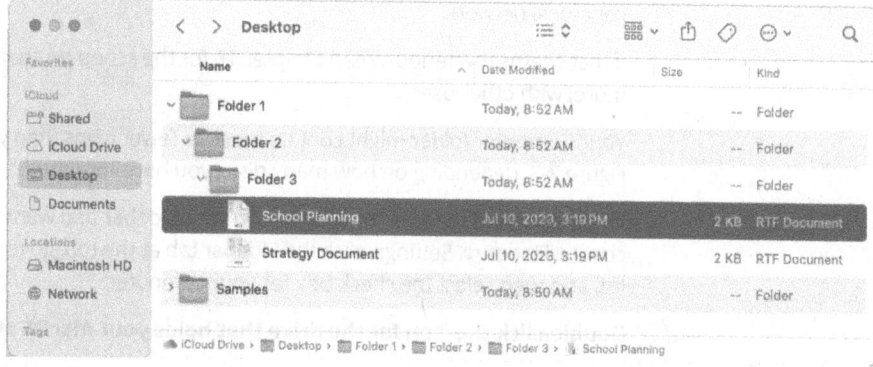

FIGURE 7-2: Nested folders, going four levels deep.

You can see the following in Figure 7-2:

>> The Desktop is the top-level folder in this example; all other folders and files you see reside in the Desktop folder.

>> Folder 1 is inside the Desktop folder, which is one level deep.

>> Folder 2 is inside Folder 1, which is one level deeper than Folder 1, or two levels deep.

>> Folder 3 is inside Folder 2 and is three levels deep.

>> The two files inside Folder 3 are four levels deep.

REMEMBER

If the preceding list makes sense to you, you're golden. What's important here is that you grasp the path to Folder 3: To get to files inside Folder 3, you open Folder 1, open Folder 2, and then open Folder 3.

The Computer folder

The Computer folder is the top level of the folder hierarchy. The Computer folder shows all the storage devices (hard drives, CD- or DVD-ROMs, USB flash drives, and so forth) connected to your Mac. The following steps show how you can start at the Computer folder and drill down through the folder structure:

1. **Choose Go ⇨ Computer, press ⌘ +Shift+C, or click your computer's name in the sidebar's Locations section.**

   Now you're at the Computer folder. In Figure 7-3, the Computer folder is called Guy's Mac mini (look in the title bar), and it contains a drive icon (Macintosh HD) and a Network icon, from which you can access servers or other computers on your local network.

   If that seems mysterious, read Chapter 16 for the scoop on sharing files (and more) with other users.

   Your Computer folder might contain more or fewer icons than you see in Figure 7-3, depending on how many disks you have mounted.

   If you don't find the icon for your Mac in your sidebar and want to add it, choose Finder ⇨ Settings, click the Sidebar tab at the top, go to the Locations list, and then select the check box for your computer.

2. **Double-click the icon for the drive that holds your macOS stuff.**

   Technically, this drive is called your *boot drive*. In Figure 7-3, that drive is called Macintosh HD. This is the default name, so your Mac's boot drive will be called Macintosh HD unless you've renamed it.

3. **Check out the folders you find there.**

   You should see at least four folders on your boot drive. The next few sections walk you through what you can find in each one.

FIGURE 7-3:
Click the
computer's name
in the sidebar to
display its drive
and the
Network icon.

The Applications folder

To access the Applications folder, located at the root level of your boot drive (the one with macOS installed on it), click the Applications icon in the sidebar, choose Go ⇨ Applications from the menu bar, or press ⌘+Shift+A. This folder contains apps and utilities that Apple includes with macOS, as well as most (if not all) third-party apps and utilities that you've installed.

Most Mac users have access to all the items in the Applications folder, with the exception of managed accounts or accounts restricted by Screen Time settings, as discussed in Chapter 10.

The Library folders

The Library folder, at the root level of your macOS hard drive, is like a public library. It stores items available to everyone who logs into any account on this Mac.

There are three (or more) Library folders on your hard drive:

>> At the root level of your macOS disk (the /Library folder)

>> In the root-level System folder (the /System/Library folder)

>> In each user's Home folder (the ~/Library folder; here, ~ is shorthand for your Home folder, so the folder's location is /Users/*Username*/Library)

TECHNICAL STUFF

macOS hides your ~/Library folder from view to discourage you from making changes, because they might interfere with how your Mac runs. See the section "Opening your own Library folder," later in this chapter, to learn how to make this folder visible.

Here's the scoop on your various Library folders:

>> **/Library:** The Library folder at the root level contains a bunch of folders. Most of them contain files that you never need to open, move, or delete. The subfolder that gets the most use is the Fonts folder, which houses many of the fonts installed on the Mac.

>> **/System/Library:** This folder is the nerve center of your Mac. You should never have to touch this particular Library folder.

WARNING

Leave the /System/Library folder alone. Don't move, remove, or rename it, or do anything within it unless you're absolutely certain you know what you're doing, because doing so might prevent macOS from running.

>> **~/Library (in each user's Home folder):** This folder is where macOS stores configuration and preferences files for each user account.

Figure 7-4 illustrates the locations of these libraries.

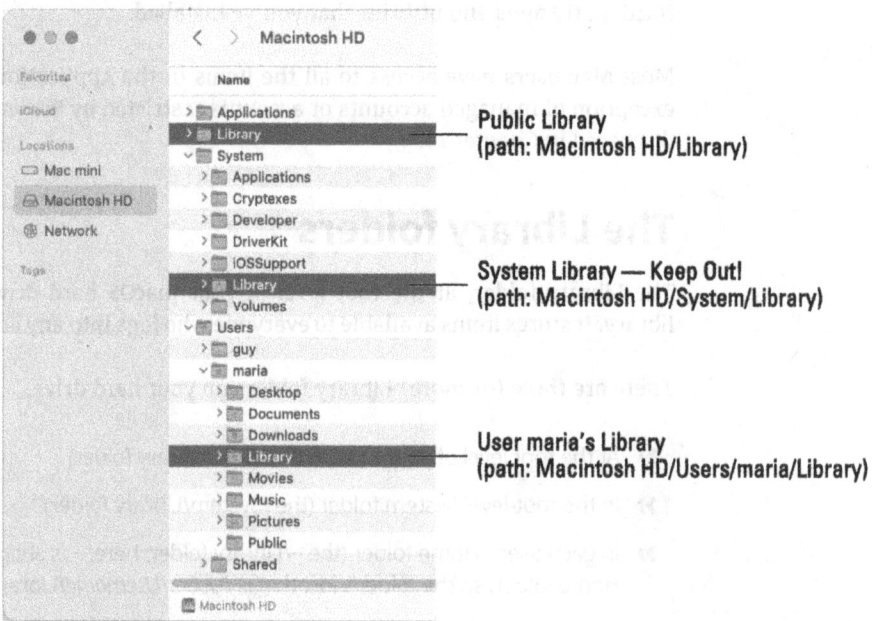

FIGURE 7-4:
A guide to
which Library
folder is which.

Only users with administrator (admin) privileges can put stuff in the public (root-level) Library folder. (For more information on admin privileges, check out Chapter 16.)

The System folder

The System folder contains the files that macOS needs to start up and keep working.

WARNING

Leave the System folder alone. Don't move, remove, or rename it or anything within it. It's part of the nerve center of your Mac.

So now you can forget everything outside your Home folder, because with few exceptions, that's where all *your* stuff will reside.

The Home folder

Your Home folder is inside the Users folder. Once you've logged in to your Mac, the contents of your Home folder appear whenever you choose Go ➪ Home or press the keyboard shortcut ⌘+Shift+H with the Finder active.

REMEMBER

Your Home folder is the most important folder for you as a user — or at least the one where you stash most of your files. Always save files to a folder or subfolder within your Home folder — preferably, in subfolders in your Home/Documents folder. The advantage of doing so is that your Home/Documents folder is easy to find, and many apps use it as the default folder for opening or saving a file.

When you open your Home folder, you see a Finder window with your short user-name in the title bar. Every user has a Home folder named after their short user-name (as specified in the Users & Groups pane in System Settings). If you refer to Figure 7-1, you'll see that the example Home folder contains seven subfolders — Desktop, Documents, Downloads, Movies, Music, Pictures, and Public — and that the Home folder is named *guy*, the short name for the user account to which the Home folder belongs.

If your Mac has more than one user, you can see their Home folders in the Users folder (you can see the *kay* Home folder and the *maria* Home folder in Figure 7-1), but macOS prevents you from opening files from or saving files to other users' Home folders.

By default, your Home folder has several folders inside it created by macOS. The following four are the most important:

» **Desktop:** If you put items (files, folders, apps, or aliases) on the desktop, they're actually stored in the Desktop folder.

» **Documents:** This folder is the place to put all the documents (letters, spreadsheets, recipes, novels, and so on) that you create.

- » **Library:** As mentioned earlier in this chapter, macOS hides this Library folder; you see how to change that in the next section. Even though it's hidden, this folder is still one of the most important in your Home folder, containing preferences (files containing the settings you create in System Settings and individual apps' preferences), fonts available only to you, and other stuff that you — and only you — expect to use.

- » **Public:** If others on your local area network (LAN) use file sharing to connect with your Mac, they can't see or use the files or folders in your Home folder unless you explicitly share them, but they can share files you store in your Home folder's Public folder. (Read more about file sharing and Public folders in Chapter 16.)

You can create more folders, if you like. In fact, every folder you create on this particular hard drive or volume *should* be within your Home folder. You learn to create folders and subfolders and organize your stuff inside them later in this chapter.

TIP

Keep these two points in mind as you dig around your Home folder:

- » If you decide to get rid of an item on the desktop, delete it by dragging its icon from the Desktop folder to the Trash or by dragging its icon from the desktop itself to the Trash. Both techniques move the file to the Trash, where it remains until you empty the Trash. Or if you don't want the file on the desktop anymore but don't want to get rid of it, you can drag it from the desktop into any other folder you like.

- » The other four folders that you should see in your Home folder are Downloads, Movies, Music, and Pictures. All these folders are empty until you (or apps such as Music, GarageBand, Photos, or iMovie, which create files inside these folders automatically the first time you launch them) put something in them.

Opening your own Library folder

The invisible Library subfolder of your Home folder contains everything that macOS needs to customize *your* Mac to *your* tastes. You won't spend much time (if any) adding things to the Library folder or moving them around within it, and that's why macOS hides it from sight. Still, it's a good idea for you to know what's in your Home/Library.

As mentioned earlier in this chapter, the root-level (public) Library folder (refer to Figure 7-4) is used to specify preferences for all users on this Mac. The Library folder in your Home folder, however, is all about you and your stuff.

WARNING

Be cautious with all Library folders. macOS is persnickety about how the folders and files within it are organized. You can safely add items to and remove items from most public or Home/Library folders, but *leave the folders themselves alone.* If you remove or rename the wrong folder, you could render macOS inoperable.

To find your hidden Home/Library folder, do this:

1. Click the Go menu and then press the Option key.

The (formerly) invisible Library folder appears on the Go menu as long as you hold down the Option key.

2. Click Library and then release the Option key.

You should see many folders in the Home/Library folder; the exact number depends on the software that you install on your Mac. Many of the folders have esoteric names, such as Daemon Containers and IntelligencePlatform, but other folders have easier-to-grasp names, such as Mail, Safari, Logs, Preferences, and Printers.

TIP

If you don't want to do this dance every time you open your Home/Library folder, open your Home folder in Finder and choose View ➪ Show View Options (or press ⌘+J). Select the Show Library Folder check box near the bottom of the View Options window, and your Home Library will be visible.

Some of the most important standard folders in the Library folder include the following:

» **Application Support:** Some apps store their support files here; others store theirs in the main (root-level) public Library folder.

» **Fonts:** This folder is empty until you install your own fonts here. The easiest way to install a font is to double-click its icon or name and let the Font Book utility handle it for you, as described in Chapter 19.

TIP

Avoid adding too many fonts for two reasons. First, the Fonts menu will become long and unwieldy. Second, and worse, installing too many fonts may make your Mac run more slowly.

» **Preferences:** The files here hold the information about whichever things you customize in macOS or in the apps you run. Whenever you change a system or app setting, that info is saved to a file in the Preferences folder.

WARNING

Don't mess with the Preferences folder! You should never need to open or use this folder unless something bad happens — say, you suspect that a particular preferences file has become *corrupted* (that is, damaged).

Saving Your Document

Now that you understand the macOS folder structure, let's look at how to save documents and where to save them. You can create as many documents as you like, but if you want to keep a document, you need to save it. You can save to your Mac's drive, to an external drive or USB thumb drive, or to iCloud. Saving documents to iCloud enables you to easily access them on all your Apple devices. Chapter 8 discusses iCloud in greater depth.

Understanding Auto Save and Versions

Saving a document is straightforward, as you'll see shortly, but macOS gives you greater protection by providing an Auto Save feature that saves versions of your work as you work, when you pause, and every 5 minutes. A *version* is a snapshot of the state of the document at that point in time, but it is saved within the same document file rather than as a separate file. The version contains enough information for the app to revert the document to that state.

If you're working in an app that supports Auto Save, a new version of the document is created each time you save the document explicitly and each time Auto Save runs. This is much easier for you than using the File ⇨ Save As command to save a separate copy of the file under a different name or duplicating files in Finder and then renaming the duplicates. The file containing versions is also smaller than the multiple separate documents.

To access a previous version of a document, choose File ⇨ Revert To ⇨ Browse All Versions within the app, or choose Enter Time Machine from the Time Machine icon on the menu bar while the document is active on-screen. (See Chapter 21 for more on Time Machine.)

Sad to say, even though macOS has offered Auto Save and Versions for more than a decade now, only some third-party apps use these features. Other apps rely on you to keep any extra copies you need of your documents.

REMEMBER

The following sections show you how to save your masterpieces. Prevent unnecessary pain in your life by developing good saving habits, so save your work (or save a version in apps that support Versions)

>> Every few minutes

>> Before you switch to another app

>> Before you print a document

>> Before you leave your Mac

TIP

The keyboard shortcut for Save in almost every Mac app is ⌘+S, and it works with Auto Save and Versions as well as with Save and Save As. Train your finger muscles to press ⌘+S automatically every time you've made a change you wouldn't want to have to make again.

Stepping through a basic save

This section walks you through the steps you use the first time you save a document. The process is the same whether your app supports Auto Save and Versions or not. It's only after the initial save that Auto Save and Versions come into play.

DOES THIS APP HAVE AUTO SAVE AND VERSIONS OR NOT?

The easiest way to tell whether an app uses the Auto Save feature and the Versions feature is to look at the title bar of a document open in the app. If it displays a little downward caret (like a *v*) to the right of the document's name when you hover your cursor over it (as shown at the top of the illustration here), and a pop-up window appears if you click the caret, the app supports Auto Save and Versions. (You read more about the options in the pop-up window later in this chapter.)

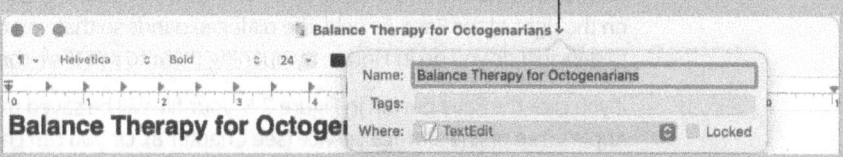

Click the downward caret

Alternatively, open the File menu. If the Save As command appears, the app is old-school and likely doesn't support Auto Save and Versions. If the Duplicate command appears, the app likely supports Auto Save and Versions. The keyboard shortcut for either Duplicate or Save As (whichever command appears) is typically ⌘+Shift+S. If the Duplicate command appears, you can hold down Option to display the Save As command instead.

You can also check whether the app has the Rename command and the Move To command on its File menu. If it doesn't, it's old-school; if it does, it's Auto Save and Versions-savvy.

Saving a file works pretty much the same way in any app you use to create documents. This example uses the macOS text-editor app, TextEdit, but the process will be similar in Microsoft Word, Adobe Photoshop, Apple Keynote, or any other app.

TIP

To follow along on your Mac, click Launchpad on the Dock to display the Launchpad screen, then click the TextEdit icon to open the TextEdit app. Click the New Document button or choose File ⇨ New to create a new document, and then type a few words in the Untitled document that appears.

When you choose to save a file for the first time (choose File ⇨ Save or press ⌘+S), a Save As dialog appears in front of the document that you're saving, as shown in Figure 7-5. This dialog is the *basic* Save As dialog (as opposed to the *expanded* Save As dialog, which you'll meet in a moment):

1. **In the Save As field, type a name for your file.**

   When a Save As dialog appears for the first time, the Save As field is active and displays the name of the document. The document name (usually, Untitled) is selected; when you begin typing, the name you type replaces it.

2. **If the Where pop-up menu lists the location where you want to save your file, choose that location and proceed to Step 5; if not, click the disclosure button (labeled in Figure 7-5).**

   You can choose among a short list of folders and volumes listed on the basic Save As dialog's Where pop-up menu (which are the same devices and favorites you see in the sidebar of Finder windows). Or if you click the disclosure button on the right of the Save As field, the dialog expands so that you can navigate folders just as you do in Finder: by opening them to see their contents.

   If you click the Save button in Figure 7-5, your file will be saved to iCloud Drive, Apple's free online storage service (see Chapter 8). Or you can choose another location from the Where menu before you click Save and save the file elsewhere.

   If you switch to expanded view (shown in Figure 7-6) by clicking the disclosure button, a standard Save As dialog appears so that you can save your file in any folder you like.

   Note that the Where menu in the expanded Save As dialog in Figure 7-6 doesn't have a Favorites section; instead, it displays the path to the folder in which the file will be saved (Documents). To access Favorites in the expanded Save As dialog, you use the sidebar instead.

TIP

Switch between the basic and expanded Save As dialogs a few times by clicking the disclosure button. Make sure that you see and understand the difference between what you see on the Where menu in a basic Save As dialog (Figure 7-5) and what you see on the Where menu in an expanded Save As dialog (Figure 7-6). The steps that follow assume you're using the expanded Save As dialog.

3. **To make it easier to find the folder in which you want to save your file, click the View icon and click your preferred view on the pop-up menu.**

In Icons view, you double-click a folder to open it. List view offers disclosure brackets for folders and drives; click the disclosure brackets of folders to see their contents. In Columns view, you click an item on the left to see its contents on the right, just as you do in a column-view Finder window.

You can also use the Forward and Back icons or the sidebar, both available only in an expanded Save As dialog, to conveniently navigate your Mac's filesystem. You can use the Sort By pop-up menu or the Group By pop-up menu to sort or group the files and folders. Many of these navigation aids work just like the ones in Finder; see Chapter 4 for more details. You can enlarge the Save As dialog by dragging one of its corners or edges.

TIP

If you can't find the folder in which you want to save your document, type the folder name in the Search box, which works just like the Search box in a Finder window, as described in chapters 4 and 8. You don't even have to press Return; the Save As dialog updates itself to show you only items that match the characters as you typed them.

4. **Choose the folder where you want to save your file from the Where pop-up menu or in the sidebar.**

5. **If you want to create a new subfolder of the selected folder to save your file in, click the New Folder button (labeled in Figure 7-7), give the new folder a name, and then save your file in it.**

In Figure 7-7, an existing folder named Outgoing is selected. You can tell that it's selected because its name is displayed in the Where menu and highlighted below that in the second column.

The keyboard shortcut for New Folder is ⌘+Shift+N, regardless of whether you're in a Save As dialog or in Finder. In the example in Figure 7-7, clicking the New Folder button or pressing the keyboard shortcut would create a folder inside the Outgoing folder.

6. **In the File Format pop-up menu (which says Rich Text Document in Figure 7-7), make sure the format selected is the one you want.**

7. **Click the Save button to save the file to the active folder.**

TIP

After you save a file for the first time, choosing File ⇨ Save or pressing ⌘+S won't open the Save As dialog. Instead, what happens next depends on whether the app supports macOS's Auto Save and Versions. If the app *doesn't* support Auto Save and Versions, Save and its shortcut (⌘+S) merely resave your document in the same location and with the same name. If you want to save a unique version with a different name, you have to choose the Save As command and save the file under a new name.

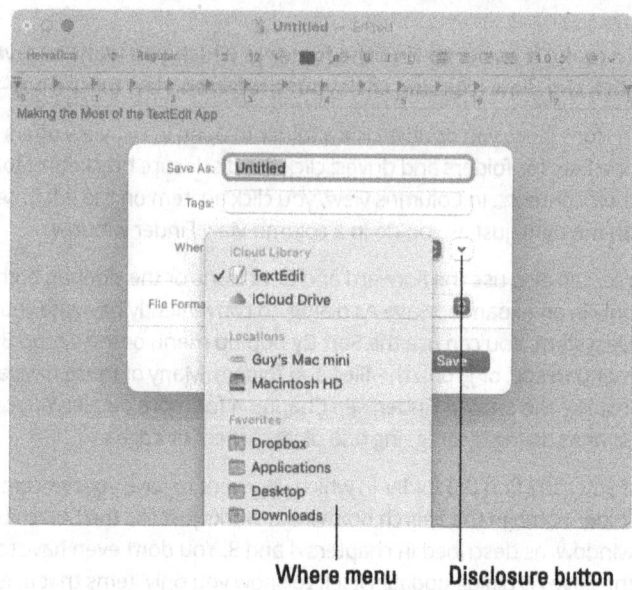

FIGURE 7-5:
A basic Save As
dialog looks like
this example.

Where menu   Disclosure button

Forward   Group By/Sort By (pop-up menu)

Back   View (pop-up menu)   Where menu

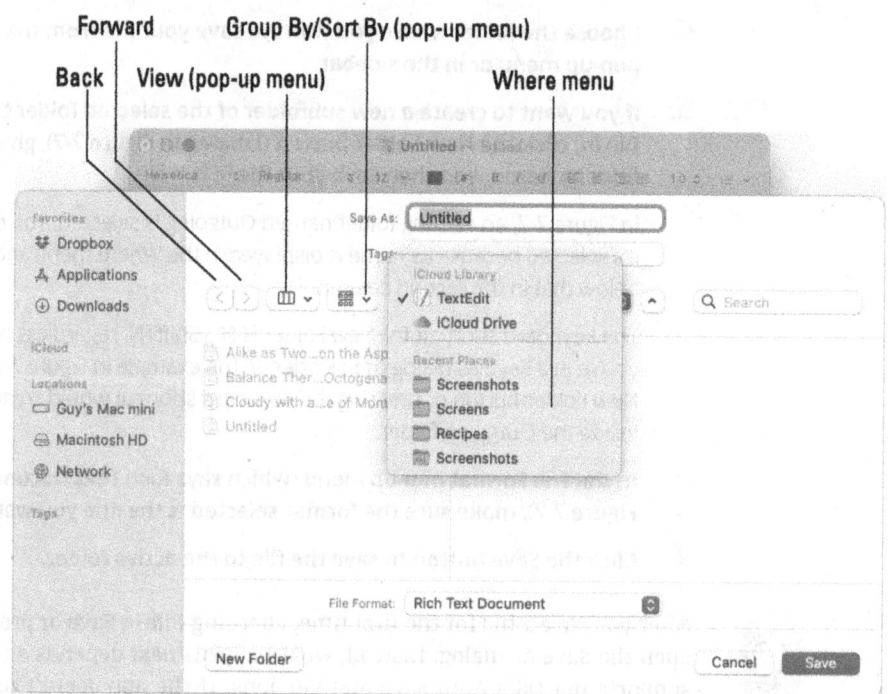

FIGURE 7-6:
An expanded
Save As dialog
looks similar to
this one (shown
in Columns view).

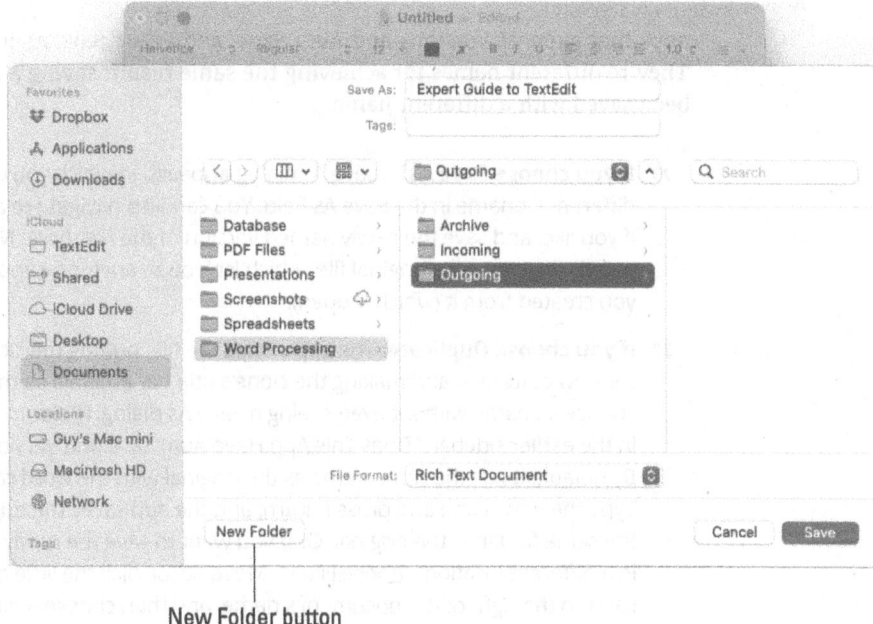

 **WARNING**

FIGURE 7-7:
Saving a file in the
Outgoing folder
(which is in a
subfolder of
the Documents
folder).

New Folder button

If the app *does* support Auto Save and Versions, however, the following section explains how things work.

When creating a document in an app that doesn't support Auto Save and Versions, press ⌘+S whenever you've made changes you don't want to have to make again. Figures 7-5, 7-6, and 7-7 show the Save As dialog for TextEdit as an example. In apps other than TextEdit, the Save As dialog might contain additional options, fewer options, or different options, and therefore might look slightly different. For example, while many apps include the File Format menu, some do not; and some include other options. Don't worry. The Save As dialog always works the same way, no matter what options it offers.

Save As versus Duplicate: Different names for the same result

The two commands File ⇨ Duplicate and File ⇨ Save As serve the same purpose and achieve the same result. The difference is that you'll find File ⇨ Duplicate in apps that support Versions and Auto Save, and File ⇨ Save As in apps that don't. They're different names for achieving the same result: saving a file that's already been saved with a different name.

>> **If you choose Save As:** A Save As dialog appears, in which you can type a different filename in the Save As field. You can also navigate to another folder, if you like, and save the newly named version of the file there. Now you have two distinct files: the original file (which isn't open anymore) and the new file you created from it (which *is* open).

>> **If you choose Duplicate:** The app clones the file, putting the clone in a window of its own and making the clone's title bar editable so that you can change its name without even seeing a Save As dialog. (Refer to the illustration in the earlier sidebar, "Does This App Have Auto Save and Versions or Not?") By default, it has the same name as the original with the word *copy* appended. Type the new name and press Return, and the app saves the duplicated file in the same folder as the original. Or if you want to save the newly renamed file in a different location, choose File ⇨ Move To, or click the little downward caret to the right of the document's name, and then choose a different location from the Where menu.

TIP

Another way to create a copy of a file is to duplicate it in Finder by choosing File ⇨ Duplicate or pressing ⌘+D. You can then rename the copy, open it, and make changes to it, as needed. When you finish making changes, you can save the document without worrying about Save As or Duplicate.

If you prefer to use Save As, just press the Option key before you click the File menu, and Duplicate magically changes to Save As.

Versions gives you the benefits of Save As without any action on your part, but many apps still lack support for Auto Save and Versions more than a decade after their introduction.

REMEMBER

If the app you're using supports Versions, you can revert to an earlier version of the document. Choose File ⇨ Revert To ⇨ Browse All Versions or click the Time Machine icon on the Dock while the document is active on-screen. Either way, Time Machine displays versions of the document side by side, as shown in Figure 7-8. See Chapter 21 to learn about working with Time Machine.

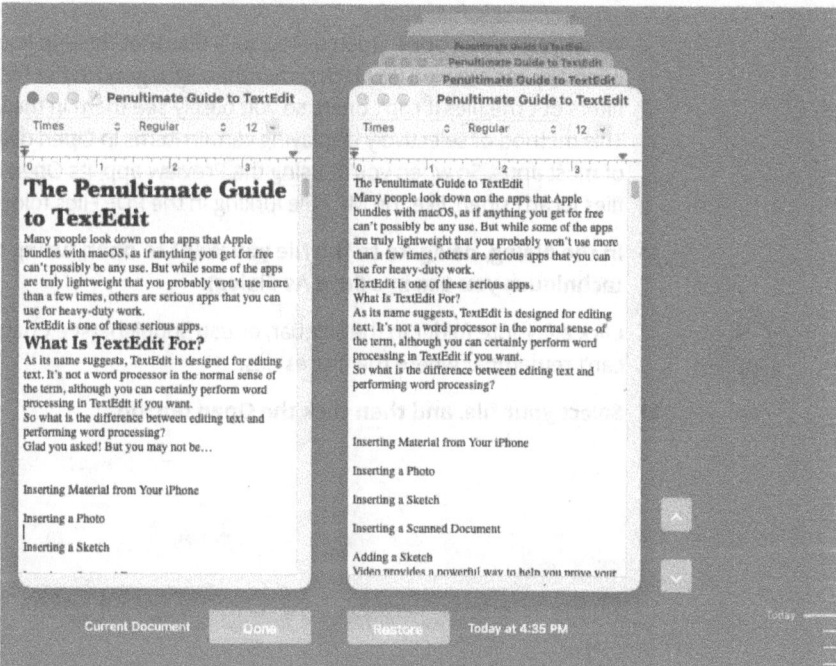

Penultimate Guide to TextEdit
Penultimate Guide to TextEdit
Penultimate Guide to TextEdit

FIGURE 7-8:
Browse All
Versions lets you
compare all
versions and
revert to an
earlier version.

Open, Sez Me

You can open any item in Finder — whether it's a file or a folder — in at least six ways:

» Double-click the item. This is usually the easiest way.

» Click the item to select it, and choose File ⇨ Open.

» Select the item, and then press either ⌘+O or ⌘+↓.

» Control-click or right-click the item, and choose Open from the contextual menu.

» If the item is a document, drag it onto the Dock icon of an app that can open that type of document.

» If the item is a document, right-click or Control-click it, and choose an app from the Open With submenu of the contextual menu.

You can also open any document from within an app like this:

» **In the app, choose File ⇨ Open, or press the shortcut ⌘+O.**

An Open dialog appears, like the one shown in Figure 7-9.

When you use an app's Open dialog, only files that the app knows how to open appear enabled (in black rather than light gray) in the file list. The app filters out the files it can't open, so you barely see them in the Open dialog. This method of selectively displaying certain items in Open dialogs is a feature of most apps. So when you're using the Preview app, its Open dialog dims all files it can't open, like the MP3 file lurking in the PDF Files folder in Figure 7-9.

» **In the dialog, navigate to the file you want to open (using the same techniques you use in a Save As dialog).**

Click a favorite folder in the sidebar, or use Spotlight (see Chapter 10) if you can't remember where the file resides.

» **Select your file, and then click the Open button.**

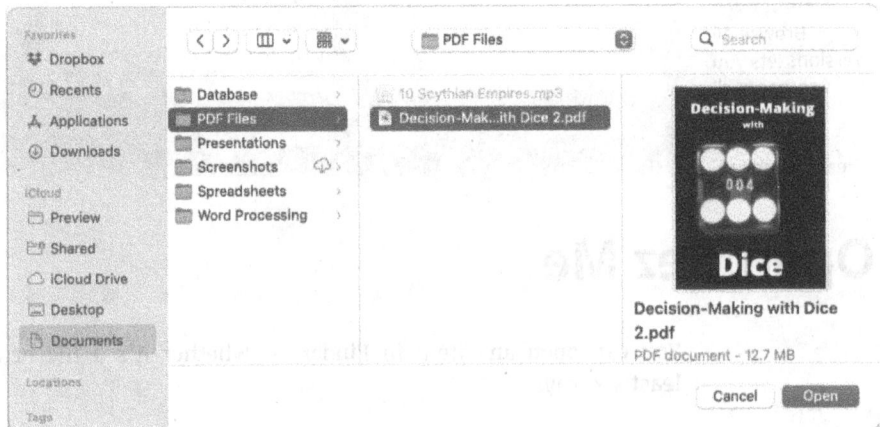

FIGURE 7-9:
The Open dialog
in Columns view.

Some apps allow you to select multiple files in their Open dialogs by clicking the first file and then holding down either Shift (for contiguous selections) or ⌘ (for noncontiguous selections). If you need to open several files, it's worth a try; the worst thing that could happen is that it won't work, and you'll have to open the items one at a time.

Some apps, including Microsoft Word and Adobe Photoshop, have a Show menu or a Format menu in their Open dialogs. This menu lets you specify the type(s) of files you want to see as available in the Open dialog. When an Open dialog has such a menu, you can often open a file that initially appears dimmed; choose All Documents from the menu, and then see if the file is listed in black rather than gray.

With drag-and-drop

You can open a document by dragging it onto the icon of a suitable app. If you've got a Word document on your desktop, for example, you can drag it onto the Microsoft Word app icon on the Dock. The app launches (or becomes active if it is already open) and opens the document.

With Quick Look

The Quick Look feature (which you meet in Chapter 10) can display the contents of many types of files. For now, know that you can use Quick Look to peek at the contents of most files in Open dialogs. Just Control-click or right-click the file, and choose Quick Look from the contextual menu; or select the file and press ⌘+Y; or select the file and press the spacebar. Up pops an overlay showing the file's contents, all without launching an app.

When your Mac can't open a file

If you try to open a file, but macOS can't find an app to open that file, macOS prompts you with an alert window. Click Cancel to abort the attempt to open the file, or click the Choose Application or Search App Store button to select another application to open this file.

If you click the Choose Application button, a dialog appears, displaying the apps in your Applications folder. macOS dims any apps it thinks can't open the file. For a wider choice of apps, click the Enable pop-up menu, and then choose All Applications instead of Recommended Applications.

REMEMBER

You can't open every file with every app. If you try to open an MP3 (audio) file with Microsoft Excel (the spreadsheet app), for example, it just won't work; you get an error message or a screen full of gibberish. Sometimes, you just have to keep trying until you find the right app; at other times, you don't have an app that can open the file.

TIP

When in doubt, search online for information about the file extension. You can quickly find out which apps create such files and which apps can open them.

With the app of your choice

Sooner or later, you'll likely run into a file created by an app you don't use — perhaps even an app you've never heard of. macOS lets you specify the app in which you want to open a document in the future when you double-click it. More than that, you can specify that you want all documents of that type to open with the specified app.

Assigning a file type to an app

Suppose that you want all .jpg files that usually open in Preview to open instead in Adobe Lightroom, a heavy-duty third-party app for organizing and editing photos. Here's what to do:

1. **Click one of the files in Finder.**

2. **Choose File ⇨ Get Info (or press ⌘ +I).**

   Or right-click, Control-click, or tap the file with two fingers, and then choose Get Info from the contextual menu.

3. **In the Info window, click the disclosure arrow to disclose the Open With pane.**

4. **From the pop-up menu, choose an app that macOS believes will open this document type.**

   If you choose Lightroom, as in Figure 7-10, Lightroom will open each time you open this file (instead of the default app, Preview).

5. **(Optional) If you click the Change All button at the bottom of the Open With pane, as shown in Figure 7-10, you make Lightroom the new default app for all .jpeg files that would otherwise be opened in Preview.**

   Notice the alert that appears when you click the Change All button. Click the Continue button if you're sure you want to make this change.

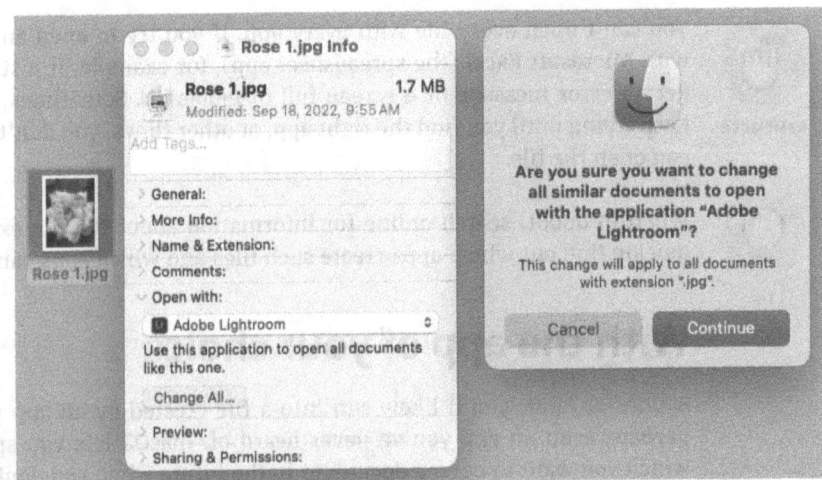

FIGURE 7-10:
Changing the app that opens this document and all others like it (that is, .jpeg files).

Opening a file with an app other than the default

TIP

When you want to open a document with an app other than its default, drag the file onto that app's icon or alias icon or Dock icon, and the file opens in the app. For example, double-clicking an MP3 file normally opens it in the Music app and copies the file to your Music library. But if you just want to listen to the MP3 file, you can drag it onto QuickTime Player's icon in the Applications folder or its Dock icon (if it's on the Dock) to make QuickTime Player play the file.

TIP

Only apps that *might* be able to open the file should highlight when you drag the file on them. That doesn't mean the document will be usable — just that the app can *open* it.

To open a file with an app other than its default (and not change anything for the future), right-click the file, and then choose another app from the contextual menu, as shown in Figure 7-11.

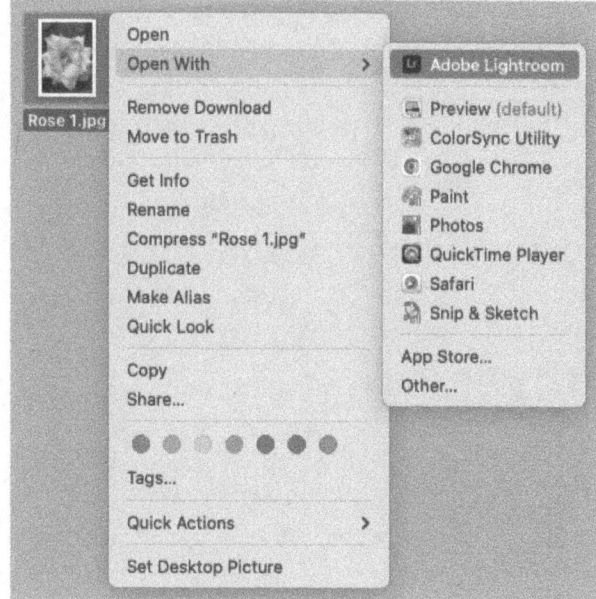

FIGURE 7-11:
To open a file with an app other than its default, right-click the file, and then choose the app you desire.

TIP

You can also change the default app to open *this* file by pressing Option after you right-click the file, which causes the Open With command to change to Always Open With.

IN THIS CHAPTER

» Getting organized with folders

» Moving around files and folders

» Using iCloud, iCloud+, and iCloud Drive

Chapter **8**

Managing Files and Folders the Smart Way

You'll eventually accumulate a lot of files on your disk(s): tens, hundreds, thousands, even millions of files.

In Chapter 7, you read about Finder and opening and saving files. In this chapter, we take a look at how to organize all those files so you can find them when you need them.

Organizing Your Stuff in Folders

Organizing your files is as personal as your taste in music; you develop your own style with the Mac. But this section provides some ideas about how you might want to organize things, plus some suggestions that can make organization easier for you.

The following subsections explain the difference between a file and a folder, show you how to set up nested folders, and cover how some special folder features work.

What's the difference between a file and a folder?

Let's start by sorting out the difference between a file and a folder. A *file* is a named container that holds a specific item, such as a document, an app, or an alias. If you open Microsoft Word, create a document, and save it, the document is saved in a file.

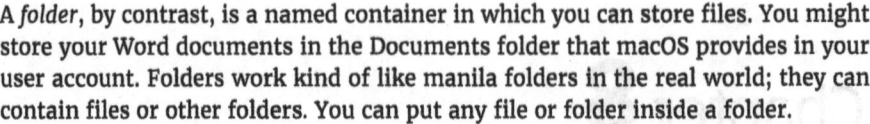

A *folder*, by contrast, is a named container in which you can store files. You might store your Word documents in the Documents folder that macOS provides in your user account. Folders work kind of like manila folders in the real world; they can contain files or other folders. You can put any file or folder inside a folder.

Organizing your stuff with subfolders

To organize your stuff, you can put folders inside folders. A folder you place inside another folder is a *subfolder* or a *nested folder*. As you know from Chapter 7, macOS sets up your user account with a default folder structure. Your Home folder (the folder that bears your short username) contains various subfolders, including the Desktop folder, the Documents folder, and the Downloads folder.

You can create subfolders according to whatever system makes sense to you. In case no system makes sense yet, here are four organizational topic ideas and naming examples for subfolders:

>> **By type of document:** Word Processing, Spreadsheets, Graphics

>> **By date:** Documents May–June, Documents Fall 2024

>> **By content:** Memos, Outgoing Letters, Expense Reports

>> **By project:** Project X, Project Y, Project Z

When you notice your folders filling with enough files to make them hard to navigate, subdivide them again by using a combination of these methods that makes sense to you. Suppose that you start by subdividing your Documents folder into multiple subfolders. Later, when those folders begin to get full, you can subdivide them further.

Allow your folder structure to grow as you need it to grow. Don't let any single folder get so full that it's a hassle to deal with. Create new subfolders when things start to get crowded. (You learn how to create folders in the next section.)

If you use a particular folder a lot, give yourself easy access to it in as many of these ways as you find helpful:

>> **Dock:** Drag the folder to the right side of your Dock.

>> **Home folder:** Put an alias to the folder in your Home folder.

>> **Desktop:** Place an alias to the folder on your desktop.

>> **Sidebar:** In Finder, select the folder and choose File ⇨ Add to Sidebar or press ⌘+Control+T. The folder is then available in the sidebar in Open and Save dialogs as well.

See Chapter 4 for more information about aliases.

TIP

If you create your own subfolders in the Documents folder, you can click that folder on the Dock to reveal them, as shown in Figure 8-1. List view enables you to access the documents most easily. Chapter 3 shows you how to customize the Dock.

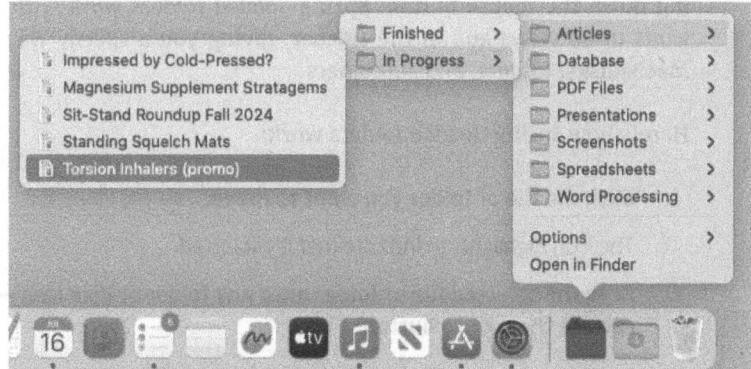

FIGURE 8-1: Place your Documents folder on the Dock to gain quick access to your documents.

Creating new folders

macOS creates your user account with a decent fistful of folders, but you're pretty much guaranteed to need more folders to keep your files organized the way you prefer. You can create a new folder in moments by following these steps:

1. **Open a Finder window to the folder in which you want to create the new folder.**

   If you want to create a new folder in your Documents folder, open a Finder window showing the Documents folder. If you want to create a new folder right on the desktop, you can work directly on the desktop or open a Finder window to the Desktop folder in your user account.

2. **Choose File ⇨ New Folder (or press ⌘ +Shift+N).**

A new folder appears in the folder with its default name selected.

3. **Type a descriptive name for the folder, and then press Return.**

If you accidentally click anywhere before you type the folder name, the name becomes deselected. To select it again, click the name and press Return.

REMEMBER

For folders and files that you might share with users of non–Mac computers, follow this rule to maximize compatibility: Use no punctuation and no Option-key characters in the folder or filename. Other operating systems may disallow periods, slashes, backslashes, and colons in file and folder names. Option-key characters are special characters that you enter using the Option key, such as ™ (Option+2), ® (Option+R), and ¢ (Option+4).

Navigating with spring-loaded folders

A *spring-loaded folder* pops open when you drag something onto it and keep holding down the mouse button. Spring-loaded folders work with all folder or disk icons in all views and in the sidebar, giving you a speedy way to navigate your Mac's disks, folders, and subfolders.

Here's how spring-loaded folders work:

1. **Click the file or folder you want to move.**

The icon highlights to indicate that it's selected.

2. **Drag the selected file or folder onto any folder or disk icon — but don't release the mouse button.**

In a second or two, the highlighted folder or disk flashes twice and then springs open, right under the pointer. If you don't want to wait, press the spacebar to open the folder immediately.

3. **After the folder springs open, perform any of these actions:**

- Continue dragging if you want to traverse your folder structure this way. Subfolders continue to spring open until you release the mouse button.

- Release the mouse button to drop the item into the folder that's currently active. The Finder window remains open.

- To cancel a spring-loaded folder, drag the pointer away from the folder icon or outside the boundaries of the sprung window. The folder springs shut.

TIP

If spring-loaded folders don't work, or if the springing is too fast or too slow, open the System Settings app, click Accessibility in the sidebar, and then click Pointer Control in the Motor section of the Accessibility pane. In the Mouse & Trackpad area of the Pointer Control pane, make sure that the Spring-Loading switch is set to On (blue) to enable the feature, and then drag the Spring-Loading Speed slider along its Tortoise–Hare continuum to adjust the speed.

Using smart folders

A *smart folder* lets you save search criteria that specify exactly what files and folders you want to round up. macOS continuously updates each smart folder, so it displays all the files on your computer that match its search criteria set even if you add or delete files.

Figure 8-2 shows a smart folder that gathers all PNG image files with *Nature* in their name that have been opened in the past 15 days. Or, you can create a smart folder that displays spreadsheet files, but only the ones bigger (or smaller) than a specified file size. Then all those files appear in one convenient smart folder.

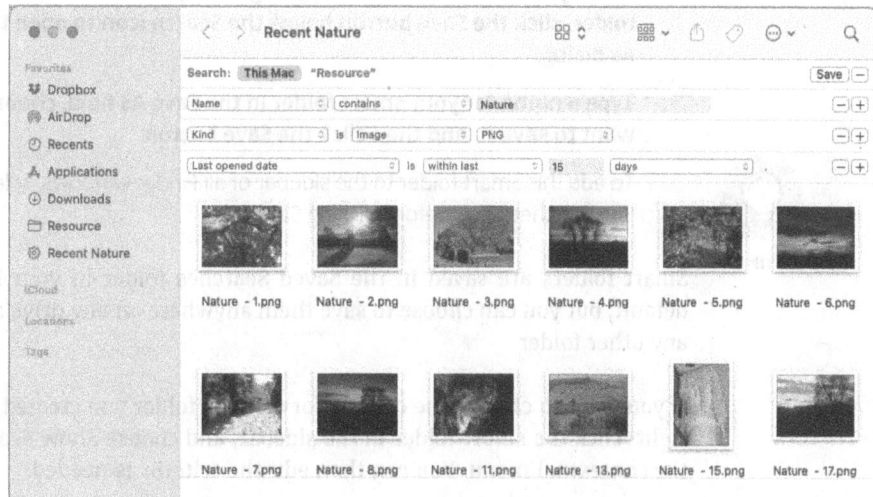

FIGURE 8-2:
A smart folder that displays PNG files opened in the past 15 days whose names contain the word *Nature*.

Smart folders don't gather the files in a separate place; they gather search results. The actual files remain in the folders in which you stored them.

Smart folders are so useful that Apple provides four ways to create one. The following steps show you how:

1. **Start your smart folder by using any of the following methods:**

   - Choose File ⇨ New Smart Folder.
   - Choose File ⇨ Find.
   - Press ⌘ +F.
   - Type at least one character in the Search box of a Finder window.

   WARNING

   If you have Recents selected in the sidebar, you can't use the last method, because Recents is a smart folder itself — one with a weird icon, but a smart folder nonetheless.

2. **Enter your first search criterion in the line of controls that appear.**

   In Figure 8-2, the first criterion is *Name contains Nature*.

3. **Add further criteria for your search by clicking the + button to add a criterion or the – button to delete one.**

4. **When you're satisfied and ready to gather your criteria into a smart folder, click the Save button below the Search icon to open the Save As dialog.**

5. **Type a name for your smart folder in the Save As field, choose where you want to save it, and then click the Save button.**

   TIP

   To add this smart folder to the sidebar of all Finder windows, select the Add to Sidebar check box before clicking Save.

Smart folders are saved in the Saved Searches folder in your Library folder by default, but you can choose to save them anywhere on any drive and use them like any other folder.

If you want to change the criteria for a smart folder you created, Control-click or right-click the smart folder in the sidebar, and choose Show Search Criteria from the contextual menu. You can then edit the criteria as needed.

When you finish changing the criteria, click the Save button to resave your folder. (If you try to close a modified smart folder without saving your changes, macOS prompts you to save it.) When you do save, macOS may ask whether you want to replace the previous smart folder of the same name; usually, you do.

Smart folders (except the sidebar's Recents, which has a clock icon) display a gear icon, making them easy to tell apart from regular folders.

Working with Files and Folders

Sometimes, keeping files and folders organized means moving them from one place to another. At other times, you want to copy them, rename them, or compress them to send to a friend. This section explains all those things and more.

TIP

The techniques in this section work in List view, Columns view, and Gallery view as well as in Icon view. The figure in this section uses Icon view because it's the best view for pictures to show you what's going on. List view and Columns view usually are much better for moving and copying files.

Moving files and folders

You can move files and folders around within a window to your heart's content as long as that window is set to Icon view. Just click and drag any icon to its new location in the window.

TIP

If the icons won't move, make sure View ➪ Arrange By is set to None. You can't move icons around in a window displayed in List, Columns, or Gallery view. Even in Icon view, you can't move icons around in a window that's under the spell of the Arrange By command.

macOS provides various ways of moving files and folders into folders or onto other disks. These are the two easiest ways:

REMEMBER

>> **Drag the item onto a folder.** Drag one or more folders or files onto another folder (or disk), releasing the mouse button when the second folder or disk is highlighted. The files or folders land inside the second folder or disk. This technique works regardless of whether the second folder is open in a separate window or tab.

   If you *don't* release the mouse button when the second folder is highlighted, the second folder will spring open, allowing you to see its contents before you commit to moving the item or items by releasing the mouse button.

>> **Drag the item into an open folder's window.** Drag one or more folders or files into the open window of a second folder (or disk), and release the mouse button when the second folder's window is highlighted.

REMEMBER

If you want to move an item from one disk to another disk, you can't use the preceding methods, because dragging the item between disks copies the item rather than moving it. To move a file or folder from one disk to another, hold down the ⌘ key while you drag the item from the disk it's currently on to the one you want to move it to. You'll know immediately if you've gotten this right, because you'll see the Moving Files window rather than the Copying Files window.

Selecting multiple items

You can easily copy or move several items to the same destination. You just need to select the items first. To select all the items in the active folder, choose Edit ⇨ Select All or press ⌘+A. To select just some of the items in the active folder, take one of the following actions:

>> **Draw a selection rectangle around the items.** In Icon view, click open space in the folder window and drag the pointer to draw a box, called a *selection rectangle*, around the items, as in Figure 8-3. Finder highlights each item within the box or touching it. You can also use this technique on the thumbnails at the bottom of the window in Gallery view.

>> **Select a contiguous range of items.** In any view except Icon view, click the first item, hold down the Shift key, and then click the last item. Finder selects the first item, the last item, and all the items between them.

>> **Select a noncontiguous range of items.** In any view, click the first item and then hold down the ⌘ key while you click each other item you want to add to the selection. To deselect a selected item, hold down the ⌘ key and click the item.

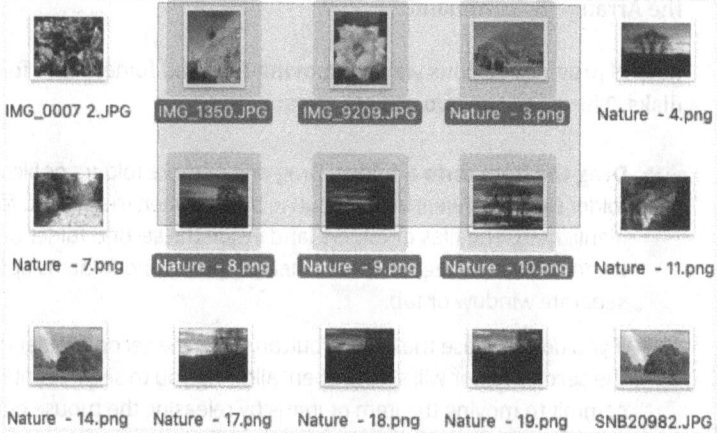

IMG_0007 2.JPG   IMG_1350.JPG   IMG_9209.JPG   Nature - 3.png   Nature - 4.png

Nature - 7.png   Nature - 8.png   Nature - 9.png   Nature - 10.png   Nature - 11.png

Nature - 14.png   Nature - 17.png   Nature - 18.png   Nature - 19.png   SNB20982.JPG

FIGURE 8-3:
The six items touched by the selection rectangle become selected.

After selecting the items, you can drag them to move or copy them.

TIP

To move two or more items to a new folder, select the items and choose File ⇨ New Folder with Selection. Alternatively, press ⌘+Control+N, or Control-click or right-click one of the selected items and choose New Folder with Selection from the contextual menu. All three techniques will create a new folder, move the selected items into it, and select the default name of the new folder (which will be New Folder with Items) so you can type its new name and press Return.

Renaming items

To rename an item, you can either click the item's name directly or click the item's icon and then press Return once to open the name for editing. Type the new name over the existing name, or edit the name by clicking the I-beam pointer to place the insertion point at the appropriate point, and then make the change. To apply the name, press Return or click outside the name.

TECHNICAL STUFF

If an item is locked or busy (such as an app that's currently open), or if you don't have the owner's permission to rename that item (see Chapter 16 for details about permissions), you can't rename it. Similarly, you should never rename macOS system items such as the Library folder, System folder, and Desktop folder.

WARNING

Don't change the name of a folder that contains open files, because you might mess up the saving process and possibly cause data loss.

Renaming multiple items at once

To rename a group of files, giving them related names, first select them all; then right-click anywhere in your selection and choose Rename from the contextual menu. A dialog appears with options for adding or replacing text in the existing filename, or creating a custom format with indexes, counters, and dates before or after whatever new filename you choose.

TIP

For more complex renaming, use a renaming utility, such as A Better Finder Rename (https://www.publicspace.net/ABetterFinderRename/).

Compressing files

TIP

If you're going to send files attached to an email message, creating a compressed archive of the files first and sending the archive instead of the originals usually saves you time sending the files and saves the recipient time downloading them. To create this compressed archive, select the file(s) or folder(s) and then choose File ⇨ Compress. This command creates a compressed file in the widely used zip format containing the files or folders you selected. If those items are compressible, the zip file is smaller than the original items, sometimes substantially smaller; if the items aren't compressible, the zip file may actually be bigger than the items — but even so, it's easier to handle. Double-click a zip file to decompress it.

Getting rid of files and folders

To get rid of a file or folder, simply drag it onto the Trash icon in your Dock. See the section "Trash talkin'" in Chapter 3 for instructions on emptying the Trash and recovering items from it.

REMEMBER

Trashing an alias gets rid of only the alias, not the parent file. But trashing a document, a folder, or an app icon puts it in the Trash, where it will be deleted permanently the next time you empty the Trash.

Using iCloud, iCloud+, and iCloud Drive

iCloud has been around in various forms for years providing Internet-based storage for Macs, iPhones, iPads, and other Apple devices. iCloud Drive is a component of iCloud that lets you store files of any type in iCloud and access them from any device via your iCloud account. iCloud Drive is built into macOS, so it works like any other folder on your Mac. That means you can drag documents of any type into it, organize them with folders and tags (see Chapter 4) if you care to, and find them with Spotlight (see Chapter 9).

The best part is that the files are available not only on your Mac but also on your iPhone, iPad, or Windows PC as well. That's the good news. The bad news is that if you need more than the 5GB of free storage space that you get in a standard iCloud account, you need to move up to the paid tier, which is called iCloud+. As of this writing, iCloud+ storage costs 99 cents per month for 50GB, $2.99 per month for 200GB, $9.99 per month for 2TB, $29.99 per month for 6TB, and $59.99 per month for 12TB. You can also get extra iCloud+ storage as part of an Apple One subscription bundle (https://www.apple.com/apple-one/).

iCloud Drive is normally enabled by default. To check, open a Finder window, expand the iCloud category if it's collapsed, and then look for the iCloud Drive item. If you don't see it, you may need to enable iCloud Drive: Click the System Settings icon on the Dock, click the Apple ID icon in the sidebar, and then click the iCloud button to display the iCloud screen. Now click the Drive button to open the iCloud Drive dialog, and then set the Sync This Mac switch to On (blue). Before you close the iCloud Drive dialog, set the Desktop & Documents Folders switch to On (blue) if you want to use iCloud to sync these folders. Then click the Done button to close the dialog.

If you've set the iCloud Drive switch to On but still don't see iCloud Drive in your sidebar, Finder may be set to suppress iCloud Drive. With a Finder window active, choose Finder ⇨ Settings to open the Finder Settings window, click the Sidebar tab at the top, and then select the iCloud Drive check box in the iCloud section of the Show These Items in the Sidebar box.

Chapter 9

Eight Terrific Time-Saving Tools

S equoia is packed with time-saving apps and shortcuts. This chapter shares what you need to know to exploit eight key tools in full. You start with Siri, the voice-driven virtual assistant that taps into Apple Intelligence; touch on the Clipboard and the Universal Clipboard; and then move on to peeking at files with Quick Look, searching for files and folders with the Find feature, and searching for pretty much anything with Spotlight.

After queries, quizzing, and search, you move on to management. You learn to manage apps, windows, desktops, and spaces with the Mission Control feature, and then get the hang of using Stage Manager to marshal your recent apps and flip among them. Last, we touch on two essential tools you have already met: Control Center and Launchpad.

Getting to Grips with Siri

Siri, Apple's intelligent digital assistant, helps you get things done by using your voice, including capabilities designed specifically for your Mac. That means you can search for information, find files, send messages, and do much, much more with only your voice. As you'd imagine, your Mac needs an Internet connection for Siri to search online.

Siri is optimized to work well with your Mac's built-in microphones, so you don't have to buy or connect a mic. Despite this optimization, you'll typically find that Siri, along with other voice-driven features such as Dictation and Voice Control, works even better with a headset microphone. (More on this in Chapter 20.) A headset microphone is especially helpful if you're using Siri in a noisy environment.

What Siri can do for you

Here are examples of things you can ask or tell Siri to do:

» "Open the Microsoft Word document I worked on yesterday."

» "Remind me to take the pizza out of the oven in 14 minutes."

» "Add a meeting to my calendar at 11 a.m. tomorrow with Dr. Spock."

» "Call Anna Connor with FaceTime."

» "Play songs by the Beatles." (This one works only if you have songs by the Beatles in your iTunes Library or you subscribe to Apple Music.)

» "Call my wife on her cellphone."

» "What song is this?" (Siri uses the Shazam technology to identify songs.)

» "Send a message to Martina to reschedule dinner tomorrow."

» "Find an ATM near here."

» "Schedule a meeting with my project team."

» "Show me pictures I took in Florence, Italy" or "Show me all the pictures I took on Thanksgiving."

» "What is the Dow at?"

» "Send a tweet: 'Going on vacation. Smiley-face.'" (Siri will replace "Smiley-face" with a smiley-face emoji in the tweet.)

» "I need directions to House of Blues."

» "Who was the 19th president of the United States?"

- "How many calories are in a blueberry muffin?"

- "What are my upcoming deadlines?"

- "Who is pitching for the Yankees tonight?"

- "Who won the Academy Award for Best Actor in 2018?"

- "Help me draft a message to my manager updating them on the project status and telling them we need a bigger budget."

By leveraging Apple Intelligence, Siri understands many things in context. So if you ask Siri to "find documents related to the fourth-quarter marketing campaign," Siri can search your files and your email messages to find relevant information and present it to you. Better yet, Siri now retains the context of your recent requests, so you can make follow-up requests without having to repeat yourself as much as you used to in pre–Apple Intelligence versions of Siri.

You can also ask things such as "What's the traffic like around here?" or "Where can I get cheap gas around here?" Siri knows precisely where "here" is based on your Mac's current location (assuming you have enabled Location Services).

Now that you know what Siri can do for you, take a look at how to use Siri.

(Oh, if you're playing along: Rutherford B. Hayes; 400–500 calories, if you're lucky; Gary Oldman for *Darkest Hour*.)

Working with Siri

You can summon Siri in six easy ways. The first four ways are to click its menu-bar icon or its icon in Launchpad (shown in the margin), double-click its icon in the Applications folder, or use its keyboard shortcut (press and hold ⌘+spacebar by default or whatever you selected in the Siri System Preferences pane). The fifth way is available only if you have a MacBook that includes the Touch Bar control strip above the keyboard, and it's set to display the expanded control strip; if so, tap the Siri icon in the Touch Bar.

TIP
If you pressed and held down ⌘+spacebar, and Spotlight appeared instead of Siri, you didn't press and hold down long enough. Keep both keys pressed for two or three seconds, and Siri will be at your beck and call. Pressing and releasing them any faster summons Spotlight, not Siri.

The sixth way is to say, "Hey Siri" or simply "Siri." If you want to summon Siri this way, choose System Settings ⇨ Siri, open the Listen For pop-up menu, and then click either the "Siri" or "Hey Siri" item or the "Hey Siri" item. (The first item configures Siri to listen for either plain "Siri" or "Hey Siri"; the second item to listen only for "Hey Siri.")

Whichever way you use to summon Siri, a bubble will appear near the top-right corner of your screen, waiting for your input, as shown in Figure 9-1.

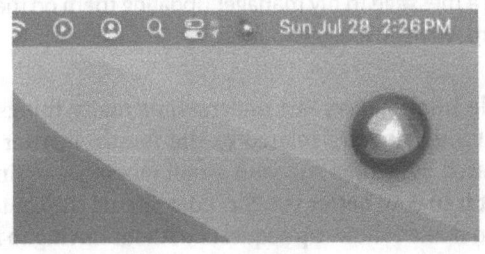

FIGURE 9-1:
Speak to Siri now, or forever hold your peace.

Making Siri your own

Using Siri couldn't be easier: You summon Siri, ask or tell Siri to do something, and then wait for Siri to deliver. But you can tweak Siri to sound and behave the way you prefer.

To manage Siri, choose System Settings ⇨ Siri. In the Siri pane, you can configure these settings:

>> **Siri:** Make sure this switch is set to On (blue) if you want to use Siri.

>> **Listen For:** In this pop-up menu, specify the word or phrase your Mac should listen for. Choose the "Siri" or "Hey Siri" item, the "Hey Siri" item, or the Off item.

>> **Allow Siri When Locked:** Set this switch to On (blue) or Off (white), as needed. Being able to use Siri when your Mac is locked can be convenient, but it compromises your security. If you set Listen For to Off, this setting doesn't appear.

>> **Keyboard Shortcut menu:** If you don't care for the default ⌘+spacebar keyboard shortcut, this menu lets you change it to Option+spacebar, Fn+spacebar, or a keyboard shortcut of your choosing (click Customize).

>> **Language menu:** Use this menu to choose the language Siri will speak and understand. The list is a long one, including nine varieties of English; four varieties each of Chinese, French, and Spanish; and dozens of other languages.

Siri is known to have difficulty understanding people with strong accents. If Siri has trouble understanding you, try setting a different version of your language on the Languages menu.

>> **Voice row:** The readout shows the selected voice variety (such as American) and Siri voice (such as Voice 2). Click the Select button to display the Siri Voice dialog. In the Voice Variety list, click the voice variety, such as American or Australian if you set Siri to use the English language. Then choose one of the voices offered for that voice variety. The number of voices you see here depends on which language and voice variety you choose.

>> **Delete Siri & Dictation History button:** If you say something you shouldn't have said and want to eradicate any record of it, click this button, and then click the Delete button in the confirmation dialog.

>> **Siri Suggestions & Privacy button:** Click this button to display the Siri Suggestions & Privacy dialog. In the left pane, click the app you want to configure; then, on the right, choose options by setting the switches to on or off, as needed. Each app has the Learn from This Application switch; some apps have the Show Siri Suggestions in Application switch as well. Click Done when you're finished.

>> **Siri Responses button:** Click this button to display the Siri Responses dialog. Here, you can set the Voice Feedback switch to On (blue) or Off (white) to control whether Siri gives you voice feedback; set the Always Show Siri Captions switch to On (blue) or Off (white) to control whether what Siri says appears on-screen; and set the Always Show Speech switch to On (blue) or Off (white) to specify whether what Siri thinks you've said appears on-screen. Again, click Done when you finish.

Introducing the macOS Clipboard

The *Clipboard* is a temporary storage area for the last thing you selected and then cut or copied. That copied item can be text, a picture, a portion of a picture, an object in a drawing app, a column of numbers in a spreadsheet, any file or folder (except a drive), or just about anything else that can be selected. You can then paste the Clipboard's contents into an app.

If you want to see what's on the Clipboard, open a Finder window or click the desktop, and then choose Edit ⇨ Show Clipboard. The Clipboard window opens (see Figure 9-2), showing the type of item (such as text, an image, or sound) on the Clipboard, as well as either the item itself or a message letting you know that the item on the Clipboard can't be displayed.

FIGURE 9-2:
The Show
Clipboard
command displays
whatever is on
the Clipboard
if it can.

When you cut or copy an item, that item remains on the Clipboard until you cut or copy something else; you log out of your Mac, restart it, or shut it down; or your Mac crashes. When you cut or copy something else, the new item replaces the Clipboard's contents.

If you want to preserve something you've cut or copied, put it in longer-term storage rather than leaving it on the Clipboard. You could paste the cut or copied item into a note in your Notes app, for example (or into any other document, as long as that document is saved somewhere).

TIP

Various third-party Clipboard enhancers remember the last 100 things (or more) that you copy or cut to the Clipboard. These utilities also preserve their contents when you log out of your Mac or shut it down (or if it crashes). Here are two utilities well worth a try: CopyClip from FIPLAB (free) and its more powerful successor, CopyClip 2 ($9.99), both available from the Mac App Store (see Chapter 20).

REMEMBER

The Cut, Copy, and Paste commands on the Edit menu are enabled only when you can use them. If the selected item can be cut or copied, the Cut and Copy commands on the Edit menu are enabled (black). If the selected item can't be cut or copied, the commands are unavailable and are dimmed (gray). If the Clipboard is empty, or the current document can't accept what's on the Clipboard, the Paste command is dimmed. And when nothing is selected, the Cut, Copy, and Paste commands are all dimmed.

Note that Finder doesn't let you cut files and folders, only copy them. So when a file or folder is selected, the Cut command is always gray. However, once you've copied a file or folder, you can issue the Move Here command to move the item to the folder you specify. This has the effect of cutting and pasting the item.

Copying files and folders

The Clipboard gives you an easy way to copy files and folders from one place to another. Select a file or folder, or select multiple items; then choose Edit ⇨ Copy (or use its shortcut, ⌘ +C) to copy what you've selected to the Clipboard. To paste the copied item or items in another location, navigate to that other location and then choose Edit ⇨ Paste (or use its shortcut, ⌘+V). The result is that you'll have two copies of the files or folders in two places.

Other methods of copying files and folders from one place to another include these:

>> **Option-drag the file or folder from one folder onto the icon of another folder.** Release the mouse button and Option key when the second folder is highlighted. This technique works whether or not the second folder is open in a window.

When you copy something by Option-dragging, the pointer changes to include a little plus sign (+) next to the arrow, as shown in the margin.

When you drag an item to a different disk, macOS copies the item rather than moves it, whether or not you hold down the Option key. But you can move an icon from one disk to another by ⌘-dragging rather than plain dragging.

>> **Option-drag a file or folder into the open window for another folder.** Drag the file or folder that you want to copy into the open window for a second folder (or other hard drive or removable media, such as a USB flash drive).

>> **Choose File ⇨ Duplicate (⌘+D), or Control-click or right-click the item you want to duplicate and then choose Duplicate from the contextual menu that appears.** This command makes a copy of the selected item, adds the word *copy* to its name, and then places the copy in the same window as the original item. You can use the Duplicate command on any item except a disk.

You can't duplicate an entire disk onto itself. But you can copy an entire disk (call it Disk 1) to any other actual, physical, separate disk (call it Disk 2) as long as Disk 2 has enough space available. Just Option-drag Disk 1 onto Disk 2's icon. The contents of Disk 1 are copied to Disk 2 and appear on Disk 2 in a folder named Disk 1.

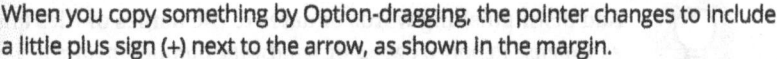

⚠️ **WARNING** If Disk 1 is a *start-up disk* (meaning that macOS has been installed on the disk, and it can start your Mac), Disk 2 will contain the same files but won't be a bootable start-up disk (that is, the disk cannot start a Mac). Also, some files may not be copied properly due to macOS permissions issues. See Chapter 16 for the story on permissions. If you need to copy a start-up disk, see Chapter 21.

You can cut an item's name, but you can't cut the item; you can only copy an item.

There are two ways to achieve the same effect as cutting an item:

>> Select the item, copy it to the Clipboard, paste it in its new location, and then move the original item to the Trash.

>> Move the item via Copy and Paste, but press Option to make Finder replace the Paste command on the Edit menu or the contextual menu with the Move Item Here command. Click this command to paste the item and remove it from its source folder. You can also press ⌘+Option+V to move items from one location to another.

TIP

Add distinguishing words or dates to the names of files and folders you copy, such as *Expense Report Q3 2024* or *Landscape Bunnies Invoice 4-1-2025*.

You can have lots of files with the same name on the same disk (although it's probably not a good idea). But your Mac won't let you have more than one file with the same name and extension (.txt, .jpg, .docx, and so on) in the same folder.

Pasting from the Clipboard

To place the item that's on the Clipboard someplace new, click where you want the item to go, and choose Edit ⇨ Paste or press ⌘+V to paste it.

REMEMBER

Pasting doesn't remove the contents of the Clipboard. Instead, an item stays on the Clipboard until you cut or copy another item; you log out, restart, or shut down your Mac; or your Mac crashes. This means that you can paste the same item over and over again, which can come in handy at times.

Most apps support the Clipboard, so you can usually cut or copy something from a document in one app and paste it into a document in another app.

Expanding your horizons with the Universal Clipboard

The Universal Clipboard lets you copy or cut an item on one device (say, your Mac), and then paste it on another device (say, your iPhone or iPad). Because it performs this magic by using iCloud, the requirements are as follows:

>> Both devices involved must have an Internet connection (wired or wireless).

>> Bluetooth must be enabled on each device.

>> Both devices must have Handoff enabled. On your Mac, choose System Settings ⇨ General ⇨ AirDrop & Handoff, and then set the Allow Handoff Between

This Mac and Your iCloud Devices switch to On (blue). On your iPhone or iPad, choose Settings ⇨ General ⇨ AirPlay & Continuity, and then set the Handoff switch to On (green).

>> Both devices must be logged into the same iCloud account.

>> The devices must be within a few feet of each other.

When these conditions are met, Universal Clipboard just works. If you cut or copy something on one device, you can paste it on another device for approximately 2 minutes after you cut or copy it; after a couple of minutes, however, it may or may not work.

If Universal Clipboard doesn't work for you, check the Apple website (www.apple.com/macos/continuity) to make sure that both devices meet the system requirements. If both are supported, and you still can't make Universal Clipboard work, try turning off Handoff on both devices, waiting a minute or two, and then turning it back on. You might also try logging out of iCloud on both devices, restarting them, and then logging back into iCloud on both. Finally, some older Macs have issues with the set of features Apple calls Continuity, which include the Handoff and Universal Clipboard features, even though these Macs meet the specifications.

If you can't get Universal Clipboard to work, save the cut or copied material to a note in the Notes app. As soon as iCloud syncs the note, you can open it on the other device.

Taking Actions from Quick Look

The Quick Look command displays the contents of the selected file in a floating window, letting you see what's in a file without opening it and without launching an app. Quick Look is great for when you want to take a quick peek at the contents of a file.

To use Quick Look, select a file or folder and then do any of the following:

>> Press the spacebar.

>> Press ⌘ +Y.

>> Choose File ⇨ Quick Look.

>> Control-click or right-click the file's icon, and choose Quick Look from its contextual menu.

>> Choose Quick Look from the Action menu on the toolbar.

Quick Look is especially useful for a folder full of images, such as the one shown in Figure 9-3.

TIP

While the Quick Look window is open, you can select different icons in the Finder window — use the arrow keys to select the next or previous icon — and see their contents in the Quick Look window.

Although Quick Look works with many types of files — Microsoft Office, Apple iWork, plain text, PDF, TIFF, GIF, JPEG, PNG, and most types of audio and video files — it doesn't work with *all* files. You'll know it doesn't work if Quick Look shows you a big document, folder, or app icon instead of the contents of that file.

If you select multiple items before you invoke Quick Look, as in Figure 9-3, the Previous icon (<) and the Next icon (>) appear at the top of the Quick Look window near the left side, enabling you to navigate to the previous item or the next item; you can also press the left-arrow key to display the previous item or the right-arrow key to display the next item. To the right of the current item's name is the Index Sheet icon, which shows four small squares. You can click Index Sheet to view all selected items as an index sheet of thumbnails.

REMEMBER

You can invoke Markup from the Quick Look window. Click the Markup icon to display the Markup tools. See Chapter 5 for more information on Markup.

Close window

Full screen

Previous   Look Up   Rotate image   Four selected icons

Next   Index sheet   Markup Share   Open with

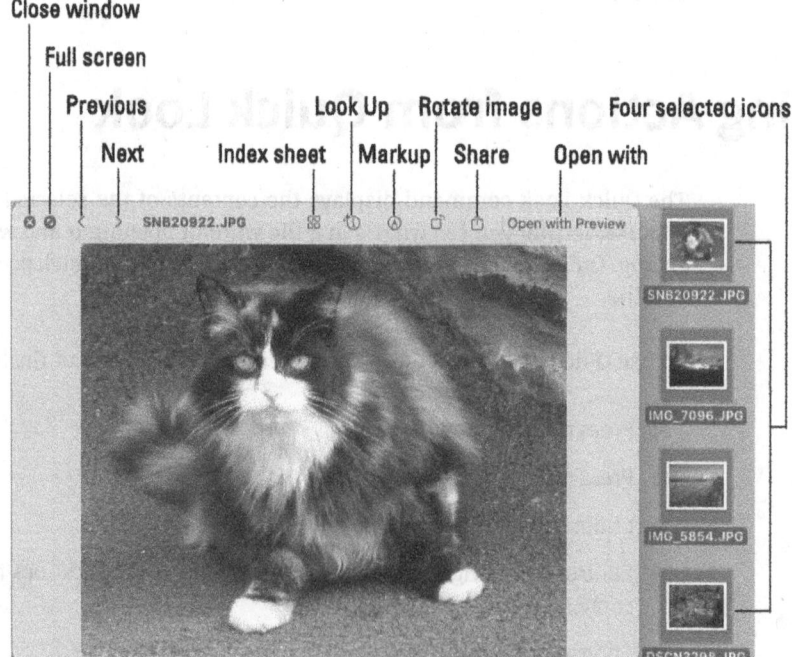

FIGURE 9-3:
The Quick
Look window
displaying an
image from one
of the four
selected icons in
a folder full
of pictures.

Share and share alike with the Share menu

 macOS makes sharing items easy. Clicking the Share icon (shown in the margin) opens the Share menu, which gives you seven or more options (depending on the type of file you selected):

>> **Mail:** Launches the Mail app and attaches the selected file to a blank message, ready for you to address and send.

>> **Messages:** Launches the Messages app and puts the selected file in an outgoing message, ready for you to address and send. You get to know the Messages app in Chapter 15.

>> **AirDrop:** Sends the selected file to users of iPhones, iPads, or other Macs via Bluetooth and Wi-Fi Direct.

>> **Notes:** Sends the selected file to the Notes app, where you can add it to an existing note or create a note for it. (You meet the Notes app in Chapter 10.)

>> **Add to Photos:** Adds the selected item to the All Photos album in the Photos app.

>> **Freeform:** Opens the selected item in the Freeform whiteboarding and collaboration app.

>> **Reminders:** Creates a new reminder in the Reminders app (see Chapter 10).

>> **More:** Lets you add other services (such as Vimeo or LinkedIn) and apps (such as Photos or Aperture) to your Share menu. To manage these extensions, choose Edit Extensions from the Share menu. Alternatively, choose System Settings ⇨ General, click the Login Items & Extensions button, and then click the *i*-in-a-circle icon to the right of Sharing in the Extensions pane. In the Select Extensions for Sharing with Others dialog that opens, select the switch for each extension you want to enable to On (blue), and then click Done.

If the file or folder you select is on your iCloud Drive, you'll see an additional option that lets you share the file or folder with others. You specify who can see it, who can modify it, and who can share it with others before sending them an invitation via Mail, Messages, Link, or AirDrop.

Slide into Slideshow (full-screen) mode

Quick Look really shines in its Slideshow (full-screen) mode, which you can start with any of these techniques:

>> Hold down Option and choose File ⇨ Slideshow.

>> Press ⌘ +Option+Y.

>> If your file is already open in the Quick Look window, click the full-screen icon, as labeled in Figure 9-3 and shown here in the margin.

When you're in Slideshow mode, a completely different set of controls appears on-screen automatically, as shown in Figure 9-4.

FIGURE 9-4:
The Slideshow
controls appear
automatically in
full-screen
Slideshow mode.

Previous   Next   Index   Exit full screen

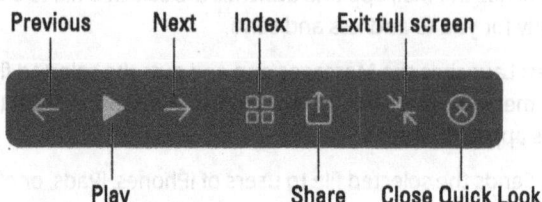

Play   Share   Close Quick Look

TIP

The Slideshow controls disappear after a few seconds of inactivity; if you don't see them when you need them, just wiggle the pointer anywhere on-screen to make them pop up.

To exit Slideshow (full-screen) mode, press Esc or click the Exit Full Screen icon to return to the Quick Look window, or click the Close Quick Look icon to both exit Slideshow mode and quit Quick Look.

When you're finished with the Quick Look window, click the X icon in the top-left corner (refer to Figure 9-3). If you're in full-screen mode, click the X icon on the control bar, as shown in Figure 9-4, or press ⌘+Y, which works in either mode.

Finding Files and Folders Fast with Spotlight

When you lose track of a file or folder, turn to Spotlight, the powerful search technology built into macOS. Spotlight indexes your files and their contents while your Mac is idle, enabling you to search for:

>> Files

>> Folders

>> Text inside documents

>> Files and folders by their metadata (creation date, modification date, kind, size, and so on)

Spotlight quickly finds what you're looking for and then organizes its results logically.

Spotlight is both a technology and a feature. The technology is pervasive throughout macOS and is the underlying power behind the Search boxes in many Apple apps and utilities, such as Mail, Contacts, System Preferences, and Finder. You can also use it by clicking the Spotlight menu — the little magnifying glass on your menu bar. Finally, you can reuse Spotlight searches in the future by turning them into smart folders (see Chapter 8).

The following subsections explain how to search using the Search box on the Finder toolbar and using the main Spotlight menu.

REMEMBER

Searching in Finder windows searches only your Mac's filesystem. Searching with the Spotlight menu searches both your Mac and the web.

TIP

You can ask Siri to search for items you need. When searching, Siri leverages the power of Spotlight, but it also benefits from the assistance of Apple Intelligence.

Using the Find command

Here's how to use the Find feature to find things on your Mac:

1. **Control-click or right-click the Finder icon on the Dock, and then click Find on the contextual menu.**

    macOS opens a new Finder window and places the insertion point in the Search box.

    To limit the search to a specific folder and its subfolders, open that folder first, and then click its Search box or press ⌘+F.

    You can search for files by clicking the This Mac button or the button showing the active window's name, if that button appears. When you open a new window, Find uses This Mac as the search scope by default, as shown in Figure 9-5.

2. **Type a single character in the Search box.**

    The window starts displaying the search results. Figure 9-5 shows the result of typing the letter *s*.

    At the same time, a menu drops down below the Search box to offer search suggestions, in categories such as Filenames, Content, and Kinds, as shown in Figure 9-5. If any of the suggestions look helpful, click its item on the menu to narrow the scope of your search. If not, type additional characters: The more you type, the fewer matches and suggestions you'll see.

Spotlight's default behavior is to search files' contents if it can (and it can search the text inside files created by many popular apps).

Third-party Spotlight plug-ins are available that let you search the contents of file types not supported by Sequoia, including old WordPerfect and QuarkXPress files and many others. Search the Internet for *Spotlight plug-ins*, and you'll find plug-ins for dozens of popular apps.

If you know all or part of the file's name, you can limit your search to filenames (that is, exclude text in files and search only for files by name). Just choose Name Contains (it's *s* in Figure 9-5) from the drop-down menu.

3. **When you find the file or folder you want, open any item in the window by double-clicking it.**

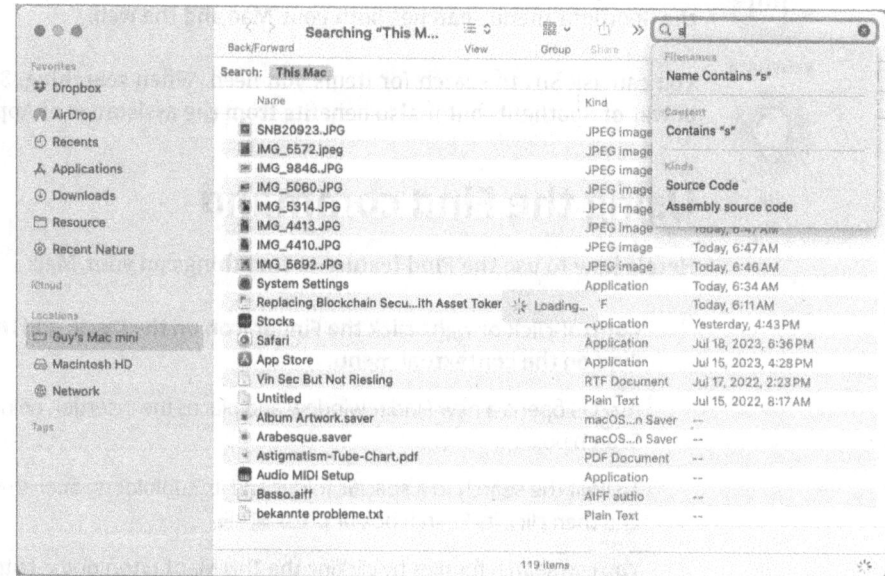

FIGURE 9-5:
Type one character in the Search box, and the magic begins.

Keep these points in mind when you perform a search:

>> You have a choice of where to search. This Mac is selected in Figure 9-5 and Figure 9-6.

>> You can choose additional search criteria — such as the kind (Text with the subcategory Rich Text in Figure 9-6) and the date the file or folder was last opened (Within Last 2 Days in Figure 9-6) — as well as other attributes, including Modification Date, Creation Date, Keywords, Label, File Contents, and File Size.

>> To add another criterion, simply click the + button on the right side of the window.

>> To save a search for reuse in the future, click the Save button in the top-right corner of the window.

FIGURE 9-6:
Search your entire Mac or a specific folder (and its subfold-ers) and then narrow your search by using one or more criteria.

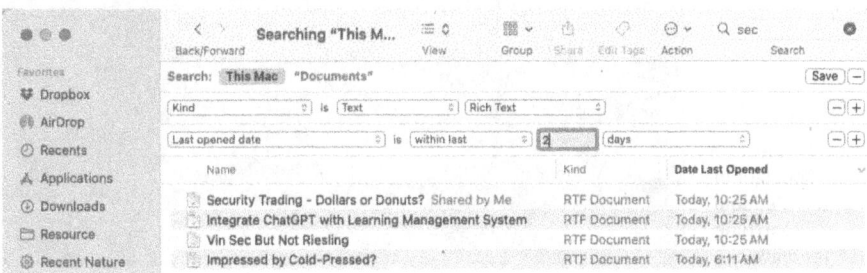

FIGURE 9-6:
Search your entire Mac or a specific folder (and its subfold-ers) and then narrow your search by using one or more criteria.

TIP

Try choosing different options from the window's Group menu — Name, Kind, Date Last Opened, and so on — to see the search results presented in different ways.

Using the Spotlight menu and its keyboard shortcut

When you want to search both your Mac and the web, use the Spotlight menu. Click the magnifying-glass icon at the far-right end of your menu bar (shown here in the margin) or press the keyboard shortcut ⌘+spacebar to open the Spotlight Search box. Then type a character, word, or series of words in the Search box to begin your search.

Spotlight floats elegantly in the middle of your screen, as shown in Figure 9-7, displaying a search for *apple m3*. As you can see, Spotlight brings in results from external sources, as well as results from your Mac.

TIP

The Spotlight Search keyboard shortcut, ⌘+spacebar, could hardly be easier to remember. But if you prefer a different shortcut, you can change it in System Settings: Click Keyboard in the left pane, click Keyboard Shortcuts in the Keyboard pane, and then click Spotlight in the sidebar.

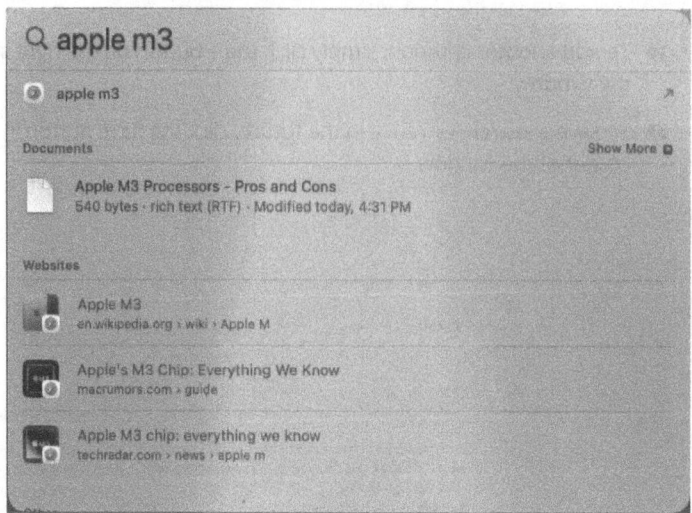

FIGURE 9-7:
Spotlight in
Sequoia
searching
for *apple m3*.

Blasting Off with Mission Control

If you use your Mac extensively, chances are that you'll use lots of apps at the same time and that some of those apps will have multiple windows open. Some apps may be full-screen. You may have multiple desktops as well.

To navigate among your open windows, apps, and desktops, you can use Mission Control, discussed here. (You can also use Stage Manager, discussed in the upcoming section, "All the World's a Stage . . . and You're the Manager.")

Mission Control's eponymous feature shows you big thumbnails of your open windows, apps, full-screen apps, and desktops so you can organize them or navigate swiftly to the one you want. Mission Control can also display all the open windows for the active app, which is great for navigating inside that app; this feature is called App Exposé. Less excitingly but still usefully, Mission Control can display the desktop, enabling you to get at the items you've parked on it; this feature is called simply Show Desktop.

Before you start using Mission Control, you might want to configure it. Open the System Settings app, click the Desktop & Dock item in the sidebar, and then scroll down to the Mission Control section at the bottom of the Desktop & Dock pane.

Setting Mission Control parameters

The Mission Control section of the Desktop & Dock pane contains four switches: Automatically Rearrange Spaces Based on Most Recent Use; When Switching to an Application, Switch to a Space with Open Windows for the Application; Group Windows by Application; and Displays Have Separate Spaces. These long-winded switch names will all make sense when you start using Mission Control. Experiment with the settings, turning them on and off, to see which way you prefer them.

Below these four switches are two buttons: Shortcuts (discussed here) and Hot Corners (discussed in the next subsection, "Setting actions for hot corners").

Click the Shortcuts button to open the Keyboard & Mouse Shortcuts dialog for Mission Control. This dialog has three sections: Mission Control, Application Windows, and Show Desktop. Each section contains two pop-up menus, the Keyboard Shortcut pop-up menu and the Mouse Shortcut pop-up menu, enabling you to set a keyboard shortcut and a mouse shortcut for each of the three features for arranging windows.

TIP

Hold down the ⌘, Option, Control, or Shift key (or any combination of the four) when you choose an item from any of the shortcut menus to add modifier keys to the shortcuts you create. So you could hold down ⌘+Shift when you choose F11 from one of the Keyboard Shortcut pop-up menus to set the keyboard shortcut for that feature to ⌘+Shift+F11. Similarly, you could hold down ⌘+Option when you choose Secondary Mouse button from one of the Mouse Shortcut pop-up menus to set the mouse shortcut for that feature to ⌘+Option–Control-click (or ⌘+Option–right-click).

Armed with this knowledge, open the Keyboard Shortcut pop-up menu in the Mission Control section, and then set the shortcut you want for this feature, pressing ⌘, Option, Control, or Shift if you want to add one or more modifier keys to the item you choose from the menu. Next, open the Mouse Shortcut pop-up menu in the Mission Control section, and choose your mouse shortcut (if you want one). Repeat these moves for the Application Windows section and the Show Desktop section, and then click the Done button to close the Keyboard & Mouse Shortcuts dialog.

Most Apple keyboards and many Mac-specific third-party keyboards include a dedicated Mission Control shortcut key (on the F3 or F4 key). If you see a tiny picture of three windows (shown in the margin) on your F3 or F4 key, you can use that key in addition to the other shortcuts discussed in this section.

Here's how you use the Mission Control features:

» To see all open windows that aren't minimized or hidden in all open apps (as shown in Figure 9-8), press Control+↑ (up arrow). This view is Mission Control view.

» To see all open windows belonging to the active app in a similar display, press Control+↓ (down arrow). This view is App Exposé view.

TIP

» If you hover your pointer over a thumbnail in Mission Control, a blue border appears around it.

If you press the spacebar while a thumbnail is highlighted, you'll see an overlay with a larger preview of the window's contents, which is especially helpful when a window is partially obscured by another window.

» To hide all open windows so you can see icons on the desktop, press F11 or Fn+F11. This view is Show Desktop view.

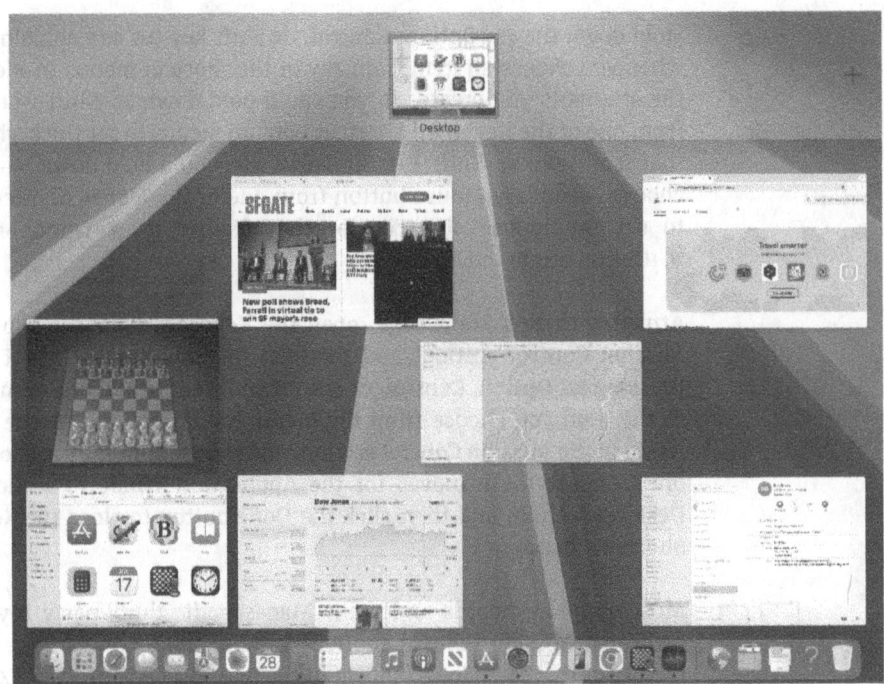

FIGURE 9-8:
Mission Control (Control+↑) gives you quick access to all your open windows.

When you're using Mission Control, windows appear as thumbnails. Hold the pointer over a thumbnail in Mission Control view to display the name of the app or window. Hold the pointer over a thumbnail in App Exposé view to display the window's name below its thumbnail. Click a thumbnail to exit Mission Control or App Exposé and make that app or window active.

If you use a trackpad, check out the More Gestures tab of the Trackpad pane in System Settings, where you can enable gestures to invoke Mission Control, App Exposé, Launchpad, and Show Desktop.

TIP

Setting actions for hot corners

In the bottom-right corner of the Mission Control section of the Desktop & Dock pane in System Settings is the Hot Corners button. Click this button to open a dialog that lets you designate any or all of the corners of your screen as hotspots to trigger Mission Control, App Exposé, Show Desktop, Notification Center, Launchpad, Quick Note, Screen Saver, Display Sleep, or Lock Screen. Click the menu for a corner, and then select the feature you want to associate with that corner. Then, whenever you move your pointer to that corner and leave it there for a second or two, the feature executes.

Hot corners can be great, but if you tend to park the mouse pointer in a particular corner of the screen as you work with the keyboard, you may find you trigger the hot corner unintentionally. If this happens, either don't set a hot corner for that corner or add one or more modifier keys to the hot corner, as explained in the next tip.

WARNING

Mission Control is enabled by default, but you can disable any or all of its features by turning off its trigger: Just choose the minus sign from a pop-up menu instead of a keyboard shortcut.

Hold down the ⌘, Option, Control, or Shift key (or any combination thereof) when you choose an item from any of the Active Screen Corner menus to add modifier keys to the hot corners you create. So if you hold down ⌘+Shift when you select Mission Control as the shortcut assigned to the top-left corner, you'll press ⌘ and Shift and move the pointer to the top-left corner to trigger it. Or if you hold down Shift when you choose Application Windows from the pop-up menu, you'll hold down Shift when you move the pointer to the top-left corner to invoke the command. If you don't press a modifier key when you select an item from a hot-corner menu, merely moving the pointer to that corner invokes the command.

TIP

Organizing desktops and spaces with Mission Control

As well as helping you organize your windows, Mission Control lets you manage spaces and desktops and switch among them with a keystroke or a trackpad gesture.

Desktops and spaces are fantastic, but the terminology is awkward. A *desktop* is an area on which you can arrange windows, as you're used to doing on the main desktop. A *space* is either an app running full-screen or multiple app windows arranged to take up a full screen. So, depending on how you look at it, a desktop is a special kind of space — or a space is a special kind of desktop.

Before you slap your forehead in frustration, take a look at Figure 9-9. Here, you see three desktops called Desktop 1, Desktop 2, and Desktop 3. So far, so clear. But there are also two spaces: one called Safari & Finder, in which those two apps split the screen 50–50, and one called TextEdit, in which your favorite text editor gets to hog the whole screen.

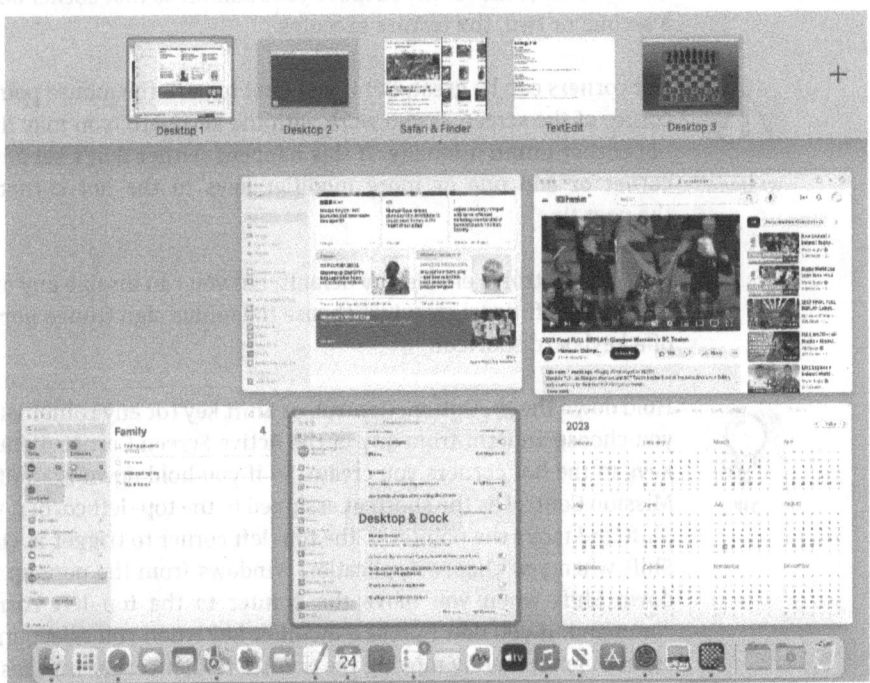

FIGURE 9-9: Mission Control showing off three desktops and two spaces.

TIP

If you find yourself spending too much time moving and resizing windows on-screen, consider setting up desktops and spaces for specific tasks. You might have one desktop dedicated to a specific project, a full-screen space for web surfing, a second desktop for email and scheduling, and a third desktop for media. In each desktop and space, you can keep the windows arranged just the way that works best for you.

To navigate your desktops, invoke Mission Control by pressing the keyboard shortcut (by default, Control+↑ or the dedicated F3 or F4 key). If you have a track-pad, you can also swipe upward with three fingers (unless you've disabled this gesture).

At first, the bar at the top of the screen shows each desktop and space as just a name with no thumbnail: Desktop 1, Desktop 2, Safari & Finder, and so on, continuing the preceding example. Move the pointer up over the bar to display the thumbnails of the desktops and spaces, as in Figure 9-9. Then you can take the following actions:

TIP

REMEMBER

>> **Add a new desktop.** Click the Add (+) button at the right end of the bar.

   To add a new desktop containing a particular window, drag that window to the Add (+) button.

>> **Delete a desktop.** Move the pointer over the desktop's thumbnail and then click the X-in-a-circle button that appears at the upper-left corner of the thumbnail.

   When you delete a desktop, macOS moves all its windows to the previous desktop.

>> **Rearrange your desktops and spaces.** Grab a desktop or space, and drag it left or right along the bar.

>> **Reduce a space to windows.** Move the pointer over the space's thumbnail and then click the Exit Full Screen button (two diagonal arrows butting heads) that appears. The space vanishes, and macOS migrates the windows to the previous desktop.

>> **Move a window to a different desktop.** Drag the window's thumbnail to the desktop's thumbnail.

>> **Display a desktop or space.** Click the desktop or space. Mission Control closes.

>> **Return to the desktop or space whence you came.** Press Esc, the Mission Control key, the Mission Control keyboard shortcut, or the Mission Control mouse shortcut (if you set one).

TIP

To move quickly among your desktops and spaces with the trackpad, swipe left or right with three fingers. If this gesture doesn't work, open System Settings, click Trackpad in the left pane, click the More Gestures tab, and then configure the Swipe Between Full Screen Applications setting.

macOS takes full advantage of multiple displays no matter how many displays are connected to your Mac. So you can work in Finder's desktop on one display and use a full-screen app on another, for example. Each display has its own exclusive set of Mission Control desktops and spaces associated with it.

TIP

If you use multiple displays, you can drag and drop a desktop or space from one display to another.

All the World's a Stage . . . and You're the Manager

Stage Manager is macOS's newest means of multitasking. It overlaps with Mission Control in some respects, but altogether is a very different beast.

If you're feeling that the Dock, the app switcher, and Mission Control provide quite enough multitasking firepower for you — yes, you have a point. But even if you're happy multitasking with those tools, spend a little while playing with Stage Manager, because you may find it helpful. If not, don't use Stage Manager.

TIP

If you've used Stage Manager on an iPad, you'll find that it works pretty much the same way on the Mac.

Enabling Stage Manager

To get started, open a handful of apps — at least five of your choice — to give Stage Manager enough raw material to work with. Figure 9-10 shows a bunch of apps jostling for space on a small screen. The app windows overlap, and though you can bring any window to the front by clicking it (or using the Dock, the app switcher, or Mission Control), the effect is cluttered, and the use of desktop real estate is poor.

To bring order to your desktop when it's like this, enable Stage Manager. Choose System Settings ➪ Desktop & Dock to display the Desktop & Dock pane in System Settings (see Figure 9-11), and then set the Stage Manager switch to On (blue). If macOS displays the Stage Manager dialog, which briefly explains the feature, click the Turn On Stage Manager button to dismiss the dialog and enable Stage Manager.

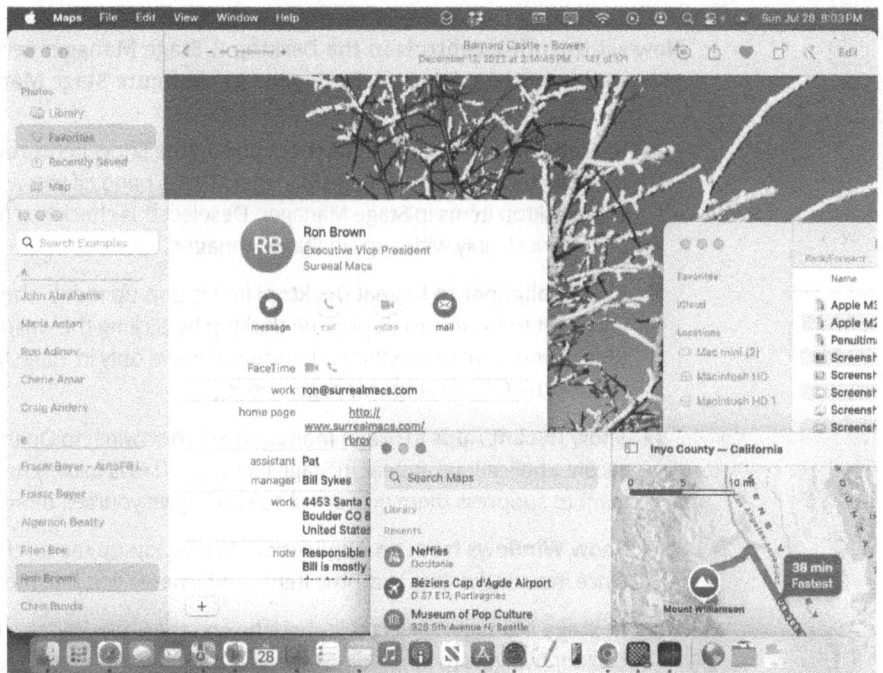

FIGURE 9-10:
A cluttered
desktop — the
problem Stage
Manager was
built to solve.

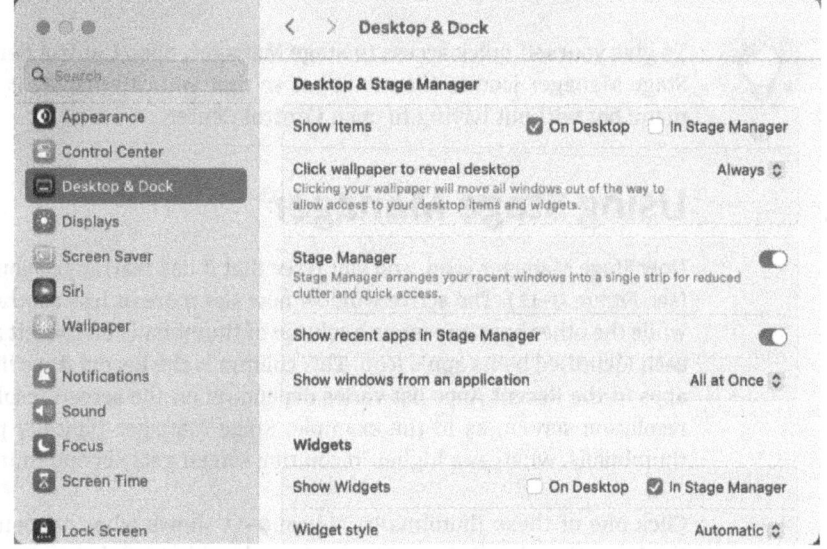

FIGURE 9-11:
In the Desktop &
Dock pane of
System Settings,
choose which
items to display
in Stage Manager
and how to
handle multiple
windows
in an app.

Now set the other controls in the Desktop & Stage Manager section and the Widgets section of the Desktop & Dock pane to configure Stage Manager:

>> **In Stage Manager:** Select this check box on the Show Items row to have desktop items appear in Stage Manager. This is handy if you want to work with desktop items in Stage Manager. Deselect this check box (white) if you plan to work only with apps in Stage Manager.

>> **Click Wallpaper to Reveal Desktop:** In this pop-up menu, choose Always if you want to be able to display the desktop by clicking the wallpaper at any time. If you want to use this click-to-reveal move only in Stage Manager, choose the Only in Stage Manager setting.

>> **Show Recent Apps in Stage Manager:** Set this switch to On (blue) to have recent applications appear in Stage Manager. This is usually helpful, but you may want to suppress them on a small screen to give yourself more space to work in.

>> **Show Windows from an Application:** In this pop-up menu, choose the All at Once item or the One at a Time item — whichever you find most helpful.

>> **In Stage Manager:** Select this check box on the Show Widgets row if you want desktop widgets to appear in Stage Manager.

When you've made your choices in the Desktop & Dock pane, close System Settings.

TIP

To give yourself quick access to Stage Manager, open Control Center, and drag the Stage Manager icon to the menu bar so that you can display it directly from the menu bar without having to open Control Center.

Using Stage Manager

Now Stage Manager is on, and you'll see that it has rearranged your recent windows (see Figure 9-12). The active window now sits more or less centrally on the screen, while the other apps appear as a column of thumbnails on the left side of the screen, each identified by its app's icon. This column is the Recent Apps list. The number of apps in the Recent Apps list varies depending on the screen resolution. For a low-resolution screen, as in the example, Stage Manager typically provides four app thumbnails, whereas a higher-resolution screen gets six app thumbnails.

Click one of these thumbnails. Figure 9-13 shows what happens when you click the Maps thumbnail: Stage Manager displays that window centered on the screen, replacing the previous window, which it displays as a thumbnail where the new app's thumbnail was in the Recent Apps list. Stage Manager resizes the central app window as needed to provide space for the Recent Apps list. Stage Manager also leaves some space free on the right side of the screen, perhaps to create the illusion of balance.

FIGURE 9-12:
Stage Manager
quickly imposes
order, placing the
active window
centrally and
lining up the
other windows in
the Recent Apps
list on the left of
the screen.

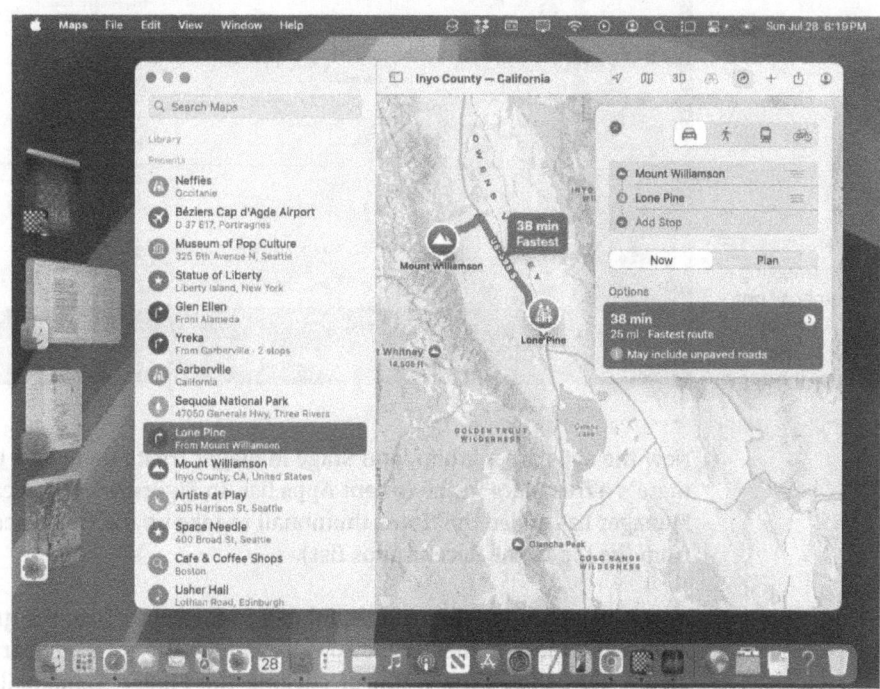

FIGURE 9-13:
Clicking a window
brings it to the
central position,
moving the
previous active
window to a
thumbnail on the
Recent Apps list.

TIP

You can resize the central window as needed by dragging its borders. You can expand the window to take up the space on the right side of the screen, for example. Or you can expand it to the left, taking up the space the Recent Apps list occupies; when you do, Stage Manager hides the Recent Apps list to get it out of your way.

Now try dragging an app thumbnail on top of the central window. Figure 9-14 shows the result of dragging the Contacts thumbnail: The two apps appear together in the central position. You can rearrange them as necessary. You might position the apps so that you can see the contents of both their windows, for example.

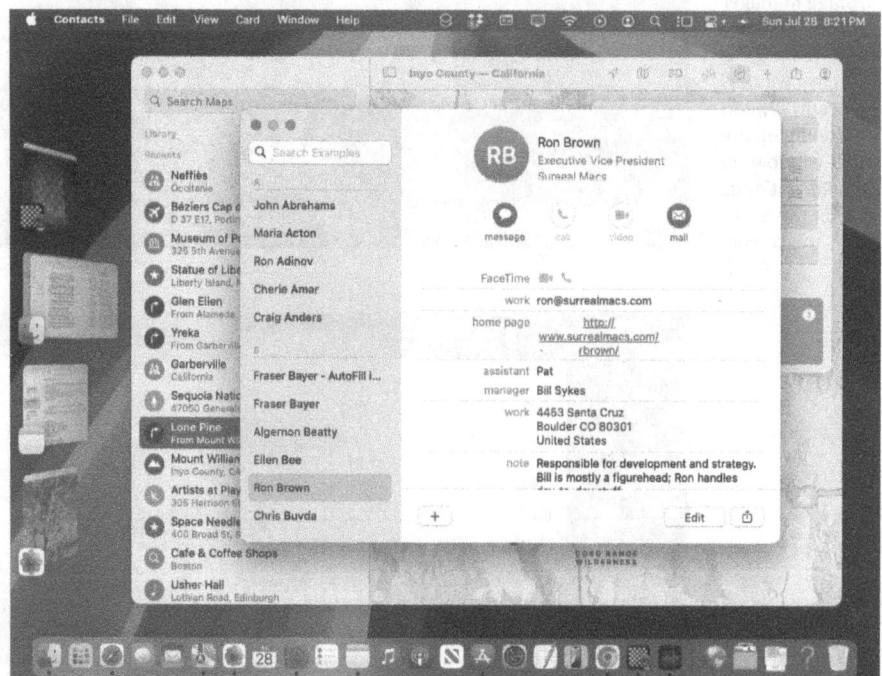

FIGURE 9-14:
Dragging a thumbnail onto the central window groups the apps.

Now the apps are a group, and Stage Manager treats them as a unit. That means there's a free place in the Recent Apps list. In Figure 9-14, you can see that Stage Manager has added the Notes thumbnail to take up the free place (the third place from the top in the Recent Apps list).

Now if you click another app thumbnail to make it active, the grouped apps that were active move to the Recent Apps list, where the group appears as a thumbnail. Figure 9-15 shows the result of clicking the Finder thumbnail to make Finder active: The Maps-and-Contacts group appeared as a thumbnail.

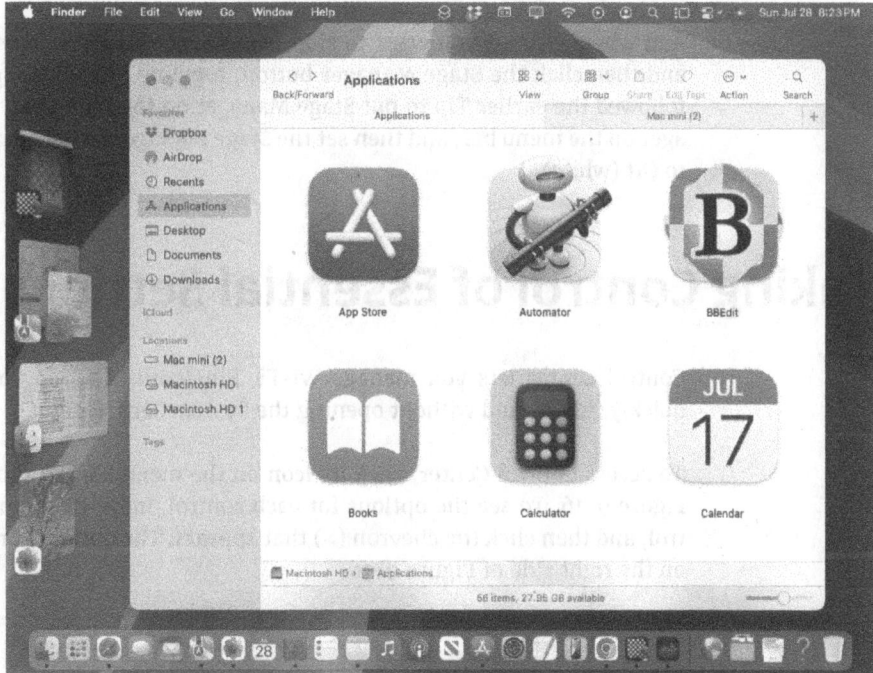

FIGURE 9-15:
When you make
another app
(Finder here)
active, the
grouped apps
appear as a
thumbnail in the
Recent Apps list.

Now you know how to use Stage Manager to flip among your recent apps. Here are four more things that are helpful to know to make the most of Stage Manager:

» If your desktop contains files, folders, drives, and so on, Stage Manager hides them to help keep the view uncluttered. If you need to work with them, click open space on the desktop, and Stage Manager hides the active app. Click open space on the desktop again when you're ready to summon the active app back.

» If you don't want to dedicate space to the Recent Apps list, hide the list. Choose System Settings ⇨ Desktop & Dock, and then set the Show Recent Apps in Stage Manager switch to Off (white).

» If you open three or more windows of the same app, Stage Manager automatically shuffles them into a group.

» To switch to another app that's not in the Recent Apps list, you can use Launchpad, the Dock, or the app switcher, as usual. Stage Manager works well with Mission Control, with desktops and spaces, and with the Dock. You can even position the Dock on the left side of the screen, where it will coexist peacefully with the Recent Apps list (whether you've chosen to show this list or to hide it).

And when — if — you want to stop using Stage Manager, open Control Center, and then click the Stage Manager button, toggling Stage Manager off. Or, if you followed the earlier Tip to put Stage Manager on the menu bar, click Stage Manager on the menu bar, and then set the Stage Manager switch on the pop-up menu to Off (white).

Taking Control of Essential Settings

Control Center lets you manage Wi-Fi, Bluetooth, AirDrop, and other settings quickly, easily, and without opening the System Settings app.

To access Control Center, click its icon on the menu bar, as shown on the left in Figure 9-16. To see the options for each control, move the pointer over the control, and then click the chevron (>) that appears. The options for Wi-Fi are shown on the right side of Figure 9-16.

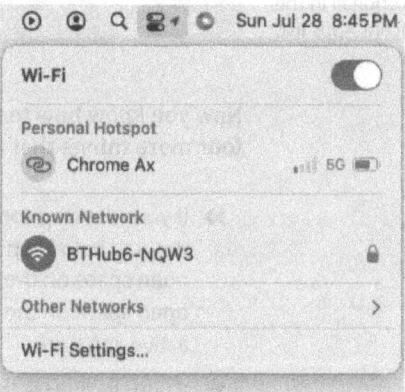

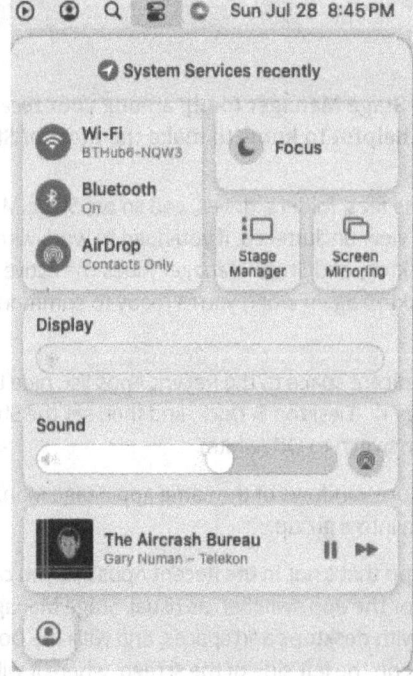

FIGURE 9-16:
The default Control Center (left) and its Wi-Fi controls (right).

To add controls to Control Center, open the System Settings app, and click Control Center in the sidebar. Then go to the Control Center Modules list and use the pop-up menus to specify which items appear in the menu bar.

Configuring Launchpad to Launch Apps Quickly

Launchpad presents all the apps in your Applications folder in a view that looks somewhat like the home screen of an iPhone or iPad.

 Click the Launchpad dock icon (shown in the margin). It fills your screen with large app icons, as shown in Figure 9-17.

FIGURE 9-17:
Launchpad, in
all its glory.

If your Launchpad has more than one page of apps, you'll see dots near the bottom of the screen. To switch pages, click a gray dot; press ⌘+right arrow (→) or ⌘+left-arrow (←) to move to the next or previous page, respectively; or click anywhere (except on an icon) and click left or right. Trackpad users can also use a three-finger swipe left or right to move from page to page.

To launch an app, click its icon. Launchpad disappears, and the app replaces it on your screen.

You can configure Launchpad by rearranging the app icons, organizing them in folders, and deleting them. These are the moves you need to know:

» **To find an app:** Type the first few characters of its name in the Search box at the top of the screen.

» **To rearrange app icons on a page:** Drag the app to its new location.

» **To move apps to the next or previous page:** Drag the app to the left or right edge of the screen, and then pause. When the next page of apps appears, drag the app to its new location on that page.

» **To add an app to your Dock:** Drag the app onto the left side of the Dock.

» **To create a folder for apps:** Drag one app's icon on top of another app's icon to create a folder. macOS gives the folder a default name, but you can change it by selecting it, typing the name you want, and then pressing Return.

» **To add an app to a folder:** Drag the app onto that folder to add it.

» **To move an app out of a folder:** Click the folder to open it and drag the app out of the folder to a new location.

» **To change a folder's name:** Click to open the folder, click the current name, and then type a new name.

» **To uninstall apps:** Click an app's icon, but don't release the mouse button until all the icons begin to wiggle. Apps that can be uninstalled display a Delete icon (X); click to uninstall the app.

» **To stop the wiggling:** Press Esc or click the background.

TIP

Many Apple apps don't have a Delete icon because they're integral pieces of macOS and cannot be removed.

Chapter **10**

Organizing Your Life

acOS Sequoia includes a folder full of apps that you can use to do everything from surf the Internet to play movies to perform numeric calculations. In this chapter, you learn to use three of these apps — Calendar, Reminders, and Notes — to organize and simplify your everyday affairs. You also explore applying the Focus feature to minimize distractions and maximize productivity, as well as tracking your own activity or a family member's activity with the Screen Time feature.

Keeping Track with Calendar

Calendar is a powerful app that provides appointment calendars with alerts. You can keep multiple color-coded calendars; several types of visual, audible, and emailed alerts; repeating events; and more. You can publish your calendars on the web for others to view (which requires an Apple Account or access to another server that uses the WebDAV protocol), and you can subscribe to calendars published by other Calendar users. In the following subsections, you meet Calendar's most useful features.

Navigating Calendar views

Calendar lets you display the main Calendar window just the way you like it. You can find the following useful items (most of which have shortcuts) on the View menu, which provides close control of what you see and how you navigate:

>> **To move back or forward:** Click the arrow buttons on either side of the Today button (top right), or use the keyboard shortcuts ⌘ +left arrow (←) and ⌘ +right arrow (→), respectively. Then you see the previous or next week in Week view, yesterday or tomorrow in Day view, and so on.

>> **To go to today's date:** Click the Today button or use its keyboard shortcut, ⌘ +T.

>> **To add a new calendar:** Choose File ⇨ New Calendar or use its keyboard shortcut, ⌘ +Option+N.

>> **To view your calendar by day, week, month, or year:** Click the Day, Week, Month, or Year button at the top of the calendar. Figure 10-1 shows Week view (keyboard shortcut: ⌘ +2). Other views on the View menu include By Day, By Month, and By Year; you can use the keyboard shortcuts ⌘ +1, ⌘ +3, and ⌘ +4, respectively.

Calendar list   Events   Selected event   Event info for selected event   Today button

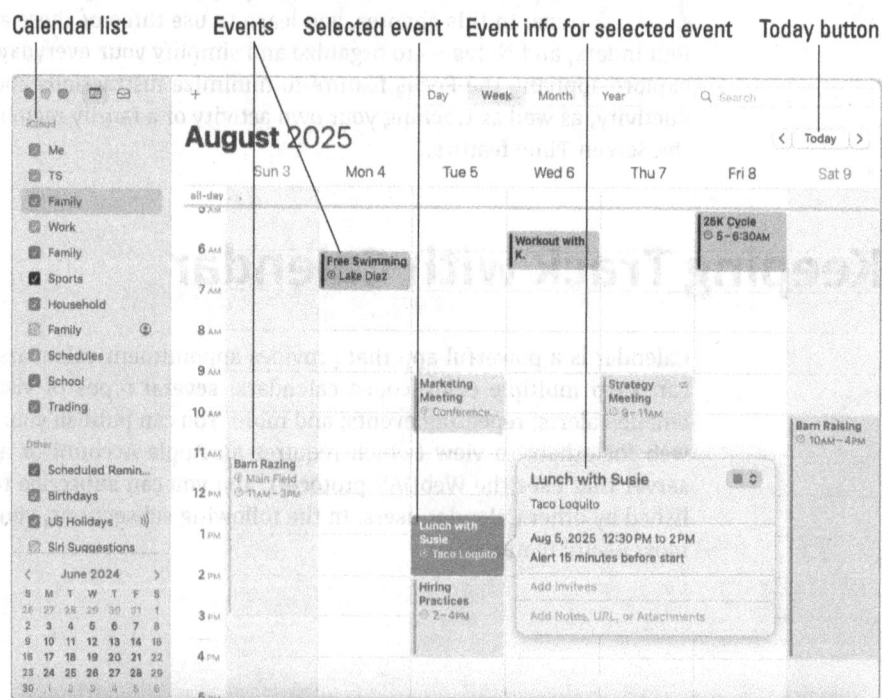

FIGURE 10-1: The Calendar main window displaying Week view.

Understanding the Calendar list

In Figure 10-1, you can see the Calendar list in the sidebar on the left. Here, the Calendar list includes two categories: iCloud and Other. The iCloud category contains the calendars in your iCloud account — in the example, calendars such as Family, Work, Household, and School. The Other category contains the Scheduled Reminders calendar, which contains reminders you've scheduled; the Birthdays calendar, which Calendar creates and maintains automatically from the birthday dates in your contact data; the US Holidays calendar, which is a public shared calendar; and Siri Suggestions, which presents potential dates that Siri has gleaned from incoming messages in the Mail app, the Messages app, and similar sources.

If you've set up another Internet account that includes calendaring, that account appears as another category in the Calendar list, with its calendars listed below the category name. You can add another account in the Internet Accounts pane of System Settings (choose System Settings ⇨ Internet Accounts) or in the Accounts pane of Calendar Settings (choose Calendar ⇨ Settings ⇨ Accounts).

In the Calendar list, select a check box to include the calendar's events in the main pane; deselect a check box to hide the calendar's events. Displaying only the calendars you need to see can help you focus on work, leisure, or whatever.

Creating calendars

To create a calendar in Calendar, follow these steps:

1. **Choose File ⇨ New Calendar.**

   If you have more than one account enabled, choose File ⇨ New Calendar ⇨ iCloud (or whichever account you want to use for this calendar).

   TIP

   Some third-party account providers don't let Calendar create new calendars. If you find the New Calendar command isn't available for the third-party account in which you want to create a calendar, go to the account provider's site and create the calendar there.

   Calendar creates a new calendar named Untitled and adds it to the appropriate account in the sidebar.

2. **Type a descriptive name for the calendar over the default name, Untitled.**

3. **To change the default color that Calendar assigned, Control-click or right-click the new calendar in the Calendar list, and then choose a color from the contextual menu.**

   The contextual menu offers seven preset colors — red, blue, green, and so on — but you can click Custom Color to open the Colors window, whose five tabs let you create any color you can visualize.

Sharing and publishing calendars

If you have an iCloud account (or access to another server that supports the Web-DAV protocol), you can share your calendars with specific people or publish them to the web so that anyone can view them. To share a calendar, follow these steps:

1. **Control-click or right-click the calendar in the Calendar list, and then choose Share Calendar from the contextual menu to display the Share dialog.**

2. **Click the Share With line, and start typing the email address of the first person you want to share with.**

   Calendar displays matching results from your contacts. Click the one you want, and it appears as a button in the Share dialog.

3. **Move the pointer over the button, click the downward caret at the right end to open a pop-up menu, and then choose View Only or View & Edit.**

   View & Edit is the default setting, but you may want to put some people in the View Only category.

4. **Repeat steps 2 and 3 until you've added everyone you want to share the calendar with.**

5. **Click Done to close the Share dialog.**

   Calendar sends an invitation to each person you specified. If they accept, they can view your calendar and edit it if you specified View & Edit for them.

If you want the whole world to be able to view your calendar, Control-click it or right-click it in the Calendar list, choose Share Calendar from the contextual menu, select the Public Calendar check box in the Share dialog, and click Done. Then you can tell everyone about the calendar by Control-clicking or right-clicking it; from the contextual menu, choose Send Publish Email to send out an email, or choose Copy URL to Clipboard if you want to share the web address via another means, such as social media.

Deleting a calendar

To delete a calendar, select it in the list and press ⌘+Delete. A confirmation dialog opens to ask if you're sure.

This alert has a useful button, Merge, which lets you merge the calendar with another calendar rather than just blowing it (and all its events) away. You can only merge calendars that live in the same account, not calendars from different accounts. For example, you can merge two iCloud calendars, but you can't merge an iCloud calendar with a Google calendar.

Click Merge to select another calendar to merge this one with, click Delete to delete it, or click Cancel to do neither thing. You can't merge calendars in the Other category; you can only suppress their display by deselecting their check boxes.

WARNING

When you delete a calendar, all the events and reminder items in that calendar are also deleted. Although you *can* undo a deleted calendar (choose Edit ➪ Undo or press ⌘+Z), you must do so before you quit Calendar. If you quit Calendar without undoing a calendar deletion, everything on that calendar (or calendars) will be gone forever (unless you have Time Machine or another backup, covered in Chapter 21).

WARNING

If you sync your calendars with iCloud or another cloud-based service, deleting the calendar will delete it from all your devices.

Creating and managing events

The heart of Calendar is the event. To create a new one, follow these steps:

1. **Choose File ➪ New Event, press ⌘+N, double-click a date or time on the calendar in any view, or drag up or down anywhere on a date in Week view or Day view.**

    TIP

    If you double-click or click and drag on the day of the event, you can skip Step 2, and you don't need to specify the date in Step 3.

    NEW

    From the dialog that opens when you choose File ➪ New Event or press ⌘+N, you can click New Reminder to start creating a new reminder right from the Calendar app.

2. **If the event doesn't appear in the proper place, just click it and drag it wherever it belongs.**

3. **To edit an event quickly, double-click it to open a bubble containing its details.**

    You can edit any of the details. Click the date or time to change it, for example. The other items — Repeat, Travel Time, and Alerts — are pop-up menus. The colored square in the top-right corner of the event's Info window is a pop-up menu that lets you assign this event to a different calendar.

    TIP

    The Travel Time item lets you add travel time to and from an event (and blocks out that time on your calendar) while preserving the event's start and end times.

4. **When you've fixed all the details, press Return or click anywhere outside the event bubble.**

Editing an event's details in a bubble is easy enough, but Calendar offers you two alternatives: the Info window and the Inspector window. Confusingly, the Inspector window has the title Info, so it looks the same as the Info window — but there is a big difference:

>> **Info window:** Control-click or right-click the event, and then choose Get Info from the contextual menu; alternatively, click the event and then press ⌘ +I or choose Edit ➪ Get Info. Each event has its own Info window, and you can open as many Info windows as you need, which makes the Info window good for comparing the details of different events. Just open an Info window for each event, and you're in business.

>> **Inspector window:** Click the event, and then choose Edit ➪ Show Inspector or press ⌘ +Option+I. There's only one Inspector window, and it displays the details of the selected event. Click another event to display its details. The Inspector window is great for working with a series of individual events, because you can park the window in a handy part of the screen and simply click each event in turn.

Inviting others to attend an event

To invite other people to your event, open the Contacts app (choose Window ➪ Contacts) and drag the contacts onto the event in Calendar. Alternatively, you can type the first few letters of the name in the Invitees field for an event, and names that match magically appear. Figure 10-2 shows the result of typing the letters *ja*: a list of two contacts with names that start with those letters. (If you're unfamiliar with Contacts, flip to Chapter 14 for details.)

FIGURE 10-2:
Invite people to
your event.

After you add one or more invitees, click the Send button to invite them to the event. If the invitees have a compatible calendar app (Calendar, Microsoft Outlook, and most calendar apps on most platforms), they can open the enclosure (included with your invitation email), which adds the event to Calendar with Accept, Decline, and Maybe buttons. All they have to do is click the appropriate button, and you receive an email informing you of their decision along with an enclosure that adds their response to the event in Calendar.

Invitations don't always work with some third-party mail apps, but the majority of people use Apple Mail, Google Calendar, or Microsoft Outlook, which can handle Calendar invitations.

If the invitee doesn't have a compatible calendar app (or doesn't open the invitation), they have to respond the old-fashioned way: by replying to your email, texting, or calling you on the telephone.

Setting an alert

What's the point of putting an event on your calendar if you forget it? If you set an alert, Calendar won't let you forget. To set an alert, click None (just to the right of the word *alert*) in the Info window or Inspector window for an event. Choose a time for the alert from the menu, or choose Custom, which lets you set Calendar to display a message with a sound, send you a reminder email, or open a file. Opening a file can be particularly effective; you're much less likely to put off updating your Microsoft Excel time sheet if Calendar opens it right in your face.

Depending on the calendar account, you can usually create multiple alerts for an event. When you add the first alert to an event, a +-in-a-circle appears to its right when you hover the pointer over the alert pop-up menu; click the + to create a second (or third or further) alert. If the + no longer appears, you've likely hit the limit for the calendar account.

To remove an alert, click the pop-up menu to the right of the word *alert* and choose None from the pop-up menu.

TIP

You can choose separate default alerts for Events, All Day Events, and Birthdays in Calendar Settings. Choose Calendar ⇨ Settings or press ⌘+, (⌘ and the comma key) and then click the Alerts tab at the top of the window.

Calendar on your Mac alone is pretty helpful, but syncing your events and alerts with all your devices — your iPhone, iPad, and Apple Watch as well as your Mac — is the killer feature. Create an event on one device, and it appears on all the other devices within seconds, thanks to the magic of iCloud.

Staying Organized with Reminders

Unlike an event, a reminder item isn't necessarily associated with a particular day or time (although it can be). Furthermore, reminders can be associated with a location, which is handy on a MacBook but even handier on an iPhone, iPad, or Apple Watch. Each reminder can have a priority level of low, medium, high, or none.

If you have multiple Apple devices and sync with iCloud, Microsoft Exchange, or Microsoft 365, your reminders will appear simultaneously on all your Apple devices — other Macs, iPhones, iPads, and Apple Watches — which means that you should never miss a reminder.

To get started with Reminders, launch the app by clicking the Reminders icon on the Dock; if it's not there, click the Launchpad icon on the Dock, and then click Reminders on the Launchpad screen.

The first time you launch Reminders, the app asks to use your current location. Click Allow so that you can use arriving at or leaving a location as the trigger for receiving a reminder.

Getting started with Reminders

The Reminders app enables you to divide your reminders into different lists. You might want a Home list, a Work list, a Shopping list, a Dreams list, and so on, so you can keep home tasks separate from work tasks and avoid shopping for dreams. Reminders starts you off with a default list called simply Reminders, but you can rename it or delete it if you want.

To create a new list, follow these steps:

1. Click the Add List (+) button in the bottom-left corner of the window — or choose File ⇨ New List, or press ⌘ +Shift+N — to open the New List dialog (see Figure 10-3).

2. Click the New List tab at the top.

   When you've created list templates containing your preferred settings for lists, you can click the Templates tab and choose a template there.

3. Type a descriptive name in the Name box.

4. Click the color you want the list to have.

5. In the Icon area, click either the Emoji icon (the smiley) or the Glyph icon (which shows a house in Figure 10-3), and then click the emoji or glyph you want on the pop-up panel.

6. In the List Type pop-up menu, select the list type.

Choose Standard for a regular list. Choose Smart List for a list you want to be able to organize by using tags and filters. Choose Groceries for a grocery list.

7. Click OK.

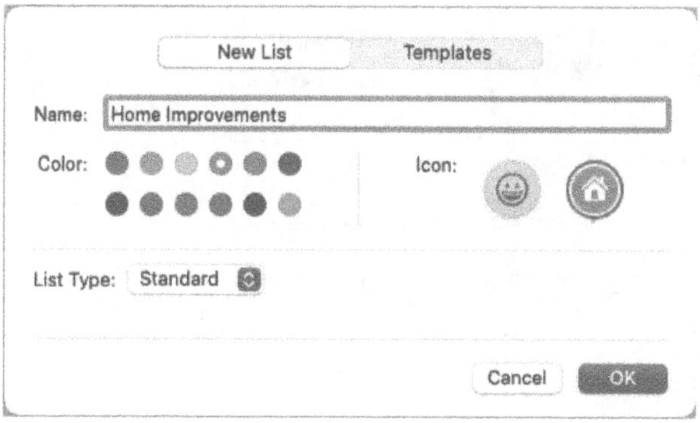

FIGURE 10-3: When you create a list, assign it a name, a color, and an emoji or glyph.

When you've completed a task, click the circle before its name to mark it as completed. Reminders displays the filled-in circle for a moment, as you see for the *Unblock the garage drain* reminder in Figure 10-4, and then moves the reminder to the Completed section.

To see completed items in the active list, choose View ⇨ Show Completed or press ⌘+Shift+H. When shown, completed items appear at the end of the list below uncompleted items. To hide the completed items again, View ⇨ Hide Completed or press ⌘+Shift+H again.

To see all the items you've completed, click the Completed button in the sidebar.

Here are three other helpful techniques for working with lists:

>> **Rename a list:** Control-click or right-click the list, choose Rename from the contextual menu, type the new name, and then press Return. Or select the list, press Return, type the new name, and then press Return again.

>> **Display a list in a separate window:** Double-click the list name, or Control-click or right-click the list, and choose Open List in New Window from the contextual menu.

>> **Show or hide the sidebar:** Choose View ⇨ Show/Hide Sidebar or press ⌘+Option+S.

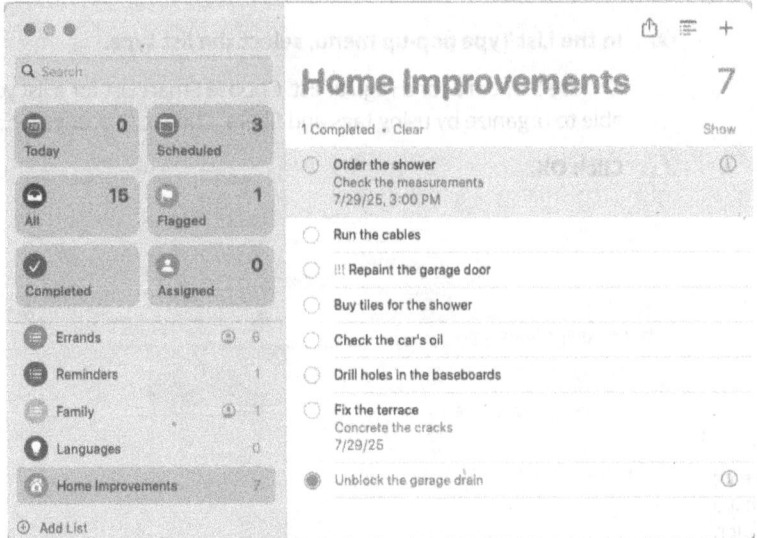

The boxes near the top of the sidebar — Today, Scheduled, All, Flagged, Completed, and Assigned (which appears only if one or more tasks is assigned to you by someone else or by you to someone else) — are preconfigured smart lists. To hide a smart list, Control-click or right-click the list and then choose Hide from the contextual menu. Alternatively, choose View ⇨ Show Smart List and then click the smart list to remove its check mark.

Creating and managing reminders

Now that you've set up your lists, create some reminders to go in them. Click the list to which you want to add the new reminder and then choose File ⇨ New Reminder; press ⌘+N; click the + in the top-right corner of the Reminders window; or click the first blank line in a list and begin typing.

Type the text for the reminder — its name, if you will. Then you can do more, including

>> Reminding you at a specific time on a specific date (as shown in Figure 10-4)

>> Repeatedly reminding you at a specified interval

>> Reminding you at a specific location (as shown in Figure 10-5)

If you have an iPhone, location-based reminders are the best for making sure that you don't miss completing tasks. As you can see in Figure 10-5, the alert triggers not just at a particular day and time, but also on arrival at Marin Ace Hardware, which should make ordering the shower impossible to forget.

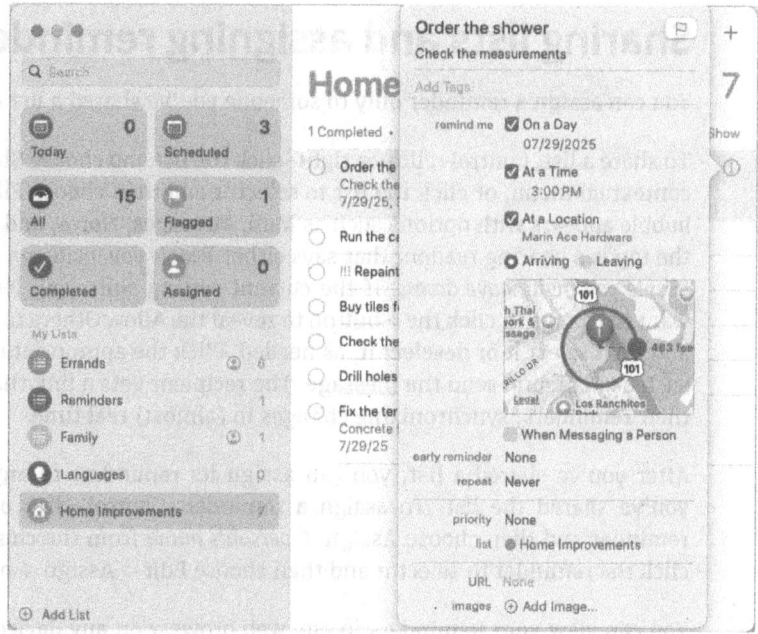

FIGURE 10-5:
Location-based
reminders trigger
when you arrive
at the specified
location or when
you leave it.

As well as text notes, which you can type in on the line after the reminder's name, a reminder can also have a priority, a URL, and images. To access these features, move the pointer over the reminder and click the *i*-in-a-circle that appears on the right; you can also click in the reminder and choose View ⇨ Show Reminder Info. Either way, the info bubble opens. Then you can open the priority pop-up menu at the bottom and assign the priority, click in the URL field and add a URL, or click Add Image and add an image either from the Photos app or by scanning or shooting with your iPhone's or iPad's camera.

To change the order of reminders in a list, choose View ⇨ Sort By and then choose Due Date, Priority, Creation Date, or Title. Or choose Manual and control the item order yourself by clicking a blank spot on any reminder and then dragging the reminder to its new position on the list.

Reminders can have subtasks, which you create by choosing Edit ⇨ Indent Reminder or pressing ⌘+]; to promote a subtask, choose Edit ⇨ Outdent Reminder or press ⌘+[. If the subtask is below the wrong reminder, click a blank spot on the subtask and drag the subtask to where you want it. You can show all subtasks by choosing View ⇨ Show All Subtasks or pressing ⌘+E, and hide all subtasks by choosing View ⇨ Hide All Subtasks or pressing ⌘+Shift+E.

Sharing lists and assigning reminders

You can assign a reminder only to someone you've shared a list with.

To share a list, Control-click or right-click the list and choose Share List from the contextual menu, or click the list to select it and then choose File ⇨ Share List. A bubble appears with options such as Mail, Messages, Notes, and Invite Link. Near the top is a sharing readout that says either *People you invite can add others* or *Only people you invite have access*. If the current setting suits you, leave it, but if you want to change it, click the > button to reveal the Allow Others to Invite check box, and then select it or deselect it, as needed. Click the appropriate sharing method, such as Mail, and send the message. The recipient gets a link that adds the list to their reminders, synchronizing changes in (almost) real time.

After you've shared a list, you can assign its reminders to anyone with whom you've shared the list. To assign a reminder, Control-click or right-click the reminder and then choose Assign ⇨ *person's name* from the contextual menu, or click the reminder to select it and then choose Edit ⇨ Assign ⇨ *person's name.*

REMEMBER

You can view your Reminders in any web browser on any device by logging in to www.icloud.com and clicking Reminders. You'll see the same lists and reminders that you see on your Mac and Apple devices. You can't share lists or assign reminders (at this time), but you can manage existing reminders or create new ones, which can be handy when you're stuck somewhere without your Apple devices.

Everything You Need to Know about Notification Center

Notification Center (see Figure 10-6) manages and displays alerts from any app that supports Apple's notifications protocol. You can show or hide Notification Center by clicking the clock icon in your menu bar or by swiping left from the right edge of your trackpad with two fingers.

Tweaking Notification settings

You manage which apps display notifications by using the Notifications pane of System Settings. Choose System Settings ⇨ Notifications to display the main Notifications pane and then navigate to its subpanes as necessary.

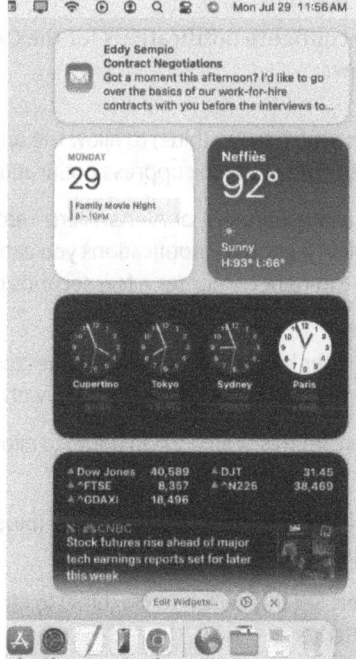

FIGURE 10-6:
A Mail alert banner (top), Calendar's Up Next widget (second row, left), Weather widget (second row, right), the World Clock widget, and the Stocks widget (bottom).

Start by configuring the following four settings in the Notification Center section at the top of the main Notifications pane:

>> **Show Previews:** Open this pop-up menu, and choose Always, When Unlocked, or Never, as needed. Always is indiscreet and Never is close-lipped, so When Unlocked usually is the best choice. This is the default setting for notification previews. You can choose a different setting for any app's or feature's previews.

>> **Allow Notifications When the Display Is Sleeping:** Set this switch to On (blue) or Off (white), as needed.

>> **Allow Notifications When the Screen Is Locked:** Set this switch to On (blue) or Off (white), as you prefer.

>> **Allow Notifications When Mirroring or Sharing the Display:** Set this switch to On (blue) or Off (white). Off usually is the better choice unless you're demonstrating how to deal with notifications.

Next, move on to the Application Notifications section of the main Notifications pane, which contains a button for each app or feature for which you can configure notifications. Click the button to display the pane for the app or feature, such as displaying the Calendar pane to configure notifications for the Calendar app. Then you can choose settings as follows:

>> **Allow Notifications:** Set this switch to On (blue) to allow the app to raise notifications. Set the switch to Off (white) to suppress notifications.

>> **Alert Style:** In the box, click None, Banners, or Alerts. Alerts remain on-screen until you dismiss them, so they're good for notifications you can't afford to miss; banners appear in the top-right corner for a few seconds before disappearing.

TIP

To make a banner reappear after it disappears, just click the clock on your menu bar or swipe left from the right edge of the trackpad with two fingers.

>> **Allow Time Sensitive Alerts:** Set this switch to On (blue) to allow time-sensitive alerts to clamor for your attention.

>> **Show Notifications on Lock Screen:** Set this switch to On (blue) to display this app's notifications on the Lock screen.

>> **Show in Notification Center:** Set this switch to On (blue) to include this app's notifications in Notification Center.

>> **Badge Application Icon:** Set this switch to On (blue) to have the app's Dock icon display a red badge showing the number of notifications.

>> **Play Sound for Notification:** Set this switch to On (blue) to allow the app to accompany a notification with a sound.

>> **Show Previews:** Open this pop-up menu and choose Default, Always, When Unlocked, or Never. Choose the Default item to have this app use your choice in the Show Previews pop-up menu in the main Notifications pane.

>> **Notification Grouping:** Open this pop-up menu and choose Automatic, By Application, or Off to control how macOS groups notifications for this app.

Managing Widgets 101

To manage the Widgets displayed in Notification Center, click the clock to display Notification Center and then click the Edit Widgets button at its bottom. (You may need to scroll down to reach the Edit Widgets button.) Alternatively, Control-click or right-click the desktop, and then click Edit Widgets on the contextual menu. Either way, the Widgets dialog opens, and you can work as explained in the section "Adding Widgets to Your Desktop" in Chapter 5.

You can drag widgets freely between the desktop and Notification Center.

Using Notification Center

Here's how to use Notification Center:

>> **To respond to a notification:** Click the banner or alert before it disappears. Or open Notification Center and then click the notification to launch its app.

Hold the pointer over a banner to display additional options such as the ability to reply to an email or message without launching Mail or Messages.

>> **To repeat a notification in 9 minutes:** Click its Snooze button.

>> **To clear all notifications for an app:** Hold the pointer over a notification. If the app has more than one notification, the little X in its top-left corner (which would clear only this notification) changes to a Clear All button. Click Clear All to clear all notifications from that app.

Getting focused

For several years, Apple has been improving macOS's features for helping you work undisturbed. The Do Not Disturb feature, which silenced all alerts and notifications, led the way, but has now been replaced with Focus, a wider-ranging feature that enables you to create various different types of leave-me-alone settings. You can now not only allow some apps and contacts to interrupt your focus, but also create focus filters that control how key apps (such as Mail and Messages) behave when Focus is on.

To set up and manage your focuses, choose System Settings ⇨ Focus, and then work in the Focus pane. Here, you'll find several standard focuses, such as Do Not Disturb, Driving, and Sleep, set up and ready to go. You can activate other canned focuses (such as Reading, Gaming, and Mindfulness) that typically lurk shyly at first, and you can create your own custom focuses from scratch. Better yet, you can configure each focus to specify exactly which apps you're prepared to acknowledge and which Hollywood agents you might be interested in taking calls from while you're meditating.

If the Focus pane doesn't show the focus you want, click Add Focus to open the What Do You Want to Focus On? dialog. If the focus you want appears here, click it; macOS closes the dialog, adds the focus to the list in the Focus pane, and displays the focus's configuration screen, where you can proceed as explained next. If the dialog doesn't show the focus you want, click Custom. In the Custom dialog that opens, type the name for the focus, click a color circle, click the emoji or glyph you want to use (just like creating a list in Reminders), and then click OK. The Custom dialog closes, the new focus takes its place in the Focus pane, and the focus's configuration screen appears.

If you just want to configure one of the focuses that was already in the Focus pane, click it there, and its configuration screen appears.

You're ready to configure the focus.

Use the Allow Notifications section to specify which people and apps (if any) can notify you while the focus is enabled.

To add a person or group, click the Allowed People button, and work in the Allowed People dialog. From the pop-up menu at the top, choose the Allow Some People item or the Silence Some People item. Then click Add (+), and add people to the list. If you chose Allow Some People, you can open the Allow Calls From pop-up menu and choose Everybody, Allowed People Only, Favorites, Contacts Only, Colleagues, or Friends, as appropriate. You can also set the Allow Repeated Calls switch to On (blue) to let someone interrupt the focus by calling twice within 3 minutes (which might signal an emergency). If you chose Silence Some People, set the Allow Calls from Silenced People to On (blue) or Off (white), as appropriate. Click Done when you finish working in the Allowed People dialog.

To add an app, click the Allowed Apps button, and work in the Allowed Apps dialog. From the pop-up menu at the top, choose either Allow Some Apps or Silence Some Apps. Then click Add (+), and add apps to the list. Set the Time Sensitive Notifications switch to On (blue) or Off (white), as needed. Click Done when you finish working in the Allowed Apps dialog.

Back on the configuration screen for the focus, click the Add Schedule button in the Set a Schedule section if you want to run this focus on a schedule rather than enable and disable it manually.

In the Focus Filters section, click Add Filter if you want to add a focus filter. In the App Filters dialog, click the app you want to affect, such as Safari. In the following dialog, which varies depending on the app, choose suitable options for the focus. In Safari, for example, you can allocate a specific tab group or Safari profile to the focus; for a tab group, you can decide whether to allow opening links that lead outside that tab group. Click Add to add the focus filter to the configuration screen for the focus.

 To enable or disable a focus, click the Control Center icon on the menu bar (and shown in the margin), click Focus, and then click the focus you want to use.

Taking Notes with the Notes App

Notes is an electronic notepad for your Mac. A note is a convenient place to jot quick notes, recipes, phone numbers, or whatever. Figure 10-7 shows some notes.

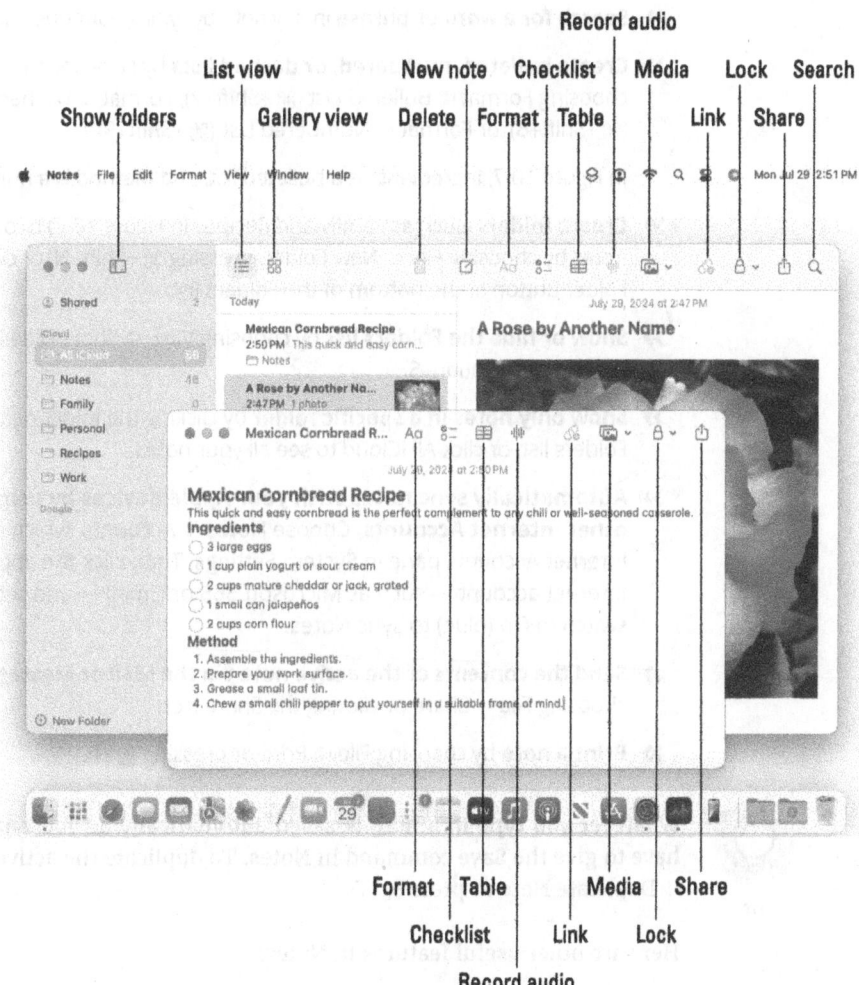

To create a new note, choose File ⇨ New Note; press ⌘+N; or click the New Note button, the button with the little square and pencil, on the toolbar.

Notes is supremely flexible. Here are the moves you need to get started:

>> **Double-click a note to open it in its own window** so you can drag it around on-screen by its title bar.

After opening a note in its own window, if you want the note to float in front of other windows so it's always visible, choose Window ➪ Keep on Top.

>> **Change the text** to any font, color, size, and style by selecting it and using the myriad tools on the Format menu and the Format pop-up menu (the Aa icon) on the toolbar.

>> **Search for a word or phrase** in any note by typing your query in the Search box.

>> **Create bulleted, numbered, or dashed lists** by selecting the text and choosing Format ➪ Bulleted List (⌘+Shift+7), Format ➪ Dashed List (⌘+Shift+8), or Format ➪ Numbered List (⌘+Shift+9).

In Figure 10-7, Ingredients is a bulleted list, and Method is a numbered list.

>> **Create folders** (such as Family and Recipes in Figure 10-7) to organize your notes by choosing File ➪ New Folder, pressing ⌘+Shift+N, or clicking the New Folder button at the bottom of the Folders list.

>> **Show or hide the Folders list** by choosing View ➪ Show/Hide Folders or pressing ⌘+Option+S.

>> **Show only notes in a specific folder** by clicking the folder name in the Folders list, or click All iCloud to see all your notes.

>> **Automatically sync notes with your Apple devices by using iCloud or other Internet Accounts.** Choose Notes ➪ Accounts, which opens the Internet Accounts pane in System Settings. Then click the appropriate Internet account — such as Microsoft 365 or Gmail — and set its Notes switch to On (blue) to sync Notes.

>> **Send the contents of the active note via the Mail or Messages app** by choosing File ➪ Share or clicking the Share icon.

>> **Print a note** by choosing File ➪ Print or pressing ⌘+P.

Whatever you type in a note is saved automatically as you type it, so you don't have to give the Save command in Notes. To duplicate the active note, choose File ➪ Duplicate Note or press ⌘+D.

Here are other useful features in Notes:

>> You can record audio and have Notes transcribe it automatically for you. Start a new note and give it a title, and then click the Record Audio icon on the toolbar or choose Edit ➪ Record Audio. The New Recording pane appears to the right of the note. Click the red Record button to start recording, and then

speak the content you want to record. If you want to pause recording, click the Pause button; you can then click the Resume button to resume recording. Click the Transcript button to display the automatic transcript of the recording (see Figure 10-8). Click the Stop button to stop recording, and click the Done button to finish working with the audio note.

» You can drag and drop photos, PDFs, videos, and other files into any note.

» The Attachments browser displays every external file you've dragged into every note in a single place, making it easier to find things. Choose View ⇨ Show/Hide Attachments Browser or use its keyboard shortcut ⌘+3 to see the Attachments Browser in action.

» Use the Share menu in apps such as Safari and Maps to add content to Notes.

» You can add checklists (in addition to bulleted, numbered, and dashed lists) by clicking the Checklist icon on the toolbar (shown in the margin), by choosing Format ⇨ Checklist, or by using the shortcut ⌘+Shift+L.

» You can add a table to any note by choosing Format ⇨ Table; by using its keyboard shortcut, ⌘+Option+T; or by clicking the Table icon on the toolbar (shown in the margin).

» You can format text as a title, heading, or body by choosing Format ⇨ Title, Format ⇨ Heading, or Format ⇨ Body, or by using the keyboard shortcut ⌘+Shift+T, ⌘+Shift+H, or ⌘+Shift+B, respectively.

» In Sequoia, Notes enables you to collapse and expand sections that start with the Heading style or the Subheading style. Move the pointer over a Heading paragraph or a Subheading paragraph to display a downward caret; click this caret to collapse the section. To expand the section again, move the pointer over the heading or subheading, and then click the > icon that appears.

NEW

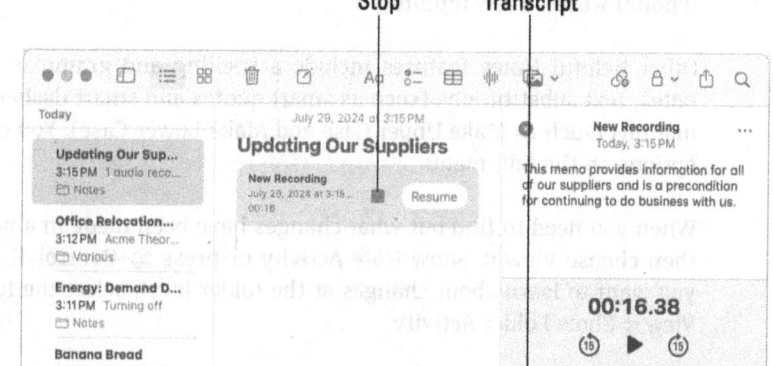

FIGURE 10-8:
You can record audio into a note and have Notes automatically transcribe it for you.

To specify the style with which each new note starts, choose Notes ⇨ Settings and choose the style in the New Notes Start With pop-up menu.

» In Sequoia, Notes enables you to highlight text in different colors. Select the text you want to highlight, click the Style button on the toolbar to display the Style pop-up menu, click the color circle, and then click the highlight color you want to apply.

» The Math Notes feature lets Notes perform math for you. For example, if you type **735/13 =** in a note, Notes suggests 56.53846. You can insert the result by pressing the Tab key. If you want Notes to enter the result rather than suggesting it, choose Format ⇨ Math Results ⇨ Insert Results, moving the check mark from the default setting, Suggest Results, to the Insert Results item. To turn off results, choose Format ⇨ Math Results ⇨ Off.

» Notes appear in the list in chronological order with the most recently edited note on top. You can pin a note to the top of the list, where it remains until you unpin it. To pin or unpin a note, click it once to select it and then choose File ⇨ Pin Note (or Unpin Note). Or Control-click or right-click the note in the list and choose Pin Note (or Unpin Note) from the contextual menu. The note appears in the Pinned section at the top of the list.

You can also share your notes with others and allow them to edit them. Here's how the process works: Select the note, and click the Share icon on the toolbar to open the Share panel. At the top, choose Collaborate from the pop-up menu. (The other choice is Send Copy.) Then choose how you'd like to send your invitation: Mail, Messages, Invite with Link, or AirDrop.

If the people you invite are also running Sequoia or another recent version of macOS, they'll see the note in their copy of Notes; if they're running any other operating system, the note will open in the iCloud website for editing. When they're done, you'll see their edits in Notes on your Mac (and on your iPad and iPhone) within a few minutes.

Other helpful Notes features include a spelling and grammar checker, spoken notes, text substitutions (such as smart quotes and smart dashes), and transformations (such as Make Upper Case and Make Lower Case). You can find all these options on the Edit menu.

When you need to find out what changes have been made in a note, select it and then choose View ⇨ Show Note Activity or press ⌘+Control+K. Similarly, when you want to learn about changes at the folder level, select the folder and choose View ⇨ Show Folder Activity.

When you're feeling logical, folders can be a great way to organize your notes. But when you need more flexibility, use tags instead to not only organize your notes, but also filter them. To create a tag, simply put # before the tag word, such as *#Sequoia* or *#efficiency*. After you create a tag, it appears in the sidebar's Tag Browser as a button that you can click to display all notes that bear that tag. Or click All Tags to see notes that have any tag.

TIP

If you've created one or more tags but don't see buttons in your sidebar, hover your pointer over the word Tags and click the > that appears to its right.

One more thing: Don't forget that you can use your iPhone or iPad as a camera or scanner by using Continuity Camera. (Chapter 20 has the details.)

Taking a Quick Note with Quick Note

When you need to jot down a note instantly, use Quick Note. To do so, move the pointer to the bottom-right corner of your screen, and click the blank note that appears. The Notes app launches (if it's not already open), and a new note appears in the middle of the screen.

If you click the link icon, you can add an app link to the note. Then, because Notes knows which website you're on, what story you're reading in the News app, who you're communicating with in the Messages app, and much more, the next time you visit that website or store or correspond with a person, Notes will automatically display that Quick Note in the bottom-right corner.

The links are contextual, so the Quick Note will appear when Notes thinks you need it. You can also access all your Quick Notes by clicking the Quick Notes smart list in the Notes app.

Tracking Activities with Screen Time

We can all use a break from our digital devices, and Apple's solution is Screen Time. Although Screen Time includes the parental controls that used to appear in the Parental Controls System Preferences pane in older versions of macOS, Screen Time also encourages you to police your own behavior.

If you have an iPhone or iPad, you're probably familiar with Screen Time, which provides insight into how you spend your time on your iPhone or iPad, including which apps you use and websites you visit, and for how long. On the Mac, Screen Time manifests itself as a pane in System Settings, so choose System Settings ⇨ Screen Time to get started.

Next, go to the Limit Usage box and click the App & Website Activity button. In the Keep Track of Your Screen Time? dialog, click the Turn On App & Website Activity button.

Near the bottom of the Screen Time pane, set the Share Across Devices switch to On (blue) if you want Screen Time to report data for every iPhone, iPad, and Mac that signs in to this iCloud account. This setting usually is what you want; there's no sense monitoring your teenager's Mac use closely while letting them run riot on their iPad.

Also at the bottom of the Screen Time pane, set the Lock Screen Time Settings switch to On (blue), and follow the prompts to set a four-digit password that will prevent anyone from switching off or reconfiguring Screen Time without your okay.

Now use the ten buttons in the main part of the Screen Time pane to view usage and set suitable restrictions:

>> **App & Website Activity:** Displays details about the apps the user used and how long they used them.

>> **Notifications:** Displays the number of notifications the user received on this day and the times received.

>> **Pickups:** Shows you how many times the user picked up their devices.

>> **Downtime:** Sets a schedule for times when only apps specifically allowed during downtime are available. A reminder appears 5 minutes before downtime starts.

>> **App Limits:** Sets time limits for apps and app categories such as Social, Games, and Productivity & Finance.

>> **Always Allowed:** Specifies the contacts and apps available to the user during downtime.

>> **Screen Distance:** Set the Screen Distance switch to On (blue) to have Screen Distance alert the user when they hold a Face ID iPhone or iPad too close to their face for a long time.

>> **Communication Limits:** Specifies who is allowed to contact the user via phone, FaceTime, or iMessage during Screen Time and downtime.

>> **Communication Safety:** Set the Communication Safety switch to On (blue) to have Messages attempt to detect nude photos before your child sends them or views ones they have received.

>> **Content & Privacy:** Replaces the Parental Controls options in earlier versions of macOS. You can enable or disable content by type and apply restrictions to the Apple online store and specific apps. You can also allow or disallow passcode changes, account changes, and other options for which you may want to restrict changes.

Chapter **11**

Finding Your Way with Maps

 I f you know how to use the Maps app on your iPhone or iPad, you already know most of what you need to know to use Maps on your Mac. But if you don't have an iPhone or iPad, don't worry — this chapter will get you up to speed in next to no time.

Finding Your Current Location

 If you're wondering where you are, Maps can set you straight. Launch Maps from the Dock or from Launchpad, and then click the Current Location icon, which is a little arrowhead (shown in the margin) on the toolbar at the top of the window. A blue dot indicates your location.

REMEMBER

If you click or drag the map, your Mac continues to update your location but won't re-center the blue dot, so the blue dot can scroll (or zoom) out of the window. If that happens, click the Current Location icon again to center the map on your current location again.

This feature and many other Maps features rely on an active Internet connection and having Location Services enabled. The first time you launch Maps, macOS displays the "Maps" Would Like to Use Your Current Location dialog to prompt you to enable Location Services; click the Allow button to do so. After that, you can check about Location Services like this: Click System Settings on the Dock, click Privacy & Security in the sidebar, click Location Services to display the Location Services screen, and then set the Location Services switch to On (blue). Set the switch on the Maps row to On (blue) as well.

If Maps displays the Get Notified When Friends Share Their ETAs dialog, click Enable Notifications if you want to see notifications about their estimated times of arrival and updates about photos and reports. Otherwise, click Not Now. You can configure Maps' notifications later in the Notifications pane in System Settings.

TIP

Use the – and + icons in the bottom-right corner (or the scroll control on your mouse or trackpad) to zoom in and out on the map.

Finding a Person, Place, or Thing

To find a person, place, or thing with Maps, choose Edit ⇨ Find, press ⌘+F, or click the Search field in the sidebar (where it says Search Maps) and then type what you're looking for. You can search for addresses, zip codes, intersections, towns, landmarks, and businesses by category and by name, or combinations, such as *New York, NY 10022, pizza 60645,* or *Texas State Capitol.*

TIP

If the letters you type match names stored in your Contacts list (see Chapter 14), the matching contacts for whom you have street addresses appear in a list below the Search field. Click a name to see a map of that contact's location.

If you don't find a match in the list, press Return, and with any luck, a map will appear within a few seconds. If you search for a single location, it's marked with a single bubble. If you search for a category (*coffee 02108,* for example), you may see multiple bubbles, one for each matching location (a terrifying number of coffee shops in Boston), as shown in Figure 11-1.

To find out more, click a name in the list below the Search field or click a pin. A *card* — an information window with details — appears (refer to Figure 11-1). The card sometimes contains reviews, photos, or both (only photos are visible in Figure 11-1), so scroll down through the card to see everything that's available.

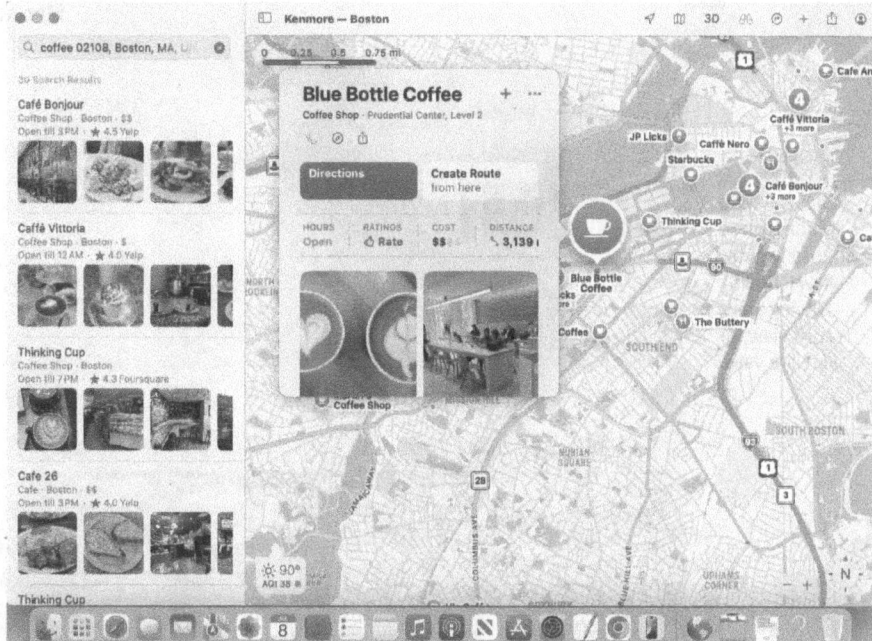

FIGURE 11-1:
Bubbles indicate
matching
locations; click a
bubble to see
its details.

Viewing, Zooming, and Panning

Once you've found the location you're interested in, you can change views, zoom in or out, or pan around.

Click the Map Mode icon on the toolbar to choose Explore view, Driving view, Transit view, or Satellite view (see Figure 11-2), all of which can also be viewed in 3D. Satellite view uses satellite imagery, as you see in Figure 11-3; this figure also uses 3D view, which lets you look at the map from an angle rather than from directly overhead.

WARNING

3D maps aren't available in every area. It appears that the more populated an area is, the more likely it is to be available in 3D.

3D

To display a 3D map, click the 3D icon on the toolbar (shown in the margin), choose View ➪ Show 3D Map, or press ⌘+D. You may have to zoom in for the map to appear in 3D.

Map Mode

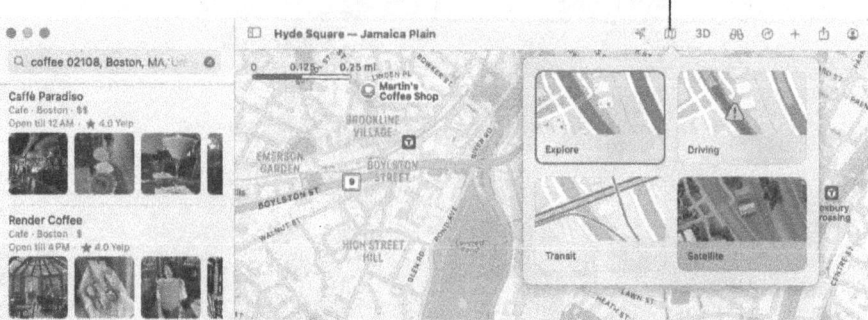

FIGURE 11-2:
Click the Map
Mode icon to
choose Explore
view (shown),
Driving view,
Transit view, or
Satellite view.

FIGURE 11-3:
A 3D satellite
view.

Zoom In button   3D angle slider

Zoom Out button   Rotate Map compass

You can use these tools in all views, in 2D or 3D:

>> **To zoom in:** Choose View ➪ Zoom In or press ⌘ ++ (plus sign). If you have a trackpad, you can also expand (spread two fingers) to zoom in, just like on an iPhone or iPad.

>> **To zoom out:** Choose View ➪ Zoom Out or press ⌘ +– (hyphen). If you have a trackpad, you can also pinch to zoom out, again like on an iPhone or iPad.

TIP

If you have a scroll-wheel mouse, you can use the wheel to zoom in and out. You can also click the Zoom In (+) button and Zoom Out (–) button in the bottom-right corner of the window. If you want to get back to the default zoom percentage, choose View ➪ Default Zoom or press ⌘ +0.

To get to Maps' Globe view, zoom out as far as you can. Then you can manipulate the globe with your mouse or trackpad and zoom in wherever you like to see additional details.

>> **To pan:** Drag left, right, up, or down. If you have a trackpad, place two fingers on the trackpad and slide them in the direction you want to drag the map. Flick those two fingers across the trackpad to fly over the ground.

>> **To rotate the map:** Drag the compass in the bottom-right corner. You can also place two fingers (or your thumb and a finger) on the trackpad and rotate them.

Finally, to adjust the viewing angle in 3D views, press Option and drag the map (or press Option and drag with two fingers on a trackpad), or drag the little slider in the bottom-right corner (refer to Figure 11-3).

Using Maps with Contacts

Maps and Contacts (see Chapter 14) go together like peanut butter and jelly. If you want to see a map of a contact's street address, for example, type a few letters of the contact's name in the Search field, and click the name in the list that automatically appears.

If you're in the Contacts app, the process is even easier: Hover your pointer over a street address, and click the little blue pin that appears to its right, as shown in Figure 11-4. Maps opens, showing a pin at the address.

FIGURE 11-4:
Click the little
blue pin to
see this
address
in Maps.

After you find a location by typing an address in Maps, you can add that location to your contacts.

First, click the location's bubble on the map; then click the ellipsis (. . .) in the top-right corner of the card and choose Create New Contact from the menu that appears.

You can also get driving directions to and from most locations, including a contact's address, to most other locations, including another contact's address. You see how in the "Getting Smart with Maps," later in this chapter.

Saving Time with Library, Guides, and Recents

The Maps app offers three tools in its sidebar that can save you from having to type the same locations over and over.

Library

NEW

Maps used to have bookmarks for storing locations you wanted to be able to revisit easily. Then bookmarks changed to favorites. Now, in macOS Sequoia, the Library feature replaces favorites.

To add a location to Library, click its bubble on the map, and then click the + (Add) button in the upper-right corner of the card. The + changes to a check mark to indicate that Maps has added the location (and to prevent you from trying to add it again).

You can also start adding a location from the sidebar. Move the pointer over the Library heading in the sidebar, and then click the + sign that appears. In the Add Pin dialog that opens, either click one of the locations in the Siri Suggestions list or enter your search term in the Search Maps text box and identify the location manually.

After you add a location to Library, you can return to it at any time by clicking it in the Library section of the sidebar. If the sidebar is hidden, click the Toggle Sidebar button to display it; if the Library section is collapsed, expand it by moving the pointer over it and clicking the > button that appears.

The first locations you should add to Library are your home address and work address. You'll use these addresses all the time with Maps, so add them now to avoid typing them over and over. Library provides a Home location and a Work location at the top of the list until you set them up; just click the Add link under the Home location and use the Set Up Home dialog to specify the location, then repeat for the Work location.

When you no longer need a location in Library, Control-click it or right-click it, and then click Delete on the contextual menu.

Guides

Guides are collections of places that you can create and share with others. A few big cities, such as San Francisco, New York, London, and Los Angeles, have guides created by "brands you trust" (at least, according to Apple). The cool thing about guides is that they update automatically, so if you share them with others, their guides will update when you add or delete locations.

The Locations button appears just above the Recents heading in the sidebar. The Locations button doesn't show the word *locations* — instead, it shows the number of places, guides, and routes, such as 12 Places, 6 Guides, 3 Routes. Clicking the Locations button opens the Library window.

To create a guide, follow these steps:

1. **Click the Locations button in the sidebar to display the Library window.**

2. **Click the Guides button to display the My Guides window.**

3. **Click the + (Add) button in the lower-right corner to open the New Guide dialog.**

4. **Type a descriptive name for the guide.**

5. **Click the photo icon, and then select a photo in the window that opens. Move and scale the photo in the Choose Photo dialog, and then click the Use button.**

6. **Back in the New Guide dialog, click the Create button.**

   Maps creates the guide and adds it to the My Guides window.

7. **Click the new guide to display its window.**

8. **Click Add a Place to display the Save to My Guides dialog.**

9. **Add places by searching or from the Recently Viewed list.**

10. Click the Done button to close the Save to My Guides dialog.

11. Click the Close (X) button to close the new guide's window.

The My Guides window appears again.

TIP

To delete a guide, click the Edit button in the My Guides window, click the red delete icon to the left of the guide's name, and then click the textual Delete button that appears to the right of the guide's name.

To share a guide, you share a link to it. Open the guide's window, and then click the Share icon at the bottom. If Maps warns you that anyone with access to the guide link will be able to view its contents, click the Share Guide button. The Share sheet then appears at the bottom of the guide's window. Click the means of sharing, such as Messages or Mail, and then follow through the resulting prompts.

TIP

To send a guide to one of your devices, open the guide's window, and then choose File ⇨ Send to Device, and then click the device on the continuation menu.

Recents

The Maps app's Recents list automatically remembers every location you've searched for in Maps either on your Mac or on any other device that signs in to your iCloud account. That includes the locations you'd rather forget. Expand the Recents list to see your recent searches; click the item's name to see it on the map.

To remove a single location from your Recents list, Control-click or right-click it, and then click Delete on the contextual menu.

To clear the Recents list, go to the very bottom of the list, and then click Clear Recents. There's no confirmation dialog for this action.

Getting Smart with Maps

The Maps app enables you to get route maps and directions for driving, walking, cycling, or taking public transportation. What's more, you can create your own routes that go exactly where you want. You can also get real-time information about traffic conditions, explore places with flyovers and look arounds, and access handy information on the card.

Getting route maps and driving directions

You can get route maps and directions to any location from any other location in a couple of ways. Maps usually displays driving directions at first, but you can click the Driving icon (which shows a car) if you get a different kind of directions.

>> **If a bubble is already on the screen:** Click it and then click the Directions button on its card. Click in the My Location field to choose where the directions begin.

>> **When you're looking at a map screen:** Click the Directions button on the toolbar (shown in the margin). The Directions window appears, with From and To fields at the top. When you click either field, a drop-down list appears with your current location and a few recent locations. If you don't see what you need, type a few letters and choose the location from the list that appears. To swap the From and To locations, drag one or both to reverse their positions.

If you need to change the From or To location, click it, click the little x-in-a-circle to the right of its name to erase it, and try again.

Many journeys need only a start location and a destination, but for others, you'll want to add stops along the way. Click Add Stop, type the location, and then select the appropriate match. Drag the stops into the appropriate order by using the handles at the right end of their buttons; Maps updates the route with the best fit, as shown in Figure 11-5.

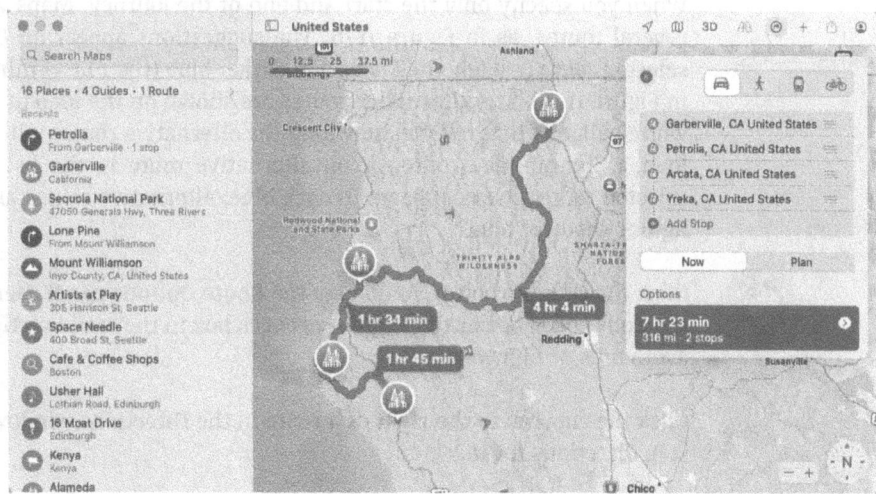

FIGURE 11-5: Click Add Stop to add a stop along the way. Drag the stops into your preferred order.

When the From and To fields have been filled, press Tab or Return, and step-by-step directions appear, as shown in Figure 11-6.

FIGURE 11-6:
When Maps
offers multiple
routes, the
selected route
appears in
darker blue.

When you specify only the start and end of the journey, Maps will often suggest several routes, as in Figure 11-6. The suggestions appear on the map with the selected route (usually the fastest) in darker blue (the 1 hr 3–min route is selected in Figure 11-6). The alternative routes are shown on the map in lighter blue, with white balloons that tell you how long the alternative routes will take. Click a balloon, a lighter-blue route, or an alternative route in the list to select it. The selected route always appears in dark blue; alternative routes always appear in a lighter shade of blue.

TIP

Click the Options button to display the Route Options panel. Here, you can select the Tolls check box or the Highways check box in the Avoid section to tell Maps to avoid tolls or highways.

Click the chevron to the right of a route in the Directions window to see step-by-step directions for it.

After you've selected your route, you can print the directions (File ⇨ Print or ⌘+P), share them (File ⇨ Share), or send them to any nearby Apple device (File ⇨ Send to Device).

When you're finished with the step-by-step directions, click the Directions button to close the Directions window.

Getting walking directions

For step-by-step directions for walking, click the Walk icon above the Start and End fields. Walking directions generally look a lot like driving directions except for your travel time.

WARNING

Check through walking directions carefully before attempting to follow them. Apple keeps improving the directions, but verify that they don't involve any impossible moves. Pedestrian-free tunnels and bridges have been sore points in the past.

Getting directions for public transportation

Maps offers directions for using public transportation in more cities than ever, but mostly large cities. To get public-transit directions, specify your start and end points as usual, and then click the Public Transit icon (the train icon) at the top of the Directions window. Maps suggests as many viable routes via public transit as it can identify.

TIP

If you zoom in far enough, you can see the entrances to transportation facilities, such as train stations. Also, to see the effect of leaving at a time other than right now, click the Plan tab, and specify a departure or an arrival time.

Getting cycling directions

Maps offers cycling directions for some journeys. To get them, click the Cycling icon (the bicycle) at the top of the Directions window. As with walking directions, check through cycling directions carefully before using them.

Creating custom routes

NEW

A great new feature in Maps in macOS Sequoia is creating custom routes that go exactly where you want. To create a custom route, follow these steps:

1. **On the map, navigate to the area for the route, such as a national park.**

   You can search for a national park, a trail, or a trailhead by name.

   Once you're in the right place, zoom in or out as needed.

2. **Click the location, such as a trailhead, to display its card.**

   This location will be the start of the route you create.

3. **Click the Create a Custom Route button to display the Create a Custom Route window.**

4. **Click each turning point for the route in turn.**

   Maps draws the route on the map, as you see in the example in Figure 11-7. The Create a Custom Route window displays the route's current distance, approximate time to hike, and total ascent and descent measurements. The longitudinal profile at the bottom of the Create a Custom Route window shows the route's elevations, plus the gradients and where they occur.

TIP

   To remove a point, click it, and then click Remove Point. This works for the start point and end point as well as for the intermediate points.

5. **At the top of the Create a Custom Route window, click the buttons, as needed:**

   - *Reverse Route:* Click to reverse the route direction.

   - *Out & Back:* Click to change the route to going out and coming back on the same track.

   - *Close Loop:* Click to make Maps figure out the route from the current end point (the last point you've placed) back to the start point, closing the loop.

6. **Click the Save button to display the Save to Library dialog.**

   If you're creating a route in your immediate vicinity and just want to use it rather than save it, click the Go button instead of the Save button. The Go button appears when you're at the route's location, replacing the Directions button, which offers you directions to a route that's elsewhere.

7. **Type a descriptive or memorable name for the route.**

8. **Click in the notes field and type any notes about the route.**

9. **Click the Done button to save the route.**

   The route appears in the Routes window. You can then close the window by clicking the Close (x) button.

Get traffic info in real time

You can find out the traffic conditions for whatever map you're viewing by choosing View ⇨ Show Traffic. When you do, Maps color-codes major roadways to inform you of the current traffic speed. It also displays markers indicating any known hazards, such as roadwork or accidents.

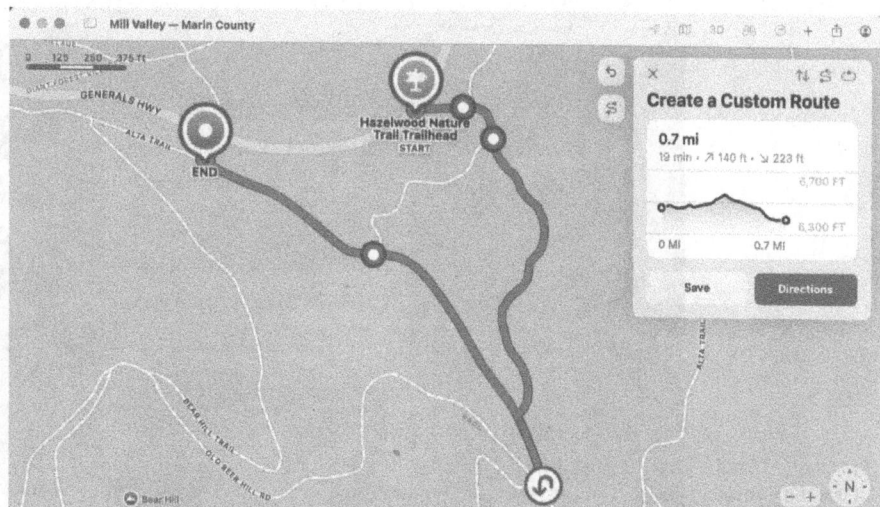

FIGURE 11-7:
Creating a
custom
route in Maps.

TIP

Reverse this process to hide traffic.

Here's the key to those colors: Orange means 25 to 50 miles per hour; red means under 25 miles per hour; and no color means that no data is available at this time.

WARNING

Traffic info isn't available in every location, but the only way to find out is to give it a try. If color codes don't appear, assume that traffic information doesn't work for that particular location.

Enjoying flyovers and look arounds

Certain cities and landmarks include cool additional features such as 3D flyover tours and *look arounds*, which you can use to explore select cities in an interactive 3D experience, panning 360° and moving smoothly through streets.

Flyovers

To try a flyover, first search for a city or landmark by name and select it. If a 3D flyover tour is available for it, you'll see the Flyover Tour button on its card, as shown in Figure 11-8. Click the button to watch the flyover tour; click the little x-in-a-circle at the bottom of the window to end the tour.

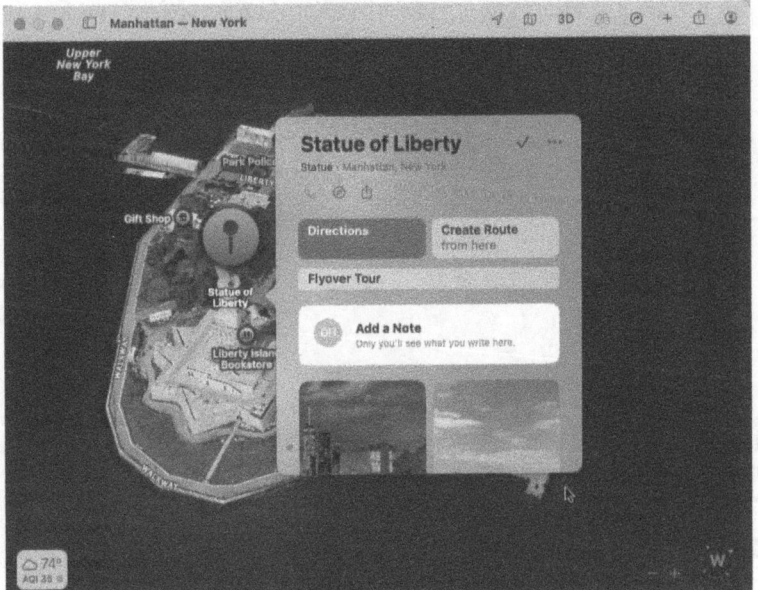

FIGURE 11-8:
Click the Flyover
Tour button to
watch the 3D
flyover tour of the
Statue of Liberty.

Look arounds

Look arounds are rare but interesting when you find them. You can start a look around by clicking the Look Around icon on the toolbar. The map screen changes to look around view, where you can click to move (or look) in any direction, as shown in Figure 11-9. If the Look Around icon is light gray and nothing happens when you click it, there's no look around for that location.

Doing more on the card for a location

After clicking a location's bubble to display its card, you can get directions to or from that location, add the location to your favorites or contacts, or create a new contact from it. But you can also do three more things with a location from its card:

>> Click the phone number to call it.

>> Click the email address to launch the Mail app and send an email to it.

>> Click the URL to launch Safari and view its website.

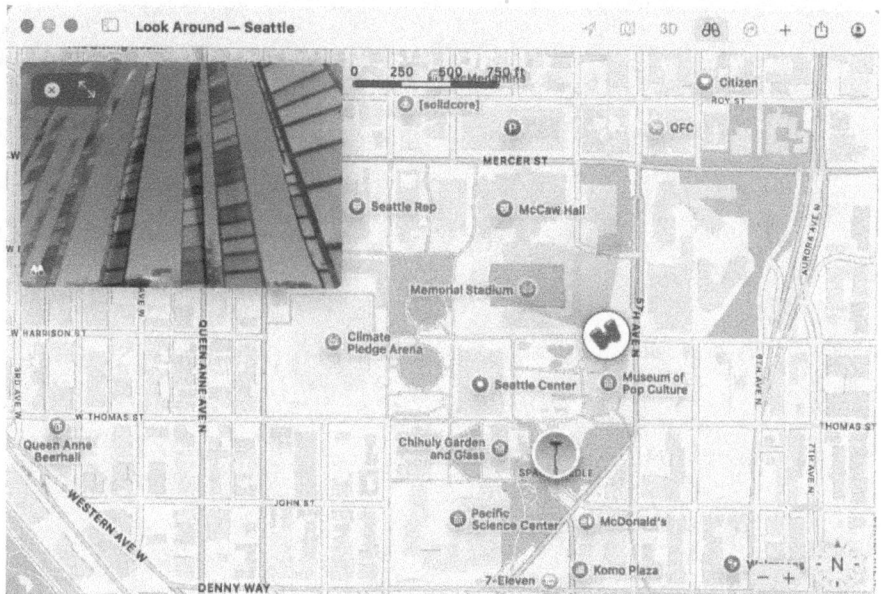

FIGURE 11-9:
A look around view of the Museum of Pop Culture in Seattle.

IN THIS CHAPTER

» Tracking your stocks with Stocks

» Staying current with News

» Making voice memos with
  Voice Memos

» Automating repetitive tasks
  with Shortcuts

Chapter **12**

Using Stocks, News, Voice Memos, and Shortcuts

This chapter covers four useful apps that launched on the iPhone and iPad before moving to the Mac:

» Stocks lets you monitor information about specific stocks and the market in general.

» News gathers stories from myriad publications in one convenient place.

» Voice Memos enables you to record memos with your voice.

» Shortcuts allows you to automate repetitive tasks.

Tracking Your Stocks

 The Stocks app makes it easy to view stock quotes, interactive charts, and top business news (from Apple News, which is covered in "Keeping Current with News," later in this chapter).

When you launch Stocks for the first time, it displays a default set of quotes and indexes that Apple thinks you might appreciate, as shown in Figure 12-1. Note that if you have an Apple ID and have already selected securities in the Stocks app on your iPhone or iPad, your selections will appear in the Mac app.

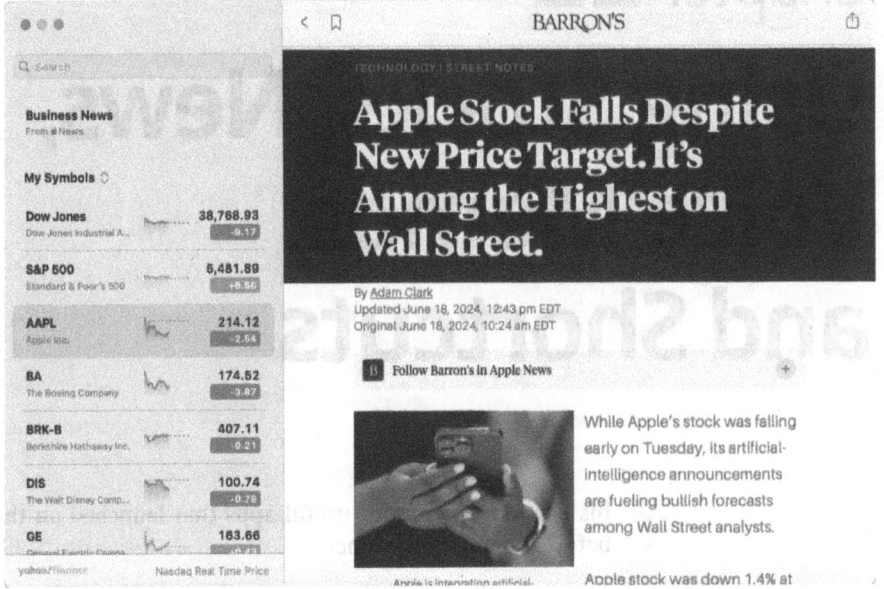

FIGURE 12-1:
The Stocks app comes stocked with a short list of securities and indexes chosen by Apple.

The default stocks, funds, and indexes appear in the sidebar on the left; news items appear in the pane on the right. You may need to scroll either the sidebar or the right pane to see all the data available.

When you open the Stocks app, it displays the latest price for the listed items, as long as your Mac has a working Internet connection.

WARNING The prices that Stocks displays are in near real time — in other words, they are not absolutely up to date. Do not use them for real-time trading.

Your stocks also appear by default in Notification Center. If you don't see the Stocks widget in Notification Center, and you want to see it, click the Edit Widgets button at the bottom of Notification Center, and then add the Stocks widget. Alternatively, you could add the widget to the desktop. (See Chapter 10 for instructions on adding widgets.)

Adding and removing stocks, funds, and indexes

Your chance of owning the default group of stocks, funds, and indexes is slim, so you'll likely want to add your own stocks, funds, or indexes and delete any or all default ones.

Here's how to add a stock, a fund, or an index:

1. **In the Search field in the top-left corner of the Stocks window, type the name of the item you want to add.**

   As you type, the list updates with companies, indexes, and funds that match what you've typed so far, with items already in your watchlist appearing in a separate section.

2. **Do one of the following:**

   - Click the Add to Watchlist icon, the little + sign in a circle to the left of the item's name.

   - Control-click or right-click the item you want to add, and choose Add to Watchlist from the contextual menu.

3. **When you finish adding items, click the Done (X) button to the right of the Search field to return to your watchlist.**

To remove an item, select it, press Delete, and then click Remove in the confirmation dialog that opens. Alternatively, Control-click or right-click the item and choose Remove from Watchlist from the contextual menu. Or you can click the item and then click the Remove from Watchlist icon, the check-mark icon in the top-right corner of the Stocks window.

TIP To change the order of the items on your watchlist, drag an item up or down to its new place in the list.

The devil is in the details

To see the details for an item, click it; the right side of the window offers additional information on the item. The interactive chart described in the next section appears at the top of the pane. Scroll down for additional news; click See More Data from Yahoo! Finance for even more additional news.

Charting a course

When you select a stock, fund, or index, you'll see a graph with the following numbers and letters above it: 1D, 1W, 1M, 3M, 6M, YTD, 1Y, 2Y, 5Y, 10Y, and ALL. These symbols stand for 1 day, 1 week, 1 month, 3 months, 6 months, year to date, 1 year, and 2, 5, 10, and all recorded years, respectively. These numbers and letters are labels; click one, and the chart updates to reflect that period of time.

You can do two other neat things with charts:

>> Hover your pointer over the chart to see the value for that point in time.

>> Click and drag to see the difference in values between 2 days.

By default, the Stocks app displays the change in a stock's price in dollars. You can see the change expressed as a percentage instead or as the stock's market capitalization. Just open the View menu, click or highlight the Watchlist Shows continuation menu, and then click Price Change, Percentage Change, or Market Cap, as needed.

While the View menu is open, check out its other Stocks-related commands:

>> Refresh (⌘ +R)

>> Hide Sidebar (⌘ +Control+S)

>> Back (⌘ +[)

>> Next Story (⌘ +→)

>> Previous Story (⌘ +←)

>> Actual Size (⌘ +Shift+0)

>> Zoom In (⌘ +plus sign)

>> Zoom Out (⌘ +minus sign)

>> Enter Full Screen (⌘ +Control+F)

Finally, Stocks lets you open multiple windows (choose File ⇨ New Window) or tabs (choose File ⇨ New Tab) to keep more information available on the screen. You can create another watchlist by choosing File ⇨ New Watchlist, and manage your various watchlists by choosing File ⇨ Manage Watchlists.

Keeping Current with News

 The Apple News app gathers articles, images, and videos you might be interested in and displays them in a visually appealing fashion. Participating publishers include ESPN, *The New York Times*, Hearst (publisher of various newspapers), Time Inc., CNN, Condé Nast, and Bloomberg.

What are your interests?

The first time you open the News app, the Follow Your Favorites screen appears and walks you through selecting news channels that interest you. Any time after that, you can customize what appears in the News app by choosing File ⇨ Discover Channels and working in the Discover Channels dialog. Click the red plus sign for each source you want to follow, changing the plus sign to a red selection circle containing a white check mark.

If you select an item by mistake, click the check mark to change it back to a small red plus sign.

When you've clicked all the sources you want to follow, click Done, and they'll appear in the Following section of your sidebar.

To remove an item from the sidebar's Following section, do one of the following:

» Control-click or right-click the item, and choose Unfollow Channel from the contextual menu.

» Select the item, and choose File ⇨ Unfollow Channel.

» Select the item, and press ⌘ +Shift+L.

How News works

News creates a customized near-real-time news feed based on the sources you're following, highlighting stories it expects you to be interested in. The more you read, the better its suggestions become, or so Apple says.

Click a story to read it; click < (Back) at the top of the pane to return to the main News screen. Or use the handy commands and shortcuts on the View menu, including the following:

» Check for New Stories (⌘ +R)

» Next Story

- » Previous Story

- » Actual Size (⌘+Shift+0)

- » Zoom In (⌘+plus sign)

- » Zoom Out (⌘+minus sign)

Managing your news

In addition to the useful commands in the View menu, the News app's File menu offers several commands that help you manage your news.

To help News find stories you'll enjoy, choose File ⇨ Suggest More Stories Like This (⌘+L) if you love the story you're reading; choose File ⇨ Suggest Fewer Stories Like This (⌘+D) if you don't love it. The more you use these two commands, the more insightful News will be when suggesting stories of interest.

Choose File ⇨ Save Story (⌘+S) to save the story for future reading. To return to the story, click the Saved Stories category in the sidebar to display the Saved Stories list, and then click the story.

TIP

The History category in the sidebar can help you find that story you read the other day and now want to share.

Finally, check out the other commands on the File menu, which can help fine-tune what you see in News, including the following:

- » Follow Channel (⌘+Shift+L)

- » Block Channel (⌘+Shift+D)

- » Manage Notifications & Email

- » Manage Blocked Channels and Topics

- » Manage Subscriptions

Apple offers a subscription news service called News+ that gives you access to hundreds of newspapers and magazines for $12.99 a month. Click News+ in the sidebar for more information or to begin a free 1-month trial.

TIP

You can also get access to News+ by taking out a subscription to the Apple One service, which bundles up to six services in a single subscription payment. Depending on which other Apple services you want, getting them via Apple One might cost less than getting them individually.

Recording Memos with Voice Memos

Voice Memos lets you record, play back, and share short audio recordings. Any time you need to capture audio quickly, fire up Voice Memos, and you're in business.

Recording a voice memo

Launch Voice Memos, and you'll see a simple window with a sidebar that lists any previous recordings you've made and a big red button.

TIP

Recordings use your Mac's built-in microphone by default. If you prefer to use a different microphone, select it on the Input tab in the Sound pane of the System Settings app before you begin recording.

To record a voice memo, click the big red button. To pause the recording, click the red Pause button, which becomes the Resume button, as shown in the lower-left corner in Figure 12-2. Click Resume to continue recording, or click Done to finish and save the recording.

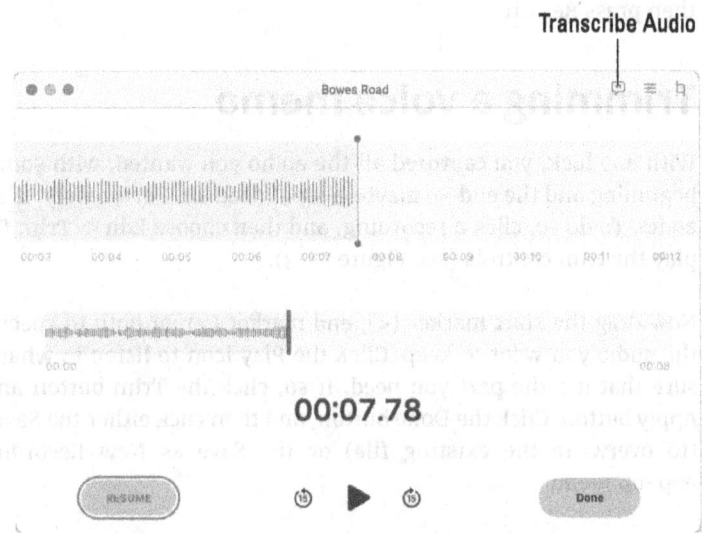

Transcribe Audio

FIGURE 12-2:
You can pause at any time and then click Resume or Done.

00:07.78

Listening to a voice memo

After you capture your thoughts or musings, you'll probably want to play them back. To do so, just click the voice memo you want to hear and then click the triangular Play icon to listen.

TIP

You can drag the playhead (the vertical blue line in the middle of the waveform) to move forward or back in the memo.

Transcribing a voice memo

NEW

To have Voice Memos transcribe the audio in a voice memo, select the memo and then click the Transcribe Audio button in the upper-right corner of the window. The text appears, and you can select all or part of it, copy it, and use it elsewhere, as needed.

Naming a voice memo

When a memo is added to your list of recordings, it shows up with the date and length of the recording and the uninspiring title New Recording. If you've allowed Voice Memos to access Location Services, Voice Memos gives each memo a name based on the location it detects for you, but these names quickly get repetitive, too.

To keep your voice memos straight, give each memo a descriptive name as soon as you've recorded it and decided to keep it rather than trash it. Click the memo in the sidebar, double-click the existing name to select it, type the new name, and then press Return.

Trimming a voice memo

With any luck, you captured all the audio you wanted, with some dead air at the beginning and the end — maybe a lot of dead air. Fortunately, it's easy to trim the audio. To do so, click a recording, and then choose Edit ➪ Trim Recording to display the trim controls (see Figure 12-3).

Now drag the start marker (<), end marker (>), or both to specify the portion of the audio you want to keep. Click the Play icon to listen to what's left and make sure that it's the part you need. If so, click the Trim button and then click the Apply button. Click the Done button, and then click either the Save Recording item (to overwrite the existing file) or the Save as New Recording item on the pop-up menu.

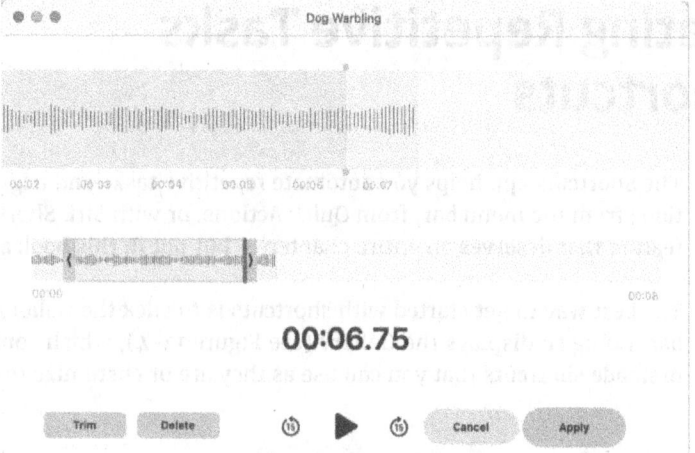

FIGURE 12-3:
Voice Memos
enables you to
trim a memo
quickly and
accurately.

TIP

If you make a mistake, choose Edit ⇨ Undo immediately to restore the audio you trimmed.

You may want to share a Voice Memo with others. No problem. Just click a Voice Memo to select it and then click the share icon (shown in the margin) on the toolbar. You have the option to email the memo or send it in a message. Or you can share it instantly with Mac, iPhone, or iPad users via AirDrop (covered in Chapter 4), or add it to the Notes app or the Reminders app.

When you have no further use for a recording, you can remove it from the Voice Memos app by selecting it in the sidebar and then either clicking the Delete icon on the toolbar or pressing Delete (or Backspace on a non-Apple keyboard).

TIP

To share your voice memos across your Apple devices, do one of the following:

>> **On your Mac:** Open System Settings, click Apple ID in the sidebar, and click iCloud to display the iCloud screen. In the Saved to iCloud section, click the See All to open the More Apps Using iCloud dialog. In the list of apps, set the Voice Memos switch to On (blue), and then click the Done button.

>> **On your iPhone or iPad:** Tap Settings ⇨ Apple ID (the button bearing your name) ⇨ iCloud to display the iCloud screen. In the Saved to iCloud section, click the See All button to display the Saved to iCloud screen, and then set the Voice Memos switch to On (green).

Automating Repetitive Tasks with Shortcuts

 The Shortcuts app helps you automate repetitive tasks and trigger those automations from the menu bar, from Quick Actions, or with Siri. Shortcuts is a powerful feature that deserves an entire chapter — but not in this book and not today.

The best way to get started with shortcuts is to click the Gallery item in the sidebar. Doing so displays the Gallery (see Figure 12-4), which contains hundreds of premade shortcuts that you can use as they are or customize to suit your needs.

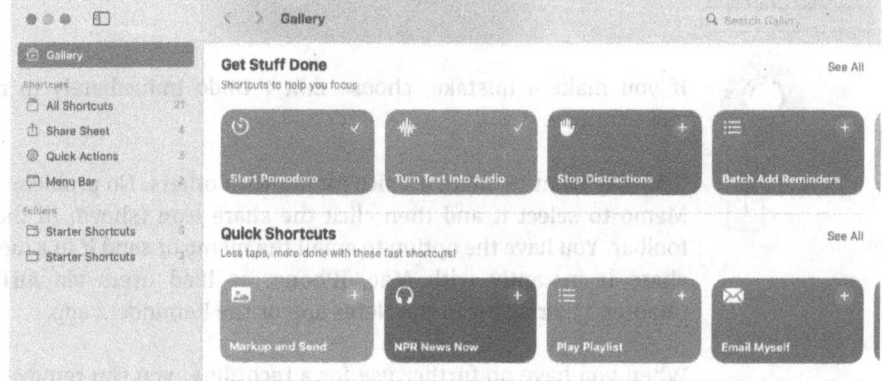

FIGURE 12-4:
Explore more than 300 made-for-you shortcuts in the Shortcuts Gallery.

Click any shortcut to see a description of what it does. For example, if you click the Start Pomodoro shortcut (the first shortcut in the Get Stuff Done category in the Gallery), you see the Start Pomodoro screen (see Figure 12-5). If you like it, click the Add Shortcut button. Depending on how the shortcut is configured, you may just see the message *Shortcut Added*, or the Setup dialog may open so that you can configure the shortcut for your Mac.

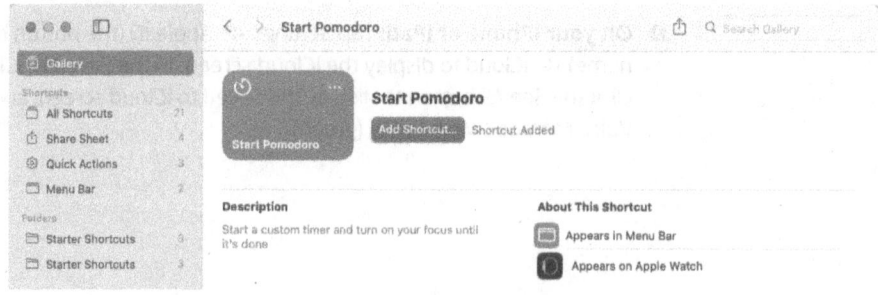

FIGURE 12-5:
On the details screen for a shortcut, click Add Shortcut if you want to use the shortcut.

After you've added a shortcut, drag it from your All Shortcuts folder to the Quick Actions folder if you want to be able to trigger the shortcut from the contextual menu, or to the Menu Bar folder if you want to run the shortcut from the menu bar. You can also ask Siri to perform the shortcut by name.

Apps you install on your Mac may add extra capabilities via shortcuts. For example, depending on the hardware involved, you may be able to use shortcuts to take actions such as managing your yard's sprinkler system or heating up your hot tub right from your Mac.

When you've whetted your appetite with built-in shortcuts, you can graduate to creating custom shortcuts of your own. To get started, choose File ⇨ New Shortcut or press ⌘ +N.

3
Getting Along with Others

Connect your Mac to the Internet.

Surf the web with Safari.

Explore video chatting with FaceTime and SharePlay.

Make apps such as Mail, Contacts, and Messages work for you.

Share files and more.

Chapter **13**

(Inter)Networking

macOS Sequoia offers built-in Internet connectivity right out of the box. Sequoia comes with the following:

» Apple's Safari web browser, which you use to navigate the web, download remote files, and more

» The FaceTime app for video chats with other users of Macs, iPhones, iPads, Vision Pro headsets, and even Windows PCs

» The Messages app, used for instant messaging (text), audio and video chatting, screen sharing, and file transfers

» The Mail app (for email)

This chapter and the two that follow cover the top things most people use the Internet for: surfing the web and video and audio chatting. You discover Safari in this chapter, Contacts and FaceTime in Chapter 14, and Mail and Messages in Chapter 15.

First, we need make sure your Mac is connected to the Internet. If you're already able to surf the web, send and receive email, or send and receive text messages, you're connected and could skip many (if not most) of the steps in the following section.

Getting Connected to the Internet

Before you can use (or surf) the Internet, you need to connect to the Internet. If you're a typical home user, you need three things to surf the Internet:

>> **A connection to the Internet,** such as a cable connection, digital subscriber line (DSL) connection, fiber-optic connection, or a satellite Internet service. This connection will normally manifest itself as a physical device that establishes the Internet connection, maintains it, and shares it with your devices via a local area network. In technical terms, this physical device is usually a router and switch combined, and will often be a wireless access point as well. This section uses the term *Internet router* to refer to this type of device.

The local area network via which your Internet router shares its Internet connection with your Mac and your household's other devices can be a wired network, a wireless network, or both. Almost all wired networks use the Ethernet family of standards. Almost all wireless networks use the Wi-Fi family of standards.

All Mac models have Wi-Fi, from the sveltest MacBook Air up to the heavyweight Mac Pro. Recent iMac models have optional Ethernet built into their external power brick. Monitor-free desktop Macs — the Mac mini, the muscle-bound Mac Studio, and the Mac Pro — have built-in Ethernet ports. Not content with one Ethernet port, the Mac Pro boasts two.

>> **An account with an Internet service provider (ISP),** such as AT&T or Comcast.

If you like taking a minimalist approach, you can get online with free Wi-Fi, which is available almost everywhere — in stores, restaurants, parks, libraries, and other places. Instead of an ISP account, you can go a long way with a free email account from Apple's iCloud, Microsoft's Outlook.com, Google's Gmail, or Yahoo! Mail.

>> **A Mac,** preferably one running macOS Sequoia.

After you set up each of these components, you can launch and use Safari, Mail, Messages, and any other Internet apps.

Choosing an Internet service provider (ISP)

You may have to select a company to provide you access to the Internet: an Internet service provider, or ISP for short. The prices and services that ISPs offer vary, often from minute to minute. Keep the following in mind when choosing an ISP:

>> **If your connection comes from a cable or telephone company, your ISP is probably that company.** In effect, the choice of ISP is pretty much made for you when you decide on cable, fiber, or DSL service.

>> **Broadband access to the Internet starts at around $40 per month.** If your service provider asks for considerably more than that, find out why.

If you think you're paying too much for Internet service or you don't like your current provider, do your homework and determine what other options are available in your neighborhood.

Generally speaking, ISPs are getting better at setting up Internet connections so that they work reliably and don't require you to bug the ISPs' tech-support departments constantly. But before your Internet connection flatlines, make sure you know how to get in touch with your ISP's tech-support department via phone or another means that doesn't involve your Internet connection.

As you know, the Number One solution to computer problems is *power cycling* — switching the wretched thing off, cursing freely, and then switching it back on. Well, guess what: The Number One solution to Internet router problems is also power cycling. (You can even use the very same curses.)

TIP

Connecting your Mac to a network via Wi-Fi

Once your network is up and running, you can connect your Mac to it via Wi-Fi either via Control Center or via the Wi-Fi pane in System Settings. Let's start with Control Center, because this is the method you'll probably want to use when you're out and about.

1. **Click the Control Center icon (shown in the margin) on the menu bar to open Control Center (shown on the left in Figure 13-1).**

2. **Click Wi-Fi to display the Wi-Fi panel (shown on the right in Figure 13-1).**

   Make sure the Wi-Fi switch at the top is set to On (blue).

3. **Click the network's name in the Other Networks list.**

   Control Center closes. A dialog opens to prompt you for the Wi-Fi network's password.

4. **Type the password in the Password box.**

   If you want to see the characters you're typing, select the Show Password check box. Seeing the characters can be a lifesaver when you're entering a murderously complex password.

5. **Click the Join button.**

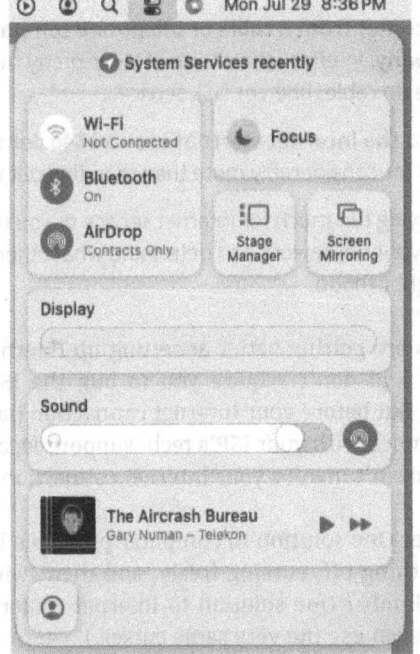

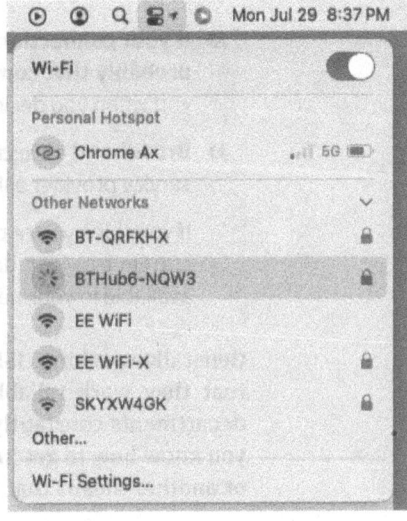

FIGURE 13-1:
Click Wi-Fi in
Control Center
(left), and then
click the network
in the Wi-Fi
pane (right).

If the Wi-Fi network you want to join doesn't appear in the Other Networks list, but you know the network exists, it's probably set to hide its name (in technical terms, its Service Set Identifier, or SSID). Click Other to open the Find and Join a Wi-Fi Network dialog (see Figure 13-2). Fill in the Network Name field and the Password field, and then click the Join button.

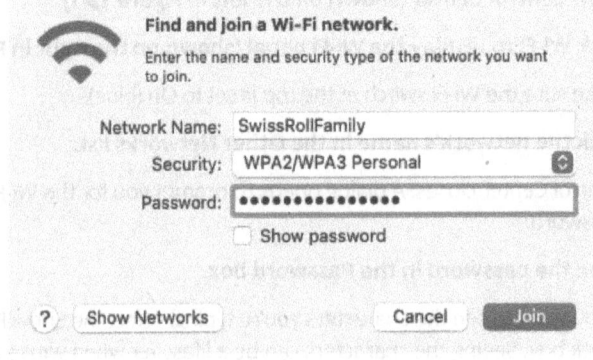

Find and join a Wi-Fi network.
Enter the name and security type of the network you want to join.

Network Name: SwissRollFamily

Security: WPA2/WPA3 Personal

Password: ●●●●●●●●●●●●●●●

☐ Show password

? Show Networks   Cancel   Join

FIGURE 13-2:
Use the Find and
Join a Wi-Fi
Network dialog to
join a Wi-Fi
network that
hides its name.

TECHNICAL STUFF

Most home Internet routers are set to use a technology called Dynamic Host Configuration Protocol (DHCP), which automatically provides connection information to computers on the network. This connection information includes the Internet Protocol address (IP address), a number that identifies the computer; the subnet mask, a number used to organize the network; and the IP address or name of the Internet router, which tells the computer where to find the on-ramp to the Internet.

To connect your Mac to a Wi-Fi network via the Wi-Fi pane in the System Settings app, follow these steps:

1. **Open System Settings — for example, click the System Settings icon on the Dock or on the Launchpad screen.**

2. **Click Wi-Fi in the sidebar to display the Wi-Fi pane.**

   Make sure the Wi-Fi switch at the top is set to On (blue).

3. **In the Other Networks list, move the pointer over the Wi-Fi network you want to join, and then click the Connect button that appears on the right (see Figure 13-3).**

   A dialog opens to prompt you for the Wi-Fi network's password.

4. **Type the password in the Password box.**

   To see the characters you're typing, set the Show Password switch to On (blue).

5. **Click the Join button.**

   Once macOS has established the connection, the network's name appears near the top of the Wi-Fi pane, just under the Wi-Fi switch.

Managing your Wi-Fi networks

If your Mac connects to only a single Wi-Fi network, you may not need to perform any management — you can just let it connect with default settings. But if your Mac connects to multiple Wi-Fi networks, take a minute to make yourself familiar with the controls for managing Wi-Fi networks. This is especially important if your Mac connects to two or more Wi-Fi networks in the same location — for example, if you have multiple Wi-Fi networks in your home, in your workplace, or in your favorite espresso emporium.

FIGURE 13-3:
From the Wi-Fi
pane in System
Settings, you can
set up and
configure Wi-Fi
network
connections.

Here's how to manage your Wi-Fi networks:

1. **Open System Settings — for example, choose ⬢ ⇨ System Settings.**

2. **Click Wi-Fi in the sidebar to display the Wi-Fi pane (see Figure 13-4).**

   The current Wi-Fi network appears at the top, with a green circle and a *Connected* readout. Below that, the Networks section shows three lists:

   - **Personal Hotspots:** These are hotspot Wi-Fi networks provided by devices such as your iPhone or cellular iPad.

   - **Known Networks:** These are the available Wi-Fi networks your Mac has previously connected to and for which it knows the password (if the network is secured, indicated by the lock icon). A check mark appears next to a known network to which your Mac is already connected.

   REMEMBER

   Your Mac will automatically connect to networks in the Known Networks list when they are available. If you don't want your Mac to connect to a particular known network, you need to tell macOS (we'll get to this in a moment).

- **Other Networks:** These are Wi-Fi networks your Mac hasn't previously connected to, or that it has connected to but that you've made it forget.

3. **Set the Ask to Join Networks switch to On (blue) if you want your Mac to prompt you to join an available Wi-Fi network when none of its known networks are available.**

   These prompts may be helpful, so try turning on Ask to Join Networks and see how it suits you.

4. **Set the Ask to Join Hotspots switch to On (blue) if you want your Mac to prompt you to join an available Wi-Fi hotspot.**

   These prompts also may be helpful. But keep in mind that some hotspots are run by malefactors keen to slurp up unwary users' credentials, bank information, and cookie recipes, so connecting to hotspots whose provenance you don't know may prove costly.

5. **Click the Advanced button at the bottom of the Wi-Fi pane to display the Advanced dialog (see Figure 13-5).**

6. **In the Require Administrator Authorization To section, set the Change Networks switch, the Turn Wi-Fi On or Off switch, and the Show Legacy Networks and Options switch to On (blue) or Off (white), as needed.**

   Requiring administrator authentication for all three actions might be a good idea.

TIP

   Legacies are generally a positive thing, but a *legacy network* usually means one that has poor network speeds and worse security.

   The Wi-Fi MAC Address readout shows the hexadecimal Media Access Control (MAC) address for your Mac's wireless network interface. You might need the MAC address to whitelist your Mac with your Internet router.

7. **Configure Auto-Join and prune the Known Networks list as needed:**

   - *Toggle Auto-Join for the network.* Click the ellipsis (. . .) button, and then click Auto-Join to place or remove the check mark.

   - *Remove a network.* Click the ellipsis (. . .) button, click Remove from List, and then click the Remove button in the confirmation dialog.

TIP

   The ellipsis (. . .) pop-up menu for a network in the Advanced dialog also usually contains the Copy Password command, which lets you copy a known network's password.

8. **Click Done to close the Advanced dialog.**

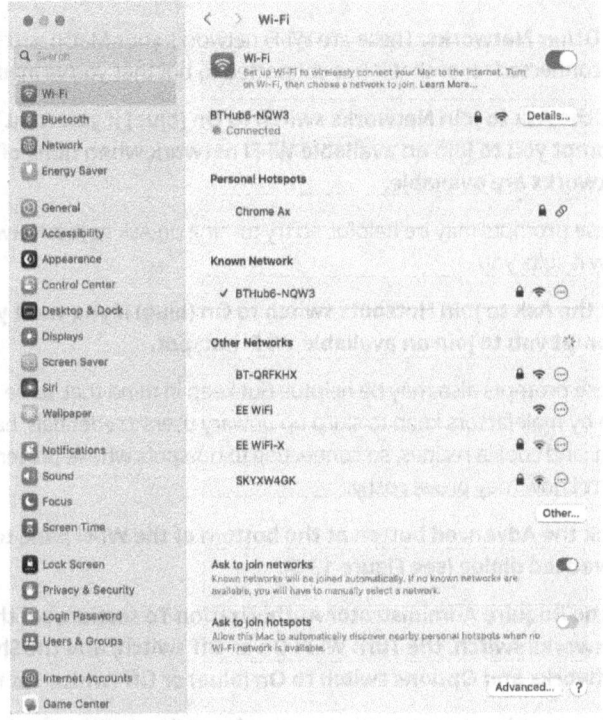

FIGURE 13-4:
In the Wi-Fi pane, choose whether to automatically join known networks and hotspots.

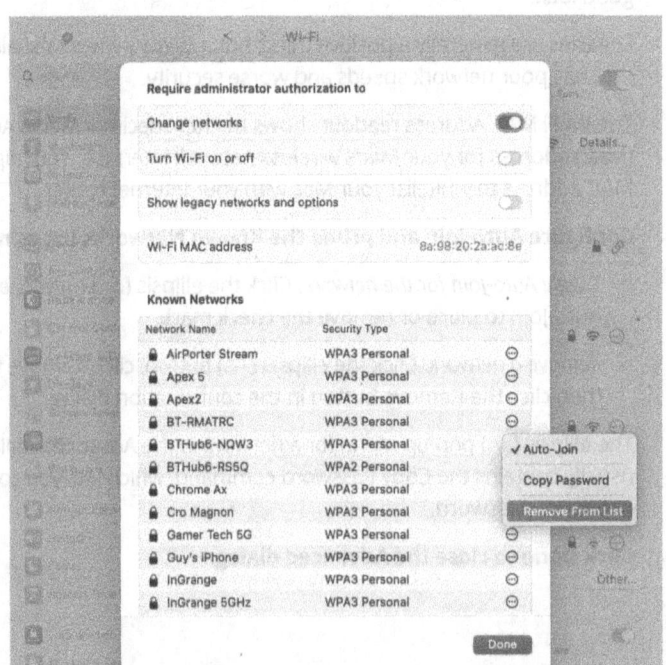

FIGURE 13-5:
In the Advanced dialog, you can control automatic joining and remove Wi-Fi networks you no longer want to use.

From the Wi-Fi pane in System Settings, you can click the Details button for the connected Wi-Fi network to display the Details dialog, which provides options for configuring that network. In this dialog, you can set these four settings:

>> **Automatically Join This Network:** This switch gives you another way to control whether your Mac automatically joins this particular network when it's available.

>> **Private Wi-Fi Address:** In this pop-up menu, choose whether to obfuscate your Mac's Wi-Fi interface's hardware address instead of providing its real address (which might enable malefactors to track your connections). Choose Off to provide the real address. Choose Fixed to use a single fake address for each connection. Choose Rotating to use a different fake address each time your Mac connects to a Wi-Fi network.

>> **Low Data Mode:** Set this switch to On (blue) to reduce your Mac's data usage as far as is practical. You'd use Low Data Mode when connecting your Mac to a metered network, such as the extortionate Internet connections some hotels provide. (If the Wi-Fi network is connected to an all-you-can-eat Internet connection, you probably won't want to use Low Data Mode.)

>> **Limit IP Address Tracking:** Set this switch to On (blue) to have macOS hide your IP address from known address trackers in Safari and Mail. Limiting tracking is usually a good idea.

TIP

The Details dialog also contains readouts showing the IP address your Mac's wireless connection is using. Lastly, there's a Forget This Network button that you can click to command your Mac to forget this network.

REMEMBER

Use only wireless networks that you know and trust, especially in public places such as hotels and airports. If you must connect your Mac to a network that might be untrustworthy, use a virtual private network (VPN) to encrypt the data your Mac sends and receives.

Finally, if you have any reservations about using public Wi-Fi, use your mobile phone's hotspot feature (if it has one) instead of a public Wi-Fi network. Cellular networks encrypt all traffic, making them more secure than Wi-Fi networks.

Also look for *https* (not *http*) at the beginning of URLs to ensure that your wireless connection to that website is encrypted (more secure).

Connecting your Mac to a network via Ethernet

If your Mac has an Ethernet port, you can connect the Mac to a network in seconds by plugging one end of an Ethernet cable into that port and the other end into your Internet router. Take a few more seconds to arrange the cable so that nobody will trip over it and your cats can't use it as a slackline.

TIP

If your Mac doesn't have an Ethernet port, you can add one by getting a USB-to-Ethernet adapter or a Thunderbolt-to-Ethernet adapter.

Once you've made the physical connection, macOS normally configures it automatically within a few seconds. To see the details of the connection, open the System Settings app, click Network in the sidebar, and then click Ethernet in the Network pane. The Ethernet pane appears (see Figure 13-6), showing the connection's details, including the IP address and the router address.

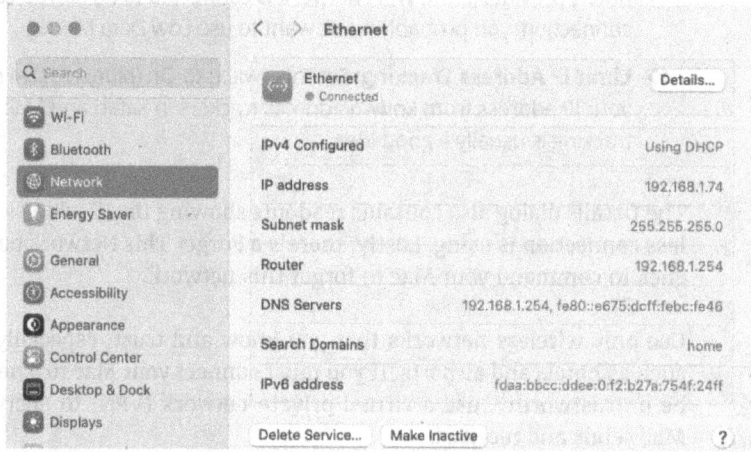

FIGURE 13-6:
Use the Ethernet pane to learn the IP address and other details of an Ethernet connection.

From here, you can click the Details button to open the Details dialog, which enables you to perform heavy-duty configuration of the connection. With the Ethernet category selected at the top of the sidebar, make sure the Limit IP Address Tracking switch is set to On (blue). Beyond this, it's best not to change the settings in the Details dialog unless a) you know what you're doing, or b) you're following directions from a network administrator to solve a particular problem.

Browsing the Web with Safari

With your Internet connection set up, you're ready to browse the web. The following sections use Safari because it's the web browser installed with macOS Sequoia.

TIP

If you don't care for Safari, check out Firefox or Chrome, which are both free browsers and have features you won't find in Safari. It never hurts to have a spare in case Safari has issues with a particular website.

To begin, open Safari in any of these ways:

>> Click the Safari icon (shown in the margin) on the Dock or Launchpad.

>> Double-click the Safari icon in your Applications folder.

>> Click a URL link in an email, an iMessage, or a document.

>> Double-click a URL link document (a .webloc file) in Finder.

The first time you launch Safari, you see a generic start page, as shown in Figure 13-7. (If you've upgraded to Sequoia from an earlier version of macOS, Safari will open to the same page it opened to before you upgraded.)

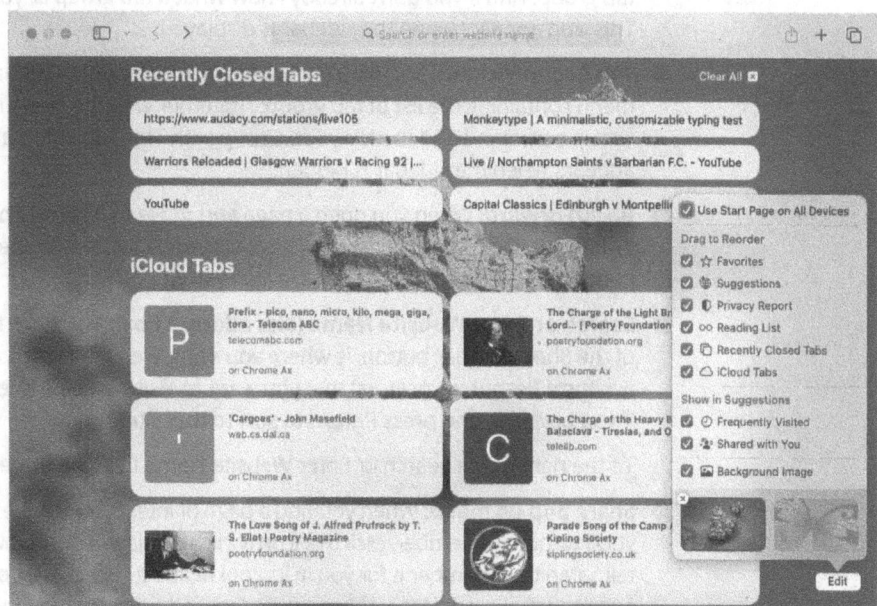

FIGURE 13-7:
Safari first displays a generic start page.

You can customize your start page by clicking the Edit button in the lower-right corner of the start page (shown in Figure 13-7). Enable or disable an item by selecting or deselecting its check box, respectively.

TIP

The Recently Closed Tabs section lists webpages that were open in tabs you've recently closed on this Mac, while the iCloud Tabs section of the start page shows webpages you've recently accessed on your other computers and devices that log into the same iCloud account.

TIP

You can choose what appears in new Safari windows and tabs by choosing Safari ➪ Settings and clicking the General tab at the top of the Settings window.

Using and customizing the toolbar

The Safari toolbar, at the top of every Safari window, consists of a narrow row of icons and the Search or Enter Website Name field. The icons do pretty much what their names imply. From left to right, they are

>> **Show/Hide Sidebar:** Click this icon (shown in the margin) to see your favorites or Reading List in the sidebar; click it again to hide the sidebar.

>> **New Tab Group:** Click this icon (shown in the margin) to create a new empty tab group. And if you don't already know what a tab group is, you will shortly. This icon appears when the sidebar is displayed.

>> **Tab Group Picker:** Click this icon (shown in the margin) to display a pop-up menu containing the list of tab groups, together with the New Empty Tab Group command and the New Tab Group with This Tab command. This icon appears when the sidebar is hidden.

>> **Back/Forward:** When you open a page and move to a second page (or third or fourth), Back takes you to previously visited pages. Remember that you need to go back before the Forward icon will work.

>> **Search or Enter Website Name (aka address box):** This field, to the right of the Show Sidebar button, is where you enter web addresses, or URLs (Uniform Resource Locators) that you want to visit. Just type one — or paste if you prefer — and press Return to surf to that site.

To the right of the Search or Enter Website Name field are three more icons:

>> **Share pop-up menu:** When you find a page of interest or a page you know you'll want to remember, click this icon (which displays a drop-down menu) to tell Safari to remember it for you in its cool Reading List or as a bookmark — two topics covered later in this chapter. Or send a link to it via Mail or Messages, both covered in Chapter 15, or post it on Facebook or tweet it on Twitter.

- >> **New Tab (+):** Click to open a new tab; press and hold down to see a drop-down menu of recently closed tabs, and then click the one you want to return to.

- >> **Show/Hide Tab Overview:** Click the Show/Hide Tab Overview icon to see previews of all your open tabs (which you learn about shortly) or all tabs in the selected tab group. If you have other Macs or Apple devices, you'll also see the open tabs in Safari on other devices that have Safari enabled in iCloud. This feature is so handy you can also access it on the View menu (View ⇨ Show Tab Overview) or by pressing ⌘+Shift+\.

TIP

You can add other useful icons to your toolbar by choosing View ⇨ Customize Toolbar and then dragging icons such as Home Page, History, Bookmarks, Auto-Fill, and Print from the Customize Toolbar dialog to the toolbar.

Using the Safari sidebar

Click the Show/Hide Sidebar icon on the toolbar, choose View ⇨ Show Sidebar, or press ⌘+Shift+L to display the sidebar, where you'll find links to your start page, tab groups, received links, and collected links (where you'll find Bookmarks and Reading List).

Click the first sidebar item, Start Page, to see your start page (as discussed previously).

Working with tab groups

Tab groups give you an easy and effective way to manage multiple tabs.

To create a new tab group, click the New Tab Group icon on the right above the sidebar (shown in the margin) and choose New Empty Tab Group. If the sidebar is not displayed, click the Tab Group Picker icon and choose New Empty Tab Group. Or, if you currently have more than one tab open, and you want to create a group containing those tabs, choose New Tab Group with x Tabs (for example, New Tab Group with 5 Tabs).

Another way to create a new empty tab group is by choosing File ⇨ New Empty Tab Group or pressing ⌘+Control+N.

You can add a webpage to a tab group in these ways:

- >> **If the sidebar is displayed:** Drag the webpage's tab from the tab bar onto the appropriate tab group in the sidebar. If the sidebar is hidden, you can display it by choosing View ⇨ Show Sidebar or pressing ⌘+Shift+L.

>> **If the sidebar is hidden:** Click in the address box to make it active, and then drag the little icon that appears left of the address to the left side of the Safari window and pause. When the sidebar slides into view, drag the icon to the appropriate tab group and drop it there.

To see the Tab Overview page for a tab group with thumbnails of all the pages it contains (as shown in Figure 13-8), move the pointer over the tab group's name, click the ellipsis (. . .) button that appears, and then click Show Tab Overview on the pop-up menu.

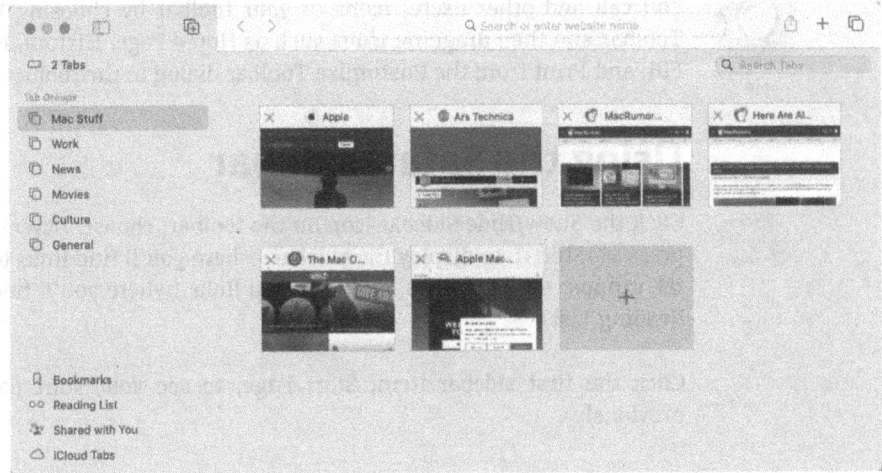

FIGURE 13-8:
The Tab Overview
for the Mac Stuff
tab group.

To activate a tab group, click its name in the sidebar. The tab group's tabs replace your current tabs.

Note that if you open a new tab when a tab group is active (selected in the sidebar), the new tab becomes part of the active group. Conversely, if you close a tab when a tab group is selected in the sidebar, the tab is removed from the group.

Shared with You: Links from others

The Shared with You entry in the sidebar automatically gathers content that's been shared with you. Click Shared with You and an overview page appears with thumbnails of all the photos, videos, articles, and more that have been shared with you by friends and family in the Messages app.

Bookmarking your favorite pages

When you find a webpage you want to return to, bookmark it like this:

1. **Choose Bookmarks ⇨ Add Bookmark, press ⌘+D, or click the Share icon and choose Add Bookmark to open the Add Bookmark dialog.**

2. **Choose where to store the bookmark from the pop-up menu.**

   By default, Safari puts new bookmarks in the Favorites folder. The Favorites folder can get full pretty quickly, so it's best to organize your bookmarks into a folder structure that suits your browsing needs.

3. **Rename the bookmark or use the name provided by Safari.**

4. **(Optional) Add a brief description in the Description field.**

5. **Click the Add button to close the dialog and save the bookmark.**

Finding your bookmarks in the sidebar

To return to a bookmarked page, click it in the Favorites bar (if you saved it there), choose Bookmarks ⇨ Show Bookmarks, press ⌘+Option+B, or click the Show Sidebar icon and then click Bookmarks to see all your bookmarks.

If you add a bookmark to the Favorites folder, it automatically appears in the Favorites bar. If you add the bookmark outside the Favorites folder in the sidebar, it will not appear in the Favorites bar but will be available at the bottom of the Bookmarks menu and in the Bookmarks sidebar.

To open a bookmarked page, click it once in the sidebar. To view the contents of a folder, click the folder name in the list.

To delete a bookmark, Control-click or right-click it and choose Delete.

TIP

⌘+click a folder in the Bookmarks window or Favorites bar to simultaneously open all the bookmarks it contains.

Managing your favorites and the Favorites bar

Below the Search or Enter Website Name field is the Favorites bar, which is populated by default with icons for webpages that Apple thinks you might enjoy, including Apple, Yahoo!, Google Maps, YouTube, and Wikipedia.

TIP

If you don't see the Favorites bar, choose View ⇨ Show Favorites Bar or press ⌘+Shift+B. If you want to access a ton of bookmarks from your Favorites bar, put folders of bookmarks rather than individual bookmarks on the Favorites bar. The Favorites bar displays the folders as drop-down menus, and you can quickly navigate down the menus to the bookmarks you want to display.

Favorites is a folder of bookmarks that appear in the Favorites bar and Favorites page. Not all bookmarks are favorites, but all favorites are bookmarks.

Keeping your Reading List

The Safari sidebar also contains your Reading List, which serves as a repository for pages or links you want to read sometime but not right now. A Reading List item is a lot like a bookmark but easier to create on the fly, which makes the Reading List perfect for pages or links you don't need to keep forever (that's what bookmarks are for).

To add the page you're viewing to your Reading List, click the Share icon and choose Add to Reading List. Alternatively, press ⌘+Shift+D.

To add a link to your Reading List without visiting the page, Shift-click that link. You'll see an animation of a round item flying up to the Show/Hide Sidebar icon. Alternatively, Control-click or right-click the link, and then choose Add Link to Reading List from the contextual menu.

Right-click any item in your Reading List for additional options, such as marking the item as read or saving the item offline so you can read it when your Mac has no Internet connection.

To delete an item from the Reading List, Control-click or right-click the item and then choose Remove Item. To remove all items from the Reading List, Control-click or right-click any item and then choose Clear All Items.

TIP

If you have other Macs or Apple devices that sync with the same iCloud account, you can sync your Reading List among your devices by enabling Safari in the iCloud pane in the System Settings app.

Website-specific settings

To specify settings for the active website, choose Safari ➪ Settings for *website name*. The website-specific settings overlay appears with the following options:

>> **Use Reader When Available:** Select this check box to use Reader view when it is available.

>> **Enable Content Blockers:** Select this check box to enable content blockers.

>> **Page Zoom:** Click this pop-up menu and set the zoom percentage at which you want to display this site.

>> **Auto-Play:** Click this pop-up menu and choose Allow All Auto-Play, Stop Media with Sound, or Never Auto-Play, as needed.

>> **Pop-up Windows:** Click this pop-up menu and choose Block and Notify, Block, or Allow, as needed.

>> **Camera, Microphone, Screen Sharing, and Location:** Open each pop-up menu and choose Ask, Deny, or Allow, as needed.

Reader view

Reader view reformats the page for easier reading while hiding ads, navigation, and other distractions. It's available for a page if the icon in the margin appears at the left edge of the Search or Enter Website Name field.

To enter Reader view, click the icon, and then click Show Reader (see the left screen in Figure 13-9). Alternatively, choose View⇨ Show Reader or press ⌘+Shift+R.

NEW

While in Reader view, you can customize the display by clicking the Reader view icon and working on the panel that appears (see the right screen in Figure 13-9). For example, you might choose a background color in the Theme section, pick a font in the Font section, or click the Zoom pop-up menu and change the zoom percentage.

To exit Reader view, press Esc, press ⌘+Shift+R, or choose View⇨ Hide Reader.

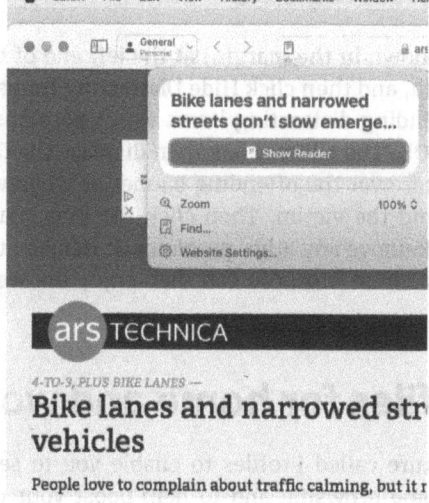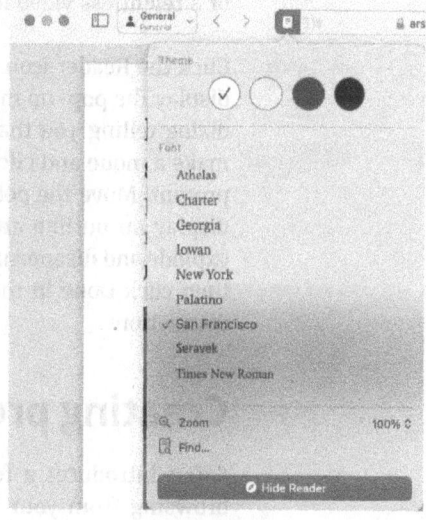

FIGURE 13-9:
Click the Reader view icon and click Show Reader (left) to enter Reader view. Click the Reader view icon to display the customization controls (right).

Browsing smarter with Safari Highlights

NEW

In macOS Sequoia, Safari introduces a new feature called Highlights that makes browsing faster and more efficient. Highlights uses Apple Intelligence and machine learning to identify, extract, and organize key information from a webpage, and then displays that information in a pop-up window, enabling you to quickly grasp what the page offers and decide whether to look at the whole page. Highlights works only for some webpages — they need to be coded in a specific way.

Before you can use Highlights, you may need to enable it. Choose Safari ⇨ Settings to open the Settings window, and then click the Advanced tab to display its contents. Select the Allow Highlights to Share Web Addresses with Apple check box, and then click Close (the red gumdrop) to close the Settings window.

Now go to a webpage and look for a purple dot on the Reader icon (shown in the margin) at the left end of the address box. This dot indicates that Highlights are available. Click the Reader icon to display a pop-up window showing the highlights, which typically include key links you might want to follow. When you're ready to close the pop-up window, click outside it.

Removing distracting items

NEW

Safari in macOS Sequoia also introduces a neat new feature for removing distracting items from a webpage. So if you're looking at a page that has a flashing banner or a relentless video loop, you can try to get rid of it.

Click the Reader icon (shown in the margin) at the left end of the address box to display the pop-up menu, and then click Hide Distracting Items. Safari displays a dialog telling you that hiding distracting items won't permanently remove ads; make a moue and click OK. The address box then displays the *Click an item to hide* prompt. Move the pointer over the offending banner or whatever, making Safari display an outline around the victim. Then click the item, and Safari makes it explode and disappear. Remove any other problematic items in the same way, and then click Done in the address box. You can then enjoy the webpage with fewer distractions.

Creating profiles for home and work

Safari introduces a feature called Profiles to enable you to separate your work browsing from your home browsing and to help boost your concentration and privacy. A Work profile is perhaps the most obvious type of profile to create, but you can create whatever profiles you need. For example, you might create a profile for each major project you work on, if keeping those projects separate from each other is helpful.

Profiles work as a sort of extension of tab groups and focus modes. Each profile maintains a separate set of history, cookies, and website data, so your work history does not get contaminated by your home history, and so on.

Creating your first Safari profile

To get started with profiles, you create a profile. You only need to create one profile because once you do, Safari creates another profile called Personal that contains the settings you've been using up till now, and makes this profile the default. So you need only create one profile to start using profiles.

To create a profile, follow these steps:

1. **Choose Safari ⇨ Settings to display the Safari Settings window.**

2. **Click Profiles on the tab bar to display the Profiles pane.**

   Until you create a profile, the Profiles pane contains only some explanatory text and the Start Using Profiles button (see Figure 13-10).

3. **Click the Start Using Profiles button to display the New Profile dialog (see Figure 13-11).**

4. **Type a descriptive name for the profile in the Name box.**

5. **Click a symbol in the Symbol line to represent the profile.**

   You can click the ellipsis (. . .) button to display a panel containing other symbols.

6. **Click the Color swatch, and then click the color for the profile.**

   Safari uses this color on the Profiles button (which you'll meet shortly) and on the profile's start page.

7. **Leave the Create New Bookmarks Folder option button selected unless you want to use an existing folder — in which case, click the Use Existing Folder option button and select the folder in the pop-up menu.**

8. **Click the Create Profile button to create the profile and close the dialog.**

   The profile appears in the Profiles pane (see Figure 13-12). The Profiles pane also shows the Personal profile, which had been hidden up till now.

9. **Open the New Windows Open With pop-up menu, and then choose Start Page, Empty Page, Same Page, or Tabs for [This Profile] (such as Tabs for Home Browsing in the example).**

10. **Open the New Tabs Open With pop-up menu, and then choose Start Page, Empty Page, or Same Page, as needed.**

11. Click the Extensions tab and specify which extensions to use with the profile.

12. If you want to create another profile, click the Add (+) button at the bottom of the left pane in the Profiles pane.

The New Profile dialog opens. Repeat steps 4 to 11.

13. When you finish creating profiles, click Close (the red gumdrop button) to close the Safari Settings window.

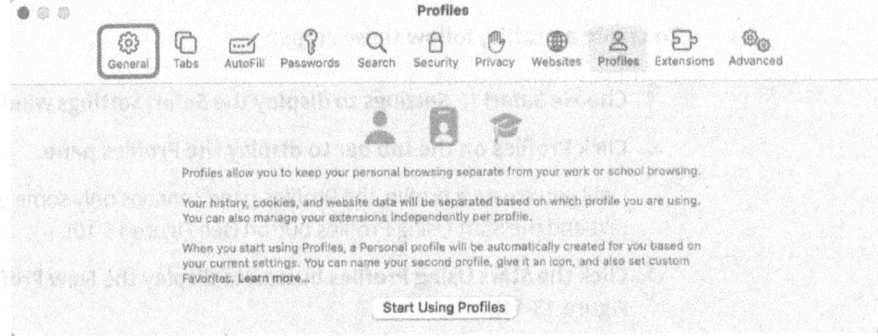

FIGURE 13-10:
The Profiles pane in Safari Settings before you create a profile.

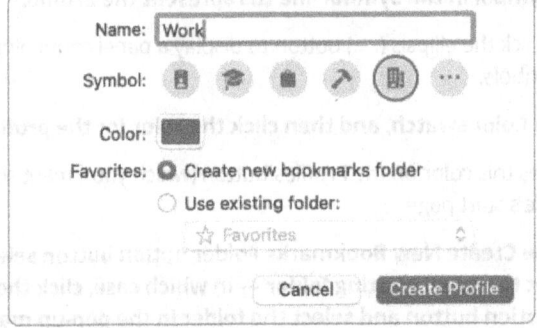

FIGURE 13-11:
Enter the profile's name and details in the New Profile dialog.

Switch from one profile to another

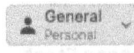

Now that you've created your profiles, the Profile pop-up menu appears on the Safari title bar to the right of the Show Sidebar button when the sidebar isn't displayed. This pop-up menu bears the name of the current tab group and the name and color of the current profile, as shown in the margin here for the Personal profile with the General tab group active.

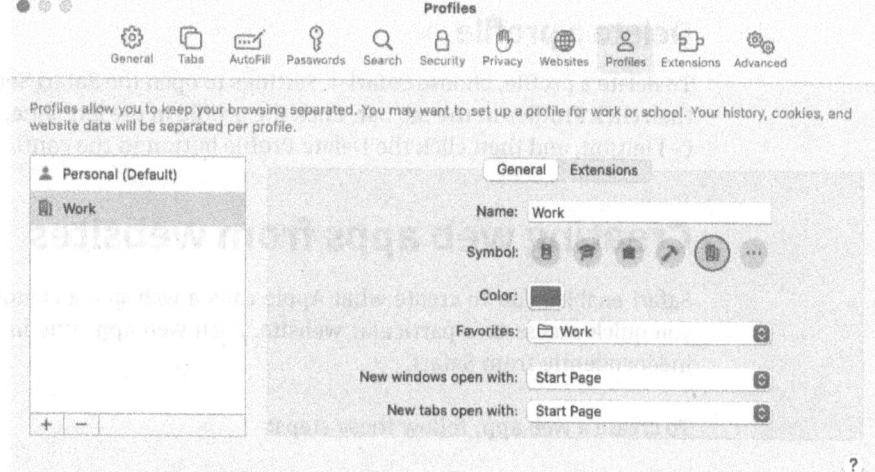

FIGURE 13-12:
The Profiles pane with a profile added and the preexisting Personal profile revealed.

To switch from one profile to another, you open a new window for the profile you want to use. For example, in Figure 13-13, the Personal profile is active. You can open a window for the Work profile by clicking the Profile pop-up menu, and then clicking New Work Window, as shown in Figure 13-13.

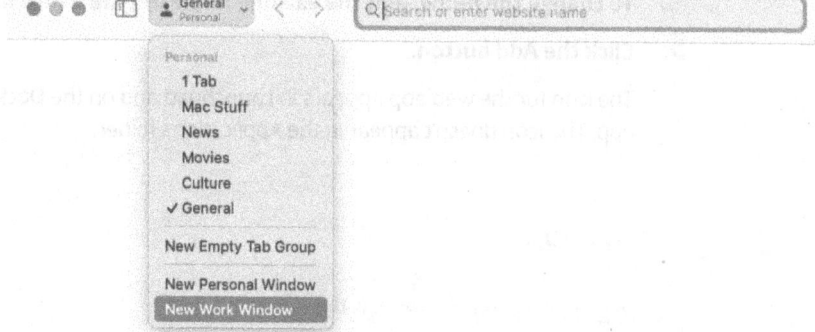

FIGURE 13-13:
Use the Profile pop-up menu to open a new window for a different profile.

TIP

You can also create a new window for a particular profile from the Safari menu bar or from the Dock. From the menu bar, click File, and then click the appropriate New Window item, such as New Personal Window. From the Dock, Control-click or right-click the Safari icon, and then click New *Profile* Window on the contextual menu, where *Profile* is the profile name.

Delete a profile

To delete a profile, choose Safari ⇨ Settings to open the Safari Settings dialog, and then click Profiles in the tab bar. Click the profile in the left pane, click the Remove (–) button, and then click the Delete Profile button in the confirmation dialog.

Creating web apps from websites

Safari enables you to create what Apple calls a *web app*, a custom app that gives you quick access to a particular website. Each web app runs in its own window, independently from Safari.

To create a web app, follow these steps:

1. **In Safari, go to the website from which you want to create a web app.**

2. **Choose File ⇨ Add to Dock to display the Add to Dock dialog (see Figure 13-14).**
   The Add to Dock dialog shows the website's default icon and name.

3. **To change the icon, click the existing icon, select the icon in the dialog that opens, and then click Choose.**

4. **To change the name, edit the existing name or type a new name.**

5. **Click the Add button.**

   The icon for the web app appears in Launchpad and on the Dock after the last app. The icon doesn't appear in the Applications folder.

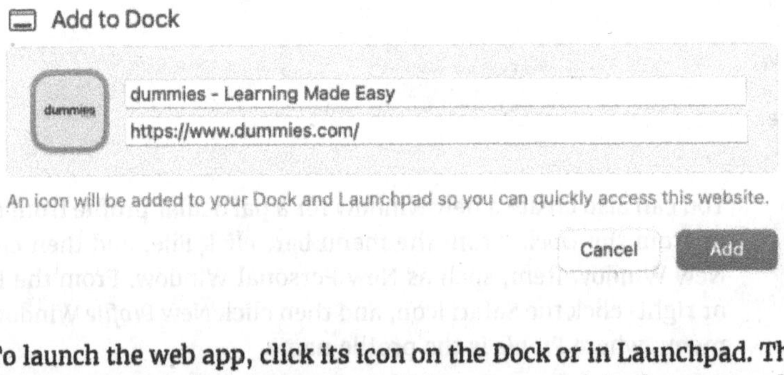

🗔 Add to Dock

| dummies | dummies - Learning Made Easy |
| | https://www.dummies.com/ |

An icon will be added to your Dock and Launchpad so you can quickly access this website.

Cancel   Add

FIGURE 13-14: Creating a web app with the Add to Dock dialog.

To launch the web app, click its icon on the Dock or in Launchpad. The app opens, showing the website's home page, and you can work in the app much as in Safari. When you're ready to quit the web app, click its application menu (which shows the web app's name), and then click the Quit command. Alternatively, press ⌘ +Q.

To delete a web app, open Launchpad, and then drag the web app's icon to the Trash. In the confirmation dialog, click the Delete button.

Controlling audio and video playback

In the bad old days of the web, a webpage could start playing audio of its own accord, leaving you leaping for the volume control or trying to find which of your hundred open tabs was emitting Gothic yodeling drenched with guitar feedback.

Apple has improved matters considerably by making Safari block audio and video from playing by default. If you want to enable automatic playback of audio and video for all sites or specific sites, follow these steps:

1. Choose Safari ➪ Settings to open the Settings window.

2. Click Websites on the tab bar at the top of the window to display the Websites pane.

3. Click Auto-Play in the sidebar to display the Auto-Play controls.

4. For each website in the Currently Open Websites list, open the pop-up menu and choose Allow All Auto-Play, Stop Media with Sound, or Never Auto-Play, as needed.

5. Open the When Visiting Other Websites pop-up menu and choose Allow All Auto-Play, Stop Media with Sound, or Never Auto-Play, as needed.

And when the noise starts (*The bells! The bells!*), go to the little blue speaker icon that appears on the right side of the address box whenever audio is playing on a webpage. Click that icon, and Safari will fall silent even if the audio is coming from an inactive tab or a hidden window.

NEW

In macOS Sequoia, Safari has a new video viewer feature that enables you to watch video in a pop-up window, reducing distractions from other content on the web-page, and control playback more easily. To use this video viewer, click a video file on a webpage.

Using passkeys

As you know, passwords are widely used as a means of authentication both online and offline, but they have various problems: Weak passwords are easy to crack, strong passwords are hard to remember (or easy to forget), and any password can easily be shared.

To help increase your security, macOS includes support for *passkeys*, an authentication method that uses biometric checks (such as face recognition or fingerprint recognition) and that replace passwords for some purposes. If you're using macOS Sonoma, iOS 17, or iPadOS 17, or a later version of any of the three, Apple automatically assigns you a passkey linked to your Apple ID. You can then use this passkey to sign in to Apple's websites and services and affiliated websites and services (see Figure 13-15). Here, you would click the Sign In with iPhone button, use your iPhone to scan the QR code displayed, and then tap the Sign In with a Passkey button on the iPhone's screen.

FIGURE 13-15: Click the Sign In with iPhone button to sign in using your passkey.

Chapter **14**

Dealing with People

I n this chapter, you learn how to use the Contacts app built into macOS to store, manipulate, and use your contacts' information. You start by adding new contacts manually; then you move on to importing contacts from other contact-management apps and services, organizing your contacts in both conventional lists and self-updating smart lists, and setting your contact information to sync itself automatically through iCloud or another service.

Toward the end of the chapter, you explore how to make audio and video calls with Apple's FaceTime communications technology and how to use macOS's innovative SharePlay feature to enjoy media — TV shows, videos, songs, and more — with the other participants in your FaceTime calls.

Collecting Your Contacts

Contacts stores and manages information about your family members, friends, companies, and any other entities you want to keep in touch with. Contacts works seamlessly with the Mail, Messages, and Maps apps, enabling you to quickly look up phone numbers, email addresses, or physical locations when you're ready to communicate with someone or visit them.

Contacts also works with many other apps, including the following:

>> In FaceTime (covered later in this chapter), use Contacts to video-chat with friends and family.

>> In Calendar (covered in Chapter 10), choose Window ⇨ Contacts to display your contacts. Then drag a person in your contacts list from the Contacts window to any date and time on the calendar to make Calendar create a meeting event for that person. The event includes a Send Invitation button that you can click to launch Mail and send the person an invitation to this meeting.

>> The Contacts app can also work with any other app whose programmers choose to make the connection or with any device that's compatible with Contacts.

>> Contacts is also available in most apps that have a Share icon or menu so you can share with your contacts via whichever method is appropriate — usually their phone number, email, or `icloud.com` or `mac.com` address (for an iMessage).

>> If you use iCloud, you can sync contacts with devices that include (but aren't limited to) other Macs, iPhones, iPads, and Vision Pro headsets. You can also sync contacts via Google, Microsoft Exchange, Microsoft 365, or any combination.

In the following sections, you find out the best ways to fill Contacts with your own contacts and how to keep those contacts organized. You start with adding contacts manually by creating new contact entries, because you'll likely need to do this now and then. But if you already have your contact data in another contacts app, skip to the "Importing contacts from other apps" section.

Adding contacts

Follow these steps to create a new contact record in Contacts:

1. **Launch the Contacts app by clicking its icon on the Dock or on the Launchpad screen.**

   The Contacts window appears. The first time you open Contacts, you see two cards: Apple Inc. and the card with whatever personal identification information you supplied when you created your account.

2. **To create a new contact record, click the + button in the bottom-left corner of any contact card, and then choose New Contact from the pop-up menu.**

   An untitled address card appears, with the First text field selected.

3. **In the First text field, type the person's first name.**

4. **Press Tab to move to the Last text field.**

TIP

   You can always move from one field to the next by pressing Tab. In fact, this shortcut works in almost all Mac apps with fields. (To move to the previous field, press Shift+Tab.)

5. **Type the last name for the person you're adding to your Contacts.**

6. **Continue this process, filling in each field for which you have the contact's information (see Figure 14-1).**

   If you're creating a contact record for a company, select the Company check box just below the Company field to make Contacts list the contact record by the company name rather than first name and last name.

TIP

   If you don't see the field you need, click Add (+) at the bottom of the card to open the pop-up menu shown in Figure 14-1. The Add Field to Card section of this menu contains frequently used fields. The More Fields submenu contains less-used fields, including Phonetic First/Last Name, Lunar Birthday, and Department. Click the field you want to add to the contact record.

7. **When you finish entering information, click the Done button to exit editing mode.**

TIP

   The up-and-down arrows between the labels and their content fields in Figure 14-1 are pop-up menus that offer alternative labels for the field. You can click the arrows next to Mobile, for example, to choose iPhone, Apple Watch, Home, Work, and so on instead.

To add more info about any contact record, click the name in the list of contacts. Click the Edit button at the bottom of the Contacts window (where the Done button appears in Figure 14-1), make your changes, and click Done.

Repeat these steps for each new contact record you want to add to your Contacts list.

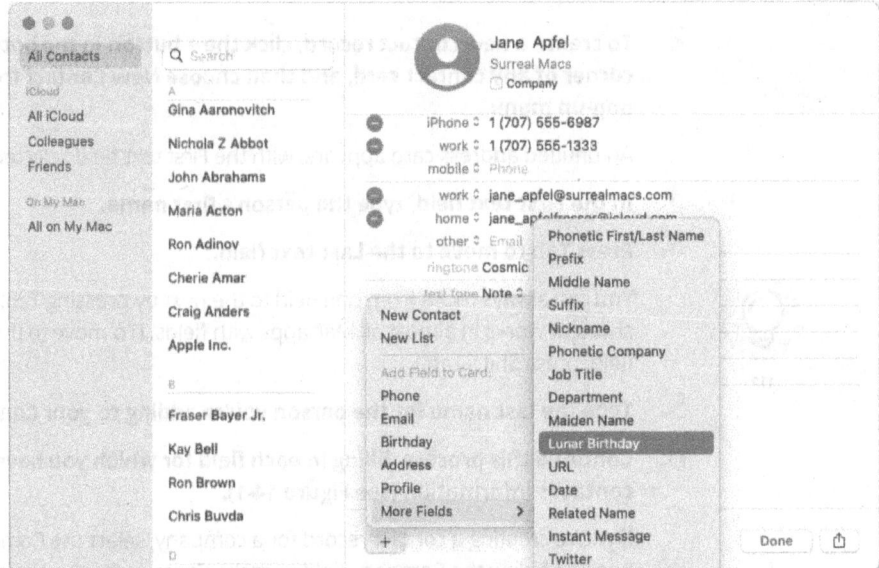

FIGURE 14-1:
Creating a
new contact
record in the
Contacts window.

Importing contacts from other apps

If your contacts are on another Mac or an iPhone or iPad, or stored by Google or Microsoft, you won't need to import your contacts. Just add the appropriate account in the Internet Accounts pane of System Settings (if you haven't added it already,) and then enable syncing for contacts.

If you have contacts in another app (such as FileMaker Pro or ACT), you can export the contact data to a file and then import it into Contacts.

Contacts can import data in five file formats:

>> **vCard:** vCard files are virtual address cards and use the .vcf file extension. A vCard can contain data for a single contact or multiple contacts. If the app that contains your contact data can export to vCard, this format is your best choice.

>> **Archive:** Early versions of OS X used archive files with the .abbu file extension. OS X has since become macOS, and Address Book has become Contacts, but the Archive format persists. If you have a file in this format, you can import it into Contacts.

>> **LDAP Data Interchange Format (LDIF):** LDAP is the acronym for Lightweight Directory Access Protocol. You might have an LDIF file (with the .ldif file extension) exported from a corporate address book.

>> **Comma-Separated Values (CSV):** This text-file format has commas separating the fields. CSV files usually have the .csv file extension. CSV files are a good

way to export contact data from a Microsoft Excel worksheet for import into the Contacts app. You may also need to create a CSV file when you're exporting from an address book that doesn't support vCard format.

>> **Tab-Separated Values:** This text-file format has tabs separating the fields. The files use the .tsv or .txt file extension. Use tab-separated values to export contact data from an app that supports neither vCard nor CSV format.

After you've exported the contact data, go back to the Contacts app. Choose File ⇨ Import, select the exported data file in the Open File dialog, and then click the Open button. The imported contacts appear, and you can start working with them.

Creating a basic list

To organize your contacts in the Contacts app, you can create lists, which macOS used to call *groups*. A list can contain whatever logical (or illogical) selection you want, such as Friends, Colleagues, or Softball Team. After you've created the list and added the appropriate contacts to it, you can treat the list as a single unit. You can send an email to the Softball Team list, for example, without having to mess about with multiple addresses and maybe miss someone.

Here's how to create a list and add contacts to it:

1. **If the Contacts app isn't running, launch it by clicking its icon on the Dock or on the Launchpad screen.**

2. **Create the new list by choosing File ⇨ New List; pressing ⌘ +Shift+N; or clicking the + icon at the bottom of the window, and then choosing New List from the pop-up menu.**

   An untitled list appears in the List pane with *untitled list* selected.

3. **Type a descriptive name for this list and then press Return.**

   This example uses *Softball Team.*

4. **Click All Contacts in the List pane to show all your contacts in the second pane.**

5. **Click the contacts you want to include in the new list.**

   To select more than one contact, click the first contact and then ⌘-click each other contact.

   TIP

   You can use the Search field at the top of the window to find a contact or contacts, and then drag them to the list to add them.

6. **Drag the selected contact names to the new list, as shown in Figure 14-2.**

   Contacts displays the number of contacts you're dragging, which is six in this example.

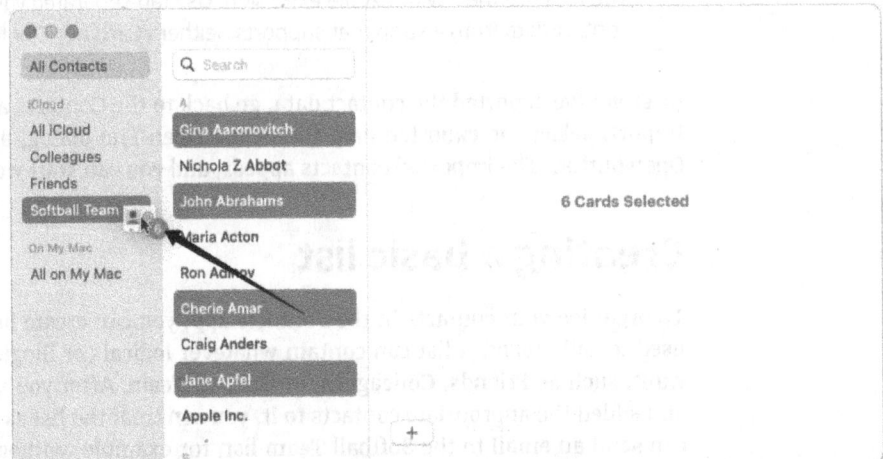

FIGURE 14-2:
Adding six contacts to the Softball Team list.

TIP

Another way to create a list is to select contacts by clicking, ⌘-clicking, or Shift-clicking them, and then choose File ➪ New List from Selection.

Setting up a smart list (based on contact criteria)

A second type of list — a smart list — might be even more useful to you because it gathers contacts in your Contacts based on criteria you specify. You might create a smart list that automatically selects contacts who have email addresses that use your company's domain name (such as surrealmacs.com).

REMEMBER

The big advantage of using a smart list instead of a regular list is that when your company hires or fires people, Contacts updates the list appropriately, with no action needed on your part.

To create a smart list, follow these steps:

1. **Choose File ➪ New Smart List or press ⌘ +Option+N.**

   The Smart List dialog opens (see Figure 14-3).

2. **Give the smart list a name.**

   This example uses Company Staff.

3. **Choose the appropriate items from the menus: Company, Contains, Email, and so on.**

   Figure 14-3 shows the criteria for a smart list that picks any contact with the company name Surreal Macs Corp. or an email address that ends with surrealmacs.com.

4. **When you're happy with the criteria specified, click OK.**

   The smart list appears in the Smart Lists section of the List pane.

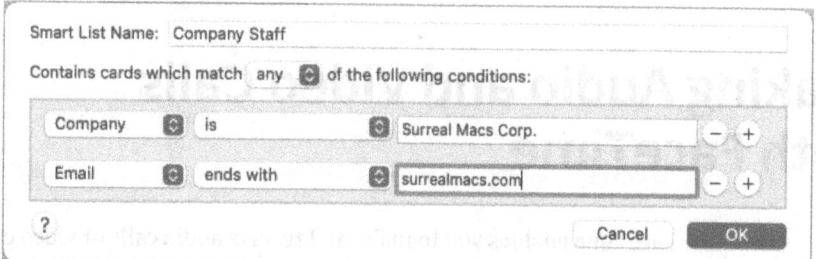

Smart List Name: Company Staff

Contains cards which match [any ◆] of the following conditions:

| Company ◆ | is | Surreal Macs Corp. | − + |
| Email ◆ | ends with | surrealmacs.com | − + |

? Cancel OK

FIGURE 14-3:
Creating a
smart list.

Deleting a list or smart list

To delete a list or a smart list from your Contacts, click to select it and then press Delete or choose Edit ⇨ Delete List.

Syncing Your Contacts Across Your Devices

To get the most out of your Mac and your other Apple devices that use the same Apple ID, you must sync your contacts — and preferably other information, such as your calendars and reminders — via iCloud or the other online service in which you store them, such as Google or Microsoft 365.

Here's how to enable cloud syncing for Contacts via iCloud:

1. **Choose System Settings ⇨ Apple ID to display the Apple ID screen in System Settings.**

2. **Click the iCloud button to display the iCloud screen.**

3. **Click the See All button to open the More Apps Using iCloud dialog.**

4. **Set the Contacts switch to On (blue).**

   While you're here, make sure that the switches are set to On (blue) for any other data you want to sync via iCloud, such as iCloud Calendars and Reminders.

5. **Click the Done button to close the More Apps Using iCloud dialog.**

6. **Choose System Settings ⇨ Quit System Settings to quit System Settings.**

TIP

To add another Internet account, such as a Google account that includes contacts, choose System Settings ⇨ Internet Accounts, and then click Add Account in the Internet Accounts pane. Follow the prompts to add the account, authenticating yourself as required. Then, on the configuration screen for the account, set the switch to On (blue) for each service you want to sync, such as Mail, Contacts, Calendars, and Notes.

Making Audio and Video Calls with FaceTime

FaceTime enables you to make and receive audio calls or video calls between Macs, iPhones, iPads, and Vision Pro headsets. You can even use Apple's SharePlay technology (discussed later in this chapter) during a FaceTime call to enjoy a movie or a game with friends or family members remotely. FaceTime works beautifully for audio calls and video calls between Macs, iPhones, iPads, and Vision Pros.

As of this writing, Apple hasn't released a version of FaceTime for Windows, let alone for other operating systems, such as Android or Linux. But you can add users of these and other operating systems to your FaceTime calls by sending them links that they open in a web browser. This approach to FaceTime is clumsy compared with the seamless implementation on Apple devices, but it does work.

Making a FaceTime call

Start by clicking the FaceTime icon on the Dock or on the Launchpad screen to launch FaceTime. The FaceTime window opens.

TIP

When you want to enjoy a FaceTime call with someone outside the Apple ecosystem, send them a FaceTime link. Click the Create Link button in the top-left corner of the FaceTime window to display the FaceTime Link pop-up panel. If the person appears as a suggestion circle near the top of the panel, marked with an icon for the type of sharing, click it. Otherwise, click the means of sharing you want to use — Copy Link (so you can paste it wherever you like), AirDrop, Mail, Messages, Notes, Freeform, or Reminders — and then complete the sharing. When you click Mail, for example, macOS starts a new message in the Mail app, embeds the FaceTime link in it, and enters the text *Join my FaceTime*. Then you address the message, type a subject line compelling enough to make the recipient open the message, and send it.

To make a FaceTime call, click the New FaceTime button. The New FaceTime dialog opens, with a field for typing the contact's name above a few suggestions. Type the contact's name or accept a suggestion, and then click the FaceTime button in the bottom-right corner to start a video call.

To make an audio FaceTime call instead of a video call, click the pop-up menu to the right of the FaceTime button and then choose FaceTime Audio from the menu. If the Call Using iPhone item also appears on this pop-up menu, you can click it to place a FaceTime call via your iPhone's cellular connection rather than via your Mac's Wi-Fi connection. Normally, you'd want to use Wi-Fi rather than burn through your cellular data allowance (unless you have an unlimited plan).

If your contact appears in the list of recent calls in the sidebar, you can click the camera icon to initiate a video call that the recipient can answer on an iPad, an iPhone, or a Mac.

When the recipient accepts the FaceTime call, you see them, they see you, and you can socialize (see Figure 14-4).

FIGURE 14-4:
A FaceTime call.

FaceTime uses Contacts, so if you have friends or family members who have a Mac or any current or recent iPhone or iPad, type the contact name in the field, select them in the resulting list, and click the FaceTime button to begin your video chat.

Using SharePlay during a FaceTime call

After establishing a FaceTime call, you can use the SharePlay feature to watch a TV show or a movie along with the other call participants, enabling each of you to hear and see the other participants' reactions to what you're watching. You can also enjoy music via the Music app.

To watch TV or a movie or to listen to a song via SharePlay, each participant must have access to the content independently, such as through a subscription to Apple TV or Apple Music. (A trial subscription is fine until it runs out.) You might wish that one participant could share their TV show or movie with everyone else, but that's not how SharePlay works. Anyone without access to the content will still be part of the FaceTime call but won't be able to see or hear the content. Instead, they'll receive prompts to get a subscription or to rent or buy the content.

To watch TV or a movie, open the TV app, and set the show or movie running. Because you're connected via FaceTime, macOS assumes that you want to use SharePlay and prompts you to confirm this desire. Click the Start SharePlay button, and you're in business. (If you click the Start Only for Me button instead, SharePlay will prompt you again next time.) The show or movie starts at the same time for each participant, and anyone can control playback by using the on-screen controls.

Sharing music via SharePlay works in a similar way. After connecting via Face-Time, open the Music app, and start playing a song to which each participant has access. The song starts at the same time for each participant, so you can all sing along. Each participant can control playback and can line up songs in the play queue.

If you want to stop SharePlay from bugging you to use it on your FaceTime calls, open FaceTime, and choose FaceTime ⇨ Settings to display the Settings dialog for FaceTime. Click the SharePlay tab, and deselect the SharePlay check box.

Chapter **15**

Communicating with Mail and Messages

I n Chapter 14, you learned to use the Contacts app to manage information about the people in your life. In this chapter, you dig into two more terrific apps — Mail and Messages — that work with Contacts to make managing your email and messages (chats) a breeze.

Sending and Receiving Email with Mail

TIP

This chapter covers a lot of material in relatively few pages, so if there's something you want to find out about Mail or Messages that it doesn't cover, try choosing Help ⇨ Mail Help or Help ⇨ Messages Help.

Mail is an app for sending, receiving, and organizing your email. Mail is fast and easy to use. Click the Mail icon (shown in the margin) on the Dock or Launchpad to launch Mail.

REMEMBER

You can use other apps to read email. The App Store has dozens of other mail readers, and most versions of Microsoft Office include the Outlook app, which handles email and more. Most email services, including Google's Gmail and Apple's iCloud, offer a web-based interface you can use in a web browser in a pinch. You can continue to use any or all of these options for your email if you like, but when you're using your Mac, Mail is likely to be your best choice.

The Mail app stores your email messages on your Mac, which means they take up disk space. The advantage of this is that you can access your messages instantly, and you can work with them when your Mac is offline. But if your Mac is short of disk space, there's an argument for using only web-based email accounts, storing all your email (and any attachments) in the cloud.

Setting up Mail

If you're launching Mail for the first time, you may need to set up your email account or accounts. If so, a set of Choose a Mail Account Provider screens appears automatically. Just follow the instructions on each screen, fill in the fields as requested, and keep clicking the Continue button until you're finished.

If you've signed into your iCloud account on this Mac, your iCloud email should be set up already. If it's not, choose System Settings ⇨ Internet Accounts to display the Internet Accounts pane in the System Settings app, click the iCloud button, and then click the Mail button. In the dialog that opens, set the Sync This Mac switch to On (blue), and then click Done.

If you've just enabled iCloud mail on this Mac for the first time, you'll also see a Mail Privacy Protection dialog the next time you launch Mail. Click the Protect Mail Activity button or the Don't Protect Mail Activity button, as appropriate, and then click Continue. Normally, you would want to click Protect Mail Activity. (To change this setting at any time, choose Mail ⇨ Settings ⇨ Privacy and select or deselect the Protect Mail Activity check box. If you deselect Protect Mail Activity, you can select or deselect the Hide IP Address check box and the Block All Remote Content check box, as needed. When the Protect Mail Activity check box is selected, Mail manages the Hide IP Address check box and the Block All Remote Content check box for you.)

TIP

If you don't know what to type in one or more of these fields, contact your Internet service provider or mail provider for assistance.

After you set up one or more email accounts, you see a Welcome message, asking whether you'd like to see what's new in Mail. If you click Yes, Help Viewer launches and shows you the What's New in Mail page; the Mail main window, which looks like Figure 15-1, appears in the background. If you click No, the Mail main window appears immediately.

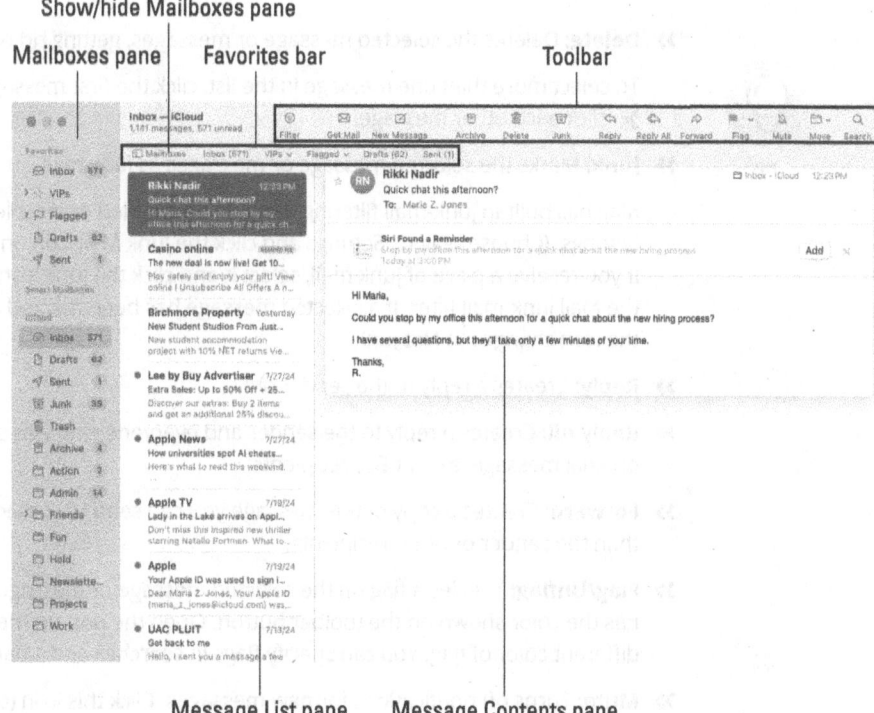

Show/hide Mailboxes pane

Mailboxes pane   Favorites bar   Toolbar

FIGURE 15-1:
The main
window in Mail.

Message List pane   Message Contents pane

TIP

The Mail main window is called a *viewer window* or *message viewer window*. You can have more than one of these windows on your screen, if you like; just choose File ⇨ New Viewer Window or press ⌘+Option+N. Using two or more viewer windows enables you to look at multiple mailboxes at the same time, which can save time over switching between mailboxes in a single viewer window.

Identifying the toolbar icons

Figure 15-1 shows the 12 icons and Search field on the viewer window's default toolbar:

>> **Filter:** Enables or disables filtering for this mailbox; click and hold down to change filtering criteria.

>> **Get Mail:** Checks for new email.

>> **New Message:** Creates a new, blank email message.

>> **Archive:** Archives the selected message or messages, putting them in a designated archive folder.

>> **Delete:** Deletes the selected message or messages, getting rid of them.

   To select more than one message in the list, click the first message; then ⌘-click each other message.

>> **Junk:** Marks the selected message or messages as junk mail.

   Mail has built-in junk-mail filtering that can be enabled or disabled in Mail Settings. (Choose Mail ➪ Settings and click the Junk Mail icon on the tab bar.) If you receive a piece of junk mail, select it and click the Junk icon to help train the Mail junk-mail filter. If a selected message has been marked as junk mail, the icon changes to Not Junk.

>> **Reply:** Creates a reply to the sender only.

>> **Reply All:** Creates a reply to the sender and everyone who was sent the original message, except Bcc recipients.

>> **Forward:** Creates a copy of this message you can send to someone other than the sender or other recipients.

>> **Flag/Unflag:** Toggles a flag on the selected message or messages. The flag has the color shown on the toolbar button. Open the pop-up menu to select a different color of flag. You can specify flags in searches and smart mailboxes.

>> **Mute:** Turns off notifications for new messages. Click this icon (or choose Message ➪ Mute, or press Control+Shift+M) to turn off notifications for new messages in the selected message thread.

>> **Move:** Moves the selected messages to the folder of your choice.

>> **Search field:** Finds a word or phrase in any item stored in Mail. When you begin typing, a pop-up menu appears so you can narrow the search to people or subjects matching your search phrase. You can click the buttons on the Favorites bar to limit the search to a specific mailbox.

If you don't see the Favorites bar, choose View ➪ Show Favorites Bar or press ⌘+Option+Shift+H. If you don't see the text labels on the toolbar buttons, Control-click or right-click the toolbar, and then click Icon and Text on the contextual menu.

The numbers next to the mailbox buttons on the Favorites bar or Mailbox pane indicate the number of unread messages in that mailbox. Mail marks a message as read after you display it for a second or two. You can also mark a message as read by Control-clicking or right-clicking it, and then clicking Mark As Read on the contextual menu.

Searching in Mail works the same way as searching in Finder. So, for example, if you want to save a search as a smart mailbox (Mail's version of Finder's smart folder), click the + icon below the search field to add criteria.

Mail populates the Favorites bar with mailboxes it expects you to use often: Inbox, VIPs, Flagged, Send Later, Drafts, and Sent. You can add your own favorite mailboxes by dragging them from the Mailbox pane to the Favorites bar or the Favorites section of the Mailbox pane.

Composing a new message

Here's how to create an email message:

1. **Click the New Message icon on the toolbar, choose File ⇨ New Message, or press ⌘ +N.**

A new message window appears for you to compose your email message, as shown in Figure 15-2.

Don't worry if your new message doesn't have a pop-up Signature menu like the one in Figure 15-2. That menu is displayed only after you've created at least one signature, as described later in this chapter.

2. **Click in the To field, and type someone's email address.**

If you're just practicing or testing Mail, you could use your own address.

TIP

If the recipient is in your Contacts, type the first few letters, and Mail displays a list of matches from your Contacts list. Click the contact you want; or use the arrow keys to select it, and then press Return.

3. **Press the Tab key twice, and type a subject for this message in the Subject text field.**

4. **Click in the main message portion of the window, and type your message there.**

TIP

If you don't finish writing the message now, or if you finish it but want to read it again later before sending it (often wise!), save the message as a draft rather than leaving it open. Click Close (the red gumdrop button) in the top-left corner of the message window, choose File ⇨ Close, or press ⌘ +W. When the Save This Message as a Draft? dialog appears, click Save; Mail saves the message as a draft in the Drafts folder. You can resume work on the message by opening the Drafts mailbox and then double-clicking the message to open it in a window. When the message is finished, click the Send button to send it.

5. **When you're finished writing your message, click the Send button if you want to send the email immediately.**

If you realize that you shouldn't have sent the message, click the Undo Send button in the bottom-left corner of the Mail window immediately (see Figure 15-3). This button disappears after 10 seconds, so you need to act quickly. When you click the button, the message opens in its own window so that you can continue editing it and fix whatever problem you discovered.

If 10 seconds isn't long enough for you to undo sending, you can increase the delay to 20 seconds or 30 seconds. Choose Mail ⇨ Settings ⇨ Composing to display the Composing pane in Mail Settings, open the Undo Send Delay pop-up menu, and choose the setting you want. (You can also choose Off to disable Undo Send.)

If you want to send the message later, click the Send pop-up menu. Then you can choose a scheduled sending time, such as Send 8:00 AM or Send 9:00 PM Tonight, or click Send Later to open the Send Later dialog (see Figure 15-4). In the Send Later dialog, select the date, specify the time, and then click the Schedule button. Mail closes the message (confusingly, it plays the Send sound, such as whooshing, immediately), lines up the message for later sending, and sends it at the date and time you specified. Mail places the message in the Send Later mailbox. You can open it and edit it if necessary (click the Edit button).

When setting the scheduled sending time in the Send Later dialog, you need to change AM to PM, or vice versa, before setting the hours and minutes if the time will otherwise be in the past. For example, if it's 10:00 AM, and you want to schedule the message for sending at 4:00 PM, you need to change AM to PM before you can change 10 to 4.

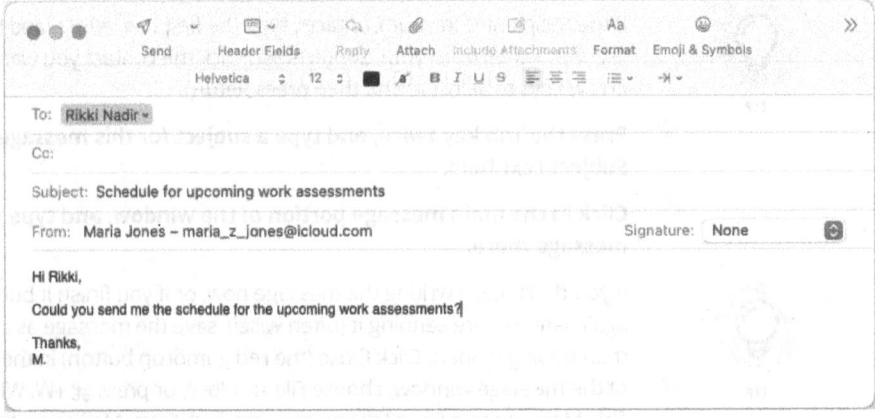

FIGURE 15-2:
Composing an email message.

FIGURE 15-3:
Made a dreadful mistake? Click the Undo Send button this instant.

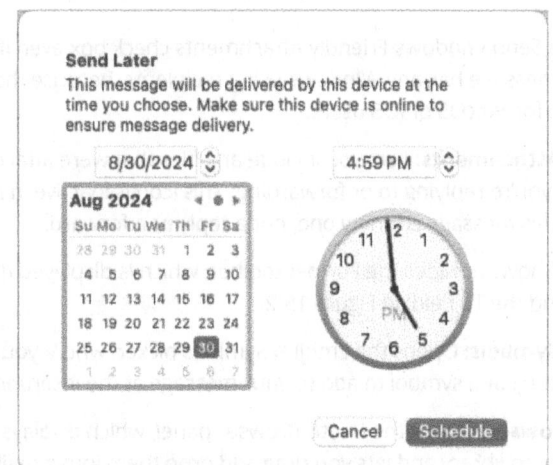

FIGURE 15-4:
Use the Send Later dialog to schedule a message to go in the mail later rather than right this moment.

Here's what you need to know about the icons on the toolbar in Figure 15-2:

>> **Send:** Sends the message right now. Click the pop-up menu to send the message later, as just explained.

>> **Header Fields:** Lets you select which header fields — Cc Address Field, Bcc Address Field, Reply-To Address Field, and Priority Field — you want to see in the message window. The Cc Address field appears by default, because many messages need Cc recipients. Fewer messages need Bcc (blind carbon copy, from the days of typewriters, when people used carbon paper to make copies), but you can add the Bcc Address Field when you need it.

TIP

Use the Reply-To Address field when you want any reply from the sender to go to a different address (which you specify in this field) rather than to the address you're using to send the message.

WARNING

Using the Priority Field to mark a message as High Priority (symbolized by two exclamation marks, !!), Normal Priority (one exclamation mark, !), or Low Priority (no exclamation marks) may seem to be helpful — but spammers have abused Priority so severely that few people pay attention to it anymore.

>> **Reply:** Lets you reply to the sender directly from the message window. This icon is inactive in Figure 15-2 because this message is brand-new, so there's no sender to reply to.

>> **Attach:** Displays a standard Open File dialog so you can choose a file or files to attach to this message. To attach multiple files, click the first; then ⌘+click each of the others.

If the recipients of this message use Windows, you probably want to click the Show Options button and select the Send Windows-Friendly Attachments check box, which appears near the bottom of the Open File dialog.

Select the Send Windows-Friendly Attachments check box even if you're not sure the message has any Windows-using recipients, because there's no downside for macOS or iOS users.

>> **Include Attachments:** Lets you include any files that were attached to the message you're replying to or forwarding. This icon is inactive in Figure 15-2 because this message is a new one, not a reply or a forward.

>> **Format:** Shows or hides the Format toolbar, which is displayed (between the toolbar and the To field) in Figure 15-2.

>> **Emoji & Symbols:** Opens the Emoji & Symbols picker, where you can double-click an emoji or a symbol to add to your message at the insertion point.

>> **Photo Browser:** Opens the Photo Browser panel, which displays the images in your photo library and lets you drag and drop them into a mail message.

Proofing and rewriting a message with Writing Tools

Alongside iOS 18 and iPadOS 18, macOS Sequoia introduces Apple's Writing Tools, a suite of powerful features designed to help you produce clear, convincing, and grammatically correct text using Apple Intelligence. Writing Tools work in a wide range of apps that let you create text, including the Mail app, the Messages app, and the Notes app.

In this section, we'll look at how you can use the Proofing feature and the Rewrite feature to improve the contents of an outgoing message before sending it. The sample message has various problems with punctuation, phrasing, presentation, and tone, as you can see in Figure 15-5.

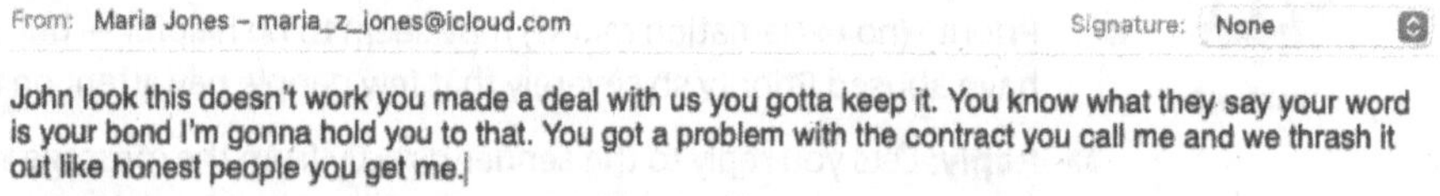

FIGURE 15-5:
A sample message ready for Writing Tools to work its magic.

From: Maria Jones – maria_z_jones@icloud.com   Signature: None

John look this doesn't work you made a deal with us you gotta keep it. You know what they say your word is your bond I'm gonna hold you to that. You got a problem with the contract you call me and we thrash it out like honest people you get me.

Select the text you want to work with (in this case, the entire message), and then open Writing Tools. You can access Writing Tools either from the menu bar (choose Edit ⇨ Writing Tools) or by Control-clicking or right-clicking in the section and then opening the Writing Tools continuation menu on the contextual menu (see Figure 15-6).

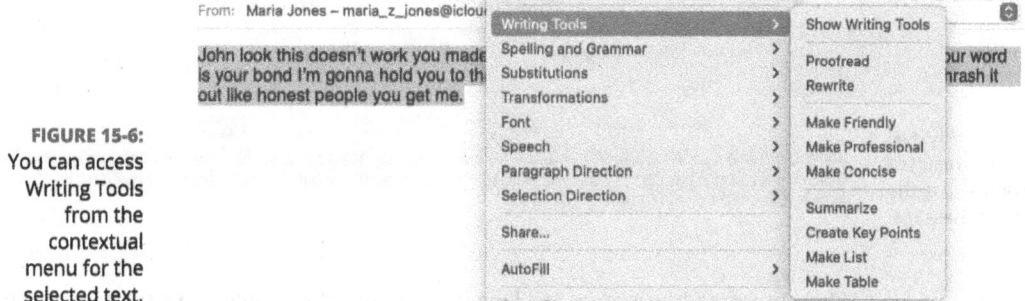

From: Maria Jones – maria_z_jones@iclou[...]

John look this doesn't work you made [...]ur word
is your bond I'm gonna hold you to th[...] [...]hrash it
out like honest people you get me.

Writing Tools	>		Show Writing Tools
Spelling and Grammar	>		Proofread
Substitutions	>		Rewrite
Transformations	>		
Font	>		Make Friendly
Speech	>		Make Professional
Paragraph Direction	>		Make Concise
Selection Direction	>		
			Summarize
Share...			Create Key Points
			Make List
AutoFill	>		Make Table

FIGURE 15-6:
You can access
Writing Tools
from the
contextual
menu for the
selected text.

You can click the Show Writing Tools item on the Writing Tools continuation
menu to open the Writing Tools pane (see Figure 15-7), which is handy when you
need to make multiple changes or play with different approaches.

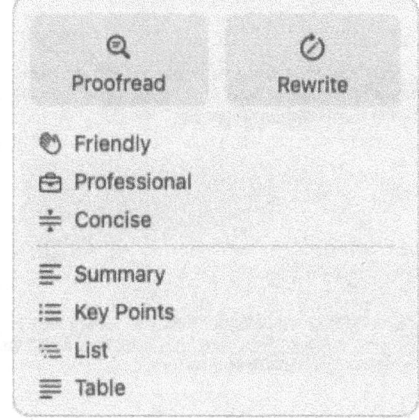

| Proofread | Rewrite |

👋 Friendly
💼 Professional
÷ Concise

⟟ Summary
⟟ Key Points
⟟ List
⟟ Table

FIGURE 15-7:
Open the Writing
Tools pane when
you need to make
multiple changes.

If you just want to proofread the text, give the Proofread command from either the
Writing Tools continuation menu or the Writing Tools pane. Figure 15-8 shows
the result of proofreading the sample message: The punctuation is fixed, but the
other problems remain.

You can click the Show Original button to display the original text; click again to
display the changes. Work your way through the changes by clicking the Next
Change button and Previous Change button, and click one of the Provide Feedback
buttons to give your thumbs-up or thumbs-down on the changes as a whole. Click
Done when you finish — or, if you don't want to keep the changes, click the
Revert button.

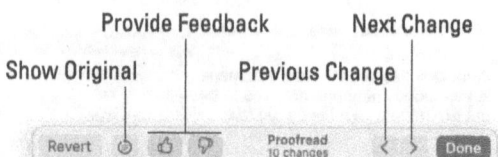

FIGURE 15-8:
The result of
proofreading the
sample message.

When proofreading proves inadequate to fixing the problems in the text, try the Rewrite feature. Click the Rewrite button on the Writing Tools panel or on the Writing Tools continuation menu, or click one of the three rewriting options — Friendly, Professional, or Concise — to request a particular approach. Figure 15-9 shows the effect of Rewrite on the sample message, while Figure 15-10 shows the Professional rewrite.

FIGURE 15-9:
The result of a
straight Rewrite
operation on the
sample message.

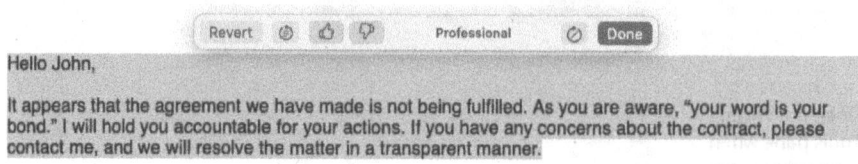

FIGURE 15-10:
A Professional
rewrite of the
message retains
its message
clearly but
changes the tone
completely.

Once you've reworked the message to your satisfaction, send it as usual.

Sending email from the Contacts app

If you're working in the Contacts app, you can quickly start an email message to a contact. With the contact record displayed, click the field label next to the email address you want to use (such as the Work label) and then choose Send Email from the pop-up menu that appears. Or move the pointer over an email address and then click the envelope icon that appears to the right of its name.

The Mail app becomes active, and a blank email message addressed to the selected contact appears on your screen. Type your email as you normally would.

The pop-up menu next to email addresses lets you do the following:

>> Send an email.

>> Send a message (see the "Communicating with Messages" section later in this chapter).

>> Send your vCard (see the following Tip) to this email address.

>> Search for this email address in documents on your Mac by using Spotlight (see Chapter 9).

TIP

You can send a contact's information to other people in an industry-standard file format known as a *vCard* (virtual business card). Choosing Send My Card works the same as Send Email, but instead of starting with a blank email message, Mail creates a message with your vCard attached. When the recipient opens the vCard file, all your contact information is added to their default contacts app in macOS or Windows.

Checking your mail

To check your mail, click the Get Mail icon on the toolbar of the main Mail window (look back to Figure 15-1), choose Mailbox ➪ Get New Mail, or press ⌘+Shift+N. The messages appear in the Message List pane, which shows a brief preview of the message.

NEW

Instead of displaying the first however-many words of the message as the preview, Mail can display previews that summarize the message content. Mail uses Apple Intelligence's Summarize feature to create these summaries. These summary previews can help you triage your messages more quickly and stay on top of your email. To switch between regular previews and summary previews, choose Mail ➪ Settings, click the Viewing tab, and then select or deselect the Summarize Message Previews check box.

>> **Read a new message.** Select it. Its contents appear in the Message Content pane.

>> **Delete a selected message.** Click the Delete icon on the toolbar or press Delete (or Backspace) on your keyboard.

You can delete a message in one other way if you have a trackpad. Swipe with two fingers from right to left on the message in the Message List until the Trash icon appears. Now you can either click the Trash icon or continue your swipe farther to the left until the Delete button takes up the full width of the Message List. Either way, the message disappears into Mail's Trash folder.

>> **Retrieve a message you accidentally deleted.** Click Trash in the Mailboxes pane, and then drag the message to the Inbox or another mailbox. If the mailbox you want is out of sight, Control-click or right-click the message to display the contextual menu, click or highlight Move To, navigate to the right mailbox on the submenus, and then click it. Mail moves the message there.

TIP

>> **Configure Mail to send and check for your messages every *x* minutes.** Choose Mail ⇨ Settings and click the General icon at the top of the Settings window. Click the Check for New Messages pop-up menu, and make a choice: Automatically; Every Minute, Every 5 Minutes, Every 15 Minutes, Every 30 Minutes, or Every Hour; or Manually. The default is to check for new messages automatically, which means every few minutes. If you don't want Mail to do that, choose Manually. You can configure your Focus settings to suppress new mail notifications, so you don't have to switch off checking for Mail to prevent the lure of new messages from interrupting a focus. (See Chapter 10 for more information on the Focus feature.)

>> **Add a sender to Contacts.** When someone who isn't already in your Contacts sends you an email message, simply choose Message ⇨ Add Sender to Contacts.

Adding a sender to your Contacts has an additional benefit: It prevents future messages from that sender from being mistaken for junk mail. If a sender appears in your Contacts, their messages will never be mistakenly marked as junk mail. In other words, your Contacts is a whitelist for the spam filter. See the following section to find out how to deal with spam.

TIP

When you receive an email containing details for an event, such as a flight or a dinner reservation, or even an invitation that says something like "Let's have brunch at 10:30 on Saturday," a smart suggestion appears between the message's header and body. Click it to add the event to Calendar.

>> **Receive a reminder to deal with a message.** Control-click or right-click the message in the Message List pane, click or highlight Remind Me on the contextual menu, and then click your choice on the Remind Me submenu, such as Remind Me in 1 Hour or Remind Me Tomorrow. To set a specific date and time for the reminder, click Remind Me Later, choose the date and time in the Remind Me dialog, and then click the Schedule button.

Dealing with spam

SPAM® is a classic lunch meat popular enough in Hawaii to be called "Hawaiian Steak," but in email, spam — junk mail — is a worldwide menace. Spammers take advantage of email's minimal costs to blast out millions of unwanted messages. Before you know it, your email Inbox is flooded with get-rich-quick schemes, advertisements for pornographic websites and chat rooms, pills and powders that claim to perform miracles, and plenty of the more traditional buy-this-now junk mail.

WARNING

Avoid opening spam messages if you can. Many of them contain trackers that tell the spammer that the message has been opened, proving that email address is valid. Spammers trade and sell their lists to each other. Valid addresses are worth more than addresses whose validity is not known.

Fortunately, Mail comes with a powerful junk-mail filter that analyzes incoming message subjects, senders, and contents to determine which ones are likely to contain bulk or junk mail. Start by choosing Mail ⇨ Settings and clicking the Junk Mail tab (see Figure 15-11). Make sure that the Enable Junk Mail Filtering check box is selected, and select the Mark As Junk Mail, But Leave It in My Inbox radio button.

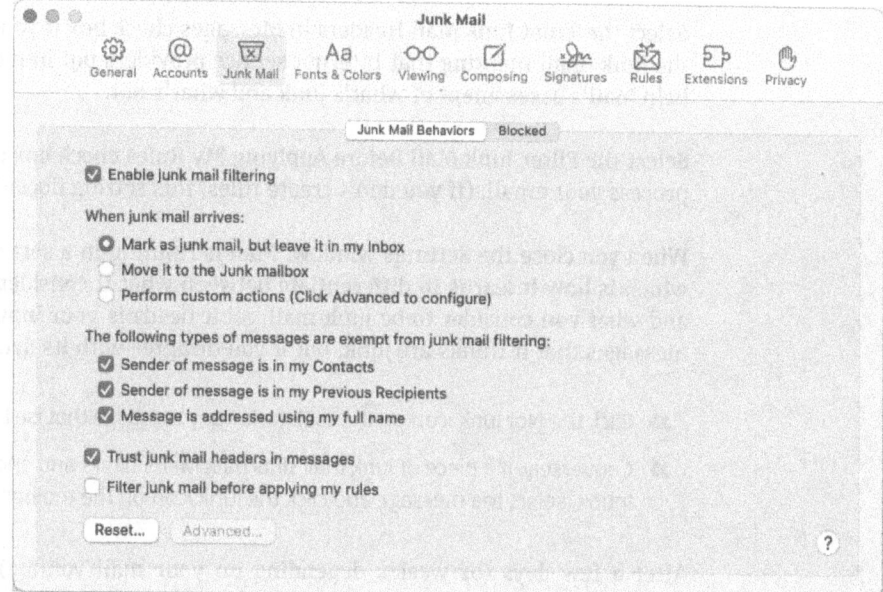

FIGURE 15-11: Configure junk-mail filtering on the Junk Mail tab of the Settings window for Mail.

In the section titled The Following Types of Messages Are Exempt from Junk Mail Filtering, select or deselect the following three check boxes, as needed:

>> **Sender of Message Is in My Contacts:** If you've added the sender to your Contacts list, Mail won't treat their messages as junk mail. Normally, you'll want to keep this check box selected.

>> **Sender of Message Is in My Previous Recipients:** Your previous recipients are the addresses to which you've sent email. So selecting this check box says

TIP

that if the sender of an incoming message is someone to whom you've sent email, that incoming message isn't junk.

To see your list of previous recipients, choose Window ⇨ Previous Recipients. Mail opens the Previous Recipients window, which shows the name, email address, and last-used date for each recipient. Click a column heading to sort the list by that heading. You can browse the list or search by terms you type to locate entries of interest. Click the Remove From List button to remove the selected entry, or click Add to Contacts to create a new contact record from the selected entry.

» **Message Is Addressed Using My Full Name:** Spammers often use email addresses without associated full names (usually because they don't have the full names). Selecting this check box says that if a message includes your full name, it's not spam. This test is less convincing than the previous two, so you may want to deselect this check box.

Select the Trust Junk Mail Headers in Messages check box if you want Mail to use the junk-mail marking that Internet service providers put in message headers to help Mail's assessment of what's junk and what's not.

Select the Filter Junk Mail Before Applying My Rules check box if you use rules to process your email. (If you don't create rules, this setting doesn't apply.)

When you close the Settings window, Mail is running in a sort of training mode, which is how it learns to differentiate between what it considers to be junk mail and what you consider to be junk mail; all it needs is your input. Mail identifies messages that it thinks are junk, but if you disagree with its decisions, do this:

» Click the Not Junk icon on the toolbar for any message that isn't junk mail.

» Conversely, if a piece of junk mail slips past Mail's filters and ends up in the Inbox, select the message and click the Junk icon on the toolbar.

After a few days (or weeks, depending on your mail volume), Mail should be getting it right almost all the time. When you reach that point, choose Mail ⇨ Settings ⇨ Junk Mail again, but this time, select the Move It to the Junk Mailbox radio button. Now Mail starts automatically moving junk mail out of your Inbox and into the Junk mailbox, where you can scan the items quickly and trash them when you're ready.

If you prefer to use your email provider or third-party spam filters, you can turn off junk-mail processing in Mail by deselecting the Enable Junk Mail Filtering check box on the Junk Mail tab of the Settings dialog. Or you can use both.

Managing your mailboxes

After reading mail, you can either delete it or file it in a mailbox. The following sections take a closer look at the two types of mailboxes you have at your disposal: plain and smart.

Plain mailboxes

Plain mailboxes are like — and look like — folders in Finder; you create them and name them, and they're empty until you put something in them. You use mailboxes to organize any messages you want to save.

Here are three ways to create a plain mailbox:

>> Choose Mailbox ⇨ New Mailbox.

>> Hold the pointer over the mailbox name (such as iCloud or Gmail) in the mailbox pane, and then click the + that appears to the right of the name.

>> Control-click or right-click the Mailboxes sidebar, and then choose New Mailbox from the contextual menu.

Whichever way you choose, the New Mailbox dialog opens. Open the Location pop-up menu, and choose the location: On My Mac to store your filed messages locally on your Mac's drive, or iCloud (or another email provider) to store filed messages remotely on the mail server.

TIP

Choosing iCloud or your email provider means that messages you move to that mailbox will be stored remotely. If you access your email from more than one device, create all your mailboxes on the email server so that they'll be available to you no matter where you are or what device you're using to check your mail.

Type the name for the mailbox in the Name box; then click OK. Mail creates the mailbox, and it appears in the Mailboxes sidebar.

If you Control-click or right-click a mailbox and choose New Mailbox from the contextual menu, the Location menu in the resulting sheet will show the name of the mailbox you clicked, enabling you to create a submailbox of the mailbox you clicked. You can create a whole hierarchy of mailboxes, if you like.

You can also drag and drop a mailbox from the top level of the list into another mailbox to turn that mailbox into a submailbox.

To delete a mailbox (and its submailboxes, if it has any), do one of the following:

» Click it to select it, and then choose Mailbox ⇨ Delete Mailbox.

» Control-click or right-click the mailbox, and then choose Delete Mailbox from the contextual menu.

Smart mailboxes

A *smart mailbox* is a mailbox that displays the result of a search, just like a smart folder in Finder displays the result of a search. The messages you see in a smart mailbox are *virtual* — they are stored in other mailboxes rather than in the smart mailbox itself, but they meet the smart mailbox's search criteria. Like smart folders in Finder, smart mailboxes are updated automatically when new messages that meet the criteria are received.

TIP

Smart mailboxes don't take up any additional disk space, so they're a great way to organize mail, automatically making it easier to find a message with no effort on your part (after you set them up).

To create a smart mailbox, do one of the following:

» Choose Mailbox ⇨ New Smart Mailbox.

» Hold the pointer over the Smart Mailboxes header in the Mailboxes pane, and then click the +-in-a-circle that appears to the right of the header.

Whichever method you choose, Mail displays the New Smart Mailbox dialog, which has a field for the smart mailbox's name, plus some pop-up menus, buttons, and check boxes, as shown in Figure 15-12. This smart mailbox gathers messages with the words *relocation* in either the body or subject.

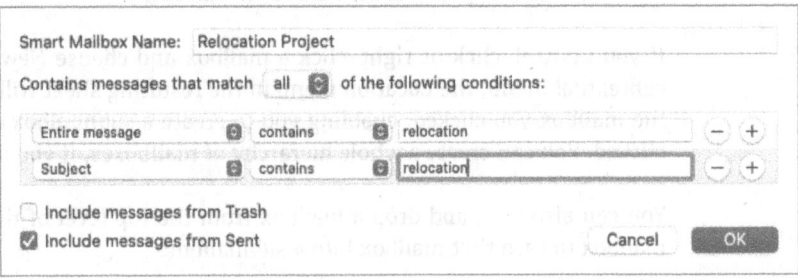

FIGURE 15-12:
Set criteria for a
smart mailbox.

Smart Mailbox Name: Relocation Project

Contains messages that match all ⬦ of the following conditions:

| Entire message ⬦ | contains ⬦ | relocation | — + |
| Subject ⬦ | contains ⬦ | relocation | — + |

☐ Include messages from Trash
☑ Include messages from Sent   Cancel   OK

Name your smart mailbox, specify its criteria by using the controls, and then click OK. The smart mailbox appears in the Smart Mailboxes section of the Mailboxes pane with a little gear icon to denote that it's smart.

TIP

When you select a mailbox or multiple mailboxes (plain, smart, or both) in the Mailboxes pane, you'll see how many mailboxes are currently selected, along with how many messages they contain, displayed above the message list.

Changing settings for Mail

Mail's Settings window (choose Mail ⇨ Settings or press ⌘ +,) is the control center for Mail, where you can do the following:

>> **Create and delete email accounts.** Visit the Accounts pane.

>> **Set the fonts and colors used for your messages.** These settings are in the Fonts & Colors pane.

>> **Turn on the Mail Privacy Protection feature.** In the Privacy pane, select the Protect Mail Activity check box. Mail Privacy Protection hides your Mac's Internet Protocol address to prevent spammers from tracking your actions by including remote images in their messages.

>> **Decide whether to send formatted mail or plain text.** Go to the Composing pane.

>> **Decide whether to turn on the spell checker.** The default setting is to check spelling as you type, which many people find annoying. This setting, too, is in the Composing pane.

>> **Decide whether to have an automatic signature appended to your messages.** Use the Signature pane, as described in the next section.

>> **Establish rules to process mail that you receive.** Visit the Rules pane (see the subsection "Ruling over your mail," later in this chapter).

The first five items are up to you to decide. The last two are the most important features of the Settings window — namely, automatically adding your signatures to outgoing messages and creating inbound-mail processing rules.

Signing your messages the smart way

Would you rather not type your entire signature every time you send an email message? Yes? That's the right answer, because you don't have to with Mail. Instead, you can create as many canned signatures as you need and then insert them into outgoing messages without typing a single character.

Here's how it works:

1. Choose Mail ⇨ Settings or press ⌘ +, (comma) to open the Settings window.

2. Click the Signatures tab to display the Signatures pane (shown in Figure 15-13).

3. In the left column, click the account for which you want to create this signature.

4. To create a new, blank signature, click the + sign below the middle column.

5. Type a descriptive name for this signature to replace the default name, such as Signature #1.

6. In the right column, type the signature exactly as you want it to appear in outgoing messages.

7. (Optional) Drag a scanned image of your signature to the appropriate place in your document.

   You can also Control-click or right-click the signature box and then insert a photo or a sketch from your iPhone or iPad by choosing the appropriate command from the contextual menu.

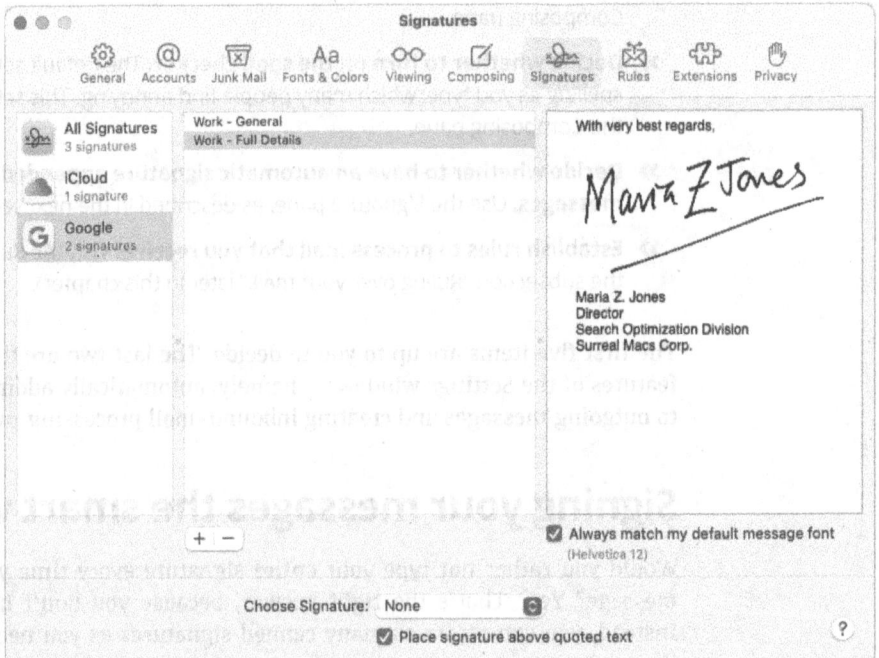

FIGURE 15-13:
You can include an image in a custom signature.

If you have more than one signature, you can select the one you want to use as the default: Select the account in the column on the left and then choose the signature from the Choose Signature pop-up menu at the bottom.

TIP

When you add your first signature, the Signature pop-up menu appears in new messages and replies, so you can choose a different signature (or no signature) in seconds.

Ruling over your mail

To really harness the power of Mail, set rules to process your messages automatically. With rules, you can automatically tag messages with a color; file them in a specific mailbox; reply to, forward, or redirect the messages automatically (handy when you're going away); or delete messages without even looking at them.

Rules are a huge topic that you'll likely want to explore in depth. This section shows you how to create a rule by specifying two conditions and the action for Mail to take when that condition is met. This example creates a rule called Mail from Boss Alert that plays an alert sound when Mail receives an incoming message from either of two specified email addresses. Figure 15-14 shows how the rule looks.

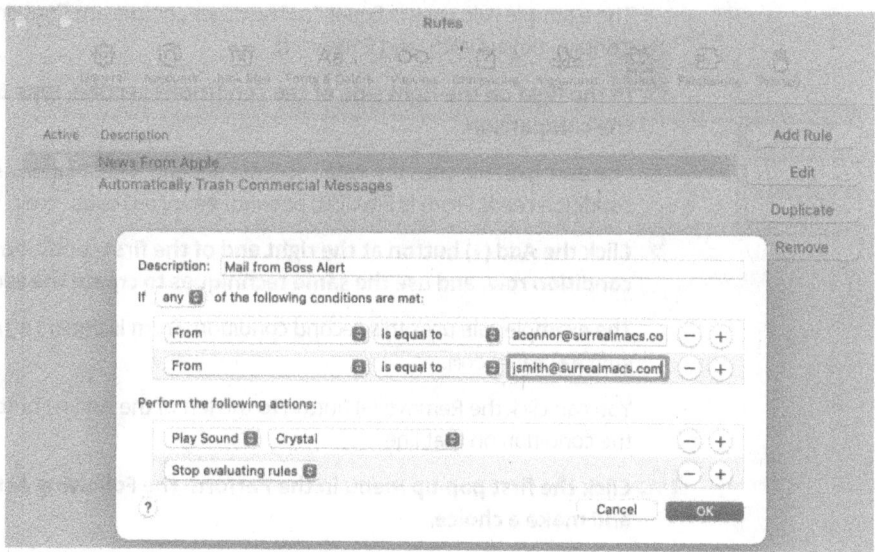

FIGURE 15-14:
Creating a rule to process email automatically.

Here are the steps:

1. **Choose Mail ➪ Settings or press ⌘ +, (comma) to open the Settings window.**

2. **Click the Rules tab to display the Rules pane.**

3. **Click the Add Rule button to open the Add Rule dialog.**

4. **In the Description field, type a description — in the example, Mail from Boss Alert.**

5. **Click the first pop-up menu (which is set to Any in Figure 15-14) to determine when to apply this rule.**

   The options are Any and All. Choose Any to make the rule run when either (of two) or any (of more than two) of the conditions is true. Choose All to make the rule run only when each condition is met. (If your rule has only one condition, choose either Any or All — it won't make any difference.)

6. **Click the first pop-up menu in the conditions section, and start defining the condition.**

   The example rule uses From, but you have a couple dozen other options: Date Sent, Date Received, Sender Is in My Contacts, Sender Is VIP, and so on.

7. **Click the second pop-up menu in the conditions section, and make a choice.**

   The example rule uses Is Equal To. The other choices are Contains, Does Not Contain, Begins With, and Ends With.

8. **In the field on the right side of the conditions section, type the text for the comparison.**

   The example rule uses the email address aconnor@surrealmacs.com, so the condition reads From Is Equal To aconnor@surrealmacs.com.

9. **Click the Add (+) button at the right end of the first condition to add a condition row, and use the same techniques to create the second condition.**

   The example rule uses this second condition: From Is Equal To jsmith@ surrealmacs.com.

   You can click the Remove (–) button to the left of the Add (+) button to remove the condition on that line.

10. **Click the first pop-up menu in the Perform the Following Actions section, and make a choice.**

    The example rule uses Play Sound. Your other choices include Move Message, Copy Message, Reply to Message, and Delete Message.

11. **Click the second pop-up menu in the actions section, and make a choice.**

    In the example, you select the sound to play: Crystal.

12. Click the Add (+) button at the right end of the first line in the actions section to add an action row.

13. Click the first pop-up menu on the new action row, and choose Stop Evaluating Rules.

Choosing this item makes the remaining controls on the row disappear, so you have no further choices to make.

If you use complex rules, the Stop Evaluating Rules action prevents another action (which you perhaps hadn't anticipated) from taking place.

14. Click OK.

Mail asks whether you want to apply your rule(s) to the selected mailboxes.

15. Choose Apply if you want Mail to run this rule on the selected mailboxes, or choose Don't Apply if you don't.

From this point forward, every time you get a message from either of the two email addresses specified in the rule, the Crystal sound alerts you.

Run a slide show from Quick Look

Like Finder, Mail has a Quick Look feature that can segue into a slide show. When you receive a message with multiple photos attached, move the pointer over the line between the message header and the message body. Click the paper-clip icon that appears, and then click Quick Look on the pop-up menu. Alternatively, click a photo in the message body, and then press the spacebar.

Click the Full Screen icon (the two arrows pointing apart) in the top-left corner of the Quick Look window to switch to full-screen. Then you can click the Play button on the floating control bar to play a slide show of the photos. When you finish viewing, click Exit Full Screen on the floating control bar to display the Quick Look window again.

To close the Quick Look window, click the X in its top-left corner or press the spacebar.

Marking up an image or PDF document

Markup lets you annotate images or PDF documents. When you're composing a message that has an image or a PDF you've attached or dragged in, hold the pointer over the picture, and a little chevron (v) appears in its top-right corner. Click it to use the Markup tools on this image.

See Chapter 5 for details on using Markup.

Transferring large files via Mail Drop

Mail Drop is an elegant solution for large email attachments. If you attach files to a message, and Mail thinks the files may be too big to send via email, it displays the Would You Like to Send This Attachment Using Mail Drop? dialog (see Figure 15-15).

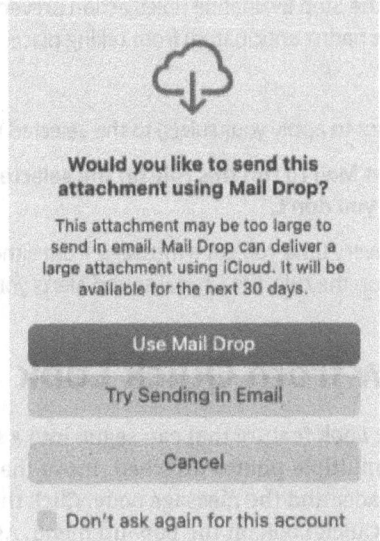

Would you like to send this attachment using Mail Drop?

This attachment may be too large to send in email. Mail Drop can deliver a large attachment using iCloud. It will be available for the next 30 days.

Use Mail Drop

Try Sending in Email

Cancel

☐ Don't ask again for this account

When this dialog appears, select the Don't Ask Again for This Account check box and then click the Use Mail Drop button. Mail uploads the file to a secure location on iCloud and sends the email recipient a link to download it. The file is available for 30 days, which should give the recipient ample time to download it.

If you click the Try Sending in Email button instead, the message might get through, but there's a good chance that a mail server along the way will bounce it back to you. Mail Drop prevents this awkwardness and lightens the load on the mail servers. Mail Drop has a file size limit of 5GB.

TIP

You can turn Mail Drop on or off manually. Choose Mail ➪ Settings ➪ Accounts to display the Accounts pane of the Settings window. Then click the account in the sidebar, click the Account Information tab, and select or deselect the Send Large Attachments with Mail Drop check box.

Unsubscribing, muting, and blocking senders

When you receive an unwanted email from a mailing list, click the Unsubscribe button (between the header and the body of the message) to unsubscribe. Couldn't be easier — at least, if the list honors unsubscribe requests, which some lists don't.

When you need to mute an email conversation, turning off notifications for new messages in the thread, select the conversation, and then click the Mute button on the toolbar, choose Message ⇨ Mute, or press Control+Shift+M.

To block a sender, Control-click or right-click their name, and then click Block Contact on the contextual menu. You'll see This Message Is from a Blocked Sender, along with a Settings button. Click the button to specify how you want your blocked mail to be handled: either marked as blocked but left in your Inbox, or moved directly to the Trash.

To unblock a sender you've blocked, choose Mail ⇨ Settings, click Junk Mail, and then click the Blocked tab. In the Enter Email Addresses to Block in the List Below box, click the blocked sender, and then click Remove (–) below the box.

Communicating with Messages

Instant messaging (IM) enables interactive communication among users all over the world. Messages gives you immediate access to all the other users of Apple's iMessage system. All you need are their screen names or email addresses, and you're set to go.

To get started, launch Messages from the Dock or from Launchpad.

What can you do with iMessage?

iMessage is Apple's inter-device messaging protocol. iMessage enables you to send unlimited messages to anyone who uses an iPhone, an iPad, or a Mac.

NEW

Cellular phone instant messaging uses three main protocols. SMS (Short Message Service) sends plain text messages, usually with a maximum length of 160 characters. These are the "text messages" that many cellphone plans include. MMS (Multimedia Messaging Service) sends text messages with attached files, such as photos, emoji, or videos; most carriers charge you extra for these messages. iOS has long supported SMS and MMS, but iOS 18 adds support for Rich Communication Services (RCS), which enhances SMS with features such as read receipts, typing indicators (you see that your contact is typing), and improved photo and video sharing.

Apple's proprietary iMessage is like MMS or RCS, but you can send and receive messages from your Mac via its network connection. An iMessage can include photos, audio recordings, videos, locations, and contacts in addition to text. If you have more than one Apple device or Mac, iMessage keeps all your conversations going across all of them. iMessage gives you delivery receipts, letting you know that your messages arrived. If the recipient has enabled read receipts, you'll get a read receipt, too.

Apple's Continuity feature in macOS and iOS allows all SMS, MMS, and RCS messages you send and receive on your iPhone via your wireless carrier's messaging system to appear in the Messages app on your Mac and iPad almost simultaneously — even if the person you're messaging doesn't have an iPhone. Better yet, you can reply from whichever device is closest to you, regardless of what kind of cellphone the person has.

For this to happen, all devices need to be using the same Apple Account for Messages, and the Enable Messages in iCloud feature must be turned on. On your Mac, choose Messages ⇨ Settings, click the iMessage tab, and then select the Enable Messages in iCloud check box.

TIP

While on the iMessage tab in Messages Settings, select or deselect the Send Read Receipts check box to control whether Messages sends read receipts. You can choose a different Send Read Receipts setting later for individual contacts.

TIP

Another way to start a new iMessage is to click a phone number in Safari, Contacts, or Calendar.

Chatting with Messages

Your chats can be one to one, or they can be group bull sessions. Messages is integrated with Contacts, so you don't have to enter your buddies' information twice.

Here's all the essential info you need to get started:

>> **Start a text chat.** Open Messages, click the New Message icon above the Search field (shown in the margin), and then begin typing a contact's name in the To field or click the little +-in-a-circle to see a list of contacts with its own search field.

If you've already chatted with someone, click their name in the list on the left to send a new message, or use the Search field to find your chat with that person.

After you've chosen a recipient, type your text in the iMessage field at the bottom of the window, and press Return or Enter to send it. Figure 15-16 shows a text chat. Below the message box, you see two suggested responses — "Sounds great!" and "Sorry, other plans on Sunday" — courtesy of Apple Intelligence. If you want to use one of these responses, tap it.

In a chat, each participant's text appears in a different color and orientation. Your words appear in blue bubbles with white text on the right, whereas the other person's words appear in gray bubbles with black text on the left. This is true only when both the sender and recipient are using Macs, iPhones, or iPads.

>> **Start a group text chat.** Click the New Message icon, and add each person you want to include as described above.

When you finish adding names to the To field, type and send your message as just described; everyone in the To field will receive it. From then on, everyone will see every message from every participant.

TIP

Click the *i*-in-a-circle at the top right to open the Info window for this conversation (see Figure 15-17). Now you can use your iPhone (if it's nearby) to call someone by tapping the Call icon below their name. Or select the Hide Alerts check box to mute notifications for this conversation only, which is great if one or more participants is a serial texter. Other options in the Info window let you share your location or your Mac's screen, send an email, or start a FaceTime video call.

>> **Attach a picture to a person in your Contacts.** Copy a picture of the person to the Clipboard in your favorite graphics app (Preview, for example). Now open Contacts, and display the card for the person for whom you want to add a picture. Click the empty picture box at the top of the card, and paste the picture from the Clipboard. Now you should see that picture on the Contacts card and also when you chat in Messages with the person.

TIP

If you've already attached a picture to a contact in Contacts, that picture will appear automatically when you chat.

>> **Format text.** Select the text you want to format, Control-click or right-click in the selection, and then click the Bold, Italic, Underline, or Strikethrough button at the top of the contextual menu.

NEW

>> **Apply text effects.** Again, select the text you want to format, then Control-click or right-click in the selection to open the contextual menu. This time, click the Text Effects continuation menu, and then click Big, Small, Shake, Nod, Explode, Ripple, Bloom, or Jitter.

NEW

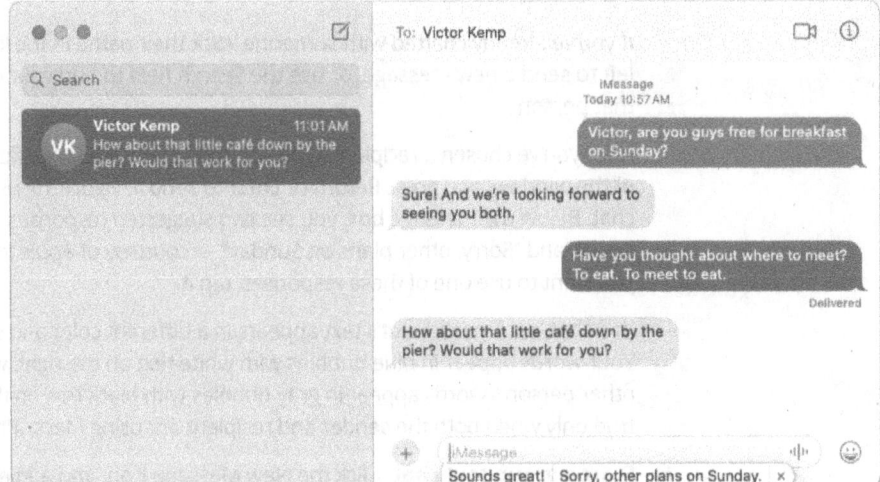

FIGURE 15-16:
A text chat in the Messages app, including two suggestions from Apple Intelligence.

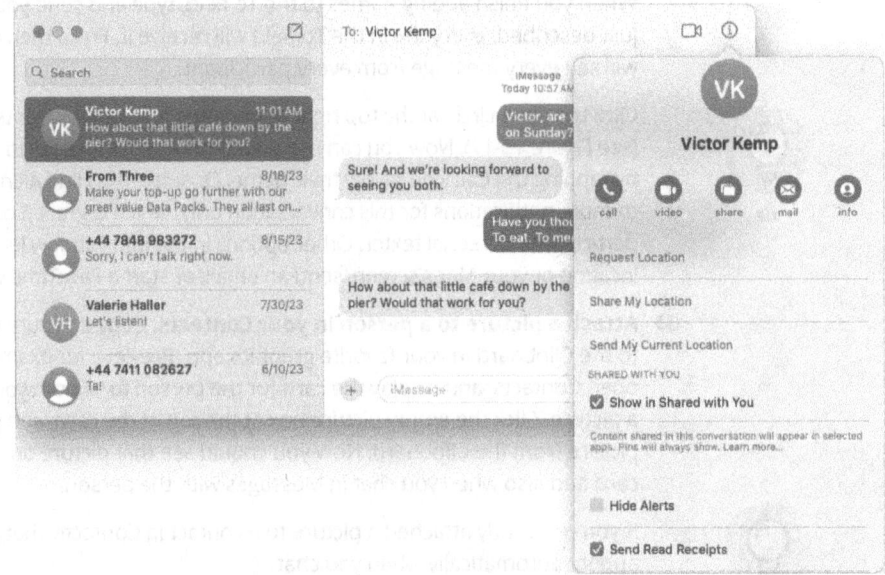

FIGURE 15-17:
In the Info window, you can start an audio call or video call, share your screen, send email, or simply hide alerts.

NEW

>> **Send a tapback.** To send a tapback, such as a thumbs-up emoji or a double-exclamation emoji, Control-click or right-click the individual message, and then click the tapback on the pop-up bar. Click the > button to display another bar's worth of tapbacks, or click the smiley-face icon to display a larger panel showing the full range of emoji.

NEW

>> **Proofread or rewrite a message.** You can use Apple Intelligence's Writing Tools to check or improve the message. See the subsection "Proofing and rewriting a message with Writing Tools," earlier in this chapter, for more information.

>> **Transfer a file or files.** Drag the file or files to the iMessage field (where you type your messages) and then press Return. This technique is a convenient way to share photos or documents without resorting to file sharing or email.

When you drag an image file to the Messages window's message box, you see an oversize semitransparent preview, letting you check that you're sending the right image, not something totally embarrassing.

You can also choose Conversation ⇨ Send File and then select the file or files in a standard Open File dialog, but drag-and-drop is faster and easier.

>> **Send a voice message.** Click the sound wave to the right of the iMessage field, and begin talking. When you finish, click the red Stop icon, and then click Send.

>> **Start a FaceTime video or audio call.** Select the person in the list on the left, and then choose Conversation ⇨ FaceTime Video or Conversation ⇨ FaceTime Audio.

>> **Share your Mac screen or ask to share a contact's screen.** Choose Conversation ⇨ Share My Screen or Conversation ⇨ Ask to Share Screen.

TIP

Screen sharing is awesome for providing technical support to other Mac users, such as members of your family. Solving a Mac problem is much easier when you can see the remote Mac's screen and control it from your Mac.

>> **Search for a person, a word, a phrase, or an image.** Click the Search field or press ⌘ +F, begin typing, and select the appropriate match in the list that appears.

>> **Pin a conversation to the top of the list.** Control-click or right-click the conversation, and choose Pin from the contextual menu. To unpin a pinned conversation, Control-click or right-click it, and choose Unpin from the contextual menu.

>> **Add message effects (balloons, confetti, lasers, and more), create a memoji, use memoji stickers, or search for images on the Internet.** Click the Apps icon on the left side of the iMessage field, and then choose Photos, Memoji Stickers, #images, or Message Effects from the pop-up menu.

>> **Send an email from Messages.** Select a conversation in the list, and choose Conversation ⇨ Send Email (or press ⌘ +Option+E). Mail launches (if it's not already open) and addresses a new message to the contact.

IN THIS CHAPTER

» Comprehending networks and file sharing

» Setting up file sharing

» Understanding access and permissions

» Connecting to a shared disk or folder remotely

» Changing your password

» Resetting the password for another account

» Configuring other types of sharing

Chapter **16**

Sharing Your Mac with Others

Have you ever wanted to grab a file from your Mac while you were halfway around the world, around the corner, or in the next room? If so, rest assured that there's nothing scary or complicated about sharing files, folders, and disks — even printers — among computers as long as the computers are Macs. And even if some of the computers are running Windows, macOS makes the sharing as painless as possible.

The first sections of this chapter provide an overview and tell you everything you need to know to set up new user accounts and share files successfully. When you've done all the required prep work, the chapter shows you how to perform the actual sharing, starting with the "Connecting to a Shared Disk or Folder on a Remote Mac" section.

Introducing Networks and File Sharing

Sequoia's file sharing enables you to use files, folders, and disks from other Macs on a network — including the Internet — as easily as if they were on your own local hard drive. If you have more than one computer, file sharing is a blessing.

Before diving in and sharing, you need to understand the following terms:

>> **Network:** For the purposes of this chapter, a *network* is two or more computers or devices connected by Ethernet cables or Wi-Fi (wireless networking).

>> **Ethernet:** This suite of network and cabling protocols lets you connect two or more computers or devices to share files, disks, printers, or whatever.

>> **Ethernet port:** This port is where you plug an Ethernet cable into your Mac (as long as your Mac has one; most desktop Macs do).

WARNING

Be careful to match the cable to its specific jack. On your Mac and printer, the Ethernet ports look a lot like a phone jack, and the connectors on each end of an Ethernet cable look a lot like phone cable connectors — but they aren't the same. Ethernet cables are typically thicker, and the connectors (RJ-45 connectors) are a bit larger than the RJ-11 connectors that you use with old-fashioned telephones. (See examples of both types of ports in the margin.)

If your Mac didn't include an Ethernet port, but you'd like to use Ethernet, you can find Thunderbolt and USB adapters that enable you to add one. Apple sells the USB-C to Gigabit Ethernet Adapter ($29.95) and the Apple USB Ethernet Adapter ($29), but there are many third-party alternatives.

>> **Local devices:** Such devices are connected directly to your computers, such as hard or optical drives. Your Mac's internal drive, for example, is a local device.

>> **Remote devices:** You access these devices over the network. The drive in a computer in the next room, for example, is a remote device.

>> **Protocols:** *Protocols* are the languages that networks speak. When you read or hear about networks, you're likely to hear the words *Bonjour*, *Ethernet*, *SMB*, and *TCP/IP*, all of which are protocols. Macs can speak several protocols, but every device (Mac or printer) on a network needs to speak the same protocol at the same time to communicate.

REMEMBER

Support for the TCP/IP protocol is built into every Mac, and macOS Sequoia includes all the software you need to set up a TCP/IP network. The hardware you provide consists of Ethernet cables and a switch (if you have more than two computers) or Wi-Fi provided by a wireless router.

>> **Switch:** A *switch* is a device for connecting the devices on an Ethernet network. You might use a switch with eight Ethernet ports into which you plug the cables from your Mac mini, your desktop PC, your printers, and so on.

TECHNICAL STUFF

A switch is similar to a hub, which also enables you to connect devices via Ethernet cables, but a switch is smarter than a hub. A hub simply blasts out all data it receives to every device on the network; the device to which the data is addressed picks it off the wire, while every other device ignores it. By contrast, a switch makes a map of which device is where and directs data only to the device to which it's addressed. This smarter means of routing data reduces the amount of data bouncing about the network and improves performance.

Understanding the essentials of home and home-office networking

A network can consist of as few as two devices, but these days, a typical home network or home-office network consists of the following:

>> A high-speed Internet connection, such as a fiber-optic connection, a digital subscriber line (DSL), or a cable connection.

>> An Internet router that shares the Internet connection on the network.

>> A wireless access point that enables computers and devices to connect to the network. Your MacBook, iPhone, and iPad might connect to the network via Wi-Fi; so might your Internet-enabled refrigerator.

>> An Ethernet switch that connects computers and devices via Ethernet cables. You might connect your desktop Macs and your printers via Ethernet rather than Wi-Fi.

REMEMBER

In many small networks, a single device plays multiple roles. For example, if your Internet connection is a DSL, you might have a single device that combines a DSL router with a built-in Ethernet switch and a Wi-Fi wireless access point. The device acts as a one-stop shop for all your network needs.

Figure 16-1 shows a simplified example of such a network — simplified in that it shows only one phone, one tablet, one laptop, and one desktop rather than multiple devices for each member of the office or household.

TIP

With the setup shown in Figure 16-1, you can set up each Mac on the network to access one another Mac's files, and each computer or device can print to the printer. Each computer or device that connects to the network can access the Internet via the shared Internet connection.

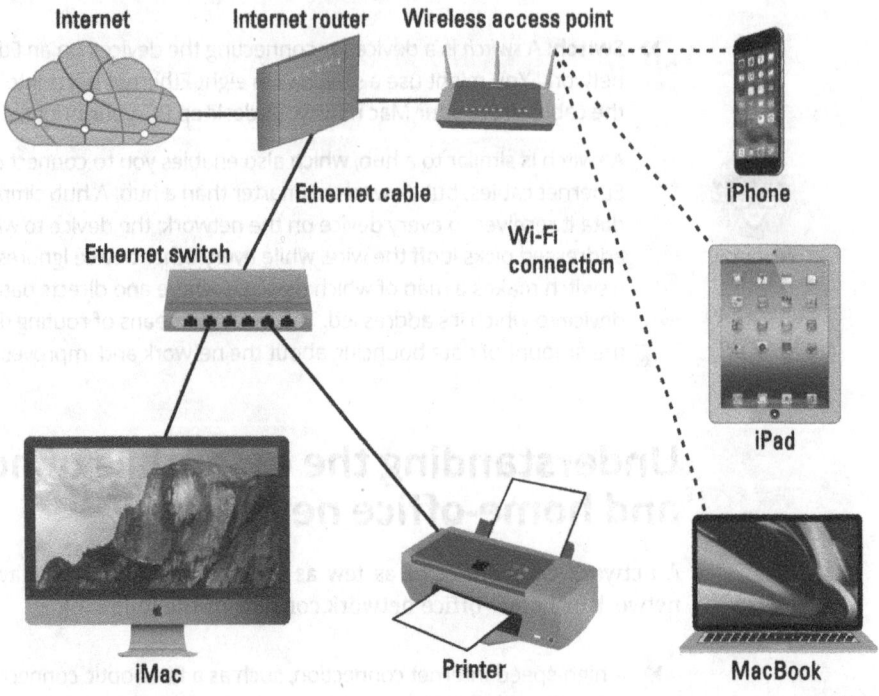

Internet   Internet router   Wireless access point

iPhone

Ethernet cable

Ethernet switch

Wi-Fi connection

iPad

FIGURE 16-1:
A typical home or home-office network includes smartphones, tablets, laptops, and desktops sharing an Internet connection, files, and printers.

iMac   Printer   MacBook

Apple Inc.

**TECHNICAL
STUFF**

A network can — and often does — have dozens or hundreds of users. Whether your network has two nodes (machines) or two thousand, the same principles and techniques in this chapter apply.

TRANSFER FILES EASILY WITH AIRDROP

Perhaps all you want to do is transfer an occasional file — not necessarily share a printer or a home Internet connection or a folder of music files or pictures. In that case, check out Apple's AirDrop, which is built into macOS, iOS, and iPadOS and which uses Bonjour, Apple's proprietary zero-configuration network protocol. Bonjour is a big part of the secret sauce in macOS that makes Mac networking so simple.

Here's how it works: If two devices speak Bonjour, you don't have to do any configuration other than possibly turning on the sharing capability (and getting the devices close to each other). Bonjour queries the other available networked devices to see what services they support and then configures the connections for you automatically.

AirDrop uses Bonjour to implement easy file transfer between Macs, iPhones, and iPads. On a Mac, AirDrop appears in the Favorites section of the sidebar in Finder windows. When you select the AirDrop favorite, as shown here, your Mac automatically locates all other AirDrop-capable Macs and devices on your wireless network.

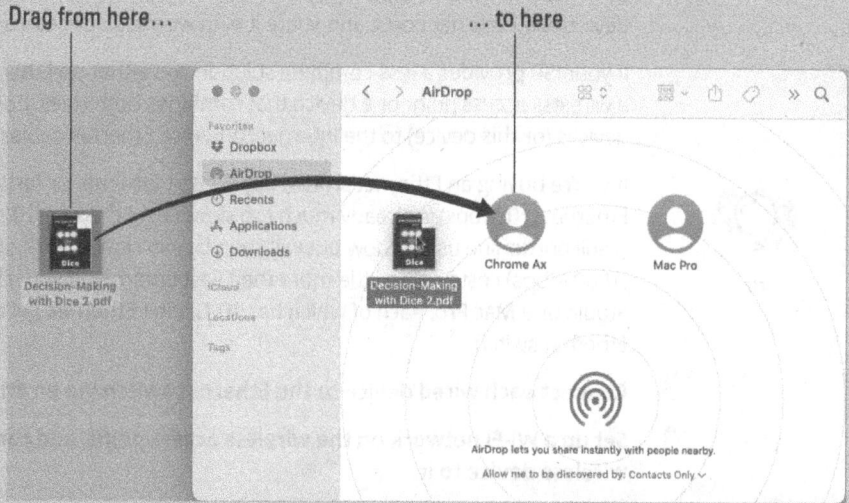

AirDrop uses both Bluetooth and Wi-Fi, and users must enable AirDrop from Control Center on iPhones and iPads. On a Mac, you can enable AirDrop either from Control Center or by selecting it in the sidebar of a Finder window.

To send one or more files or folders to the other Mac, iPhone, or iPad, just drag it (or them) onto the icon for the appropriate Mac, iPhone, or iPad. AirDrop displays a dialog on the other Mac asking whether the user wants to accept delivery; if so, the items are transferred immediately to the Downloads folder on the Mac. If you're sending to an iPad or iPhone, its user sees a dialog asking whether to accept the file, and then is asked what app to open it in using the familiar Share sheet.

When you close the AirDrop window or tab, your Mac is no longer visible to other AirDrop users.

Setting up your home or home-office network

To set up a home network or home-office network, follow these general steps:

1. Get an Internet connection that you'll share on the network.

If you've already got a high-speed Internet connection, you're good to go. If not, turn to section "Getting Connected to the Internet" in Chapter 13.

2. **Get a device for sharing the Internet connection on the network.**

For DSL, cable, and fiber connections, many ISPs provide a single device or a pair of devices that establish and maintain the connection, share it with wired devices via Ethernet ports, and share it with wireless devices via Wi-Fi.

If your ISP provides a less-complete solution, get either an Ethernet switch and a wireless access point or a device that combines both roles. Connect these devices (or this device) to the Internet router via Ethernet cables.

TIP

If you're buying an Ethernet switch, buy Gigabit Ethernet or faster. Regular Ethernet (10 Mbps) is already much too slow. Fast Ethernet (100 Mbps) is still borderline usable now but will soon be too slow, and Gigabit Ethernet (1000 Mbps) costs only a little more than Fast Ethernet. If you have a Mac Studio or a Mac Pro, each of which has 10-Gigabit Ethernet, get a 10-Gigabit Ethernet switch.

3. **Connect each wired device to the Ethernet switch via an Ethernet cable.**

4. **Set up a Wi-Fi network on the wireless access point, and connect each wireless device to it.**

TIP

Many printers support both Ethernet and Wi-Fi connections. If your printer supports both, you'll probably want to use Ethernet for reliability — unless you need to position the printer somewhere that would be awkward to reach with a cable, in which case Wi-Fi is the better choice.

Setting Up File Sharing

Before you can actually share files, you must enable the appropriate type of file sharing. Follow these steps to do so:

1. **Choose System Settings ⇨ General ⇨ Sharing to display the Sharing pane of the System Settings app (see Figure 16-2).**

At the bottom of the pane, the Local Hostname readout shows the name by which this Mac is known on the network.

2. **If you want to change the Mac's name, click Edit. In the dialog that opens, edit the name in the Local Hostname box, and then click OK.**

3. **Set the File Sharing switch to On (blue).**

4. **Click the Info (i) button to display the File Sharing dialog (see Figure 16-3).**

   Now other users on your network can access files and folders on your computer, as you see later in this chapter.

   By default, macOS shares only the Public folder that it creates automatically in your Home folder. Everyone on the network can see your Public folder but can't change its contents. Your Public folder contains a folder called Drop Box into which everyone on the network can put files but whose contents nobody but you can see. (You learn more about the Drop Box folder later in the chapter.)

TIP

   After setting the File Sharing switch to On (blue), you can access your files or folders on this computer from another computer on the network by providing your username and password; you don't need to share your folders to give yourself remote access to them.

REMEMBER

   Sharing only your Public folder is the safest setting. Don't share any other folders unless you're sure you need to.

5. **If you want all users to have full access to the Mac's disk, set the Allow Full Disk Access for All Users switch to On (blue).**

   Normally, you should leave the Allow Full Disk Access for All Users switch set to Off (white). Allowing a user full disk access means that they can enable the Full Disk Access permission for apps that need it, but such apps are rare. Full disk access doesn't mean you're giving other users carte blanche to rampage through your private files.

6. **If you want people who have accounts on your Mac to access shared files when they're using a Windows PC, click the Options button to display the Options dialog (see the left screen in Figure 16-4), and then set the Share Files and Folders Using SMB switch to On (blue).**

   For SMB to work, you must set macOS to store the user's password. To do so, select the check box to the left of the user's name in the On column of the list, type the user's account password in the Authenticate dialog that opens (see the right screen in Figure 16-4), and then click OK.

7. **Click the Done button when you're done, and proceed to the following section to continue setting up your network.**

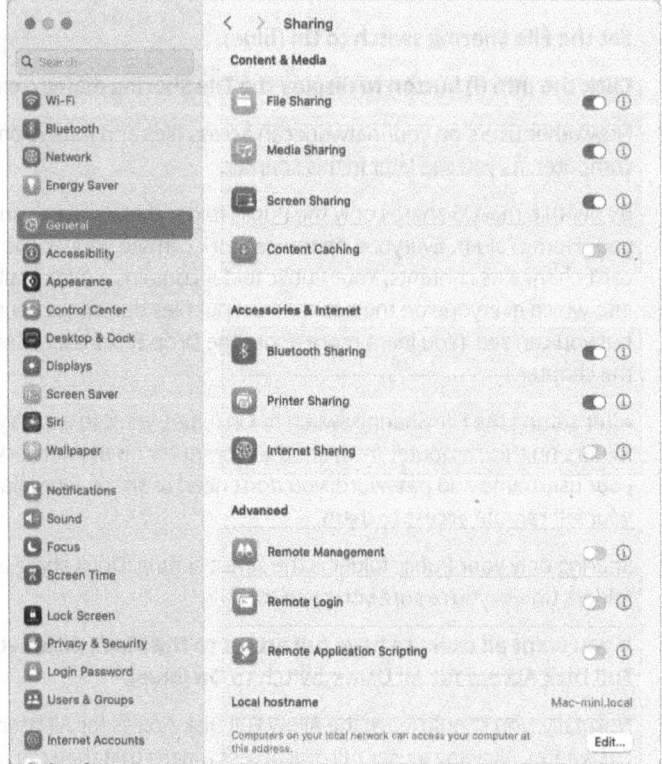

FIGURE 16-2:
At the top of the
Sharing pane,
rename your Mac
if you want and
then set the File
Sharing switch to
On (blue).

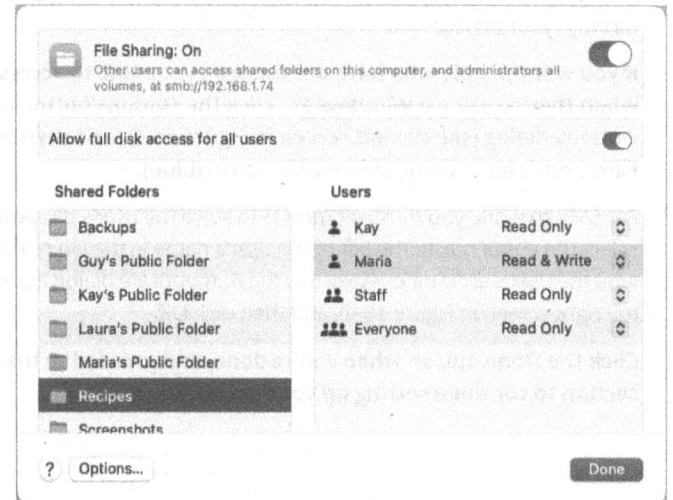

FIGURE 16-3:
In the File Sharing
dialog, choose
which folders
to share and
with whom to
share them.

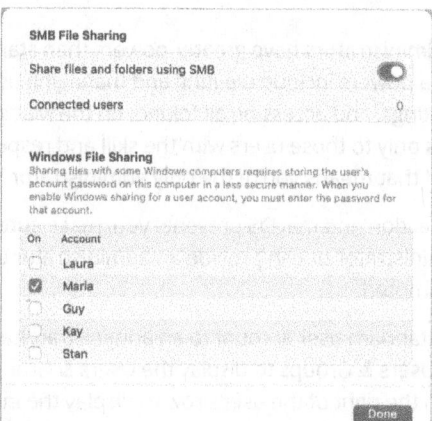

FIGURE 16-4:
In the Options
dialog (left),
specify which
users can share
files via SMB, and
provide each
user's password
in the Authenti-
cate dialog (right).

Controlling Access and Permissions: Who Can Do What

After you set up file sharing (as explained in the preceding section), tell your Mac who is allowed to see and access specific folders.

Understanding users, groups, and guests

Mac file sharing is based on the concept of users. You can share items — such as drives or folders — with no users, one user, or many users, depending on your needs. You can create groups of users to simplify administration.

Before you can understand how file sharing works, you need to know the terminology:

>> **Users:** People who share folders and drives (or your Mac) are *users*. A user's access to items on your local hard drive is entirely at your discretion. You can configure your Mac so that only you can access its folders and drives, or so that only one other person or group — or everyone — can share its folders and drives.

When you first set up your Mac, you created your first user. macOS automatically sets up this user as an administrator (see the next bullet).

TIP

A user of your Mac can be either local (sitting at the Mac and thumping the keyboard) or remote (connecting across your local network or across the Internet). Or the user can log in locally sometimes and remotely at other times.

>> **Administrators:** Administrators have greater powers than standard users. Administrators' extra powers include creating and managing users, changing sensitive system settings, and accessing all folders on the Mac's drive. Grant administrator status only to those users with the skill and responsibility to manage your Mac. If that means you're the only administrator, that's fine.

If you try to take an action and macOS prevents you, make sure that you're logged in as an administrator or can provide an administrator username and password when prompted.

You can upgrade a standard user account to an administrator account. Choose System Settings ⇨ Users & Groups to display the Users & Groups pane, click the Info (i) button on the right of the user's row to display the Info dialog, and set the Allow This User to Administer This Computer switch to On (blue). Then click OK. You'll need to restart the Mac to make the change take effect.

>> **Groups:** As you may recall, macOS is based on the Unix operating system, and *groups* are the Unix-level designations for permissions consolidation. There are groups named Staff and Everyone, for example, as well as a bunch of others. A user can be a member of multiple groups. Your main account is in the Staff, Admin, and Everyone groups (and others, too). Don't worry — you find out more about groups later in this chapter.

>> **Guests:** macOS provides a special account called Guest that allows someone without a user account to use your Mac temporarily. The Guest account has no password and provides limited functionality, the most important part of which is Internet access. A guest can't access files on your Mac. When the guest logs out, macOS automatically deletes all information and files in the Guest account's Home folder, leaving it pristine for the next guest.

To enable the Guest account, choose System Settings ⇨ Users & Groups, click the Info (i) button at the right end of the Guest User row to display the Info dialog, and then set the Allow Guests to Log In to This Computer switch to On (blue). In the Info dialog, you can also set the Limit Adult Websites switch to On (blue) to reduce your guests' access to adult websites, and you can set the Allow Guest Users to Connect to Shared Folders switch to On (blue) to enable guests to reach files in shared folders.

Creating users

Before a user can share folders and drives, they must have an account on your Mac. You can create two kinds of user accounts for them:

>> **Standard user account:** macOS sets up each user account with its own Home folder and subfolders (Desktop, Documents, Downloads, Library,

Movies, Music, Pictures, and Public). The Home folder bears the user's account name and is accessible only to that user.

>> **Sharing Only account:** macOS gives the sharing-only account access to the shared folders on the Mac — the Public folders that are shared automatically, plus any folders you've shared manually.

You can create a new *user* account only in the Users & Groups pane of System Settings. You can create a new *sharing only* account in either the Users & Groups pane of System Settings or in the Options dialog for a particular type of sharing (click the + button below the Users list).

When you add (create) a user, you need to tell your Mac who this person is. This is also the time to set a password and (maybe) administrative powers for this new user. Here's the drill:

1. **Choose System Settings ⇨ Users & Groups to display the Users & Groups pane (see Figure 16-5).**

   The Users & Groups pane displays the list of existing users. Each user's account shows its type: Admin, Sharing Only, or Standard.

2. **Click Add User, and authenticate yourself if prompted, to open the Add User dialog (see Figure 16-6).**

3. **Choose Standard from the New User pop-up menu.**

4. **In the Full Name text box, type the full name of the new user.**

   In the Account Name text box, macOS inserts a suggested account name derived from the full name — essentially, the same name, all lowercase, minus spaces and punctuation. If you enter **Peter Mann** in the Full Name text box, for example, macOS suggests *petermann* in the Account Name text box.

5. **Change the account name as needed.**

   macOS uses this name for the user's Home folder, so it's best to make the name readable. For a home or home-office network, you probably don't need a formal naming convention, so you may choose to use just the user's first name rather than the first name and last name smashed together.

TIP

   Users can connect to your Mac by using the account name, rather than having to type their full names. The account name is also used in environments in which usernames can't have spaces and are limited to eight or fewer characters. Although macOS allows account names longer than eight characters (but no spaces), you might be better off keeping your account name to eight characters or fewer, just in case.

6. In the Password field, enter an initial password for this user.

macOS insists on the password being at least four characters long, but eight characters is a more realistic minimum length for security.

7. Type the password again in the Verify text field.

8. (Optional) To help the user remember the password you assigned, type something in the Password Hint text box that will jog their memory.

TIP

If a user forgets the password and asks for a hint, the text that you type in the Password Hint field pops up. Creating a suitable password hint is difficult because you must strike a balance between preventing the user from getting locked out of their account because they can't remember the password and enabling unauthorized people to work out the password.

9. Click the Create User button to create the account.

The Add User dialog closes, and the new user appears in the Users & Groups pane.

10. (Optional) Click the account picture, and choose a different one.

TIP

macOS assigns a picture for each account, but you can select a different one by clicking the picture and working in the dialog that appears. You can select a built-in picture (from Suggestions), a memoji, an emoji, a monogram (initials), or a photo from the Photos app. Alternatively, click Camera, and take a photo with an attached or built-in camera.

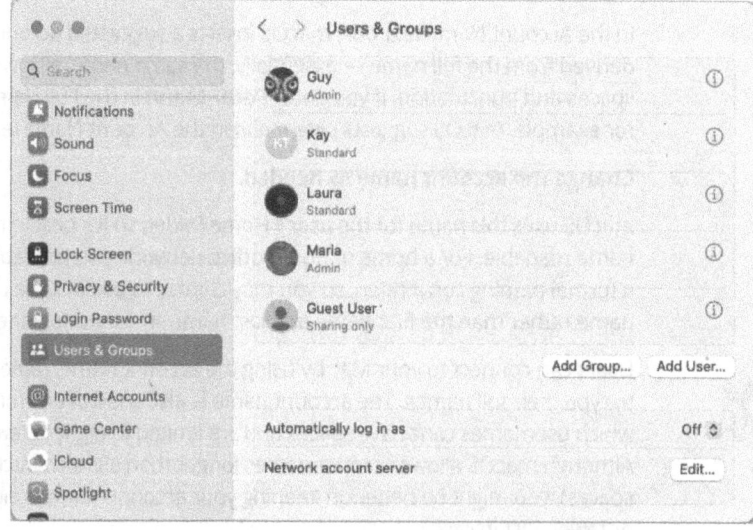

FIGURE 16-5: Click the Add User button in the Users & Groups pane to start adding a new user account.

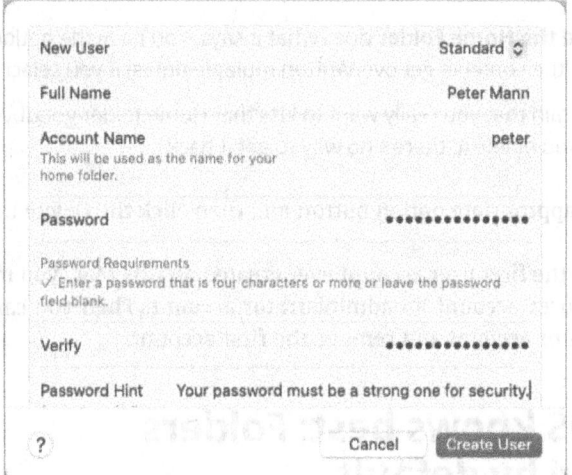

FIGURE 16-6:
Name the new
user, and your
Mac suggests a
shortened name.

Changing a user

If you have to change a user's picture or account type, do the following:

>> **Change a user's picture.** Click the user's picture, and select a replacement. Click Save when you're done.

>> **Grant a user administrator status.** Click the Info (i) icon for the user you want to modify, set the Allow This User to Administer This Computer switch to On (blue), and then click Done.

Removing a user

What if you need to delete a user? You must be logged in with an administrator account. In the Users & Groups pane, click the Info (i) icon for the user you want to delete and then click Delete User in the dialog that opens. Click OK in the first confirmation dialog. A second confirmation dialog opens, offering three choices:

>> **Save the Home Folder in a Disk Image** saves a disk image of the user's Home folder in a folder named Deleted Users (which it creates inside the Users folder).

>> **Don't Change the Home Folder** removes the user from the Users & Groups pane of System Settings and from the login screen but leaves that user's Home folder in the Users folder, macOS appends *(Deleted)* to the folder's name.

>> **Delete the Home Folder** does what it says. You have the option of a secure erase (the contents get overwritten multiple times) if you select this option.

Be certain that you really want to kiss that Home folder goodbye, because after you delete it, there's no way to get it back.

Select the appropriate option button and then click the Delete User button.

To remove the first user account ever created on this Mac, you must make at least one other user account an administrator account. Then you can log in with this administrator account and remove the first account.

macOS knows best: Folders shared by default

When you add a user account in the Users & Groups pane, macOS automatically creates a standard set of folders for that user account and makes some of them available for sharing.

Each time you add a standard or administrator user, macOS creates a Home folder hierarchy for that user in the Users folder. The user can create more folders (if necessary) and also add, remove, or move anything inside these folders. Unless you, as the owner of your Mac, give permission, the user can't see inside or use folders outside the Home folder (which has the user's name), with only three exceptions: the Shared folder in the Users folder, the top level of other user account folders, and the Public folder in every user's folder.

>> **Public:** Each user's Home folder contains a Public folder that is shared with every user who can log in to this Mac. The Public folder is also accessible to anyone who can reach your Mac by its IP address across your local network or across the Internet. Anyone who can reach your Public folder can view and copy its contents, but they can't add files or modify or delete existing files.

To prevent outsiders from accessing your Public folder, activate the macOS firewall by choosing System Settings ⇨ Network ⇨ Firewall and then setting the Firewall switch to On (blue). You can also enable the firewall on your Internet router to protect the whole of your local network; consult your router's documentation to find out how.

Inside each user's Public folder is a Drop Box folder. As the name implies, this folder is where others can drop a file or folder for that user. Only the owner can open the Drop Box folder to see what's inside — or to move or copy the files that are in it. Imagine a street-corner mailbox: After you drop your file or folder in, it's gone, and you can't get it back out.

>> **Shared:** In addition to a Public folder for each user, macOS creates one Shared folder on every Mac for all users of this Mac. You can make the Shared folder available to the Guest user by clicking the Info (i) button on the Guest row of the Users & Groups pane, setting the Allow Guest Users to Connect to Shared Folders switch to On (Blue), and then clicking OK. You find the Shared folder within the Users folder (the same folder where you find folders for each user). The Shared folder is where to put stuff that everyone with an account on this Mac might want to use. (See Chapter 8 for an introduction to the macOS folder structure.)

Sharing a folder or disk by setting permissions

As you might expect, permissions control who can use a given folder or any disk (or partition) other than the start-up disk, which you can't share because it contains the operating system.

You can set permissions for

>> The folder's owner

>> A subset of all the people who have accounts on the Mac (a group)

>> People who have the Mac's address, whether or not they have an account (guests)

Making sense of permissions

macOS distinguishes three kinds of users on the network:

>> **Owner:** The *owner* of a folder or disk can change the permissions to that folder or disk at any time. Your user account is the default owner of your Home folder and the folders it contains. Ownership can be given away (for more on that topic, see the "Applying useful settings for permissions" subsection later in this chapter). Even if you own the Mac, you can't change permissions for a folder on it that belongs to another user (unless you get Unix-y and do so as root, the superuser). The owner must be logged in to change permissions on their folders.

macOS is the owner of many folders outside the Users folder. If macOS owns a folder, you can see that "system" is its owner if you select the folder and choose File ⇨ Get Info (or press ⌘ +I).

Folders that aren't in the Users folder generally belong to system. Changing the permissions on any folder owned by system is almost always a bad idea.

WARNING

If you *must* change permissions on a file or folder, select its icon and choose File ⇨ Get Info (⌘ +I); then change the settings in the Sharing & Permissions section at the bottom of the resulting Get Info window. Never change permission settings unless you're absolutely sure of what you're doing and why. It's especially important to think twice before applying changes to all the items in a folder or disk; change permissions on the contents of the wrong folder, and you could end up with a mess. You might be able to undo permission changes by using the Revert Changes command, but be warned that it doesn't always work.

>> **Group:** In Unix systems, all users belong to one or more *groups.* The group that includes everyone who has an account with administrator permissions on your Mac is called Admin. Everyone in the Admin group has access to Shared and Public folders over the network, as well as to any folder that the Admin group has been granted access to by the folder's owner.

For the purpose of assigning permissions, you can create your own groups the same way you create a user account: Choose System Settings ⇨ Users & Groups to display the Users & Groups pane, and then click Add Group to display the Add Group dialog. Type the name of the group in the Full Name text box, and then click the Create Group button.

The group appears in the Groups list in the Users & Groups pane. To assign users to the group, click the group's Info (i) button and then set the appropriate switches in the Group Options dialog (see Figure 16-7) to On (blue). Click OK when you finish.

>> **Everyone:** This category is an easy way to set permissions for everyone with an account on your Mac at the same time. Unlike the Admin group, which includes only users with administrative permissions, the Everyone group includes everyone with an account on this Mac.

REMEMBER

If you want people without an account on this Mac to have access to a file or folder, put that file or folder in your Public folder, where the people you want to see it can log in as guests.

Sharing a folder

Suppose that you have a folder you want to share, but it needs different permissions from those set up for the Public folder, for the Drop Box folder in the Public folder, or for your personal folders. You can set suitable permissions for the folder manually.

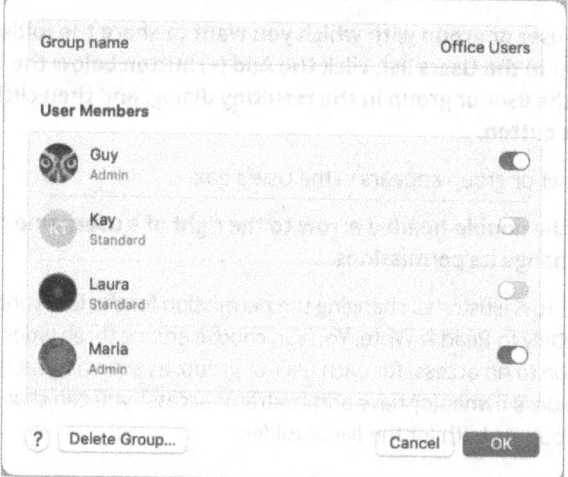

Group name	Office Users

User Members

Guy
Admin

Kay
Standard

Laura
Standard

Marla
Admin

? Delete Group...   Cancel   OK

FIGURE 16-7:
In the Group
Options dialog,
set the switch to
On (blue) for each
user you
want to add.

TIP

Share only those folders located in your Home folder (or a folder within it). Because of the way Unix works, the Unix permissions of the enclosing folder can prevent access to a folder for which you *do* have permissions. If you share only the folders in your Home folder, you'll never go wrong. If you don't take this advice, you could wind up having folders that other users can't access, even though you gave them the appropriate permissions.

You can set permissions for subfolders in your Public folder that are different from those for the Public folder itself. In fact, the Drop Box subfolder already has different permissions from the Public folder, its parent: Whereas the Public folder gives the Everyone group Read Only permission, the Drop Box subfolder gives the Everyone group Write Only (Drop Box) permission.

To share a folder with another user, follow these steps:

1. **Choose System Settings ⇨ General ⇨ Sharing to open the Sharing pane of the System Settings app.**

2. **Make sure that the File Sharing switch is set to On (blue).**

3. **Click the Info (i) icon on the File Sharing row to open the File Sharing dialog.**

   The lists of Shared folders and their users appear, as shown in Figure 16-8.

4. **Click the Add (+) button below the Shared Folders list, select the folder you want to share in the resulting dialog, and then click Done.**

   Alternatively, drag the folder from a Finder window to the Shared Folders list.

5. **If the user or group with which you want to share the folder doesn't appear in the Users list, click the Add (+) button below the Users box, click the user or group in the resulting dialog, and then click the Select button.**

The user or group appears in the Users box.

6. **Click the double-headed arrow to the right of a username or group name, and change its permissions.**

Figure 16-8 illustrates changing the permission for the Everyone group from Read Only to Read & Write. You can choose among three types of access (in addition to no access) for each user or group, as shown in Table 16-1. If you're the folder's owner (or have administrator access), you can change the owner, the group, or both for the file or folder.

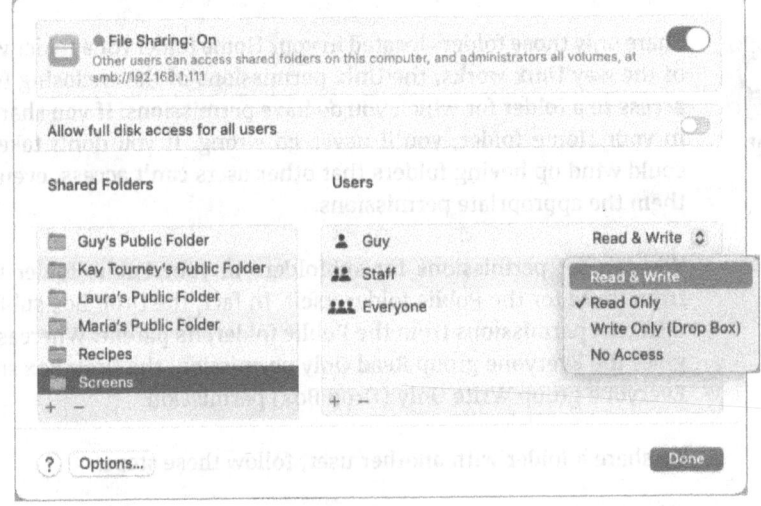

FIGURE 16-8:
Changing the
permissions of
the Screens
folder for the
group Everyone.

TABLE 16-1   ## Permissions

Permission	What It Allows
Read & Write	A user with Read & Write access can see, add, delete, move, and edit files just as though they were the owner of the files.
Read Only	A Read Only user can see and copy files that are stored in a shared folder but can't add new files or delete, move, or edit existing ones.
Write Only (Drop Box)	Users can add files to this folder but can't see what's in it. The user must have read access to the folder containing a write-only folder.
No Access	With no permissions, a user can neither see nor use your shared folders or drives.

Applying useful settings for permissions

The following sections show you some of the most common ways that you can combine permissions for a folder. You'll probably find one option that fits the way you work and the people you want to share with.

REMEMBER

Owner permissions must be at least as expansive as Group permissions, and Group permissions must be at least as expansive as Everyone permissions. So to set the Everyone permission to Read & Write, you must set the Group permission to Read & Write, and to set the Group permission to Read & Write, you must also set the Owner permission to Read & Write.

TIP

The following examples demonstrate setting permissions by working in the File Sharing dialog, which you access via the Sharing pane of the System Settings app. Another way to set permissions is to select a folder in Finder, choose File ⇨ Get Info (⌘+I), and then change the settings in the Sharing & Permissions section at the bottom of the resulting Info window. The two methods are pretty much interchangeable, so you can use whichever is more convenient.

TIP

You can also set permissions in an Inspector window. Click the folder you want to affect and then press ⌘+Option+I to open the Inspector window; alternatively, Control-click or right-click the folder, press Option to change the Get Info command on the contextual menu to the Show Inspector command, and then click Show Inspector. The Inspector window shows information for whichever folder is active, whereas the Info window shows information for only the folder for which you open it.

Here are six specific examples of setting permissions:

>> **Allow everyone access.** To give everyone access to the selected folder and let them create, modify, and delete files in it, open the pop-up menu to the right of the Everyone group and choose Read & Write.

>> **Allow everyone to read files but not change them.** To allow everyone to view files in the selected folder but not make any changes, give yourself Read & Write permission, give the Staff group Read Only permission, and give the Everyone group Read Only permission.

>> **Allow nobody but yourself access.** To allow nobody but yourself access to the selected folder, give yourself Read & Write permission, give the Staff group No Access permission, and give the Everyone group No Access permission.

>> **Allow all administrative users of this Mac access.** To give all administrative users access to the selected folder, give yourself Read & Write permission, give the Admin group Read & Write permission, and give the Everyone group No Access permission.

>> **Allow others to deposit files and folders without giving them access.** To allow others to deposit files and folders in the selected folder without letting them see its contents, set up the folder as a Drop Box. Give yourself Read & Write permission, but assign Write Only (Drop Box) permission to both the Staff group and the Everyone group.

>> **Apply the permissions to subfolders.** The Apply to Enclosed Items command (click the gear at the bottom of the Sharing and Permissions section of a Get Info window in Finder) applies the changes to all the items contained in the folder you're configuring. This feature (which is available only in Get Info windows and doesn't appear in the Sharing pane of System Settings) is a fast way to assign the same permissions to many subfolders at the same time. After you set permissions for the enclosing folder the way you like them, issue this command to apply the same permissions to all folders inside it.

WARNING

Be careful: There's no Undo command for applying a permission to subfolders.

Unsharing a folder

To unshare a folder that you own, change the permissions for every user and group to No Access. When you do, nobody but you has access to that folder.

Connecting to a Shared Disk or Folder on a Remote Mac

After you set up sharing and assign permissions, you can access folders remotely from another computer.

TIP

File sharing must be activated on the Mac that contains the shared files or folders; it doesn't have to be activated on the Mac that's accessing the files or folders. When file sharing is turned off, you can still use that Mac to access a remote shared folder on another machine as long as its owner has granted you enough permissions and has enabled file sharing. If file sharing is turned off on your Mac, others won't be able to access your folders, even if you've assigned permissions to them previously.

If you're going to share files, and you leave your Mac on and unattended for a long time, lock the screen or log out before you leave it to prevent other people from viewing your open apps and exploring your files.

REMEMBER

The following steps assume that you have an account on the remote Mac, which means you have your own Home folder on that Mac. If you need to know how to create a new user, see the "Creating users" subsection earlier in this chapter.

To connect to a shared folder on a Mac other than the one you're currently on, follow these steps:

1. **Open a Finder window.**

2. **If the Locations section of the sidebar is collapsed, click the Locations heading to expand its contents.**

3. **Click the Network item.**

    All available computers sharing files (or other services) appear in the main pane. You can see two computers in Figure 16-9: archer_d7 and Mac Pro.

4. **Click the Mac to which you want to connect — Mac Pro, in this example.**

    If the Mac is set to allow guest users to connect to shared folders, you'll see *Connected as: Guest* and a list of the shared folders, as shown in Figure 16-9.

    If the Mac is set to not allow guest users to connect to shared folders, you'll see *Not connected* and no list of shared folders. This is fine.

5. **Click the Connect As button.**

    The Connect dialog opens (see Figure 16-10). In the Connect As area, macOS automatically selects the Registered User radio button and enters in the Name field the account name under which you're logged into the Mac you're using.

6. **If your account on the remote Mac has another name, type it in the Name box.**

7. **Type your password in the Password box.**

    If your password is stored in the Passwords app, you can also click the Passwords button, which appears when you click in the Password box, and retrieve the password.

8. **Select the Remember This Password in My Keychain check box if you want macOS to store your password so you won't have to type it in for future connections to this Mac.**

9. **Click the Connect button.**

    macOS establishes the connection, and the list of available drives and folders appears in the Finder window (see Figure 16-11). Now you can navigate the drives and folders as usual and work with their contents.

When you connect to a shared folder or drive, macOS mounts it in your Mac's filesystem. When you finish using the shared folder or drive, you can eject it by clicking the Eject icon that appears to the right of its name (see Figure 16-12).

10. **When you finish using the remote Mac, disconnect by clicking the Disconnect button or by clicking the Eject icon to the right of the Mac's name in the Locations section of the Finder sidebar (see Figure 16-12).**

FIGURE 16-9:
The Mac is connected to Mac Pro as a guest and can see the Shared folder.

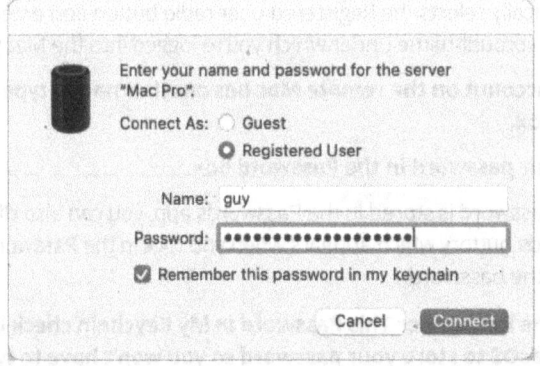

FIGURE 16-10:
In the Connect dialog, enter your password for the remote Mac.

TIP

If you've finished working for the day, and you don't leave your Mac on 24/7 or put it to sleep, choose ⇨ Shut Down or ⇨ Log Out. Shutting down or logging out automatically disconnects you from shared disks or folders. (Shut Down also turns off your Mac.)

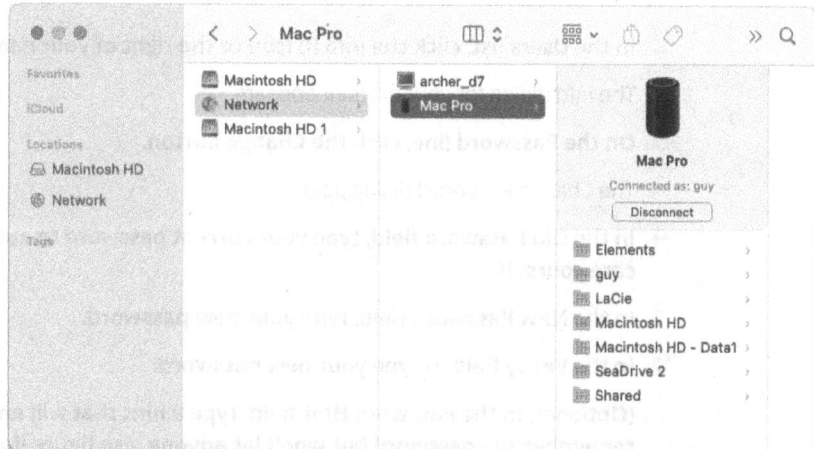

FIGURE 16-11:
The Mac is
connected to Mac
Pro as the user
named *guy* and
can see the
Mac's drives
and folders.

Click to disconnect from the remote Mac

FIGURE 16-12:
You can quickly
eject a shared
drive or folder, or
disconnect from
the remote Mac.

Click to eject a shared folder or drive

Click to disconnect from the remote Mac

Changing the Password for Your Account

You can change your account password at any time. Changing your password is a good idea if you suspect that someone else has learned your password. Follow these steps:

1. **Choose System Settings ➪ Users & Groups to display the Users & Groups pane of the System Settings app.**

2. **In the Users list, click the Info (i) icon to the right of your name.**

   The Info dialog for your account appears.

3. **On the Password line, click the Change button.**

   The Change Password dialog opens.

4. **In the Old Password field, type your current password to authenticate yourself.**

5. **In the New Password field, type your new password.**

6. **In the Verify field, retype your new password.**

7. **(Optional) In the Password Hint field, type a hint that will enable you to remember the password but won't let anyone else figure it out.**

8. **Click the Change Password button.**

   The Change Password dialog closes, returning you to the Info dialog.

9. **Click the OK button to close the Info dialog.**

10. **Choose System Settings ⇨ Quit System Settings if you've finished working with System Settings.**

Resetting the Password for Another Account

To reset the password for a different account on your Mac, follow these steps:

1. **Choose System Settings ⇨ Users & Groups to display the Users & Groups pane of the System Settings app.**

2. **In the Users list, click the Info (i) icon to the right of the account whose password you want to reset.**

   The Info dialog for that user's account opens.

3. **On the Password line, click the Reset button, and then authenticate yourself if prompted.**

   The Reset Password dialog opens.

4. **In the New Password field, type the new password.**

   The new password must be at least four characters long. Eight characters is a more secure minimum length.

5. In the Verify field, retype the new password.

6. (Optional) In the Password Hint field, type a hint.

7. Click the Reset Password button.

   The Reset Password dialog closes.

8. Click OK to close the Info dialog.

9. Choose System Settings ⇨ Quit System Settings if you've finished working with System Settings.

Exploring Other Types of macOS Sharing

Apart from file sharing, macOS offers several other types of sharing. You can configure all of them from the Sharing pane of the System Settings app (choose System Settings ⇨ General ⇨ Sharing).

Sharing another Mac's screen

Screen Sharing lets you control another Mac on your network from your Mac. You see the other Mac's screen on your Mac and control that Mac using your mouse and keyboard.

To set up Screen Sharing on the Mac you want to control remotely, follow these steps:

1. Choose System Settings ⇨ General ⇨ Sharing to display the Sharing pane of the System Settings app.

2. Set the Screen Sharing switch to On (blue).

3. Click the Info (i) button on the Screen Sharing row to open the Screen Sharing dialog.

4. On the Allow Access For line, click the pop-up menu and select the All Users item or the Only These Users item, as needed.

5. If you select the Only These Users item, click Add (+) below the list box to add the user or users whom you'll allow to use Screen Sharing.

   The Administrators group is included by default. You can remove it by clicking Administrators and then clicking Remove (–).

6. Click Done to close the Screen Sharing dialog.

To take control of your Mac from another Mac, follow these steps:

1. **Open a Finder window.**

2. **If the Locations section of the sidebar is collapsed, click the Locations heading to expand its contents.**

3. **Click the Network item.**

   All available computers sharing files or services appear in the main pane.

4. **Click the Mac to which you want to connect.**

5. **Click the Share Screen button.**

   A dialog opens, prompting you to sign in to the remote Mac.

6. **Type your username and password for that Mac.**

7. **Click the Sign In button.**

   A window with the name of the remote Mac in its title bar appears. The window shows the remote Mac's screen (see Figure 16-13).

8. **Take actions on the remote Mac.**

   Pull down a menu, or open a folder. You're controlling the remote Mac with your mouse and keyboard.

   If the remote Mac has multiple displays, Screen Sharing typically displays them all at first. This may be awkward if the Mac you're using has a small screen. If so, click the Displays pop-up menu at the right end of the toolbar, and then click the display you want to view, as in Figure 16-13.

9. **When you're finished with your session, choose Connection ⇨ Close from the menu bar to end the session. You can also simply click the red Close button to close the Screen Sharing window.**

Sharing your Mac's Internet connection

If your Mac has an Internet connection, and another computer or device nearby doesn't, you can enable Internet Sharing, and the other computer or device can share your Internet connection. To get started, choose System Settings ⇨ General ⇨ Sharing to display the Sharing pane of the System Settings app, and then click the Info (i) button on the Internet Sharing row. You then choose the network interface on which your Mac receives the Internet connection and the network interface on which to share the connection. For example, your Mac might receive the Internet connection via its Ethernet interface, and you might share the connection via the Wi-Fi interface.

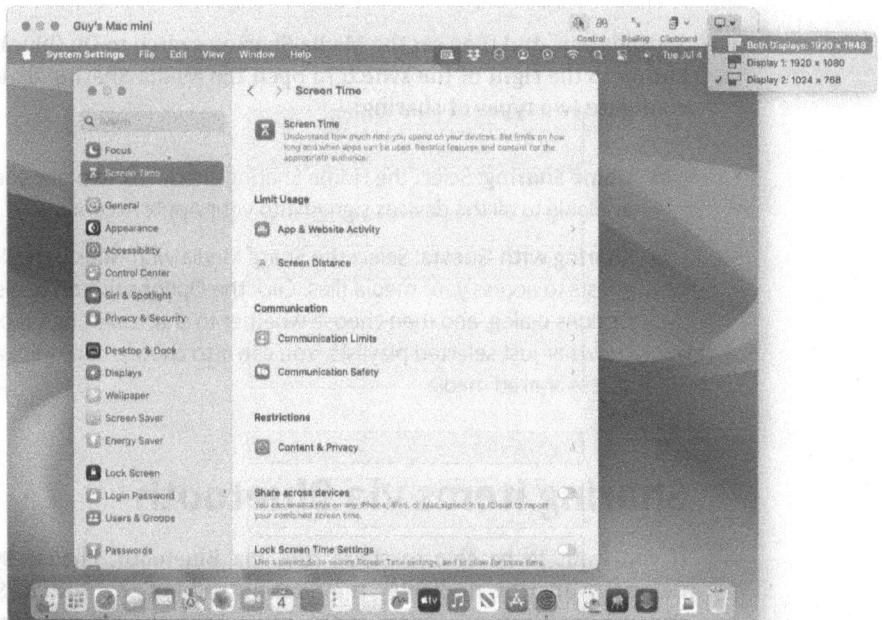

FIGURE 16-13:
Sharing a screen
on a remote Mac.

REMEMBER

The Internet Sharing feature of macOS works reasonably well, but usually, you're better off sharing your home or home-office Internet connection via a hardware device such as an Ethernet switch or a wireless access point, as explained earlier in this chapter. A typical usage scenario for Internet Sharing would be when your desktop Mac has an Ethernet connection to the Internet but no connection is available for your other computers and devices.

Sharing printers and scanners

Printer Sharing is great for printers and scanners that connect directly to your Mac rather than to the network. Choose System Settings ➪ General ➪ Sharing to display the Sharing pane of the System Settings app, and then set the Printer Sharing switch to On (blue). Click the Info (i) button to the right of the switch to open the Printer Sharing dialog, in which you can specify which printers and scanners to share.

Sharing media

If you want to allow other devices on your network to browse and play downloaded music, movies, and TV shows from your library, enable Media Sharing. Choose System Settings ➪ General ➪ Sharing to display the Sharing pane of the System

Settings app, and then set the Media Sharing switch to On (blue). Click the Info (i) button to the right of the switch to open the Media Sharing dialog. Here, you can configure two types of sharing:

>> **Home Sharing:** Select the Home Sharing check box to make your library available to all the devices signed into your Apple Account.

>> **Sharing with Guests:** Select the Share Media with Guests check box to allow guests to access your media files. Click the Options button to display the Options dialog, and then choose whether to share all songs, movies, and TV shows or just selected playlists. You can also choose to require a password to access shared media.

Sharing items via Bluetooth

If you want to be able to share files via Bluetooth, choose System Settings ⇨ General ⇨ Sharing to display the Sharing pane of the System Settings app, and then set the Bluetooth switch to On (blue). Click the Info (i) button to the right of the switch to open the Bluetooth Sharing dialog, in which you can configure the behaviors for transferring files to and from your Mac.

4
Making the Most of Your Mac

IN THIS CHAPTER

» **Understanding iTunes Match and Apple Music**

» **Becoming familiar with the Music app**

» **Working with media**

» **Playing with playlists**

Chapter **17**

Mac Machine Music

M acs have long been known for their multimedia capabilities, and macOS Sequoia proudly carries on that tradition, giving you the Music app for playing and managing music, the Podcasts app for enjoying podcasts, and the TV app for watching TV shows and other kinds of videos. This chapter digs into the Music app, and the next chapter gets you up and running with the Podcasts app and the TV app.

Before you look at Music, however, you need to know a few things about the iTunes Match and Apple Music subscription services, because what you see in your Music app might be different if you subscribe to one or both.

Understanding iTunes Match and Apple Music

iTunes Match and Apple Music are a pair of subscription music services offered by Apple.

iTunes Match is the older of the two, designed to let you store all your music in iCloud so you can stream songs to any Mac, PC, iPhone, iPad, Apple TV, or Vision Pro connected to your account. iTunes Match first determines which songs in your Music library are already available in the iTunes iCloud library. Because Apple's vast iCloud repository contains tens of millions of songs, chances are that much of your music is already there. Then iTunes Match uploads a copy of every song it *can't* match (which is much faster than uploading your entire Music library). The result is that you can stream any song in your iTunes library on any of your Macs or devices, regardless of whether the song file has been downloaded to the device.

As a bonus, all the music iTunes matches plays back from iCloud at high quality — technically, either 256 Kbps in Advanced Audio Coding (AAC) format, or the even higher-quality Apple Lossless format, and without digital rights management (DRM) restrictions — even if your original copy was lower quality. (You can even download higher-quality versions of those songs to replace your lower-bitrate copies, if you want.)

As an iTunes Match subscriber, you can store up to 100,000 songs in iCloud, and songs you purchased from the iTunes Store don't count. Only tracks or albums you specify are stored locally on your devices, saving tons of precious storage space.

At just $24.99 a year, iTunes Match is a bargain for those with extensive collections of music *not* purchased from Apple.

But Apple Music may be a better option, albeit a more expensive one. For $10.99 a month (or $16.99 a month for you and up to five family members), an Apple Music subscription provides instant access to more than 100 million songs on all your devices. Whatever you want to hear is usually just a few clicks away.

TIP

You can also get the Apple Music services as part of an Apple One subscription. If you're planning to subscribe to several Apple services, see if Apple One could save you money.

You can even ask Siri to play whatever you want to hear on your Mac, as well as on your iPhone and your iPad. Try phrases such as these:

>> "Play popular songs by Elvis Presley."

>> "Play 'Running Up That Hill' by Kate Bush."

>> "Play *Greetings from Asbury Park, N.J.* by Bruce Springsteen."

>> "Play some hair metal."

>> "Play the number 1 song on December 31, 1999."

>> "Play 'Despacito' ten times . . . No! Siri! Hey, Siri! Stop playing!"

If you find yourself with a song playing in your head (which some people call an earworm), just ask Siri to play it, and in seconds the song will be playing in real life. Usually.

TIP

Here are two quick tips. First, when asking for an album or song, include the artist's name to help Siri identify the item. So rather than saying "Play *Rubber Soul*," try saying "Play *Rubber Soul* by the Beatles." Second, before you travel by plane or commit yourself to a cruise ship, remember to click the iCloud download button (or to Control-click or right-click and choose Download from the contextual menu) for all songs, albums, and playlists you want to listen to when Internet access isn't available.

WARNING

Make a complete backup of your Music library before enabling either iTunes Match or Apple Music, just in case something goes wrong.

Both subscription services require Internet access, but as long as you're connected, you can have your entire Music library (iTunes Match) or access to a library of more than 100 million songs (Apple Music) on your Mac, iPhone, or other device. You'll never have to worry about filling all of your device's storage space with your music.

Getting Started with the Music App

To open Music, click its icon on the Dock or in Launchpad, or double-click its icon in the Applications folder. If you're opening Music for the first time, you'll probably need to click the Start Listening button on the splash screen. If an ad for the Apple Music subscription service appears, click Try It Free or Already a Subscriber (as appropriate), or press the Esc key to dismiss the ad. Once you've defeated the promo wave, the main Music window appears, as shown in Figure 17-1 with the key elements labeled.

TIP

The Music window you're looking at may appear somewhat different from the examples shown here. This is for two reasons. First, you can customize what Music displays by choosing Music ⇨ Settings and working on the General tab of the Settings dialog. Second, extra choices appear when you subscribe to Apple Music.

As usual, the sidebar on the left gives you access to different areas of the app and different categories of music. Whatever you select in the sidebar is displayed in the large pane on the right. In Figure 17-1, Songs is selected in the sidebar, so the list of songs appears in the large pane.

To play a song, double-click it, click it and then click the Play/Pause icon, or click it and choose Controls ⇨ Play.

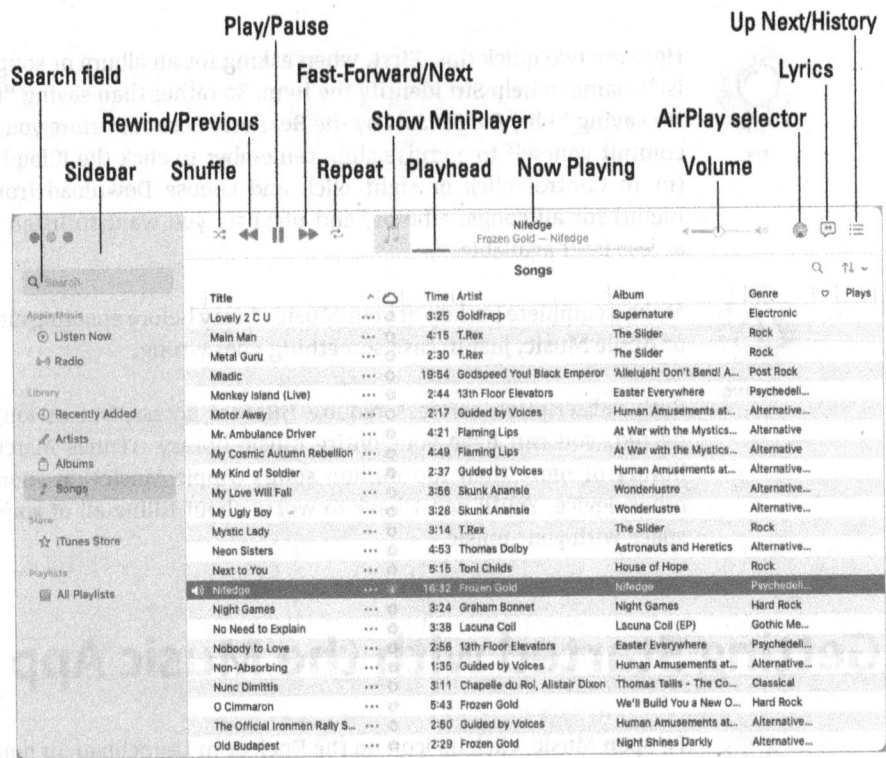

Play/Pause

Up Next/History

Search field   Fast-Forward/Next   Lyrics

Rewind/Previous   Show MiniPlayer   AirPlay selector

Sidebar   Shuffle   Repeat   Playhead   Now Playing   Volume

FIGURE 17-1:
What's what and
where in the
Music interface.

TIP

The spacebar is the shortcut for Play/Pause. When Music is the active app, this shortcut is often the most convenient way to control playback. When an app other than Music is active, pressing the dedicated Play/Pause key on your Mac's keyboard is usually best.

After you've selected a song, you can use the Fast Forward/Next, Play/Pause, and Rewind/Previous controls to manage its playback.

Here are a few more things you should know about the Music app's interface:

>> When you don't want the full Music window taking up screen real estate, switch to the more manageable MiniPlayer (shown on the left side of Figure 17-2) by clicking the Show MiniPlayer icon (labeled in Figure 17-1), choosing Window ⇨ Switch to MiniPlayer, or pressing ⌘ +Shift+M. When you give one of these commands, the main Music window hides; it comes back when you choose Window ⇨ Switch from MiniPlayer or simply press ⌘ +Shift+M again.

TIP

>> If you look at the Window menu, you'll see that as well as the Switch to MiniPlayer command you just met, there's an unvarnished MiniPlayer command (Window ⇨ MiniPlayer), which has the keyboard shortcut ⌘ +Option+M. What's it for? Well, the MiniPlayer command displays the MiniPlayer, or activates it if it's already open, but doesn't hide the main Music window. So if you want to navigate in both the MiniPlayer and the main window (don't ask why), use this command instead.

>> Music offers a ten-band graphic equalizer that can make your music (or video) sound significantly better (or worse — your choice). Just choose Window ⇨ Equalizer or press the shortcut ⌘ +Option+E to summon it on-screen. You can see the equalizer on the right side of Figure 17-2.

>> Don't miss Music's Visualizer, which offers a psychedelic light show that dances in time to the music. You turn it on by choosing Window ⇨ Visualizer or pressing ⌘ +T. If you like the default Visualizer, also check out Classic Visualizer, which you'll find on the Visualizer Settings submenu.

When you've had enough of Visualizer, choose Window ⇨ Visualizer again or press ⌘ +T again to make it disappear.

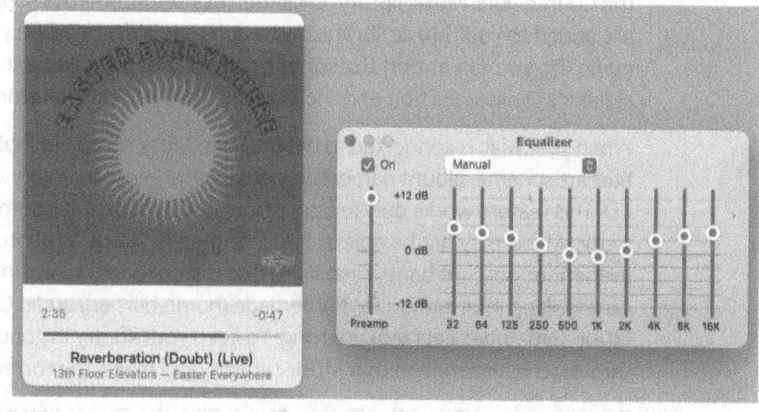

FIGURE 17-2:
The Music MiniPlayer window (left) and equalizer (right).

Working with Media

As you'd imagine, getting your music into the Music library is vital. You can acquire media in several ways, depending on the type of media and where the files reside. You can add song files that you download from websites or receive as attachments to email messages, for example, or you can add songs by ripping audio CDs. You can buy music at the iTunes Store (and from many other online vendors, including https://www.amazon.com). You can listen to all sorts of music on the Internet radio stations included with Music. Finally, Apple Music subscribers can listen to pretty much any song they can think of.

In the following sections, you discover the various ways to add music to your Music library; then you get a quick course in listening to Music's Internet radio stations.

Adding songs

You can add songs from pretty much any source, and how you add a song to Music depends on where that song comes from. Here are the main moves for adding songs:

>> **Add a song file (such as an MP3 or AAC file) from a disk drive.** Drag the file into the Music window, as shown in Figure 17-3, drag the song file (or files or folders) to the Music icon on the Dock, or choose File ➪ Import (⌘ +O) and choose the file or folder in the Open File dialog. Music doesn't support the FLAC (Free Lossless Audio Coding) audio format or the Ogg Vorbis format.

>> **Add songs from a store-bought or homemade audio CD.** Insert the CD, and Music will launch itself and offer a dialog asking whether you want to import the CD into your Music library. Click the Yes button, and the songs on that CD are added to your Music library. If you don't see a dialog when you insert an audio CD, you can import the songs on that CD by selecting the CD in the sidebar's Devices section and then clicking the Import CD button.

TIP

When your Mac is connected to the Internet, Music magically looks up the song title, artist name, album name, song length, and genre for every song on the CD. This feature works only for store-bought CDs containing somewhat-popular music; Music may not be able to find information about an obscure CD by an even-more-obscure band, even if the disc is store-bought. And in most cases, it can't look up information for homemade (home-burned) audio CDs. Finally, Music sometimes gets things wrong. To keep your library in good shape, look through the information that Music returns, and make any corrections needed.

>> **Buy your songs from the iTunes Store.** Click the iTunes Store in the sidebar to visit the iTunes Store. If you don't see the iTunes Store in the sidebar, choose Music ➪ Settings, click the General tab, go to the Show section, and then select the Show iTunes Store check box.

On the home page, you can either click a link or type the song title, album title, artist name, keyword, or phrase in the Search field. Press Enter or Return to start the search. When you find an item that interests you, double-click any song to listen to a short preview (or the entire song, if you're an Apple Music subscriber), or click the Buy button for the song or album to purchase the song or album, as shown in Figure 17-4.

>> **Buy your songs from other online vendors.** Amazon (https://www.amazon.com) has a huge downloadable music store on the web. Its MP3 Downloads section has more than a million songs, with more added every day. The prices at Amazon are often lower than the prices for the same music at the iTunes Store. If you're concerned about audio quality, read the details for each track or album carefully, and buy tracks that meet your criteria. Audiophiles insist on lossless compression, such as Apple Lossless Encoding, for their audio files, but most regular music fans find AAC audio files (which Apple uses for many songs) and MP3 audio files (which Amazon and most of the rest of the universe use) encoded at the 256 kbps bitrate to be high-enough quality for everyday listening.

WARNING

Run a quality check before buying any music tracks encoded at the 128 kbps bitrate, because they may have shortcomings that your ears can detect. Cymbal smashes, for example, may sound thin and incomplete (like the cymbals themselves after the drummer has been whaling on them).

Drag from here...   ...to here

FIGURE 17-3:
Drag and drop songs to the Music content pane or library to add them to your Music library.

Search field · Buy album · Buy song

FIGURE 17-4:
At the iTunes Store, buying music is as easy as clicking the Buy button for the song or the album.

To make a purchase from the iTunes Store, you have to create an Apple account, if you don't already have one. To do so, just choose Account ⇨ Sign In and then click the Create New Apple ID button in the Sign In dialog. After your account is established, future purchases require just one or two clicks. iTunes Store purchases made with this Apple account appear automatically on all other Apple devices that are signed into the same account.

Listening to Radio

To listen to Radio, select Radio in the Music app's sidebar. The first thing you see, at the top of the screen, are Apple's own live radio stations: Music 1, Music Hits, and Music Country (see Figure 17-5). These stations are on the air worldwide 24 hours a day, 7 days a week, offering world-class programming, interviews, and music. Scroll down to see more radio stations organized in categories such as Hosted by Artists, Discover New Shows, and Stations by Genre.

To listen to a radio station, click it. Sadly, most radio stations are available only to Apple Music subscribers.

TIP

If you can't find a particular station in the Radio section of the Music app, search for the station's website, and find the URL for tapping into its stream. Copy this URL, go back to the Music app, and choose File ⇨ Open Stream URL or press ⌘+U. In the Open Stream dialog that appears, paste the URL into the URL box, and then click OK to start the station's stream playing.

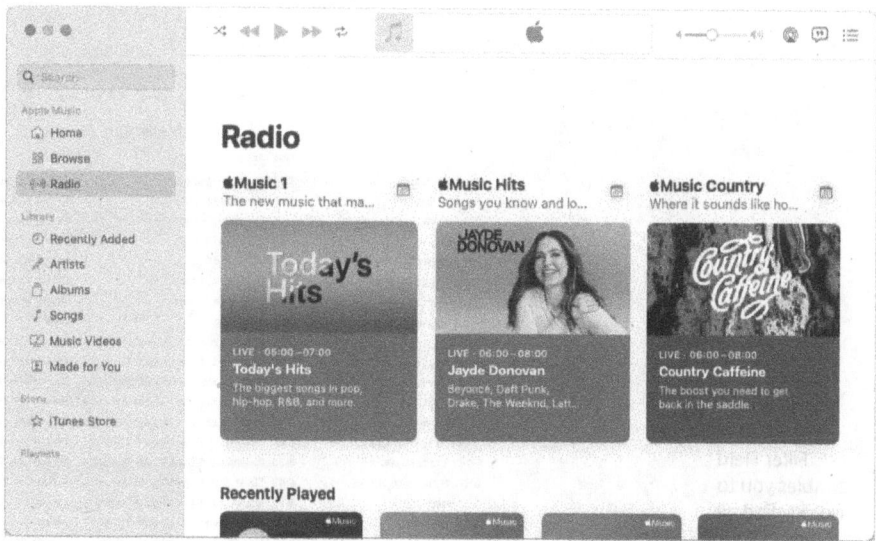

FIGURE 17-5:
Click the Radio
item in the Apple
Music section of
the sidebar to
start listening to
radio stations.

Moving right along, the more music you have in your Music library, the more you're going to love Filter Field and Column Browser.

Finding songs quickly with the Filter Field

To enable Filter Field, choose View ▷ Show Filter Field (or use its keyboard shortcut, ⌘+Option+F). The Filter Field appears in the top-right corner of the Music window. To hide the Filter Field, choose View ▷ Hide Filter Field (or press ⌘+Option+F).

Type a word or phrase in Filter Field, and all items that match that word or phrase appear below it. You can type the name of a song, an album, an artist, a genre, or a composer; the results appear instantly as you type. Figure 17-6 shows an example of using Filter Field.

Enabling and using Column Browser

To enable Column Browser, choose View ▷ Column Browser ▷ Show Column Browser (or use its keyboard shortcut, ⌘+B). To hide it, choose View ▷ Column Browser ▷ Hide Column Browser (or press ⌘+B).

The Column Browser submenu allows you to choose which categories are displayed. Genres, artists, and albums are displayed by default. Disable or enable the Composers or Groupings columns by clicking them in the Column Browser submenu. A check mark next to a category means that it's enabled.

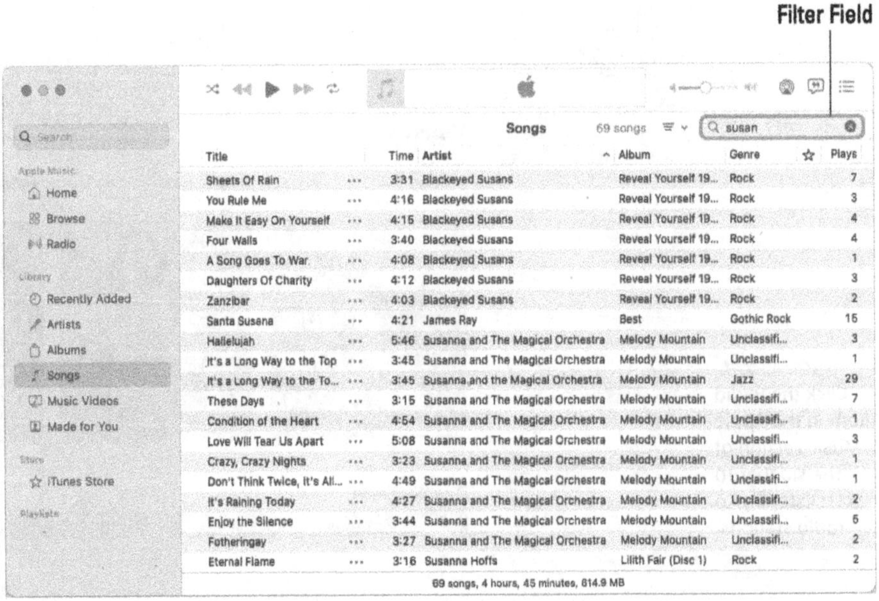

FIGURE 17-6:
Filter Field
enables you to
quickly find all
items in your
library that match
a search term.

When it's enabled, Column Browser appears above the main content area. Narrow
your search by clicking one or more items in each column. So, for example, if you
selected Hard Rock in the first column (Genre by default) and Guns N' Roses in the
second column (Artist by default), you'd see every Guns N' Roses album in every
genre in the third (Albums) column (see Figure 17-7).

FIGURE 17-7:
Column Browser
gives you an
easy way to
browse your
library swiftly.

Column Browser is an easy, visual way to narrow your search. It's especially useful if you have an extensive music library.

Making the Most of Playlists

Playlists are a big deal in Music; they let you manage otherwise-unmanageable amounts of media. Playlists let you create subsets of a large collection, so it's easier to enjoy exactly the kind of music you want in Music or on your Apple devices. If you're old enough to remember mixtapes, playlists are the high-tech equivalent.

You can create three types of playlists:

» **Regular playlists,** which contain the songs (or videos, podcasts, or radio stations) that you specify by adding them to the playlist.

» **Smart playlists,** which select songs from your library based on criteria you specify. Furthermore, you can set your smart playlists to update automatically when you add items to your library that meet the criteria. Music creates some smart playlists automatically, including the My Shazam Tracks playlist, which appears if you use Siri to identify tracks. (Siri uses the Shazam audio-recognition service.)

» **Genius playlists,** which use artificial intelligence to choose songs from your library that the Genius thinks will go great together (and often do).

TIP

If you're an Apple Music subscriber, you can use songs from your personal Music library, as well as the more than 100 million songs available to Apple Music subscribers in any type of playlist.

Creating a regular playlist

To create a regular playlist, follow these steps:

1. **Choose File ⇨ New ⇨ Playlist, or press ⌘ +N.**

   A new playlist named Playlist appears in the main pane.

2. **Type a descriptive name for the playlist over the default name.**

   If you decide not to name your playlist now, you can double-click it and type a new name any time.

TIP

3. **(Optional) In the Add Description field, type a description of the playlist.**

4. **To add a song or songs to a playlist, click an item in your library and then drag the song or songs to the playlist's name in the sidebar.**

The playlist (Morning Music in Figure 17-8) is highlighted, indicating that it's selected; the song or songs will be added to it when you release the mouse button.

Adding a song to a playlist doesn't remove it from the library; similarly, deleting a song from a playlist doesn't delete the song from your library. Furthermore, if you delete a playlist from the sidebar, the songs it contains aren't deleted from your library. Think of songs in playlists as being aliases of songs in your library.

5. **To listen to the songs in a playlist, click the playlist in the sidebar to select it; then click Play to hear all the songs in the list, or double-click a specific song to listen to it.**

...onto the playlist   Drag songs from your library...

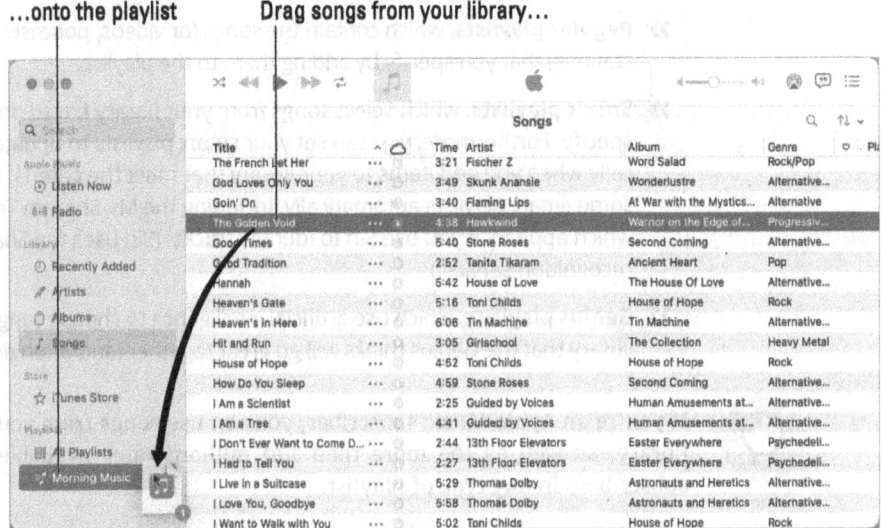

FIGURE 17-8:
Adding songs to a playlist is as easy as dragging them to the playlist.

TIP

If you don't want to drag songs to your playlist one by one, you can add them in groups: Click the first song you want to include, ⌘-click each of the other songs, and then drag the whole bunch to the playlist. You can also create a new playlist from the songs you've selected; just choose File ➪ New ➪ Playlist from Selection or press ⌘+Shift+N.

Finally, you can add any song to a new or existing playlist by Control-clicking or right-clicking it, highlighting Add to Playlist on the contextual menu, and then clicking either New Playlist or the name of the existing playlist on the continuation menu.

Working with smart playlists

To create a *smart playlist* that gathers its contents based on criteria you specify and updates itself automatically, follow these steps:

1. **Choose File ⇨ New Smart Playlist or press ⌘+Option+N.**

The Smart Playlist dialog appears, as shown in Figure 17-9.

2. **Use the pop-up menus to select the criteria — song or album name, genre, or other attributes — that will build your smart playlist.**

To add more criteria, click the + button(s) on the far right.

3. **Click OK when you're done.**

The playlist appears alongside your other playlists in the Music sidebar. You can tell that it's a smart playlist because its icon is a gear. To modify the criteria of a smart playlist after it's been created, click the playlist and then click Edit Rules (below the smart playlist's name and description in the main pane); alternatively, Control-click or right-click the smart playlist in the sidebar, and choose Edit Rules from the contextual menu.

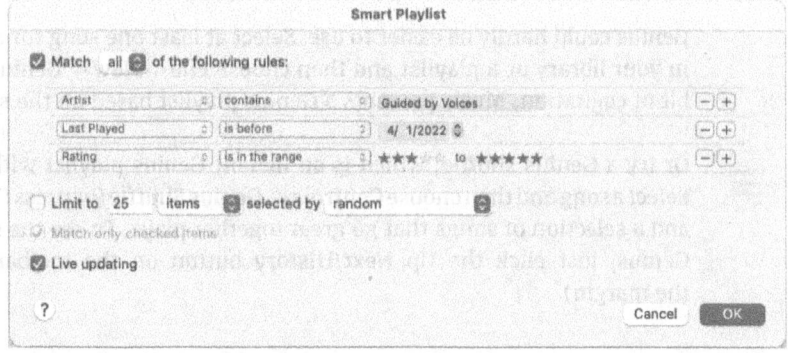

FIGURE 17-9:
Specify the criteria for your smart playlist.

TIP

Control-click or right-click any playlist to see additional options: Play, Shuffle, Play Next, Play Later, Favorite, Suggest Less, Open in New Window, Edit Rules (for a smart playlist), Burn Playlist to Disc, Copy to Play Order, Duplicate, and Delete from Library.

As you add to your music library and play the songs it contains, your smart playlists update themselves automatically, so they're always current.

Working with the Genius playlist

Regular playlists are great; smart playlists are even better; some playlists are pure Genius.

What is Genius?

Genius is a Music feature that lets you find new music (in your Music library or the iTunes Store) that's related to a song of your choice. Or, as Apple puts it: "Genius makes playlists and mixes from songs in your library that go great together. And the Genius selects music from the iTunes Store that you don't already have."

To use Genius, you must have an iTunes Store account, even though the information Genius sends to Apple about your Music library is stored anonymously, and no purchase is required. So sign in to your iTunes Store account if you have one, or create an account if you don't. After you agree to the terms of service, Genius gathers info about your Music library, sends the info to Apple, and then delivers your results. When all this is done, you can create Genius playlists and explore Genius suggestions.

How does Genius work?

Genius could hardly be easier to use. Select at least one song (or a bunch of songs) in your library or a playlist and then choose File ⇨ New ⇨ Genius Playlist. After a bit of cogitation, Music presents a Genius playlist based on the song you clicked.

 Or try a Genius shuffle, which is an instant Genius playlist without the playlist. Select a song and then choose Controls ⇨ Genius Shuffle (or press Option+spacebar), and a selection of songs that go great together plays. To see the songs selected by Genius, just click the Up Next/History button on the toolbar (and shown in the margin).

Chapter **18**

Enjoying Multimedia

macOS comes equipped to handle almost any type of media content, from movies and DVDs to graphics in a wide variety of formats. In this chapter, you learn about QuickTime Player, the TV app, the Books app, the Podcasts app, Photo Booth, and Preview.

Playing Movies and Music in QuickTime Player

QuickTime is Apple's technology for digital media creation, delivery, and playback. It's used in myriad ways by apps such as Apple's iMovie, by websites such as YouTube (www.youtube.com), and in training videos delivered on CD or DVD.

 QuickTime Player is the macOS app that lets you view QuickTime movies as well as stream audio and video, play QuickTime VR (Virtual Reality), and listen to many types of audio files. You can launch QuickTime Player by clicking its icon on

Launchpad or by double-clicking a file of a type for which it is the default app. QuickTime Player is the default app for most QuickTime movie document files.

TIP

Some QuickTime movie file types will open QuickTime Player, whereas others will open the TV app or another video player. To change the app that opens for a particular movie file type, Control-click or right-click its icon in Finder, and then choose the app you prefer from the Open With submenu. This action opens the file with that app only this one time. To make the change permanent, right-click the file, press Option to replace the Open With command with the Always Open With command, and then click Always Open With.

To play a QuickTime movie, double-click its icon, and QuickTime Player launches itself.

Using QuickTime Player couldn't be easier. All its important controls are available right in the player window, as shown in Figure 18-1.

FIGURE 18-1:
QuickTime Player
is simple to use.

TIP

QuickTime Player's controls disappear when you're not using them. So, if you don't see the controls floating in front of your video, move the pointer over the QuickTime Player window to summon the controls so you can use them.

Here are three QuickTime Player features you should know about:

» **Movie Inspector window:** Choose Window ➪ Show Movie Inspector or press ⌘ +I. This window provides a lot of useful information about the current movie, such as its location on your hard drive and the file format, frames per second, file size, and duration. Click the Close (X) icon to close the window.

>> **Trim control:** Choose Edit ⇨ Trim or press ⌘ +T. This control lets you delete frames from the beginning and end of a movie.

>> **Share/More Menu:** Click >> on the floating control bar. This menu lets you send your movies to others via the AirDrop feature (see Chapter 16) or via apps such as Mail, Messages, Notes, or Freeform; add them to your library in the Photos app; or upload them to YouTube.

See Chapter 20 for details about AirPlay Mirroring, which lets you mirror what's on your Mac screen and view it on an HDTV wirelessly. All you need is a smart TV with AirPlay or an Apple TV connected to your HDTV.

TIP

If, when you go to open a video file, QuickTime Player displays a message saying it cannot play that file type, have a look at VLC (https://www.videolan.org/). This media-player app is free and can play most kinds of video files, so it's a great tool to have either as a backup to QuickTime Player or as your main video player.

Watching TV

The TV app is macOS's app for storing and exploring video content. TV not only makes it easy to find video content to rent or buy, but also lets you add your own videos to your library (and even watch them).

The sidebar in the TV app's main window gives you quick access to various types of content. At the top of the sidebar, click Home to reach your home screen; click Apple TV+ to access the Apple TV+ subscription service, for which you may be able to get a free trial; click MLS to access the Major League Soccer subscription service; or click Store to display the video section of the iTunes Store, where you can search for, buy, or rent content. In the Library section, click Recently Added to see your latest additions; click Movies, TV Shows, or Home Videos to see the items your library has in one of those categories; click Downloaded to see items you've downloaded; or click Genres to browse your library by genres.

When you locate an item you want to watch, click its Play button. The video opens in a separate window, which you can resize as needed.

The picture-in-picture option works with most video content in the TV app, as well as videos on many websites. Click the picture-in-picture icon (shown in the margin) at the bottom of the video player to make your video float above all other pictures, as shown in Figure 18-2.

TIP

If you don't see a picture-in-picture icon on a video player, try Control-clicking or right-clicking the video. If it supports picture-in-picture, you'll see the command on the pop-up menu.

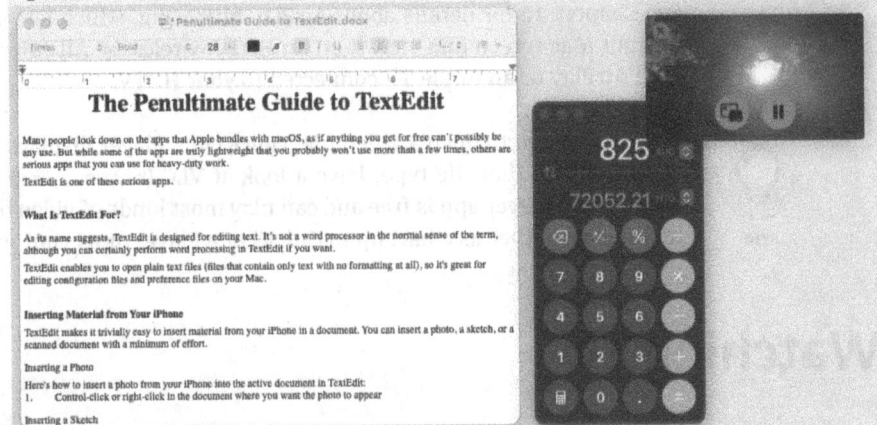

FIGURE 18-2:
The picture-in-picture video (upper right) continues to play and remains in front of TextEdit (left) and Calculator, even when one of those apps is active.

TIP

You can also add your own movies, TV shows, and home videos. To add a video file (such as MOV or MP4) from your hard drive, drag the file to the TV window or the TV Dock icon; or choose File ⇨ Import (or press ⌘ +O), and then choose the file in the Open File dialog. Whichever method you use, TV adds the file to your video library; click the Recently Added category in the Library section of the sidebar to see it.

Using the Books App

The Books app is Apple's answer to Amazon's Kindle. It's a combination ebook reader and bookstore. You can enjoy your purchases (and free downloads) on the Mac, the iPhone, and the iPad.

To use Books, you need to have at least one ebook in your library — preferably many. So the first thing to do is stock your virtual library with an ebook or two from Apple's Book Store. Don't worry — the store offers a healthy selection of free books.

Buying an ebook or audiobook

Launch the Books app by clicking Launchpad on the Dock, and then clicking Books. If this is your first time launching Books, sign in with your Apple ID and password, and then click the Get Started button.

Now, click Book Store in the sidebar. If you want audiobooks, click Audiobook Store.

TIP

If you've purchased Books from Apple in the past, they should appear automatically in your Books library.

You can look for books or audiobooks in many ways. After you select the Book Store category, scroll down to see books organized into sections, which might include For You, Featured, Top Charts, New and Trending, More to Explore, and Bestsellers by Genre. If you see the Special Offers & Free section, that can be a great place to start looking.

You can also search for a book or an author; just type a word or two in the Search field at the top of the sidebar, and then press Return. Search for *free books* to find free books.

When you see a book or ad that interests you, click it, and details will fill the screen, as shown in Figure 18-3.

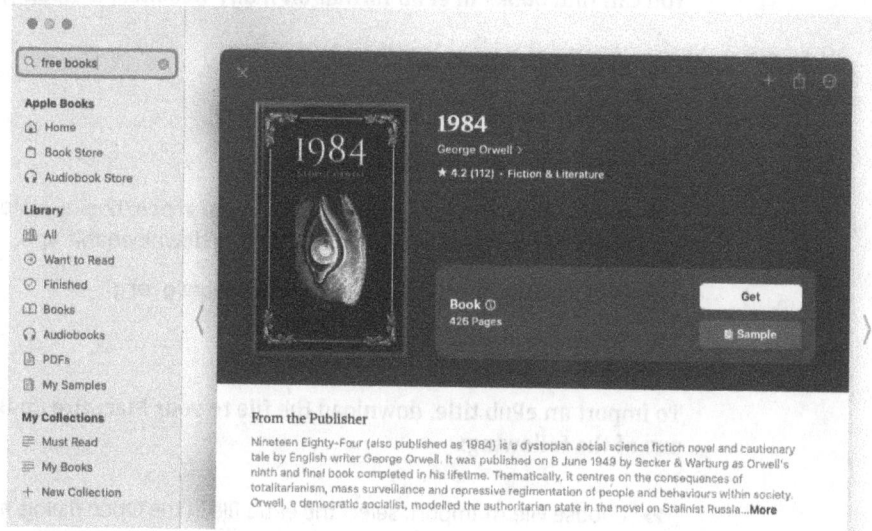

FIGURE 18-3: Buy books from the Book Store and add them to your Books library.

Click the Buy button (which shows the price) to buy the book. Or for free books, click the Get button (shown in Figure 18-3) to add the book to your library for free.

TIP

Many books offer a sample from the book that you can download for free. Click the Sample button, and a sample will appear in your Books library within minutes. If the Want to Read button appears, you can click it to add the book to your Want to Read list, which you can access by clicking the Want to Read category in the Library section of the sidebar.

The big angle brackets to the left and right of the book description in Figure 18-3 are Previous and Next buttons. Click the one on the left to see the previous book in this section; click the one on the right to see the next book in this section.

When you finish shopping, click All in the sidebar's Library section to return to your Books library.

Shopping for ebooks without Apple

Books can also handle books you acquire elsewhere. Books supports the ePub format, which is used by hundreds of thousands of free and public-domain books on the web. You can easily import such files into Books. The ePub titles must be *DRM-free*, which means free of any digital rights management restrictions.

You can find books in ePub format on many websites, including these:

>> **Baen:** www.baen.com

>> **eBooks.com:** https://www.ebooks.com/

>> **Feedbooks:** www.feedbooks.com

>> **Google Play:** https://play.google.com/store/books. Note that not all the books here are free, and Google has a downloadable app.

>> **Project Gutenberg:** https://www.gutenberg.org

>> **Smashwords:** www.smashwords.com

To import an ePub title, download the file to your Mac, fire up Books, and then do one of the following:

>> Choose File ⇨ Import, select the ePub file in the Open dialog, and then click Import.

>> Drag the ePub file from Finder into your Books library.

WARNING

You can't add books made for the Amazon Kindle to Books, not even ones that are DRM-free. To read Kindle books, download the free Kindle app from the Mac App Store. Avoid book-conversion websites that claim to be able to convert Kindle-format ebooks to ePub-format ebooks. The conversion is unlikely to work, and the sites may try to install malware on your Mac.

TIP

You *can* add PDF files to Books; it works the same as adding an ePub title. After they're imported, they appear in the PDF section of your Books library.

Finally, if you'd rather listen than read, you can make Books read text aloud:

1. **Click where you want to begin or select the text you want to hear.**

2. **Choose Edit ⇨ Speech ⇨ Start Speaking.**

   In a few seconds, a robotic voice will begin reading.

3. **To stop, choose Edit ⇨ Speech ⇨ Stop Speaking.**

It's not quite like having Mom or Dad read you to sleep, but it can be great for people with impaired vision.

TIP

You can change the voice by choosing System Settings ⇨ Accessibility ⇨ Spoken Content, and then clicking System Voice.

Finding and Listening to Podcasts with the Podcasts App

Podcasts are like radio or television shows, except when you subscribe to them, you can listen to or watch them (using the Podcasts app on your Mac, iPad, or iPhone) at any time you like. Thousands of podcasts are available and many (or most) are free.

To find podcasts, click Launchpad, click Podcasts, and then follow these steps:

1. **Click Browse or Top Charts in the sidebar.**

2. **Click a link in the content pane on the right or type a keyword or phrase in the Search field at the top of the sidebar.**

3. **When you find a podcast that appeals to you, do one of the following:**

   - Click the Follow button to receive all future episodes automatically.
   - Click the Latest Episode button to listen to the latest episode immediately.
   - Click the down-arrow button to download the current episode.

4. **Click the ellipsis (. . .) for additional options.**

Figure 18-4 shows all these things for the Mac Geek Gab audio podcast from *The Mac Observer.*

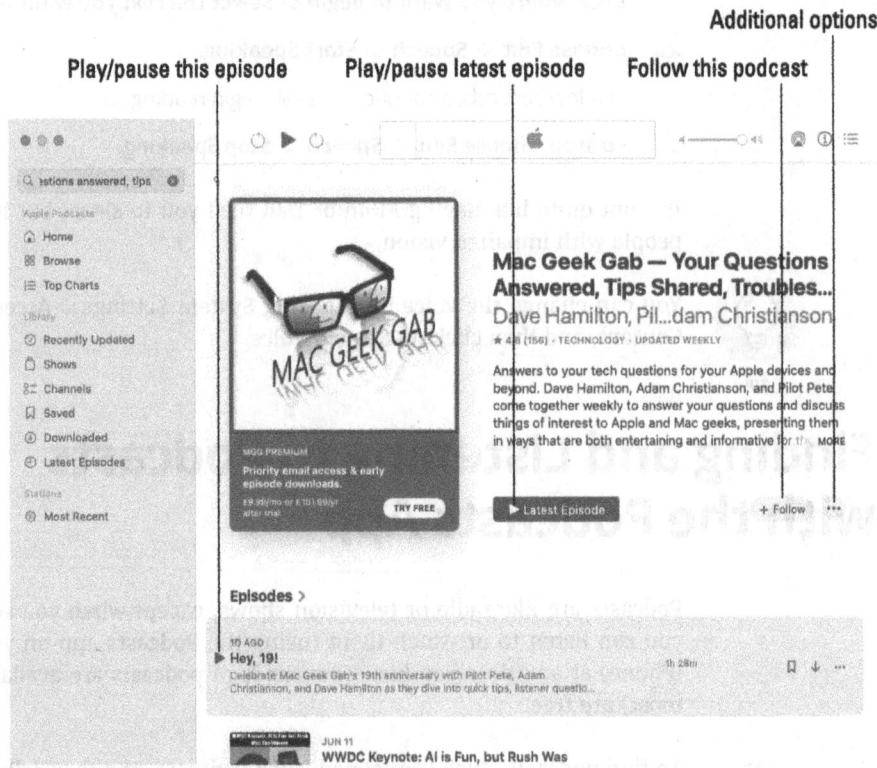

Play/pause this episode   Play/pause latest episode   Follow this podcast   Additional options

FIGURE 18-4:
The Mac Geek
Gab podcast from
The Mac Observer.

For more information on most podcasts, just move the pointer over an episode of the podcast, and then click the ellipsis that appears, as shown in Figure 18-4.

Following (formerly "subscribing to") a podcast offers several options. You can configure how often the Podcasts app checks for new episodes (hourly, daily, weekly, or manually); what to do when new episodes become available (download the most recent one, download all episodes, or do nothing); and how many episodes to keep in your Podcasts library (all, all unplayed, or a specific number between 2 and 10). To specify these settings, click a podcast you've followed in your library, click the ellipsis (. . .), and choose the appropriate option from the shortcut menu.

When you start listening to a followed podcast on your Mac in the Podcasts app and switch to an iPhone or iPad, the podcast will pick up where it left off on your Mac.

NEW

To see the transcript of a podcast episode, click the ellipsis (. . .) button on its row, and then click View Transcript on the pop-up menu.

You're the Star with Photo Booth

The Photo Booth app provides all the fun of an old-time (or new-time) photo booth, like the ones you sometimes see in malls or stores. It lets you shoot one photo, shoot a burst of four photos in a row, or shoot a movie using your Mac's built-in camera. If yours is one of the rare Macs with no built-in camera (such as the Mac mini) or you own a USB webcam better than the built-in model, rest assured that most USB webcams work with Photo Booth right out of the box with no drivers or other software necessary. Just launch Photo Booth and look in the Camera menu, where all compatible cameras appear.

TIP

If you have an iPhone, you can use it as your Photo Booth webcam by using Sequoia's Continuity Camera feature.

Photo Booth couldn't be easier to use. Start by clicking one of the three icons in the lower-left corner of the Photo Booth window — Burst (of four photos), Single Photo (selected in Figure 18-5), or Movie — and then click the red camera button to take a picture, as shown in Figure 18-5.

Before you shoot, you may want to explore the five pages of special effects — Sepia Tone, Color Pencil, Pop Art, and dozens more — by clicking the Effects button (lower right) and then clicking the particular effect you want to try. If you like it, click the red camera button and shoot a picture, pictures, or video; if you don't, click the Effects button again and click another effect. Or if you prefer to shoot with no effects, click the Normal effect in the center of any Effects page.

FIGURE 18-5:
Photo Booth
about to take a
picture of yours
truly using the
Thermal
Camera effect.

TIP

Photo Booth includes a feature called Screen Flash, which uses your computer display as a camera flash by turning the screen all-white as it shoots the photo. To turn on Screen Flash, open the Camera menu and click Enable Screen Flash. Screen Flash is disabled when you're shooting movies.

After you shoot, your pictures or movies drop into the tray at the bottom of the window (there are two photos of mutant me in Figure 18-5). You can then select one or more photos in the tray and then do any of the following:

>> **Delete them** by pressing the Delete or Backspace key.

>> **Share them** by clicking the Share button, which replaces the Effects button when one or more photos are selected in the tray.

>> **Export them as JPEG files** by choosing File ⇨ Export.

>> **Print them** by choosing File ⇨ Print or pressing ⌘+P.

>> **Drag them from the tray** to the desktop, a folder, an email, or an iMessage, where they appear as JPEG files; or drag them onto an image editor icon such as Photos (on the Dock or in the Applications folder). Because they're often suitable for blackmail, the photos are not automatically saved in your Photos library or elsewhere, so if you don't drag them somewhere, they exist only in the tray of the Photo Booth app.

Viewing and Converting Images and PDFs in Preview

You use Preview to open, view, and print PDFs as well as most graphics files (TIFF, JPEG, PICT, and so on). *PDF files* are formatted documents that can include text and images. User manuals, books, and the like are often distributed as PDF files. You can't edit the existing text in a PDF file with Preview, but you can leaf through its pages, annotate and mark it up, and print it. You can often select text and graphics in a PDF file, copy them to the Clipboard (⌘+C), and paste (⌘+V) them into documents in other apps. Preview is also the app that opens when you click the Preview button in the Print dialog (see Chapter 19).

TIP

Preview enables you to fill in PDF forms, such as those you download from the IRS and other government bodies. Filling in a PDF form is easier and quicker than printing legibly.

One of the most useful things Preview can do is change the file format of a graphic file. For example, say you're signing up for a website and want to add a picture to your profile. The website requires pictures in the JPEG file format, but the picture file on your hard drive that you'd like to use is in the TIFF file format. Preview can handle the conversion for you:

1. **Double-click the TIFF file to open it with Preview.**

   If another app (such as Adobe Photoshop) opens instead of Preview, quit it. Then either drag the TIFF document onto the Preview icon; or Control-click or right-click the file, click Open With, and then click Preview.

2. **Choose File ⇨ Export to open the Export dialog.**

3. **Click the Format pop-up menu, and then click the appropriate file format, such as JPEG or PNG.**

4. **(Optional) To make sure you don't confuse your original image with the one in the new format, change the name of your file in the Export As field.**

5. **(Optional) Add a tag or tags if you like.**

6. **Click Save.**

Preview lets you convert any file it can open to any of the following file formats: HEIC, JPEG, JPEG-2000, OpenEXR, PDF, PNG, and TIFF. Or choose File ⇨ Export as PDF to export the current file as a PDF.

HEIC is Apple's High Efficiency Image format, which creates smaller files with a higher image quality than JPEG. The upside is smaller files; the downside is that not all apps that can open a JPEG file can open an HEIC file.

TIP

Almost every macOS app with a Print command allows you to save your document as a PDF file. Just click on the PDF button (found in all Print dialogs) and choose Save as PDF from the pop-up menu. Then, should you ever need to convert that PDF file to a different file format, you can do so by using the preceding steps.

Chapter **19**

Managing Fonts
and Printing

Your Mac is great for creating attractive documents and for printing them to
create hard copies that you can share with others. In this chapter, you first
learn how to use the Font Book utility to get the fonts you need onto your
Mac so that you can use them in the documents you create with whichever apps
you prefer. You then discover how to connect one or more printers to your Mac
and print documents that look the way you want them to.

Font Mania

You can jazz up your documents, or make them a little more serious, with different fonts. To a computer user, *font* means *typeface* — what the text characters look
like. Although professional typographers will scream at this generalization, this
chapter uses that definition.

Tens of thousands of fonts are available for the Mac. macOS comes with hundreds
of fonts, which range from staid fonts, such as Times New Roman, to arty fonts,
such as Brush Script — plenty of variety to get you started with fonts.

If you really get into fonts, you can buy individual fonts and font collections anywhere you can buy software. Plenty of shareware and public-domain fonts are also available from online services and user groups. Some people have thousands of fonts. Some people even *use* thousands of fonts.

To see how to manage the third-party fonts you collect, check out the upcoming subsection, "Managing your fonts with Font Book."

Choosing font typefaces

macOS Sequoia supports a wide variety of font formats, including OpenType, Mac TrueType, Windows TrueType, bitmap, and dfont. That means pretty much any font you buy or download will probably work with macOS.

TECHNICAL
STUFF

The big exception is PostScript fonts. macOS used to support most kinds of PostScript fonts, but Apple removed this support in macOS 10.15 (Catalina). So if your Mac runs macOS Sequoia, you can't use PostScript fonts.

Managing your fonts with Font Book

macOS includes a utility called Font Book for managing your fonts. Font Book lets you view your installed fonts, install new fonts, group your fonts in collections, and activate and deactivate installed fonts. To open Font Book, click the Launchpad icon on the Dock, and then click Font Book.

TIP

By default, Font Book installs new fonts only for the current user (that's you). In this case, Font Book puts new fonts in your Home folder's Fonts folder, which is inside your hidden Library folder (~/Library/Fonts, where ~ represents your Home folder). To install fonts for all users of your Mac, choose Font Book⇨Settings, click the Installation tab of the Settings window, open the Default Install Location pop-up menu, and then click All Users instead of Current User (the only other choice). This setting makes Font Book put the fonts you install in the main Library folder (/Library/Fonts).

The easiest way to install a new font is to double-click it in Finder. Font Book opens and displays the font. Click the Install Font button to install the font.

Starting from Font Book, you can install a font by choosing File⇨Add Fonts. This command is Add Fonts to Current User if you've set the Default Install Location setting to Current User; if you've chosen All Users as the Default Install Location, the command is Add Fonts to All Users. Whichever way the command appears, you can also press ⌘+O to invoke it from the keyboard. A standard Open dialog appears. Select the font or fonts to install, and then click the Open button.

Font Book can display the font list in three views:

>> **Grid:** Choose View ▷ View as Grid, click the Grid button on the toolbar, or press ⌘+1 to switch to this view. Each font appears as a thumbnail showing a character or two; you can drag the slider on the toolbar to increase or decrease the size of the thumbnails. Grid view is useful for getting a quick overview of the available fonts.

>> **Samples:** Choose View ▷ View as Samples, click the Sample button on the toolbar, or press ⌘+2 to use this view. Each font appears in a box that shows a sample of the font. Samples view is great for seeing how each font looks, but you can see only a few fonts at a time.

>> **List:** Choose View ▷ View as List, click the List button on the toolbar, or press ⌘+3 for this view. All the fonts appear in a list, with each font family in an expandable section, like folders in List view in Finder. Click the > icon to expand a font family; click the resulting downward caret to collapse it again. Figure 19-1 shows Font Book in List view.

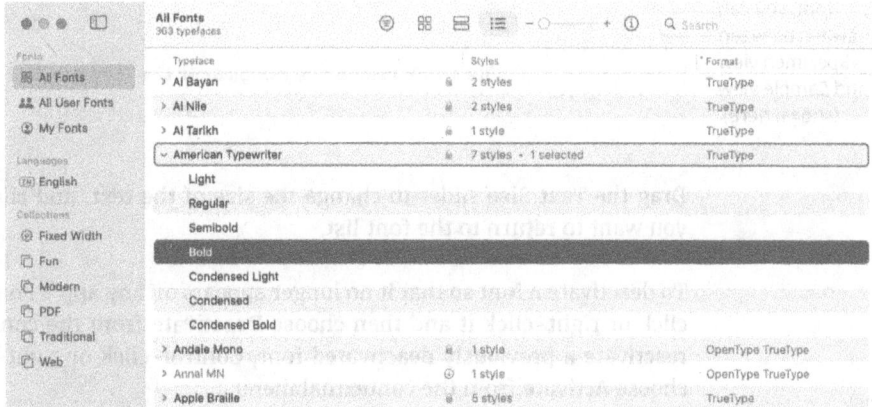

FIGURE 19-1:
Font Book in
List view.

To view or find fonts, start by clicking the appropriate item in the sidebar. The sidebar contains three expandable lists: Fonts, which lets you choose among All Fonts (really, all of them), All User Fonts (all the fonts installed for users), and My Fonts (just your fonts); Languages, which lets you choose any installed language; and Collections, which breaks the fonts into collections such as Fixed Width, Fun, Modern, Traditional, and Web.

So you might click All Fonts in the font list to display all the fonts in the main part of the window (as in Figure 19-1), or click Fixed Width in the Collections list to display just fixed-width fonts.

To view a font or font family, double-click its name in the font list. The font appears in the main part of the window, and you can switch between Specimen view (which shows a single style of the font) and Sample view (which shows all styles of the font using the *quick brown fox* sentence) by clicking the Specimen button or the Sample button on the toolbar. Figure 19-2 shows Sample view.

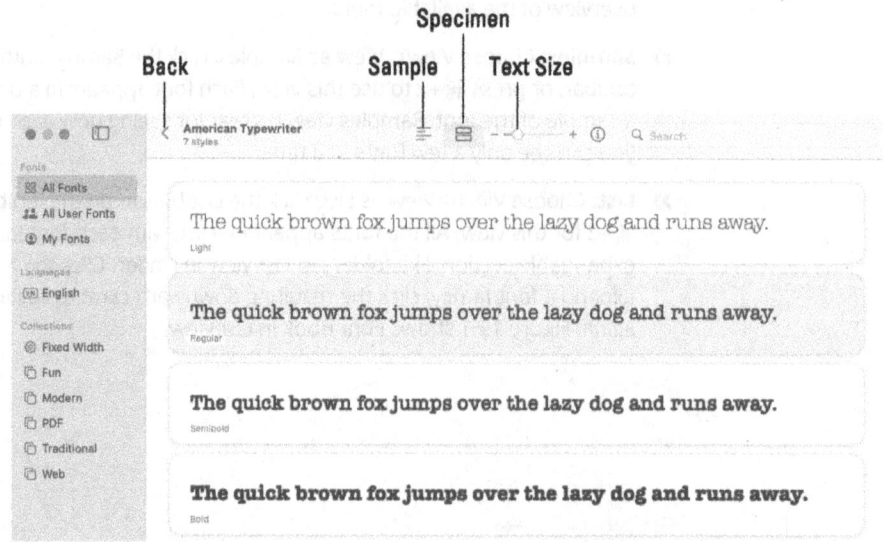

Specimen

Back   Sample   Text Size

FIGURE 19-2:
After displaying a
font, you can
switch between
Specimen view
and Sample view
(shown here).

Drag the Text Size slider to change the size of the text, and click Back (<) when you want to return to the font list.

To deactivate a font so that it no longer appears on any app's Font menu, Control-click or right-click it and then choose Deactivate from the contextual menu. To reactivate a previously deactivated font, Control-click or right-click it and then choose Activate from the contextual menu.

If a font's name is gray instead of black, that font is available but not yet downloaded to your Mac. To download and enable it, Control-click or right-click it and then choose Download from the contextual menu. After you download the font, Font Book activates it automatically, so you don't need to activate it manually.

Font Book looks out for your best interests, in that it won't allow you to deactivate or delete any fonts required by macOS itself — including (but not limited to) Lucida Grande, Helvetica, and Helvetica Neue.

TIP

Install only the fonts you need. Having tons of installed fonts can slow some apps and make the Font menu long and unmanageable. And the longer your Font menu gets, the longer it'll take the menu to appear after you click it. After installing those fonts, use them with discretion. Ransom notes have their place, but they are not widely popular.

Printing

Printing should be straightforward, but often it isn't. To make sure that you're set up to print without any headaches, this section walks you through the process of installing and configuring a printer, as though you've just gotten a new printer.

Pre-printer prep

Before you start, keep these two essentials in mind:

>> **Read the documentation that came with your printer.** Hundreds of printer makes and models that work with the Mac are available, so if your printer's manual tells you to do something different from what this chapter recommends, follow the manual's instructions first. If that approach doesn't work, try the techniques in this chapter.

REMEMBER

>> **The Print and Page Setup dialogs differ from app to app and from printer to printer.** Although this chapter's examples are representative of what you'll probably encounter, you may come across dialogs that look a bit different. The Print and Page Setup dialogs for Word, for example, include extra choices, such as Even or Odd Pages Only, Print Hidden Text, and Print Selection Only. If your Print dialog or Page Setup dialog contains commands that this chapter doesn't explain, they're specific to that app; look in its documentation for an explanation. Similarly, many graphics-related apps — such as Adobe Illustrator and Photoshop — have added their own Print dialog, which appears either before or instead of the macOS Print dialog.

Ready: Connecting and adding your printer

Before you can even think about printing something, you have to connect a printer to your Mac and tell macOS that the printer exists.

REMEMBER

If you have a printer and are already able to print documents, skip to "Set: Setting up your document with Page Setup," later in this chapter. Read this section only if you're setting up a new printer.

Connecting your printer

REMEMBER

Read your printer's documentation for specific details on how to set up your particular printer model, such as how to remove any seals from the ink or toner cartridges and how to load the cartridges into the printer.

Here are the general steps for connecting a printer to your Mac:

1. **Connect the printer to your Mac, with the cable snugly attached to both the printer and Mac.**

   Skip this step if your printer supports wireless printing and you intend to print only wirelessly. Also skip this step if your printer is a network-capable model and you've connected it to your network's switch or router with an Ethernet cable (again, snugly at each end — most Ethernet cables click into place).

   For your printer to work, you have to connect it to a data source somehow. Connecting with a cable is usually more reliable than connecting wirelessly.

2. **Plug the printer's AC power cord into a power outlet in the wall, on a power strip, or on an uninterruptible power supply (UPS).**

WARNING

   Plugging an inkjet printer into a UPS works fine, but be careful with laser printers, because they typically draw a lot of power briefly while heating their fuser rollers in preparation for printing. This power draw can swamp the UPS and rob other devices of power. To avoid this potential problem but protect your laser printer from power spikes, plug it into one of the surge-protected sockets on the UPS, not into one of the battery-powered sockets.

3. **Turn on your printer.**

   Look in the manual if you can't find the power switch. (The switch is on the printer. The manual will tell you where.)

Setting up a printer for the first time

After you connect your computer and printer and provide a power source for your printer, you're ready to configure your Mac to communicate with the printer.

REMEMBER

Many, if not all, of the steps involving the Printers & Scanners pane of System Settings require your printer to be powered on and warmed up — that is, already done with its diagnostics and start-up cycle. So make sure that your printer is not only connected to your Mac, but also ready to rock and roll.

The first time you connect your printer, you may see an alert asking whether you want to download and install software for your printer. You do, so click the Install button. At this point, you may see a License Agreement window; click the Agree button to proceed. (Clicking Disagree halts the installation process.)

TIP

If you connect a new printer, and you don't see an alert, don't worry; just follow the upcoming instructions.

After you click the Install button and the Agree button, a Software Update window may appear, telling you that it's finding software. If so, leave it alone; it disappears after a minute or two. Don't click the Stop button unless you want to abort the installation.

Here are the steps for setting up a printer for the first time:

1. **Choose System Settings⇨Printers & Scanners to display the Printers & Scanners pane of System Settings.**

2. **Click the Add Printer, Scanner, or Fax button to open the Add Printer dialog (shown in Figure 19-3 with settings chosen).**

   (Yes, the fax is still alive. There's an enduring technology for you!)

3. **At the top of the Add Printer dialog, make sure that the Default tab is displayed.**

   If it's not, click the Default button (the printer icon at the left end of the toolbar).

   The IP button (the globe icon in the middle of the toolbar) is for connecting to printers via Internet Protocol (IP). Such printers may use connections via LPD (Line Printer Daemon, a network printing protocol) or Socket (another network printing method), or may be shared across the Internet.

   The Windows button (the printer icon at the right end of the toolbar) is for connecting to printers shared by Windows computers on the network.

4. **In the list box, select the printer you want to add.**

   The printer's default details appear in the Name box, the Location box, and the Use pop-up menu.

5. **(Optional) In the Name box, change the printer's name.**

   The printer normally appears listed by its model number, which usually isn't very informative. You may want to call the printer something more descriptive, such as *Little color printer*, especially if you'll be sharing it with other people on your network.

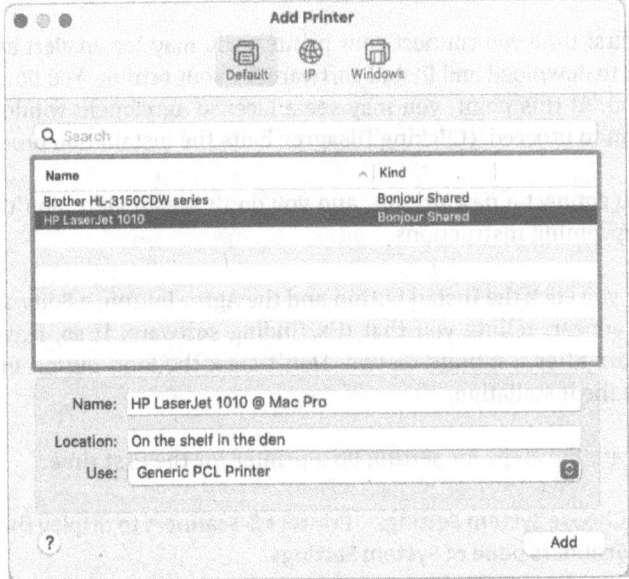

FIGURE 19-3:
Select your
printer on the
Default tab of the
Add Printer
dialog.

6. **(Optional) In the Location box, type a description of the printer's whereabouts.**

   Like the name, the location is important when you share the printer on the network. You may want to type something like **In the den** or **On top of the refrigerator** in this box.

7. **If the Use pop-up menu is set to Generic PCL Printer, try to find and choose a more-specific driver.**

   Click the pop-up menu and choose Select Software to open the Printer Software dialog (see Figure 19-4). Select the best driver match by browsing or by searching and then click OK.

   If there's no suitable match, click the Cancel button to close the Printer Software dialog. Download the latest driver from the printer manufacturer's website, and run its installer. Then open the Printer Software dialog again, select the new driver, and click OK.

   See the nearby sidebar, "Go for a Driver," for more information.

TECHNICAL
STUFF

   In case you're wondering, PCL is the abbreviation for *Printer Control Language*.

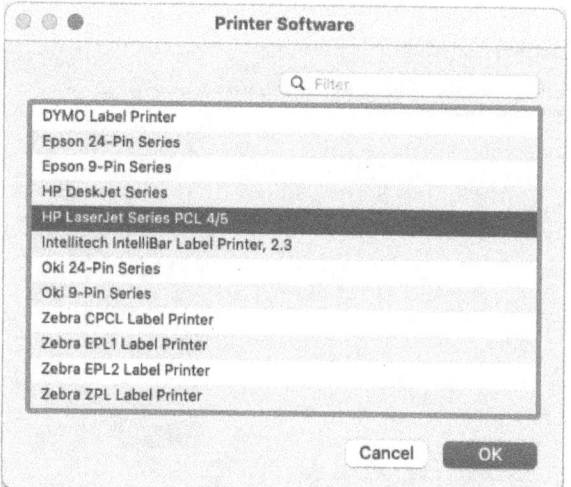

FIGURE 19-4:
Select a suitable
driver in the
Printer Software
dialog.

8. **Back in the Add Printer dialog, click the Add button.**

   If the Setting Up [printer name] dialog appears (see Figure 19-5), select or deselect the check boxes for any features that macOS suspects the printer may have, as needed. The HP LaserJet shown in the figure doesn't have a duplexer, for example, so you'd deselect the Duplexer check box.

9. **Click OK.**

   The Add Printer dialog closes, and the printer appears in the Printers & Scanners pane (see Figure 19-6).

10. **From the Default Printer pop-up menu, choose the printer you want to use by default.**

    Your choices are a specific printer (such as the printer you just installed) and Last Printer Used.

11. **From the Default Paper Size pop-up menu, choose the default paper size you want to use with this printer, such as US Letter.**

12. **Close System Settings.**

    You're ready to print your first document. Before you do, however, make sure that you have the document set up to look the way you want it. See "Set: Setting up your document with Page Setup," later in this chapter, for more info.

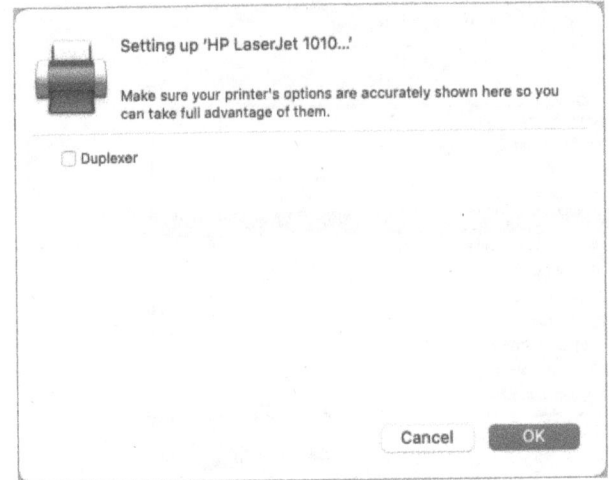

FIGURE 19-5:
In the Setting Up
[printer name]
dialog, select or
deselect the
check boxes for
printer features.

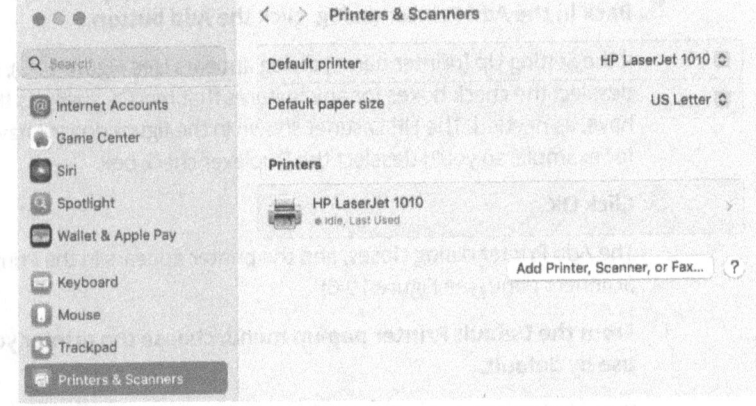

FIGURE 19-6:
The printer
appears in the
Printers &
Scanners pane of
System Settings.

GO FOR A DRIVER

macOS Sequoia includes a library of printer drivers that covers many popular printer brands and models. These drivers are installed by default. macOS also checks to see whether a newer driver is available — for every driver in its library — and if it finds one, it offers to download and install the new driver (as described earlier in this chapter).

If macOS can't find a driver for your printer, you need to install the appropriate printer drivers manually before your printer will appear in the Printers list in the Printers & Scanners pane of System Settings. So find and download the driver at the manufacturer's website, install it, and get ready to print.

Most printer manufacturers update their drivers now and then to add functionality, fix bugs, or both. If the printer included a CD, the driver on it is most likely out of date. So ignore the CD and let macOS take care of installing or updating the printer driver if possible. And if for some reason macOS can't manage it (which is rare), download the most recent version from the vendor's website rather than install the probably outdated version on the printer's CD.

Sharing your Mac's printer on the network

If you want to share a printer that's connected directly to your Mac (with others on your wired or wireless local network), choose System Settings⇨Printers & Scanners, click the printer to display its configuration dialog, and then set the Share This Printer on the Network switch to On (blue).

When you do, you may see a yellow warning triangle and the message *Printer sharing is turned off*. Click the Open Sharing Settings button to go straight to the Sharing pane of System Settings, and then set the Printer Sharing switch to On (blue). If macOS prompts you to authenticate yourself, do so.

Printer sharing is on now. Normally, that setting means that everyone on the network can print to your printer. To mitigate the onslaught of print jobs, click the Info (i) button to the right of the Printer Sharing switch in the Sharing pane and then work in the Printer Sharing dialog (shown in Figure 19-7 with the settings changed).

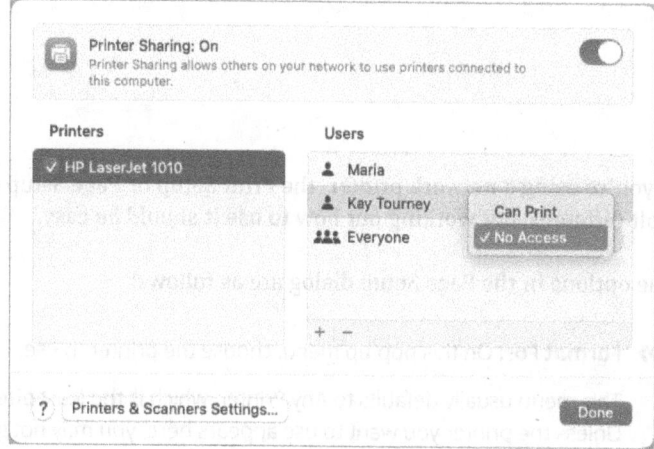

FIGURE 19-7: In the Printer Sharing dialog, choose which users can print to your shared printer.

By default, the only entry in the Users box is the Everyone group, which receives Can Print permission. To change this setting, click the Add (+) button, select the appropriate users or groups in the resulting dialog, and then click the Select button. The Users box in the Printer Sharing dialog shows the users and groups you chose without any permission entry (which means they can print — there's nothing saying they can't), and the Everyone group with the No Access permission, which means that other people can't print. Click the Done button to close the Printer Sharing dialog.

Set: Setting up your document with Page Setup

After setting up your printer, you can print — but you need to make the right choices in the Page Setup dialog to get the printout to look the way you want. This dialog enables you to choose your target printer, paper size, page orientation, and scale. To open this dialog, you usually choose File⇨Page Setup. Some apps use a different command, such as File⇨Print Setup, so be prepared to look around if necessary. Figure 19-8 shows the Page Setup dialog for the TextEdit app.

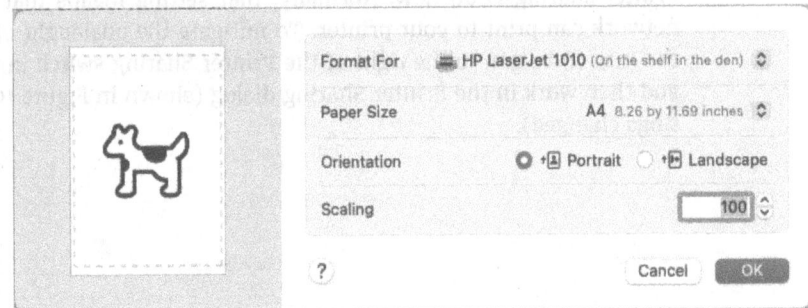

FIGURE 19-8:
The Page Setup
dialog in the
TextEdit app.

REMEMBER

If you're using a network printer, the Print Setup or Page Setup dialog might look a bit different, but working out how to use it should be easy.

The options in the Page Setup dialog are as follows:

>> **Format For:** On this pop-up menu, choose the printer to use.

This menu usually defaults to Any Printer, which is the least effective setting. Unless the printer you want to use appears here, you may not get full functionality when you print.

>> **Paper Size:** On this pop-up menu, choose the type of paper currently in the paper tray of your printer or the size of the paper you want to feed manually. The dimensions of the paper that you choose appear after its name.

>> **Orientation:** Select the Portrait radio button to print the page in portrait orientation (like a letter, taller than it is wide). Select the Landscape radio button to print in landscape orientation (wider than it is tall).

>> **Scaling:** To print your page at a larger or smaller size, change this option to a larger or smaller percentage.

REMEMBER

All these options remain in effect until you choose different settings. After you print an envelope, for example, remember to change the Paper Size setting back to Letter before trying to print on letter-size paper again.

Some apps offer additional Page Setup options. If your app offers them, they usually appear on the Settings pop-up menu in the Page Setup dialog. (Apps such as Photoshop and Word have extra options; TextEdit doesn't.)

Preview: Checking the page and setting PDF options in the Preview app

To see a preview of what your printed page will look like, click the PDF pop-up menu at the bottom of the Print dialog, and then choose Open in Preview. This command makes the Preview app display the pages that you're about to print.

TIP

macOS can save any printable document as a PDF file. To do so, click the PDF pop-up menu at the bottom of the Print dialog, and then choose Save As PDF.

If you have any doubt about the way a document will look when you print it, preview it first. When you're happy with the preview, choose File⇨Print, press ⌘+P, or click the Print button at the bottom of the Preview window. Or click the Cancel button to return to your app and make changes to the document.

Preview works with the Preview app. With the Preview feature, you can do cool things like these:

>> See all the pages in your document the way they'll be printed, one by one.

>> Zoom in or out to get a different perspective on what you're printing.

>> Rotate the picture 90 degrees to the left or right.

>> Insert (via drag-and-drop), delete, or reorder pages in Preview's sidebar.

>> Spot errors before you print something. A little up-front inspection can save paper, ink or toner, and frustration.

 Click the Show Markup Toolbar icon (shown in the margin) to display the Markup toolbar, which provides tools for marking up a document. See Chapter 5 for more information on Markup.

Check out the Preview app's View menu, where you'll find (among other things) four useful views: Content Only, Thumbnails, Table of Contents, and Contact Sheet, as well as the zoom commands (and more). Also check out Preview's toolbar, from which you can add or delete icons by choosing View⇨Customize Toolbar. And look at the items on the Tools menu, which let you rotate pages, move forward or back through multipage documents, and toggle the Magnifier (choose Tools⇨Show Magnifier or press `, the back–tick character that you'll usually find on the tilde [~] key).

Print: Printing from the Print dialog

After you connect and configure your printer and set up how you want your document to print, you need only navigate the Print dialog to print your document.

REMEMBER Most Print dialogs look like the figures shown here, but others differ — sometimes a lot. The features in the Print dialog depend on the app from which you're printing. Many apps choose to use the standard–issue Apple dialog, but not all do. If your Print dialog contains features this section doesn't explain, see the app's documentation for an explanation of the features.

Printing a document

Follow these steps to print a document:

1. **Open the document you want to print.**

2. **Choose File⇨Print (or press ⌘ +P) to open the Print dialog (see Figure 19-9).**

   Some apps locate the Print command on a different menu or use a different shortcut, but you'll find the command easily enough.

3. **Click Print.**

4. **Wait a moment for your Mac to tell the printer what to do and for the pages to print.**

5. **Pick up the printed pages from the printer.**

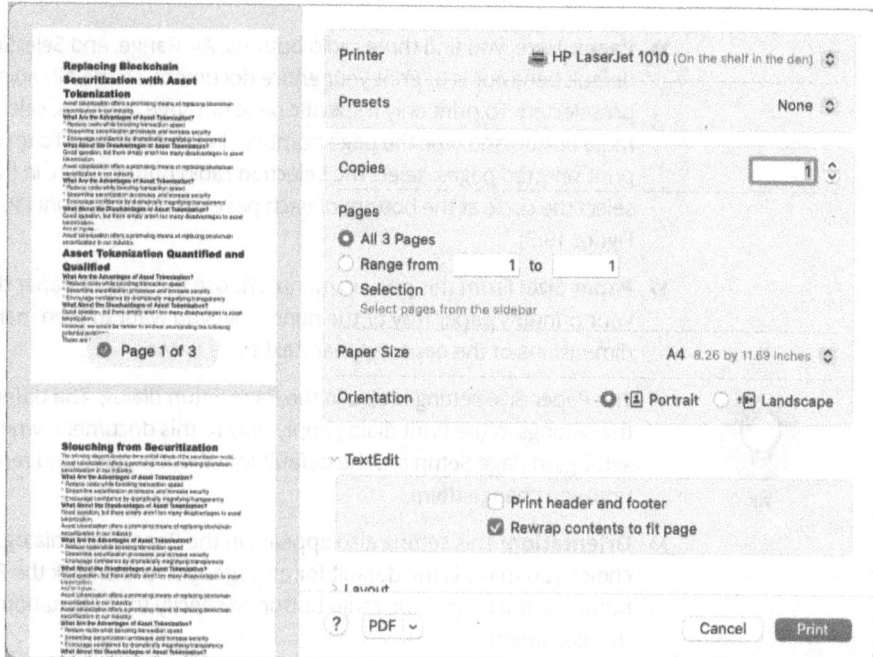

Choosing among printers

Open the Printer pop-up menu at the top of the Print dialog and choose the printer to use.

REMEMBER

You can choose only among the printers available in the Printers & Scanners pane of System Settings. This list includes printers connected to wireless base stations and routers, as well as Wi-Fi–enabled printers. After you've set up a Wi-Fi–enabled printer, Macs (and other devices) within range can print to it wirelessly.

Choosing custom settings

In addition to the drop-down Printer menu, your expanded Print dialog offers the following options:

>> **Presets:** This pop-up menu lets you manage and save print settings, as described in the next subsection, "Saving custom printer settings."

>> **Copies:** In this text field, set how many copies you want to print. The Print dialog defaults to one (1) in most apps, so if you want a single copy, you don't need to change anything. To print more copies, enter the number, either by typing it or by clicking the up- or down-arrow button.

>> **Pages:** Here, you find three radio buttons: All, Range, and Selection. The default behavior is to print your entire document, so the All radio button is preselected. To print only a specific page or range of pages, select the Range radio button and type the page numbers in the From and To text fields. To print selected pages, select the Selection radio button; then, in the sidebar, select the circle at the bottom of each page you want to print (as shown in Figure 19-9).

>> **Paper Size:** From this pop-up menu, choose the type of paper that's already in your printer's paper tray or the paper that you want to feed manually. The dimensions of the paper appear next to its name.

TIP

The Paper Size setting is also in the Page Setup dialog. The difference is that the settings in the Print dialog apply only to this document, whereas the settings in Page Setup are the default for all documents and remain in effect until you change them.

>> **Orientation:** This setting also appears in the Page Setup dialog, where the choice you make is the default for all pages you print. Click the Portrait radio button or the Landscape radio button to specify the orientation for printing this document.

REMEMBER

The settings you choose in the Print dialog apply only to this document.

Farther down the Print dialog, you can configure settings that are specific to the app you're using, as well as Layout, Paper Handling, Printer Options, and Printer Info settings:

>> **App-specific settings (here, TextEdit):** The only TextEdit-specific options are two check boxes. Select or deselect the Print Header and Footer check box to control whether the printout includes the document's header and footer. Select or deselect the Rewrap Contents to Fit Page check box to control whether TextEdit rewraps lines to fit on the page or simply prints them as they stand.

TIP

The preview in the sidebar shows the effect of selecting and clearing these check boxes.

>> **Layout:** Expand the Layout section by clicking its heading. Then you can configure the following settings:

● *Pages per Sheet:* Open this pop-up menu and choose the number of document pages to print on each sheet of paper: 1 (the default), 2, 4, 6, 9, or 16.

● *Layout Direction:* Choose one of the four icons to specify how multiple document pages are laid out on the printed page.

● *Border:* Your choices on this pop-up menu are None, Single Hairline, Single Thin Line, Double Hairline, and Double Thin Line.

- *Two-Sided:* If your printer supports two-sided (known as *duplex*) printing, the three radio buttons allow you to specify whether you're going to use two-sided printing, and if so, whether you'll be binding (or stapling) along the long or short edge of the paper or creating a booklet.

- *Reverse Page Orientation:* Set this switch to On (blue) to flip the pages upside down.

- *Flip Horizontally:* Set this switch to On (blue) to flip the pages horizontally.

>> **Paper Handling:** Expand the Paper Handling section if you want to collate the printed sheets, reverse the order in which the document's pages print, or print only the odd- or even-numbered pages. You can also specify whether the document's paper size is to be used (in which case you might have lines that break across pages) or whether the output should be scaled to fit the chosen paper size.

>> **Printer Options:** Expand this section to reach the Paper Feed button and Printer Features button. Click the Info (i) icon on the right of one of these buttons to display the Paper Feed dialog or the Printer Features dialog, in which you can choose further settings. Some printers support *duplexing*, printing on both sides of the paper.

>> **Printer Info:** Expand this section to see information about the printer: its name, location, and model (actually the printer driver, not the printer model). The most useful information here is Supply Levels, which tells you how much ink or toner the printer has left. Supply Levels data is available for only some printers.

Saving custom printer settings

After you customize your printer settings just the way you like them, you can save them for future use. Just click the Presets pop-up menu, choose Save Current Settings as Preset, and then provide a name for this preset. In the Available For area, select the radio button for the current printer to make the preset available only for that printer, or select the All Printers radio button to make the preset available to other printers as well.

From then on, the preset name appears as an option on the Presets pop-up menu. Choose your saved preset before you print any document, and all the individual settings associated with that preset are restored.

To manage your presets, display the Print dialog, click the Presets pop-up menu, and then choose Edit Preset List. The resulting list of your presets and their settings allows you to delete a preset or rename it by double-clicking the current name and typing a new one.

IN THIS CHAPTER

» Reducing eyestrain with Dark mode

» Shopping for apps with the Mac App Store

» Using your iPhone as a camera or scanner for your Mac

» Talking and listening to your Mac

» Controlling your iPhone from your Mac

» Other helpful apps and utilities you can try

Chapter **20**

Features for the Way You Work

This chapter delves into some macOS features that might improve the ways you interact with your Mac. Get ready to roll up your sleeves and dig into these features. First up: Dark mode; the Mac App Store; and Continuity Camera, which lets you use your iPhone or iPad as a camera or scanner for your Mac. After that, talking and listening to your Mac, controlling your iPhone from your Mac via iPhone Mirroring, and much more.

Going Over to the Dark Side

macOS has long been celebrated for its bright and beautiful interface, which helps make computing a pleasure. But if you sometimes find the default macOS look too bright for comfort, you can reduce the screen's brightness by enabling Dark mode. As you can see in the top screen in Figure 20-1, Dark mode completely changes the appearance of windows, buttons, menus, and other interface elements from Light mode (shown in the bottom screen).

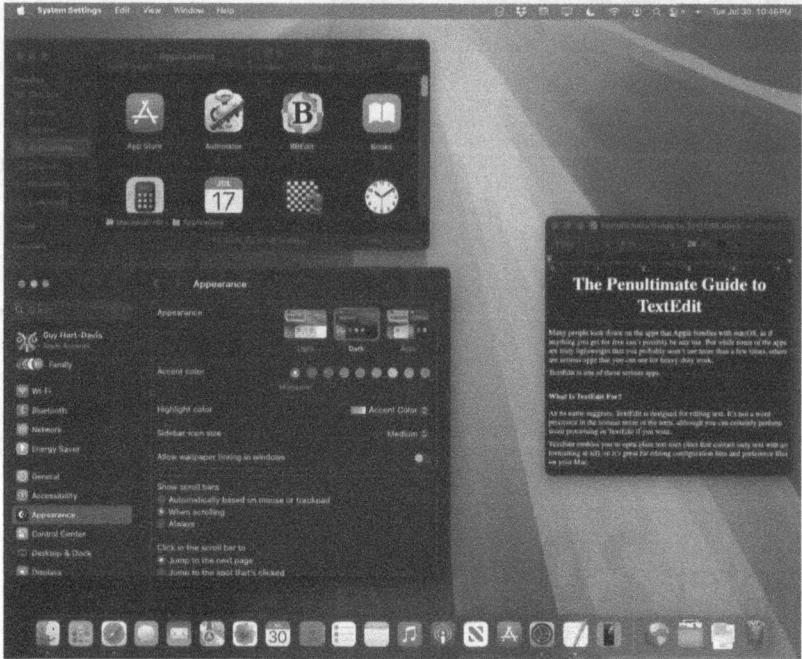

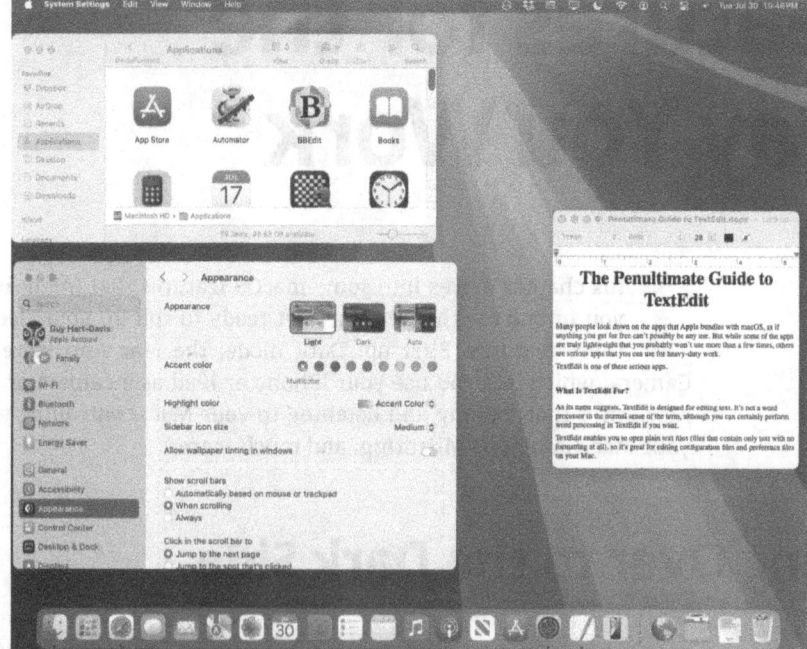

FIGURE 20-1:
Three windows,
the menu bar,
and the Dock
in Dark mode
(top) and Light
mode (bottom).

To choose Dark (or Light) mode, open the System Settings app, click Appearance in the sidebar, and then click Dark (or Light). Or click Auto to have macOS switch between the Light appearance and the Dark appearance based on the time of day. Some apps, such as iMovie, use a Dark mode look all the time and don't have a Light look.

TIP

Try changing the accent and highlight colors in Dark mode; they look slightly different than in Light mode.

App Shopping Made Easy

Introduced in 2011, the Mac App Store is the largest catalog of Mac software in the world. The App Store works in pretty much the same way as the iTunes Store (discussed in Chapter 17) and uses the credit card you have on file at the iTunes Store. If you've used the App Store on an iPhone or an iPad, you'll have no trouble using the Mac App Store.

Launch the App Store app by clicking the App Store icon on the Dock; or by opening Launchpad, and then clicking App Store. You can then navigate by clicking the categories in the sidebar:

>> **Discover:** This category displays new apps and recently updated apps.

>> **Arcade:** This category is home to the Apple Arcade subscription service, which offers more than 200 games with no ads and no additional purchases for $6.99 a month after a free 1-month trial. You can play the games on the iPhone, iPad, and even Apple TV, as well as on the Mac.

TIP

You can also get access to Apple Arcade by taking out a subscription to Apple One, which gives you access to some or all of these six services: Apple Music, Apple TV+, Apple Arcade, iCloud+, Apple News+, and Apple Fitness+.

>> **Create:** This category presents apps for video, audio, photo creation, editing, and more.

>> **Work:** This category contains any number of productivity apps.

>> **Play:** This category offers fun and games.

>> **Develop:** This category contains developer tools.

>> **Categories:** This screen enables you to browse using nearly two dozen top-level categories, such as Business, Music, and Sports (see Figure 20-2).

When you click a category, you see two recommended apps at the top of the screen, followed by a pair of lists: Top Free and Top Paid. You can see only six apps at a time in each list, but when you hover your pointer over a section, Next and Previous icons appear, looking like giant greater-than (>) and less-than (<) symbols. Click the Next or Previous icon to browse further apps.

>> **Updates:** This category shows you any available updates for your apps.

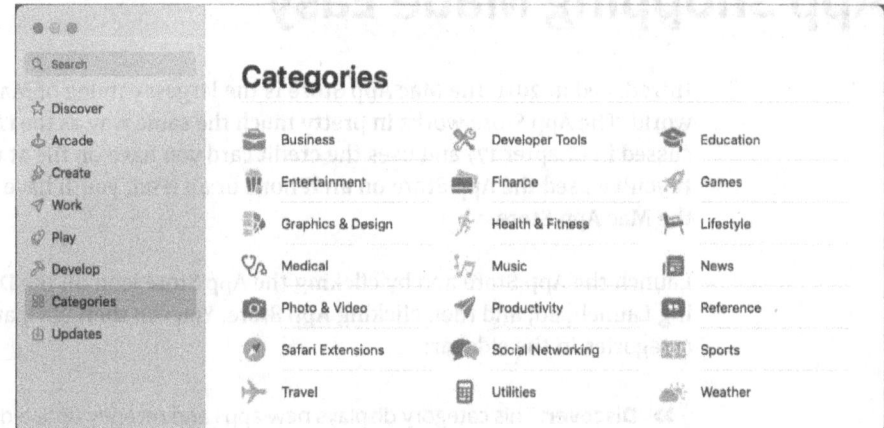

FIGURE 20-2:
The Categories tab lets you drill down into nearly two dozen categories in the App Store.

TIP

A badge (the red rounded rectangle bearing a number) on the App Store icon on the Dock means updates are available for some of your apps. Launch the App Store app and click the Updates tab to see the apps with updates awaiting them.

Using Your iPhone as Your Mac's Camera or Scanner

Continuity Camera lets you use your iPhone or iPad as a camera or scanner for your Mac. For Continuity Camera to work, both the Mac and the iPhone or iPad must

>> Be logged into the same Apple ID and using two-factor authentication.

>> Be connected to the same Wi-Fi network.

>> Have Bluetooth enabled.

If your devices meet those criteria, you can use your iPhone or iPad as a camera or scanner and have the resulting photo or scan inserted into your document or saved to the Finder in seconds.

To use Continuity Camera, Control-click or right-click anywhere an image or scan can be used (Notes, Stickies, TextEdit or Pages documents, and Finder, to name a few).

Not every app or document supports Continuity Camera, but if it's available when you Control-click or right-click, the commands appear on the contextual menu. If only one device is available, you'll see a section such as the My iPhone section (see the left screen in Figure 20-3). If two or more devices are available, you'll see the Insert from iPhone or iPad submenu (see the right screen in Figure 20-3). In this case, go to the section for the appropriate device, and then click the action you want to take, such as Take Photo.

FIGURE 20-3:
If the app supports Continuity Camera, the contextual menu contains either a section for your iPhone or iPad (left) or the Insert from iPhone or iPad submenu (right; if multiple devices are available).

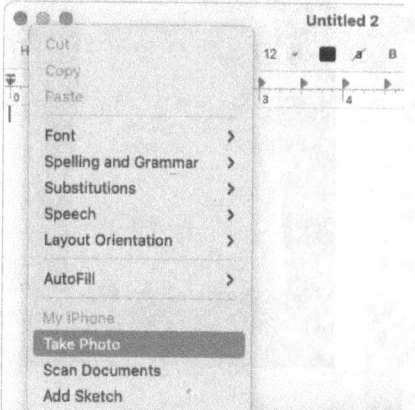
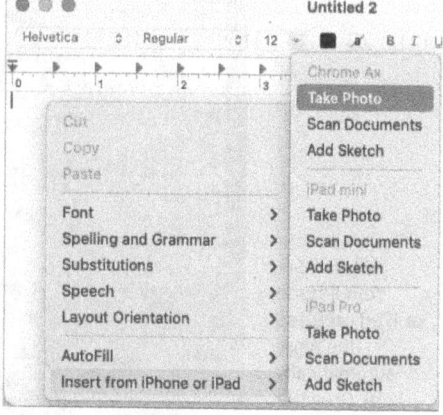

From the contextual menu or the submenu, choose Take Photo, Scan Documents, or Add Sketch, as appropriate.

If you choose Take Photo, the Camera app on your iPhone or iPad launches automatically, and you see one of two things on your Mac. If you Control-click or right-click in a document, you see an overlay below the insertion point; if you Control-click or right-click in Finder, you see a dialog instead of an overlay.

Take the photo on your iPhone or iPad by tapping the Camera app's shutter-release button in the usual fashion. After you snap a shot, a preview appears, offering two options: Retake or Use Photo. Tap Retake if you're dissatisfied with the image and want to try again. When you get a shot you're happy with, tap Use Photo, and the shot appears in the document at the insertion point or in the Finder almost immediately.

Choosing Scan Documents is similar to taking a photo, with some minor differences. You'll still see an overlay or a dialog on your Mac, but this time, the overlay or dialog says Scan a Document rather than Take a Photo.

On your iPhone or iPad, however, the Camera app works differently. In the top-right corner is a button that toggles between Auto mode and Manual mode. In Auto mode, you move the camera up, down, and all around until the blue box contains the text you want to scan, as shown on the left side of Figure 20-4. When the Camera app thinks it's nailed the subject, it takes the shot.

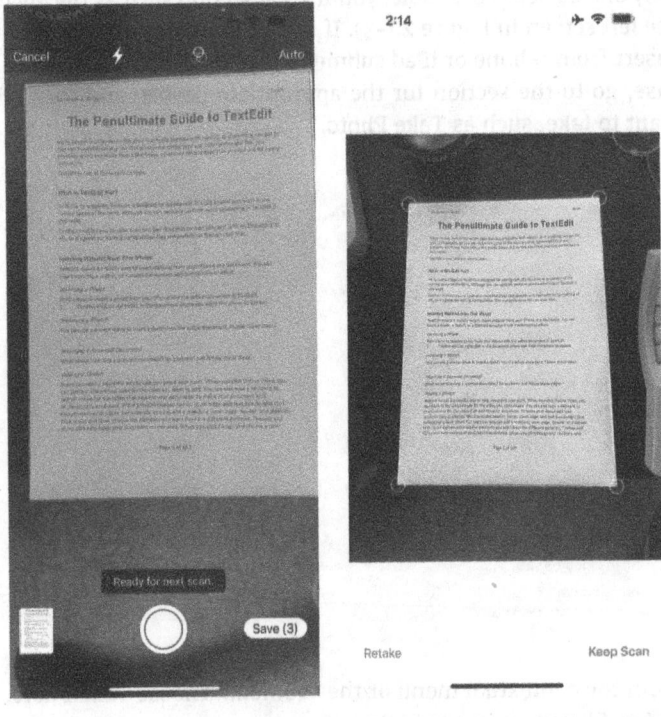

FIGURE 20-4:
Your iPhone
or iPad captures
the page
automatically
(left). Drag the
circles to contain
the text you want
to scan (right).

Or if you tap Auto (which switches the camera to Manual mode), you tap the shutter-release button to capture text.

After you capture a page, a preview of it appears, but in addition to the two buttons at the bottom of the screen (Retake and Keep Scan), a box appears, with circles at each of its four corners, as shown on the right side of Figure 20-4. Drag the circles until the box contains all the text you want to scan, and then tap Keep Scan.

After you tap Keep Scan, the camera reappears, with the message *Ready for Next Scan*. If you have additional pages to scan, continue capturing them as described. When you're finished, tap Save in the bottom-right corner.

Talking and Listening to Your Mac

Your primary methods of interacting with your Mac are typing, using the trackpad or mouse, and reading text. But you and your Mac can also communicate via voice. Your Mac has powerful built-in speech features and can talk to you as well as listen. It can both type the words you speak and obey your spoken commands.

All MacBooks and iMacs have microphones built in; if you have a Mac mini, a Mac Studio, or a Mac Pro, you'll need to add an external microphone.

Using Dictation: You talk, and your Mac types

macOS's Dictation feature can save you any amount of time and effort. Dictation doesn't suit everyone, but it's well worth trying.

First, enable Dictation. Choose System Settings ⇨ Keyboard to display the Keyboard pane, go to the Dictation section, and set the Use Dictation switch to On (blue). (The switch has a long name, of which Use Dictation are the first two words.) If the Do You Want to Enable Dictation? dialog opens, click Enable.

WARNING

Dictation processes some of your audio input on your Mac and sends other parts across the Internet to Apple's servers for conversion to text. macOS may also send other information, such as your contacts, to Apple to help your Mac understand what you're saying. If that makes you uncomfortable, you probably shouldn't use Dictation.

Make sure the Microphone Source pop-up menu shows the microphone you want to use; if not, open the menu and click the right microphone. Set the Auto-Punctuation switch to On (blue) if you want Dictation to try to punctuate your dictated text based on sense; set this switch to Off (white) if you prefer to dictate punctuation.

Once you've enabled Dictation, it's easy to use. Click where you want your words to appear in a document, dialog, web form, or whatever. Then choose Edit ⇨ Start Dictation, or press the Fn key twice in rapid succession.

TIP

If your keyboard doesn't have an Fn key, click the Shortcut pop-up menu in the Keyboard pane, and change the shortcut to one that works with your keyboard.

When you start Dictation, a blue bubble containing a white microphone icon appears (see Figure 20-5). You can then start speaking, and Dictation transcribes your words into the document after a slight delay. If your Mac is relatively recent, it will likely keep pace with your dictation unless you speak extremely rapidly.

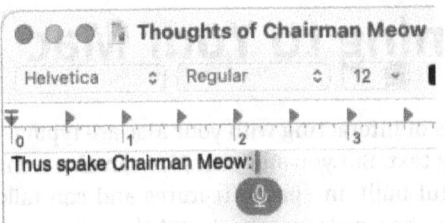

FIGURE 20-5:
The microphone
icon for Dictation.

To stop dictating, press Esc or click the microphone icon.

TIP

Save your document after you speak a few sentences or paragraphs. If you don't, the words you dictated since your last Save will be lost if the app or your Mac crashes.

You can insert punctuation by speaking its name, such as "period" or "comma." You can also perform simple formatting by saying "new line" or "new paragraph" to add space between lines.

Here are four tips for getting the best results when you dictate:

>> **Speak in a normal voice at a moderate volume level.**

>> **Avoid background noise.** If you expect to use dictation in a noisy environment or a room with a lot of ambient echo, use a headset microphone.

>> **Make sure the microphone isn't obstructed.** Check your Mac's User Guide for the location of your MacBook or iMac's built-in microphone.

>> **Make sure the input volume of an external microphone is sufficient.** If you're using an external microphone, and Dictation doesn't respond to your voice, choose System Settings ⇨ Sound, click the Input tab, and drag the Input Volume slider to the right until the meter shows a suitable response.

Commanding your Mac by voice

Voice Control enables your Mac to recognize and respond to human speech. All you need to use it is a microphone (which a MacBook or iMac has; you need to add one to a Mac mini, Mac Studio, or Mac Pro) and a voice.

Voice Control lets you issue verbal commands such as "Get my mail!" to your Mac and have it actually get your email. You can also create AppleScripts and Automator workflows, as well as Finder Quick Actions (see Chapter 5), and trigger them by voice. (AppleScripts and Automator workflows are advanced features that are beyond the scope of this book but well worth a look once you've mastered everything in the book.)

To enable Voice Control, choose System Settings ➪ Accessibility ➪ Voice Control, and then set the Voice Control switch to On (blue) in the Voice Control pane. While here, click the Commands button to display the Commands dialog (see Figure 20-6), in which you can enable or disable the available Voice Control commands.

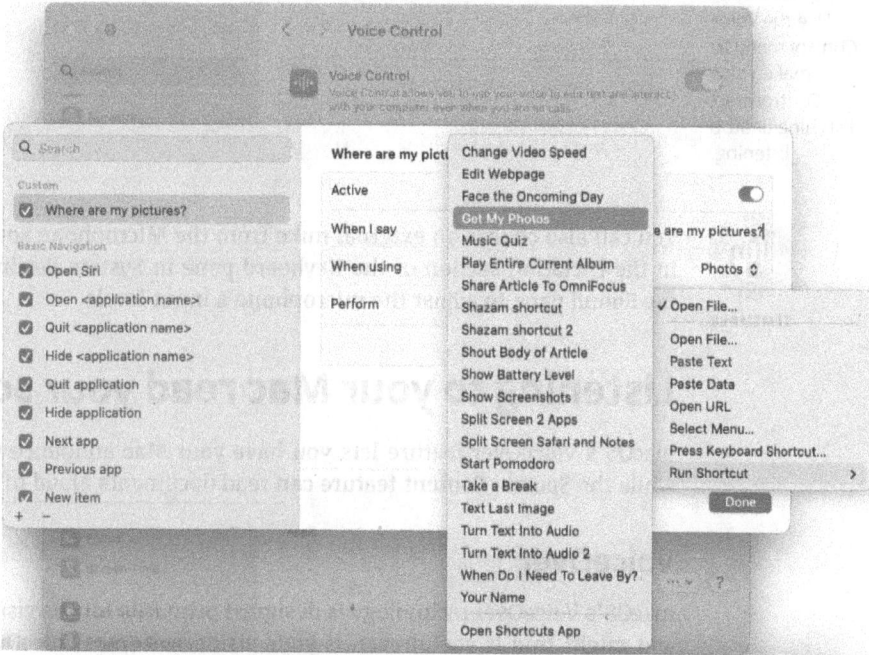

FIGURE 20-6:
The Dictation
Commands sheet
displaying some
things your Mac
will understand if
you say them.

You can then use Voice Control to control your Mac. Click the Voice Control icon on the menu bar, and then click Start Listening on the menu (see Figure 20-7). Speak your commands, and your Mac will execute them. When you want to stop using Voice Control, click the Voice Control icon again, and then click Stop Listening.

TIP

If you have a laptop or an iMac, you may get better results from just about any third-party microphone or, better still, a headset with a microphone. To use a third-party microphone, first connect the microphone to your Mac. Then choose System Settings ➪ Sound, and select the microphone from the list of sound input devices in the Input tab. Below the list is an Input Volume slider (not available with some third-party mikes) and a level meter. Adjust the Input Volume slider so that most of the dots (at least 11 out of the 15 dots) in the Input Level meter darken when you're speaking at a normal volume.

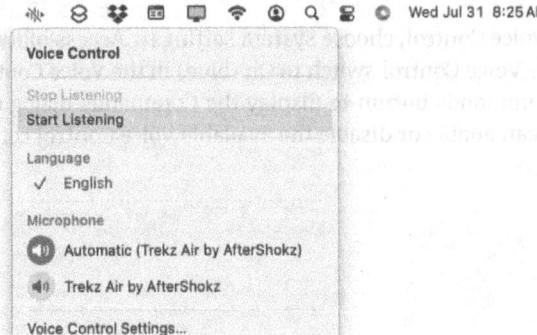

Voice Control

Stop Listening

Start Listening

Language

✓ English

Microphone

🔊 Automatic (Trekz Air by AfterShokz)

🔊 Trekz Air by AfterShokz

Voice Control Settings...

FIGURE 20-7:
Use the Voice
Control menu to
make Voice
Control start
listening or stop
listening.

REMEMBER

You can also choose an external mike from the Microphone Source pop-up menu in the Dictation section of the Keyboard pane in System Settings. As before, use the Sound pane to adjust the microphone's input levels.

Listening to your Mac read your screen

macOS's VoiceOver feature lets you have your Mac announce what's on-screen, while the Spoken Content feature can read documents aloud to you.

VoiceOver

macOS's VoiceOver technology is designed primarily for the visually impaired, but you might find it useful even if your vision is 20/20. VoiceOver not only reads what's on the screen to you, but it also integrates with your keyboard so you can navigate around the screen until you hear VoiceOver identify the item you're looking for. When you're there, you can use Keyboard Access to select list items, select check boxes and radio buttons, move scroll bars and sliders, resize windows, and so on — all with a simple key press or two.

To check out VoiceOver, choose System Settings ➪ Accessibility, go to the Vision section of the Accessibility pane, and then click VoiceOver. In the VoiceOver pane, set the VoiceOver switch to On (blue) to enable VoiceOver. Alternatively, press ⌘+Fn+F5 on Mac keyboards set to use dedicated hardware keys, or press ⌘+F5 on a keyboard that uses good old-fashioned function keys.

If the VoiceOver dialog opens, welcoming you to VoiceOver, select the Do Not Show This Message Again check box, and then click the Use VoiceOver button.

While VoiceOver is on, your Mac talks you through what is on the screen. If you click the desktop, for example, your Mac might say "Application, Finder; Column View; selected folder, Desktop, contains eight items." Here's another example: When you click a menu or an item on a menu, you hear its name spoken at once, and when you close a menu, you hear the words "Closing menu." You even hear the spoken feedback in dialogs such as Print, Open, and Save.

VoiceOver is great for the visually impaired, but it can become annoying fast if your vision is okay. You may be able to raise your tolerance of VoiceOver by choosing VoiceOver Utility ⇨ Speech, clicking the Voices tab, and then changing the voice or the speaking rate. But check out VoiceOver anyway so that you'll know what your options are. You might like it and find times when you want your Mac to narrate the action on-screen for you.

To turn VoiceOver off, press ⌘+Fn+F5 or ⌘+F5 again; or choose Settings ⇨ Accessibility ⇨ VoiceOver, and then set the VoiceOver switch to Off (white).

Spoken Content (Text to Speech)

The second way your Mac can speak to you is via Spoken Content, formerly called Text to Speech, which converts on-screen text to spoken words. Spoken Content is great if you have visual impairments or dyslexia, but it can also be good for proofreading your work — listening to what you've written makes you focus on the text in a different way from reading it. Spoken Content can also be good for relaxation (such as listening to audiobooks), for reducing your screen time, or for multitasking (such as listening to your email while performing a physical task).

Here's how to use Spoken Content:

1. **Choose System Settings ⇨ Accessibility ⇨ Spoken Content to display the Spoken Content pane.**

2. **From the System Voice pop-up menu, choose the voice you want your Mac to use when it reads to you.**

TIP

Choose Manage Voices on the System Voice pop-up menu to download additional voices. There's a huge variation in the file size of the voices, from a couple of megabytes to nearly a gigabyte for a single voice, so pay attention to the download size if your Mac is strapped for space. The larger the file size, the better the voice will sound — but that doesn't mean you'll necessarily like the voice.

3. **Click the Play Sample button to hear a sample of the voice you selected.**

4. **Drag the Speaking Rate slider to speed up or slow down the voice.**

5. **Click the Play Sample button to hear the voice at its new speed.**

6. **Drag the Speaking Volume slider to adjust the volume.**

7. **(Optional) To make your Mac speak the text in alert boxes and dialogs, set the Speak Announcements switch to On (blue).**

You might hear such alerts as "The application Microsoft Word has quit unexpectedly" or "Paper out or not loaded correctly."

8. **(Optional) To make your Mac speak text you've selected in a document, set the Speak Selection switch to On (blue).**

   The default keyboard shortcut for Speak Selection is Option+Esc, but you can assign any key combo you like by clicking the Info (i) button and typing a different keyboard shortcut.

9. **(Optional) To make your Mac describe whatever is below the pointer, set the Speak Items Under Pointer switch to On (blue).**

10. **(Optional) To make your Mac speak whatever you type, set the Speak Typing Feedback switch to On (blue).**

11. **(Optional) To explore additional options for the previous four items, click the appropriate Info (i) button.**

Now, to use Text to Speech to read text to you, copy the text to the Clipboard, launch any app that supports it (such as TextEdit), paste the text into the empty untitled document, click where you want your Mac to begin reading to you, and then choose Edit ⇨ Speech ⇨ Start Speaking. To make it stop, choose Edit ⇨ Speech ⇨ Stop Speaking.

Text to Speech is also available in the Safari web browser. The process works the same as in TextEdit, but you don't have to paste; just select the text you want to hear, and choose Edit ⇨ Speech ⇨ Start Speaking.

Controlling Your iPhone from Your Mac

NEW

If you have an iPhone, you'll likely enjoy Sequoia's iPhone Mirroring feature, which enables you to take control of your iPhone using your Mac. Once the Mac and iPhone are connected, you can run apps on your iPhone, controlling them from the Mac; receive the iPhone's notifications on your Mac desktop; and transfer photos, documents, and other files between the iPhone and the Mac.

iPhone Mirroring requires the following:

>> Your Mac and your iPhone must be physically close to each other — within Bluetooth range — and powered on.

>> Both Bluetooth and Wi-Fi must be enabled on the Mac and the iPhone.

>> You must be signed in to the same Apple Account on the Mac and the iPhone.

>> Your iPhone must be locked, so that it's not in use.

Once you've met the above criteria, launch the iPhone Mirroring app (shown in the margin) by clicking its icon on the Dock or on the Launchpad screen. The first time you launch the app, the Your iPhone on Your Mac wizard appears and walks you through the process of setting up iPhone Mirroring. Follow the instructions, clicking the Continue button to move along, until the iPhone Mirroring Is Ready to Use screen appears. Here, click the Get Started button.

To make sure it's you rather than some interloper who's connecting to your iPhone, iPhone Mirroring prompts you to enter your Mac login password. Next, the Require Mac Login to Access iPhone? dialog opens (see Figure 20-8), asking you to choose either having to authenticate (via password or Touch ID) each time you use iPhone Mirroring or authenticating automatically. To authenticate each time, which is more secure, click the Ask Every Time button. If you prefer to authenticate automatically, click the Authenticate Automatically button, enter the password in the iPhone Mirroring dialog that appears, and then click OK. Your iPhone's screen then appears in the iPhone Mirroring window (see Figure 20-9), and you can start working on the iPhone.

FIGURE 20-8:
Choose whether iPhone Mirroring should authenticate you every time or automatically.

FIGURE 20-9:
Your iPhone appears in the iPhone Mirroring window.

Here are the main moves to use with iPhone Mirroring:

>> **Resize the screen.** Choose View ⇨ Larger or press ⌘++ to make it larger, choose View ⇨ Smaller or press ⌘+− to make it smaller, or choose View ⇨ Actual Size or press ⌘+0 to make it just the perfect size for Goldilocks.

>> **Tap the screen.** Click where you would tap.

>> **Scroll the screen.** Scroll using your trackpad or mouse as usual.

>> **Display the Home screen.** Choose View ⇨ Home Screen or press ⌘+1. Alternatively, click the horizontal bar at the bottom of the screen.

>> **Display the App Switcher.** Choose View ⇨ App Switcher or press ⌘+2.

>> **Open Spotlight.** Choose View ⇨ Spotlight or press ⌘+3.

>> **Enter text in an iPhone app.** Open the app, and then type on your Mac's keyboard.

TIP

If text you type comes out garbled, make sure your Mac and your iPhone are set to use the same keyboard layout. On the Mac, choose System Settings ⇨ Keyboard and look at the *Input Sources* readout in the Text Input section of the Keyboard pane. On the iPhone, choose Settings ⇨ General ⇨ Keyboard ⇨ Keyboards to display the Keyboards pane. Here, you can change to a different keyboard layout or click Add New Keyboard to add a new keyboard.

>> **View and deal with notifications.** Notifications from your iPhone appear in Notification Center on your Mac along with your Mac's own notifications. The iPhone notifications bear a small iPhone icon to distinguish them. You can view the notifications and deal with them as usual.

>> **Transfer files.** Apple says you will be able to transfer files between your Mac and the iPhone using drag and drop. At this writing, this functionality is not yet available.

>> **End your iPhone Mirroring session.** Choose iPhone Mirroring ⇨ Quit iPhone Mirroring. Alternatively, unlock your iPhone — unlocking it terminates the connection immediately, but the iPhone Mirroring app stays open.

Other Useful Goodies

Even more neat and useful technologies are built into Sequoia. Here are several more apps and utilities you may find useful.

Accessibility pane

As you saw in the earlier subsection, "Commanding your Mac by voice," the Accessibility pane in System Settings contains features to help users with disabilities.

TIP

To see the status of all Accessibility settings on the menu bar, choose System Settings ⇨ Control Center, go to the Accessibility Shortcuts section, and then set the Show in Menu Bar switch to On (blue). If you prefer to have the Accessibility Shortcuts in Control Center, set the Show in Control Center switch to On (blue) instead.

The Accessibility pane has five main sections — Vision, Hearing, Motor, Speech, and General — each of which contains multiple buttons that take you to further panes.

In the Vision section, click the Display button to show the Display pane, which provides settings for controlling the behavior of the screen display. In the Color Filters section of the Display pane, for example, you can choose Grayscale as your filter type, which will desaturate your screen into a grayscale display.

In the top, unnamed section of the Display pane, you can set the Invert Colors switch to On (blue) to reverse the colors you see on-screen — an interesting if only occasionally useful effect. After inverting the colors, you can go to the Invert Colors Mode row and choose between the Smart and Classic radio buttons. Smart Invert Colors doesn't invert the colors of images and videos (because who would want those inverted?), whereas Classic Invert Colors simply inverts everything.

TIP

This setting is more useful: In the Pointer section of the Display pane, set the Shake Mouse Pointer to Locate switch to On (blue). Then, when you lose the pointer, wiggle the mouse back and forth a couple of times, and the pointer momentarily grows much larger. If you'd like the pointer to be bigger all the time, drag the Pointer Size slider toward the Large end.

In the Vision section of the Accessibility pane, click Zoom to display the Zoom pane. This pane is where you can enable a terrific feature called *hardware zoom*, which lets you make things on your screen bigger by zooming in on them. To control hardware zoom with the keyboard, set the Use Keyboard Shortcuts to Zoom switch to On (blue). Then you can toggle hardware zoom on and off by pressing ⌘+Option+8, zoom in by pressing ⌘+Option+= (that's the equal sign), and zoom out by pressing ⌘+Option+− (that's the hyphen key).

If your Mac uses a trackpad, set the Use Trackpad Gesture to Zoom switch to On (blue) to zoom in or out by double-tapping with three fingers, and to change the zoom by double-tapping three fingers and dragging.

If you want to zoom by using a scroll gesture while holding down a modifier key, set the Use Scroll Gesture with Modifier Keys to Zoom switch to On (blue); then open the Modifier Key for Scroll Gesture pop-up menu and choose the modifier key to use.

Next, choose a style — Full Screen, Split Screen, or Picture-in-Picture — from the Zoom Style pop-up menu. If you choose either Split Screen or Picture-in-Picture, click the Size and Location button, and then choose where the zoomed section appears on the screen.

Try Zoom even if you don't have vision problems. It can be surprisingly useful.

You've met some of the most useful Accessibility features, but there are many more we don't have space to cover here. When you have a few minutes to spare, choose System Settings ➪ Accessibility, and then explore the other features in the Accessibility pane so that you'll know what help is available should you need it. For now, you might find the following features useful:

» To make the screen flash whenever an alert sound occurs, click Audio in the Hearing section of the Accessibility pane, and then set the Flash the Screen When an Alert Sound Occurs switch to On (blue).

» To treat a *sequence* of modifier keys as a key combination, click Keyboard in the Motor section of the Accessibility pane, and then set the Sticky Keys switch to On (blue).

With Sticky Keys on, you don't have to hold down ⌘ while pressing another key. For example, you can do a standard keyboard shortcut by pressing ⌘, releasing it, and then pressing the other key. If you enable Sticky Keys, click the Info (i) button to display the Info dialog, in which you can set switches to tell you (with a beep and/or an on-screen display) what modifier keys have been pressed.

WARNING

Sticky Keys can be really awkward in apps like Adobe Photoshop, Adobe Illustrator, and other apps that toggle a tool's state when you press a modifier key.

» To adjust the delay between a keypress and its activation, click Keyboard in the Motor section of the Accessibility pane, and then set the Slow Keys switch to On (blue).

Battery pane and Energy Saver pane

The Battery pane (MacBooks) and Energy Saver (desktops) pane of the System Settings app are where you manage your Mac's energy-saving features.

All Macs are Energy Star–compliant, so the Battery pane and Energy Saver pane let you do things such as turn your Mac off at a specific time or after a specified idle period.

Battery pane (MacBooks only)

To get started, choose System Settings ⇨ Battery to open the Battery pane. You can then configure Low Power Mode, check the battery health, and view usage information:

» **Low Power Mode:** Click this pop-up menu, and then choose Never, Always, Only on Battery, or Only on Power Adapter. Choose Only on Battery for the best combination of performance and battery runtime.

» **Battery Health:** This readout shows Normal if the battery is doing okay. Click the Info (i) button for more details.

» **Histograms:** Click the Last 24 Hours tab button to see data from the last 24 hours, or click the Last 10 Days tab button to see the last 10 days of data. The *Charging* readout shows the current percentage of charge and, if the battery is charging, how long until the battery will be fully charged. The Battery Level histogram shows hour-by-hour or day-by-day battery levels, while the Screen On Usage histogram shows hour-by-hour or day-by-day usage levels.

Click the Options button to configure four more settings:

» **Slightly Dim the Display on Battery:** Set this switch to On (blue) to have the display dim slightly and use less power when running on the battery.

» **Prevent Automatic Sleeping on Power Adapter When the Display Is Off:** Set this switch to On (blue) to prevent your MacBook from sleeping when the lid is closed and the display is off.

» **Wake for Network Access:** Click this pop-up menu and then choose Never, Always, Only on Battery, or Only on Power Adapter to specify when your MacBook should wake automatically for network access.

» **Optimize Video Streaming While on Battery:** Set this switch to On (blue) to reduce battery use while you're streaming video.

Energy Saver pane (desktops only)

To start, choose System Settings ⇨ Energy Saver. Depending on the model of desktop Mac, you'll see some or all of the following settings, which are largely self-explanatory:

- » Prevent Automatic Sleeping When the Display Is Off
- » Put Hard Disks to Sleep When Possible
- » Wake for Network Access
- » Start Up Automatically After a Power Failure
- » Enable Power Nap

Bluetooth pane

Bluetooth is wireless networking for low-bandwidth peripherals, including mice, keyboards, speakers, and headphones. All Sequoia-capable Macs have Bluetooth built in, enabling you to blast music on Bluetooth speakers; input vocals via Bluetooth microphones; and connect keyboards, mice, and many other devices.

To manage your Mac's Bluetooth features, choose System Settings ⇨ Bluetooth to open the Bluetooth pane of the System Settings app.

Ink pane

Ink is the macOS built-in handwriting-recognition engine. Sadly, it works only if a third-party drawing tablet with a stylus is connected. Even more sadly, "tablet" in this sense doesn't include your iPad (at least, not so far).

To write instead of type, enable Ink in this pane, and you'll be able to handwrite anywhere your Mac accepts typing with the keyboard.

To manage your Mac's Ink features, open the Ink pane by choosing System Settings ⇨ Ink.

TIP

The Ink pane appears only if you have one of the pen-input drawing tablets that Ink supports connected to your Mac. Most of the supported drawing tablets come from Wacom (https://www.wacom.com), with prices starting under $100 for a small wireless stylus and drawing tablet.

Automatic login

If you dislike having to log in whenever you start up your Mac, you can set it to log in automatically with a specific account. Follow these steps:

1. **Choose System Settings ⇨ Users & Groups to open the Users & Groups pane of the System Settings app.**

2. **Open the Automatically Log In As pop-up menu, and choose the account you want to log in automatically.**

WARNING

Automatic login is a security nightmare, because anyone who can power on your Mac can start using it under the account you've set to log in automatically. For security, you — and every other user of your Mac — should always log in manually.

Allow your Apple Watch to unlock your Mac

If you have an Apple Watch, you'll love this feature. If your Mac has Touch ID, choose System Settings ⇨ Touch ID & Password to display the Touch ID & Password pane; if not, choose System Settings ⇨ Login Password to display the Login Password pane. In the Apple Watch section of that pane, set the switch for your Apple Watch to On (blue). You can then walk up to your Mac while wearing your unlocked Apple Watch, press a key or stroke the trackpad to wake the Mac, and be automatically logged into your user account without typing your password.

AirPlay and AirPlay to Mac

AirPlay is the screen-mirroring feature that lets you stream what's on your Mac (or iPhone or iPad) screen to an Apple TV, a smart TV with built-in AirPlay, or other compatible systems. AirPlay also includes the AirPlay to Mac feature, which enables you to stream photos or videos from a Mac or Apple device to a Mac running macOS Monterey, macOS Ventura, macOS Sonoma, macOS Sequoia, or a later version.

The Mac running Sequoia is also available as an AirPlay audio speaker, so you can stream music from another Mac (or iPhone or iPad) to a Sequoia-equipped Mac as easily as you can stream to an Apple TV or smart TV with AirPlay. First, enable the AirPlay Receiver feature by choosing System Settings ⇨ General ⇨ AirDrop & Handoff, and setting the AirPlay Receiver switch in the AirDrop & Handoff pane to On (blue). Next, click the Allow AirPlay For pop-up menu and choose Current User, Anyone on the Same Network, or Everyone to control who can use AirPlay Receiver; you can also set the Require Password switch to On (blue) and click the Set button to set a password for using AirPlay Receiver.

Once you've configured AirPlay Receiver, you can open the AirPlay Selector menu on another device, such as your iPhone, and choose your Mac as the AirPlay speaker on which to play audio.

To select a device to stream to — a Mac (running Sequoia), an Apple TV, or a smart TV with Airplay — go to the Displays pane of System Settings, and then choose the device from the Add Display (+) pop-up menu.

TIP

If you want to control screen mirroring from the menu bar, choose System Settings ⇨ Control Center to display the Control Center pane of the System Settings app. Open the Screen Mirroring pop-up menu, and then choose Always Show in Menu Bar. Then you can choose an AirPlay receiver without visiting the Displays pane of System Settings.

Handoff

The Handoff feature lets you start working on a document, an email, or a message on any Apple device and pick up where you left off on another device. To enable it, choose System Settings ⇨ General, click the AirDrop & Handoff button in the General pane, and then set the Allow Handoff Between This Mac and Your iCloud Devices switch to On (blue).

Make sure that you're signed into iCloud with the same Apple ID on your Mac and your iPhone or iPad and that Bluetooth is enabled on all devices.

Handoff works with Apple apps including Mail, Safari, Maps, Messages, Reminders, Calendar, Contacts, Pages, Numbers, and Keynote, as well as various third-party apps. When another Handoff-enabled device is nearby and using one of these apps, you'll see an icon for it at the right end of the Dock, as shown in Figure 20-10. Clicking that icon (note the tiny phone on it) opens Messages on the Mac and displays the message or reply that's currently on the iPhone screen.

FIGURE 20-10:
Handoff enables
your Mac to pick
up an active app
from your iPhone.

Universal Control

Apple's Universal Control feature enables you to use your Mac's keyboard and mouse (or trackpad) to control one or two nearby iPads or Macs. Universal Control is great for productivity, enabling you to work on your Mac and one or two additional devices without having to mess about with separate keyboards and pointing devices. You can even copy and paste material between the devices by using the Universal Clipboard feature.

Enabling and configuring Universal Control

On your Mac, follow these steps to enable and configure Universal Control:

1. **Choose System Settings ⇨ Displays to show the Displays pane of the System Settings app.**

2. **Click the Advanced button at the bottom of the pane to display the Advanced dialog (see Figure 20-11).**

3. **Set the Allow Your Pointer and Keyboard to Move Between Any Nearby Mac or iPad switch to On (blue).**

4. **Set the Push Through the Edge of a Display to Connect a Nearby Mac or iPad switch to On (blue).**

5. **(Optional) Set the Automatically Reconnect to Any Nearby Mac or iPad switch to On (blue).**

   Whether you'll want to enable this option depends on how you work. Having macOS reestablish the connection automatically can be great if you use the iPad or the other Mac consistently. If you use it only occasionally, though, having your Mac glomming onto it on sight like a lovestruck teenager can feel awkward.

6. **Click the Done button to close the Advanced dialog.**

Closing the Advanced dialog takes you back to the Displays pane of System Settings. Leave this pane open, because you're not finished there yet.

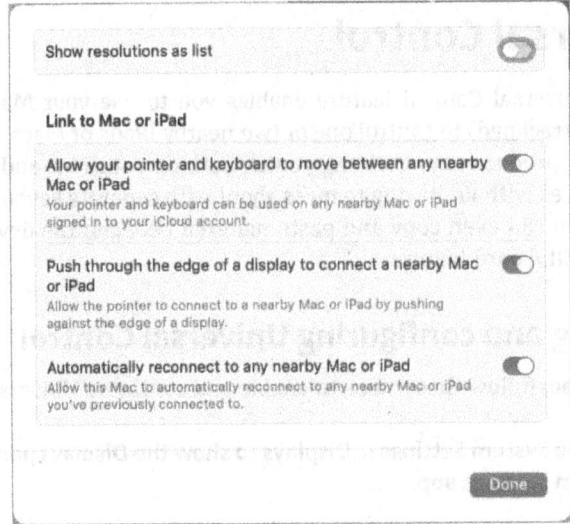

FIGURE 20-11:
Enable and
configure
Universal Control
in the Advanced
dialog for
Displays settings.

Connecting the iPad or Mac

Now fire up the iPad or the other Mac, if it's not already running, and connect it as follows:

1. **In the top-right corner of the Displays pane, click Add Display (+) to open the pop-up menu.**

2. **From the Link Keyboard and Mouse To list, choose the appropriate iPad or Mac.**

   The iPad or Mac appears at the top of the Displays pane, as you see in Figure 20-12.

3. **Click the Arrange button at the bottom of the pane to open the Arrange Displays dialog (see Figure 20-13).**

4. **Identify the display you want to move by holding the pointer over its thumbnail so that a screen tip appears.**

5. **Drag the display's thumbnail to the appropriate position to indicate how the physical displays are placed.**

6. **When all the thumbnails are suitably positioned, click Done to close the Arrange Displays dialog.**

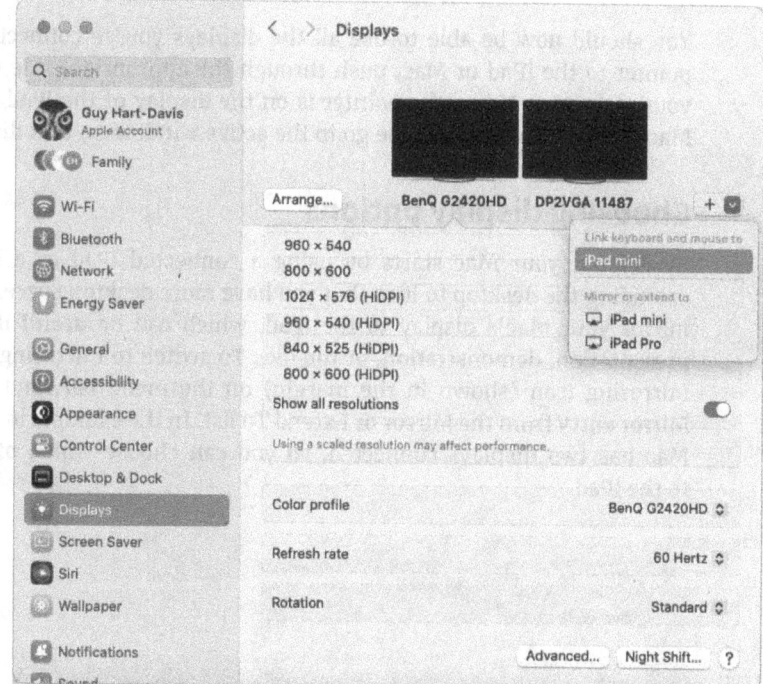

FIGURE 20-12:
In the Displays pane, click + and choose the iPad or Mac from the Link Keyboard and Mouse To list.

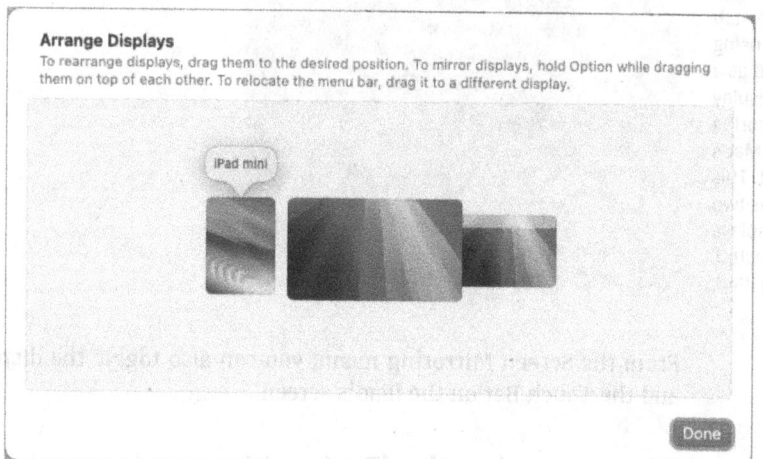

FIGURE 20-13:
In the Arrange Displays dialog, identify the display you want to move, and then drag its thumbnail to the appropriate position.

You should now be able to use all the displays you've connected. To move the pointer to the iPad or Mac, push through the appropriate side of the display on your main Mac. When the pointer is on the display of the iPad or the secondary Mac, any keystrokes you type go to the active window on that display.

Choosing display options

By default, your Mac starts by using a connected iPad as a separate display, extending the desktop to it so that you have more desktop space. But you can also mirror your Mac's display to the iPad, which can be useful if you're giving a presentation, demonstration, or the like. To switch to mirroring, click the Screen Mirroring icon (shown in the margin) on the menu bar, and then choose the Mirror entry from the Mirror or Extend To list. In the example in Figure 20-14, the Mac has two displays connected, so you can choose which of them to mirror to the iPad.

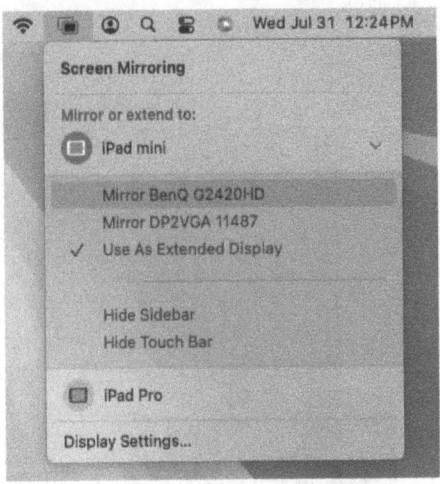

FIGURE 20-14:
Use the Screen Mirroring menu on the menu bar to switch between using the iPad as a separate display and mirroring your Mac's display to it. This Mac has two displays connected, plus the iPad.

From the Screen Mirroring menu, you can also toggle the display of the Sidebar and the Touch Bar on the iPad's screen.

Disconnecting the iPad or Mac

When you finish using the iPad or Mac via Universal Control, disconnect it as follows:

1. Click the Screen Mirroring icon (shown in the margin) on the menu bar to open the Screen Mirroring menu.

2. Click Display Settings to show the Displays pane of the System Settings app with the iPad's settings selected (see Figure 20-15).

3. Click the Disconnect button.

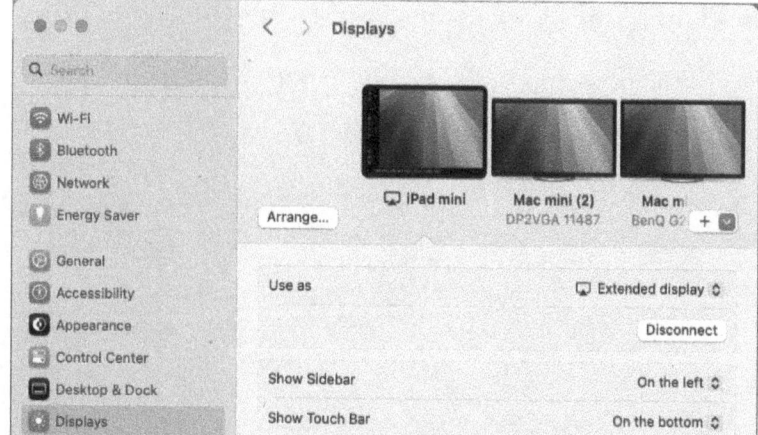

FIGURE 20-15:
Click Disconnect
in the Displays
pane of System
Settings to
disconnect
the iPad.

When you disconnect the iPad this way, macOS rounds up any windows that were on the iPad's display and returns them to the Mac's display.

Chapter **21**

Safety First: Backups and Other Security Issues

lthough Macs are generally reliable, your Mac's drive may suffer damage that causes data loss, or it might simply fail completely. To protect your data, you must back up your data consistently and often.

How often is often? That depends on how much work you can afford to lose. If losing everything you did yesterday would put you out of business, you need to back up hourly or perhaps even continuously. If you'd lose only a few unimportant documents if your Mac's drive died today, you probably can back up less often. But generally you should err on the side of caution and back up all your files frequently and consistently: It's far better to have too many backups than too few.

After explaining your backup options in depth, this chapter tells you how to protect your Mac and your data safe from viruses and other malware. Lastly, this chapter shows you how to keep other people from looking at your stuff.

Backing Up Is (Not) Hard to Do

You can back up your Mac's drive in basically three ways: the super-painless way with macOS Sequoia's excellent built-in Time Machine, the ugly way with the brute-force method, or the comprehensive way with specialized third-party backup and disk-cloning software. Read on to find out more about all three.

Backing up with Sequoia's excellent Time Machine

Time Machine is a backup system that has only become better and more reliable since Apple introduced it more than a decade ago. Time Machine is a complex technology built deep into macOS, but it manifests itself in the user interface as two parts: the Time Machine pane of the System Settings app (shown in Figure 21-1), which you use to configure the backup service; and the Time Machine app (shown in Figure 21-2), which you use to recover files from backup.

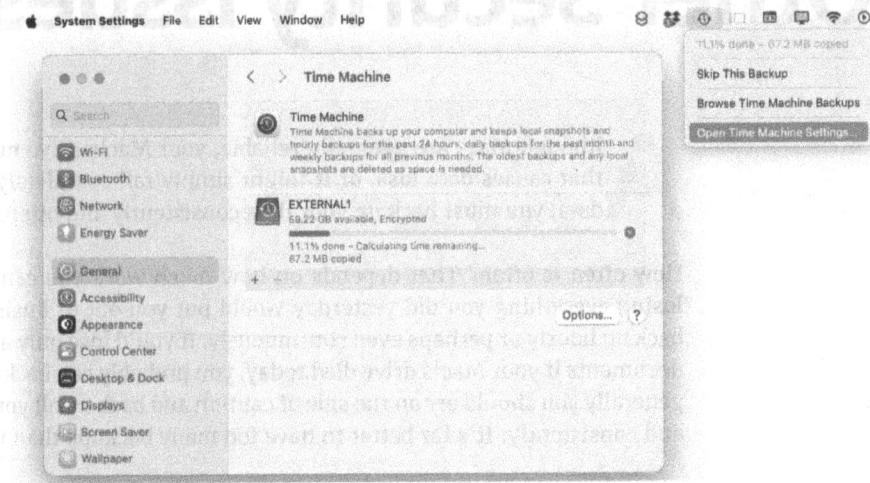

FIGURE 21-1:
The Time Machine pane of System Settings and the Time Machine menu on the menu bar.

TIP

The easiest way to get to Time Machine is to add its menu to the menu bar. To do so, open System Settings, click Control Center in the sidebar, go to the Menu Bar Only section at the bottom of the Control Center pane, open the Time Machine pop-up menu, and choose Show in Menu Bar.

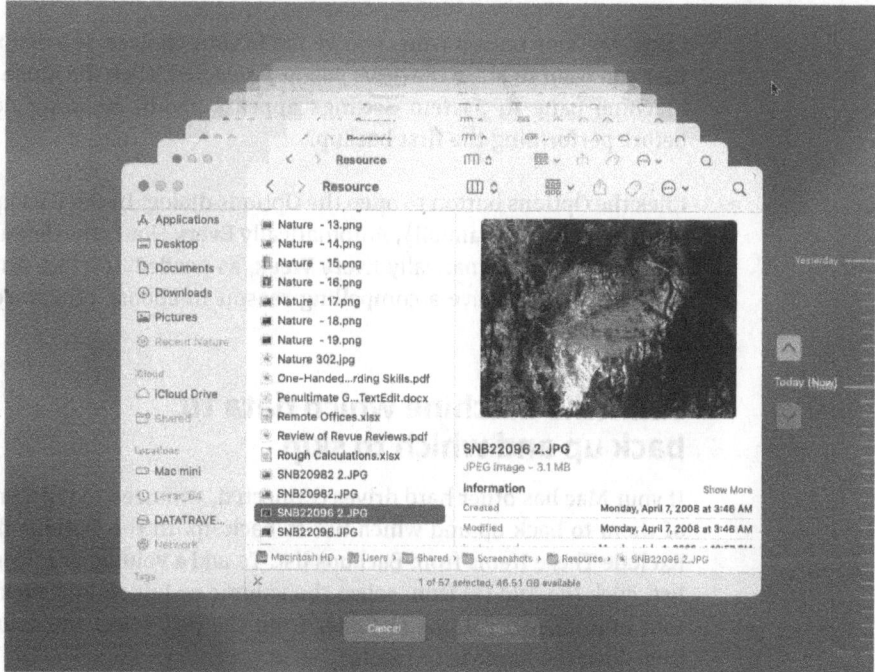

FIGURE 21-2:
The Time
Machine app is
ready to restore
an image file
in Finder.

Set Time Machine to back up your data automatically

To use Time Machine to back up your data automatically, the first thing you need is another disk that's larger than your start-up disk. The disk can connect via USB 2, USB 3, USB 4, or Thunderbolt, and it can be your choice of hard drive or SSD.

TIP

Buy the biggest backup disk you can justify. A backup disk costs a lot less than data recovery, which can run hundreds if not thousands of dollars.

To select a drive to use with Time Machine, choose System Settings ⇨ General ⇨ Time Machine; if you added the Time Machine menu to the menu bar, click the Time Machine menu, and then click Open Time Machine Settings. In the Time Machine pane, click the Add Backup Disk button, select the drive you want to use for your backups, and then click the Set Up Disk button. In the Time Machine dialog that opens, set the Encrypt Backup switch to On (blue) and enter a password to protect your backups; encrypting the backups is vital to keeping your data safe. If you want to prevent your backups from consuming the entire backup drive, select the Custom option button on the Disk Usage Limit row, and then drag the Limit Space Used for Backups slider to set the amount of space available to Time Machine. Normally, you'd dedicate the whole drive to Time Machine and leave the None option button selected on the Disk Usage Limit row.

Click the Done button when you've made your choices. If a dialog opens checking that you want to erase the drive you just selected, click the Erase button. The Time Machine pane in System Settings appears again, counting down 120 seconds before performing the first backup.

Click the Options button to open the Options dialog. In the Backup Frequency pop-up menu, choose Manually, Automatically Every Hour (the default), Automatically Every Day, or Automatically Every Week, as needed. (Choose Automatically Every Hour unless you have a compelling reason to choose otherwise.) Then read the next subsection.

Tell Time Machine which data to back up and which to skip

If your Mac has other hard drives connected, you need to tell Time Machine which of them to back up and which not to back up. In the Options dialog, look at the Exclude These Items from Backups list. To add a volume or folder to this exclusion list, click the Add (+) icon, select the volume or folder, and click the Exclude button; to remove a volume or folder from the list, select the volume or folder and then click the Remove (–) icon.

On a MacBook, the Options dialog also offers a switch to enable Time Machine backups when on battery power. This setting is set to Off (white) by default.

Assuming you selected the Automatically Every Hour backup frequency, Time Machine runs approximately once per hour and creates the following backups:

>> Hourly backups for the past 24 hours

>> Daily backups for the past month

>> Weekly backups until your backup disk is full

When your backup disk gets nearly full, Time Machine intelligently deletes the oldest backups and replaces them with new backups.

TIP

You can also tell Time Machine to create a backup at any point you want. Simply click the Time Machine icon on the menu bar and then click Back Up Now.

What does Time Machine back up?

Time Machine backs up your entire hard drive the first time it runs (apart from anything you've excluded). After that, it backs up files and folders that have been modified since your last backup. This is standard operating procedure for backup systems. But Time Machine does more. It also backs up things such as contacts, pictures in your Photos library, events in your calendars, and emails in your email accounts, not to mention its support of versions and locking. About the only thing Time Machine doesn't back up is the content of Home folders other than your own.

Those features make Time Machine unlike any other backup system.

How do I restore a file (or a contact, photo, event, and so on)?

To restore a file or any other information, follow these steps:

1. **Launch the app that contains the information you want to restore.**

If you want to restore a file, that app is Finder, which (as you know) is always running; just open a Finder window to the folder that contains the file. To restore a contact, a photo, an email message, or an event, for example, you need to launch Contacts, Photos, Mail, or Calendar, respectively.

2. **With the appropriate app running (or the appropriate Finder window open), launch the Time Machine app (refer to Figure 21-2).**

If you chose Show in Menu Bar from the Time Machine pop-up menu in the Control Center pane in System Settings, you can click the Time Machine icon on the menu bar and then click Browse Time Machine Backups (refer to Figure 21-1). Otherwise, open Launchpad, and then click Time Machine.

TIP

It will be easier to restore a file in Finder if the folder that the file is (or was) in is the *active* folder (that is, open and front-most) when you launch the Time Machine app. Otherwise, you have to navigate to the appropriate folder before you can perform Step 3.

3. **Click one of the bars with dates near the bottom-right corner of the screen *or* click the big Forward or Back arrow on the right side of the Finder window in Figure 21-2 to choose a backup to restore.**

4. **Select the file, folder, Contacts contact, Photos photo, email message, or Calendar event you want to restore.**

5. **Click the Restore button below the window.**

If the file, folder, Contacts contact, Photos photo, email message, or Calendar event exists in the same location on your start-up disk, Time Machine asks what you want to do: Replace the original, keep the original, or keep them both. Here, "original" means the current version of the file, even though the older version you're recovering is likely more "original" in the conventional sense.

TIP

You can search for files or folders in Time Machine by typing a word or phrase in the Search field of the active (front-most) window.

Backing up by using the manual, brute-force method

If you're not yet convinced you should run Time Machine, at least consider backing up important files manually. To back up this way, drag those important files a few at a time to another volume — usually, another hard drive or SSD or a Universal Serial Bus (USB) flash drive. By using this method, you're making a copy of each file that you want to protect.

WARNING

If you use an optical disc, don't forget to actually burn the disc; merely dragging those files onto the optical disc icon won't do the trick. (This is obvious, but forgetting the vital step of burning is all too easy.)

WARNING

If doing a manual backup sounds pretty awful, you're right. It is. This method can take a long, long time; you can't really tell whether you've copied every file that needs to be backed up; and you can't really copy only the files that have been modified since your last backup. Few busy people find this method viable for long.

TIP

If you're careful to save files only in your Documents folder, and those files are all you care about, you can probably get away with backing up only that folder. Or if you save files in other folders within your Home folder or have any files in your Movies, Music, Pictures, or Sites folders (which often contain files you didn't specifically save in those folders, such as your Photos app pictures and Music app songs), you should probably consider backing up your entire Home folder.

As you read in the following section, backing up your Home folder is even easier if you use special backup software.

Backing up by using commercial backup software

Another way to back up your files is to use a third-party backup app. Backup software automates the task of backing up, remembering what's on each backup disc (if your backup uses more than one disc), and backing up only files that have been modified since your last backup.

Furthermore, you can instruct your backup software to back up only a certain folder (Home or Documents) and to ignore the hundreds of megabytes of stuff that make up macOS, all of which you can easily reinstall from your Recovery disk or the Mac App Store.

Your first backup with commercial software might take anywhere from a few minutes to several hours. Subsequent backups — *incremental backups*, in backup software parlance — should be much faster.

One of the best things about good backup software is that you can set it up to automate your backups and perform them even if you forget. And although Time Machine is a step in the right direction and may be sufficient for your needs, power users may need a heavier-duty backup solution.

Why You Need Two Backups

You back up regularly. Does that make you immune to file loss or damage?

Well, picture yourself in the following scenario:

>> You leave the office one day for lunch. When you return, you discover that your office has been burglarized, struck by lightning, flooded, burned to the ground, or buried in earthquake rubble — take your pick.

>> Alas, although you did have a backup, the backup disk was right next to your Mac, which means that it was either stolen or destroyed along with your Mac and everything else.

This scenario is unlikely — but it *could* happen, and it does demonstrate why you need multiple backups. If you have several backup disks and don't keep them all in the same room as your Mac, chances are pretty good that one will work even if the others are lost, stolen, or destroyed.

TIP

For true data security, consider a backup scheme such as this one: Create at least three backups, and store at least one of them off-site. You might keep a full backup, which you update monthly, in a safe-deposit box at your bank. Next, use a cloud-based backup service such as Backblaze (https://www.backblaze.com) to create a second off-site backup that you can keep updated more frequently.

If you store all your files in the Documents folder or the desktop, you can store your Desktop and Documents folders in iCloud, which counts as another off-site backup (kinda). To do that, launch System Settings, click Apple ID, and then click iCloud. On the iCloud screen, click Drive, set the Sync This Mac switch to On (blue), and then set the Desktop & Documents Folders switch to On (blue). Click the Done button. iCloud syncs your files shortly after you make changes, which has the effect of creating a near-real-time backup.

Non-Backup Security Concerns

Backing up your files is critical unless you don't mind losing all your data some-
day. And although backing up is by far your most important security concern,
several other things could imperil your data — things such as viruses or other
types of malware, including worms, spyware, and intruder attacks. That's the bad
news. The good news is that all those things are far more likely to affect Windows
users than Mac users.

Even so, consider taking the following precautions.

About viruses and other malware

A computer *virus* is a nasty little piece of computer code that replicates and spreads
from disk to disk. A virus could cause your Mac to misbehave; some viruses can
destroy files or erase disks with no warning.

Malware (short for *malicious software*) is software that's hostile, intrusive, annoying, or disruptive. Malware is often designed to gain unauthorized access to your
computer or collect personal data (including passwords) without your knowledge, or both.

The difference between a virus and other types of malware is that a virus spreads
itself automatically, whereas other forms of malware rely on trickery, mimicry,
and social engineering to induce unsuspecting users to open a malicious file or
install a malicious app. So a virus is a type of malware, but not all malware is viral.

Almost all viruses are specific to a particular operating system. Mac viruses won't
affect Windows users, Windows viruses won't affect Mac users, and so forth. The
vast majority of known viruses affect only Windows, mostly because it's a much
larger, juicier, and more lucrative target than macOS.

The one real exception here is a "gift" from the wonderful world of Microsoft
Office (Word and Excel, for example) users: the dreaded *macro viruses* that are
spread with Word, Excel, and PowerPoint documents containing macros written
in Microsoft's Visual Basic for Applications (VBA) language. Microsoft has made
the implementation of VBA somewhat safer, but it's still wise to treat any incoming Microsoft Office file with caution.

Apple frequently releases security updates for macOS and Apple's apps to fend off
specific threats that have been detected in the wild. To keep your Mac as safe as
possible, you should allow macOS to apply security updates as soon as they become
available. See the next section for details.

Although few truly viral Mac operating system threats have been spotted in the wild so far, most malware is spread via social engineering, which is easy to protect yourself against. Here's how:

>> On the General tab in the Settings window in Safari, deselect the Open "Safe" Files after Downloading check box.

>> If a suspicious alert or window appears on your screen while you're browsing the Internet, quit your web browser immediately. If the browser doesn't respond to the Quit command, force-quit the app: Choose ⇨ Force Quit (or press ⌘ +Option+Esc) to display the Force Quit Applications window, click the browser's entry, and then click the Force Quit button.

>> If the macOS Installer launches for no apparent reason, *don't click Continue!* Don't install the software, and don't type your administrator password.

>> Don't run *any* installer — the kind built into macOS or the third-party kind — unless you're absolutely certain that it came from a trusted source.

>> Don't use credit or debit cards with unfamiliar vendors or nonsecure websites. (If you don't see *https* instead of *http* in the address bar of your browser, or if you don't see a lock icon in the address field, the site may not be secure.)

>> Allow only apps from the App Store, not apps from other sources. This is safest, but if you want to install other browsers, such as Firefox and Google Chrome, you'll need to allow apps from identified developers as well, as these browsers aren't on the App Store. To control what you can install, choose System Settings ⇨ Privacy & Security, scroll down to the Security section of the Privacy & Security pane, click the Allow Applications From pop-up menu, and then click either App Store (for greater safety) or App Store and Identified Developers (if you need apps from other developers).

REMEMBER

If you use disks or drives that have ever been inserted into a computer you don't know and trust, you may need virus-detection software. If you download and use files from the Internet, you'll be well served by virus detection as well.

You don't have too much to worry about if

>> You download files only from commercial online services, such as CNET or MacUpdate, that are conscientious about malware.

>> You buy software only from the App Store.

>> You use only commercial software and never download files from websites with strange names.

You should definitely worry about malicious infection if

>> You visit websites that offer pirated or stolen software.

>> You swap disks or USB thumb drives with friends regularly.

>> You shuttle disks or USB thumb drives back and forth to other Macs.

>> You use your disks or USB thumb drives at public computers, photo-printing machines, or other computers that are likely to have been exposed to many disks.

>> You download files from various and sundry places on the Internet.

>> You receive email with attachments (and open them). Note that you can receive malicious software in messages that look like they're from people you know and trust. This type of attack is called *spoofing*, and it's easy to accomplish, so think carefully before opening an attachment, and contact the sender if you have any doubt about the message's authenticity.

If you're at risk, do yourself a favor: Buy a commercial antivirus app. Or try a free malware scanner such as Malwarebytes, Bitdefender, or Avira. If you think you may be at risk, scan your drive with one of the free utilities before shelling out any cash. Get it if you need it; don't if you don't.

Installing security updates — or more — automatically

By default, your Mac contacts Apple's servers once a day to look for any new or updated software. To keep your Mac as safe as possible, set it to install any new security updates automatically without consulting you. You may also want to install macOS updates or app updates from the App Store automatically.

To configure checking for updates, choose System Settings ⇨ General ⇨ Software Update. Opening the Software Update pane like this forces macOS to check for any new updates, so the information you see will be up to date. When the check is complete, click the Info button (the *i*-in-a-circle icon) on the right side of the Automatic Updates button to open the Automatic Updates dialog (see Figure 21-3). Then you can configure automatic updating by setting the following four switches:

>> **Download New Updates When Available:** Set this switch to On (blue) to download updates automatically. Automatic downloading is usually helpful unless your Mac connects to metered networks, in which case you may prefer to download them manually when your Mac is connected to an unmetered network.

>> **Install macOS Updates:** Set this switch to On (blue) to install all macOS system updates.

>> **Install Application Updates from the App Store:** Set this switch to On (blue) to install all app updates issued through the App Store.

>> **Install Security Responses and System Files:** Set this switch to On (blue) to install security fixes and macOS system file updates. This category is the most important one for protecting your Mac, so install these updates automatically even if you prefer to install all others manually.

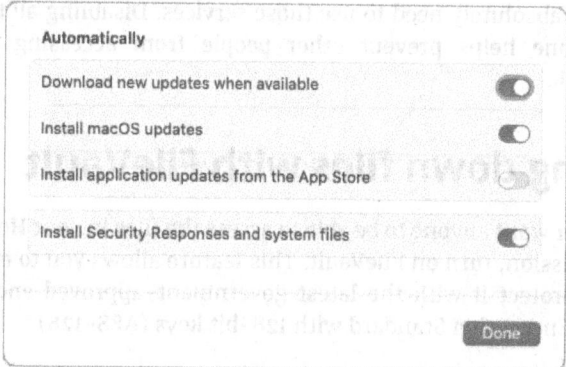

Automatically

Download new updates when available

Install macOS updates

Install application updates from the App Store

Install Security Responses and system files

Done

FIGURE 21-3:
In the Automatic Updates dialog, choose which updates to install automatically.

WARNING

Once in a blue moon, a software update has an unintended side effect: While fixing one problem, it introduces a different problem. If you're concerned that this situation might happen, set the Install macOS Updates switch and the Install Application Updates from the App Store switch to Off (white), and check an authoritative Mac tech site, such as Macworld (www.macworld.com), for headlines about faulty updates before you install any macOS updates or app updates.

Many third-party apps, including Microsoft Office and most Adobe products, use their own update-checking mechanism. Check to make sure that you have yours enabled. Many third-party apps offer a Check for Updates option on the Help menu (or sometimes another menu) or as a setting in their Settings window.

One last thing: If you see a little number on the App Store icon or System Settings icon on the Dock, you have that many updates waiting to be installed. Launch the Mac App Store and click the Updates tab, or launch System Settings, click the General icon in the sidebar, and then click the Software Update button.

Protecting Your Data from Prying Eyes

You also need to protect your files from other users on your local area network (LAN) and users who have physical access to your Mac. If you don't want anyone messing with your files, check out the security measures in the following sections.

Blocking or limiting connections

First, open the Sharing pane in System Settings by choosing ⇨ System Settings ⇨ General ⇨ Sharing and then set each of the switches to Off (white) unless you absolutely need to use those services. Disabling all the services in the Sharing pane helps prevent other people from accessing your Mac across the network.

Locking down files with FileVault

If you never want anyone to be able to access the files in your Home folder without your permission, turn on FileVault. This feature allows you to encrypt your entire disk and protect it with the latest government-approved encryption standard: Advanced Encryption Standard with 128-bit keys (AES-128).

When you turn on FileVault, you're asked to set a master password for the computer. After you do, you or any other administrator can use that master password if you forget your regular account login password.

WARNING

If you turn on FileVault and forget both your login password and your master password, you can't log in to your account — and your data is lost forever. For safety, store a copy of the master password somewhere secure.

FileVault is useful primarily if you store sensitive information on your Mac. If you're logged out of your user account, and other people gain access to your Mac, there's no way for them to access your data. Period.

Because FileVault encrypts your entire hard drive, you may be prevented from carrying out some tasks that normally access your disk. For one thing, some backup apps can choke if FileVault is enabled; Time Machine works with FileVault and is fine. Also, if you're not logged in to your user account, other users can't access your Shared folder(s).

REMEMBER

Because FileVault is constantly encrypting and decrypting files, it can slow older Macs a bit when you add or save new files, and it can take extra time before it lets you log out, restart, or shut down. If your Mac is less than 5 years old, you'll probably notice little or no delay from enabling FileVault.

To turn on FileVault, follow these steps:

1. **Choose ⇨ System Settings ⇨ Privacy & Security to open the Privacy & Security pane in System Settings.**

2. **Scroll down to the Security section at the bottom of the pane, and then click the FileVault button to display the FileVault screen.**

3. **Click the Turn On button, and then authenticate yourself with your password or Touch ID when challenged.**

   A dialog opens, giving you the choice between allowing your iCloud account to unlock your disk and reset your password, if needed, or creating a recovery key (see Figure 21-4).

4. **Select the Allow My iCloud Account to Unlock My Disk option button or the Create a Recovery Key and Do Not Use My iCloud Account option button, as appropriate.**

   Using your iCloud account gives you more flexibility, provided nobody compromises your iCloud account. Creating a recovery key gives you a long alphanumeric key that you would normally print out and store somewhere safe offline.

5. **Click the Continue button, and follow the prompts.**

FIGURE 21-4:
Choose between allowing your iCloud account to unlock FileVault and creating a recovery key you can store offline.

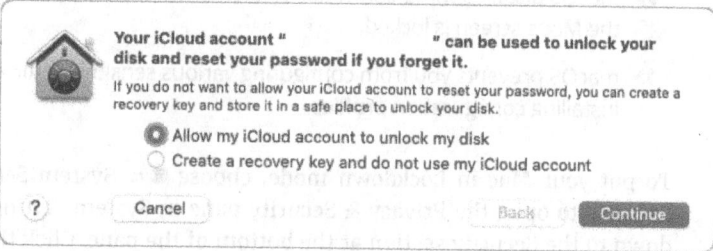

Your iCloud account "   " can be used to unlock your disk and reset your password if you forget it.

If you do not want to allow your iCloud account to reset your password, you can create a recovery key and store it in a safe place to unlock your disk.

- ● Allow my iCloud account to unlock my disk
- ○ Create a recovery key and do not use my iCloud account

(?)   Cancel   Back   Continue

To turn off FileVault, go back to the Security section of the Privacy & Security pane in System Settings, click the FileVault button to display the FileVault screen, and then click the Turn Off button on the FileVault row. Authenticate yourself, and then click the Turn Off Encryption button in the Are You Sure You Want to Turn Off FileVault? dialog.

Putting your Mac in Lockdown mode

macOS Sequoia includes a feature called Lockdown mode that enables you to fire up an extreme level of protection against someone hacking into your Mac.

Lockdown mode is designed to protect your Mac against targeted attacks using custom malware or state-sponsored spyware.

REMEMBER

iOS 16 and later versions have a similar Lockdown mode. If you need to activate Lockdown mode on your Mac, activate it on your iPhone and iPad as well.

Lockdown mode is designed for the tiny minority of users who face these types of threats. You may need to use Lockdown mode if you're a human-rights activist, a crusading journalist, or a secret agent. If you're not exposed to such threats, Lockdown mode is likely to be overkill.

To keep your Mac safe, Lockdown mode must limit some of the functionality that Mac users enjoy. Here are examples of some (only some) of the limitations that Lockdown mode imposes:

>> Messages blocks incoming message attachments, including link previews.

>> FaceTime blocks calls and invitations from people who aren't in your Contacts list.

>> Safari's just-in-time compiler for the JavaScript programming language is disabled.

>> Photos hides shared photo albums and blocks shared album invitations.

>> macOS disables wired connections to external devices or accessories while the Mac's screen is locked.

>> macOS prevents you from configuring various sensitive settings, such as installing configuration profiles.

To put your Mac in Lockdown mode, choose ⌘ ➪ System Settings ➪ Privacy & Security to open the Privacy & Security pane in System Settings, and then scroll down to the Security section at the bottom of the pane. Click the Lockdown Mode button to display the Lockdown Mode screen, and then click the Turn On button.

Setting other options for security

macOS Sequoia offers several other settings that can help keep your data safe. This section tells you where to find them and how to set them. To get started, choose ⌘ ➪ System Settings to open the System Settings app. Then you can do the following:

>> **Change your password.** Click the Login Password category in the sidebar and then click the Change button in the Login Password pane.

>> **Require a password to resume after sleep or a screen saver.** Click the Lock Screen category in the sidebar. Open the Require Password After Screen Saver Begins or Display Is Turned Off pop-up menu, and choose Immediately, After 5 Seconds, or After 1 Minute. (Don't use a longer time, because that makes your Mac less secure.)

TIP

In the Lock Screen pane, you'll also find the Show Message When Locked setting. If you want your Mac's screen to display a message when the Mac is locked, set the switch to On (blue), click the Set button, type the message in the Set a Message to Appear on the Lock Screen dialog, and then click OK. This option is popular but provides no security benefit.

>> **Limit app installation to apps from the App Store.** Click the Security & Privacy category in the sidebar, scroll down to the Security section of the Security & Privacy pane, and then click the Allow Apps Downloaded From pop-up menu. You have two choices:

- *App Store:* This setting allows you to run only apps you download from the Mac App Store. It's the safer and more restrictive setting.

- *App Store and Identified Developers:* Apple offers a Developer ID credential to certified members of the Mac Developers Program. Apple gives each developer a unique Developer ID, which allows macOS to verify that their app is not known malware and that it hasn't been tampered with. If an app doesn't have a Developer ID associated with it, macOS can let you know before you install it.

TIP

The App Store and Identified Developers option is best for most users. It allows third-party apps from Apple-vetted vendors, including Microsoft, Adobe, and thousands more. It's a lot less restrictive than the App Store option, but it still prevents you from downloading and installing apps from just anywhere.

Finally, here are three ways to tighten security from the Privacy & Security pane in System Settings:

>> **Choose which apps can use Location Services.** Click Location Services to display the Location Services screen, and you'll see a list of apps that are allowed to use your computer's current location. Set the switch for each app to Off (white) or On (blue), as needed.

>> **Limit access to your contacts, calendars, and reminders.** Click Contacts, Calendars, or Reminders in the Privacy list, and you'll see a list of the apps with access to their contents. Set the switch for each app to Off (white) or On (blue), as needed.

>> **Prune the list of apps allowed to control your Mac.** Click Accessibility in the Privacy list and then scrutinize the Allow the Applications Below to Control Your Computer list on the Accessibility screen. Set the switch for each app to Off (white) or On (blue), as needed.

Here are seven ways to protect your data:

>> Use a different strong password for each service or account.

>> Never share your passwords.

>> Don't store passwords in insecure locations (such as on sticky notes on your monitor).

>> Use a password manager (such as macOS's built-in Passwords app or a third-party app like 1Password) to store your passwords securely.

>> Don't use unsecure wireless networks.

>> Don't visit suspicious websites or open suspicious emails.

>> If you have any question about authenticity, just don't click.

Chapter **22**

Troubleshooting macOS

Macs have a great reputation for running well and just keeping on running well — and I hope your Mac does just that. But even the best hardware and software can run into difficulties sometimes, so you should be prepared to troubleshoot your Mac and its operating system at some point.

When things go wrong with your Mac, turn to the advice in this chapter. It contains tried-and-tested tips and tricks that can help you resolve many common Mac issues without a trip to the repair shop — as long as your Mac's hardware isn't dead. If it *is* dead, turn to the Apple Store or the repair shop rather than this chapter.

Before we start, you need to be clear on two key terms. First, this chapter uses the term *hard disk* generically to refer to both hard disks (mechanical disks with spinning platters) and solid-state drives, or SSDs (electronic drives with no moving parts). Second, *booting* means using a particular disk or disk partition as the *start-up disk* — the disk from which your Mac starts (or tries to).

Understanding Start-Up Disks and Booting

Although you usually see a stylish Apple logo when you turn on your computer, once in a blue moon, you may instead see a solid blue screen, a solid gray screen, a solid black screen, or something else entirely, as described in the next section.

Any of these screen types means that your Mac isn't starting up as it should. When this happens, it usually indicates that something bad has happened to your Mac or its start-up disk. Sometimes, a hardware component has bitten the dust; at other times, macOS itself has somehow been damaged.

Finding or creating a start-up disk

macOS Sequoia is available only in the Mac App Store as a download. Because you can no longer purchase a bootable installer DVD, the macOS Installer automatically creates a bootable partition named Recovery HD when you install Sequoia on a disk.

The Recovery HD partition can save your day, but you'd be wise to also make a bootable recovery disk or a clone of your Mac start-up disk in case your Mac's hard disk dies and takes the Recovery HD partition with it. If you don't, you may wish you'd done so when your Mac starts acting wonky.

WARNING

Explaining how to create a bootable recovery disk or clone is beyond the scope of this book, but you'll find full details on the Internet. Start with this Apple Support Article: https://support.apple.com/en-us/HT201372. And bear in mind that you can't start your Mac from a Time Machine backup.

TIP

A great tool for creating a recovery disk is Carbon Copy Cloner (https://bombich.com), a $49.99 app that lets you create a clone of your boot disk with a minimum of fuss. Or you can try SuperDuper! (shareware from www.shirt-pocket.com, $27.95); just add a hard disk at least as large as your boot disk, and you'll be good to go with either of these apps. Both Carbon Copy Cloner and SuperDuper! offer free trial versions that you can put through their paces.

Interpreting prohibitory signs and messages

When you turn on your Mac, it runs hardware tests, and then checks for a start-up disk containing a viable copy of macOS. If your system doesn't find such a disk on your Mac's internal hard drive, it begins looking elsewhere — on a Thunderbolt or Universal Serial Bus (USB) disk, a thumb drive, or a DVD.

When your Mac finds the (usually internal) hard drive, which contains the operating system, the start-up process continues with the subtle Apple logo and all the rest. If your Mac can't find a suitable bootable disk, the dreaded prohibitory sign appears. Think of the prohibitory sign as your Mac's way of saying, "Please provide me a start-up disk."

REMEMBER

If you have more than one start-up disk attached to your Mac, as many users do, you can choose which one your Mac boots from in the Startup Disk pane in System Settings (choose System Settings ➪ General ➪ Startup Disk) or by pressing and holding down the Option key when you start up your Mac.

If you encounter any of the warning signs shown in Figure 22-1, go through the steps outlined later in this chapter. Try them in the order listed, starting with Step 1. If one works, stop; if not, move on to the next.

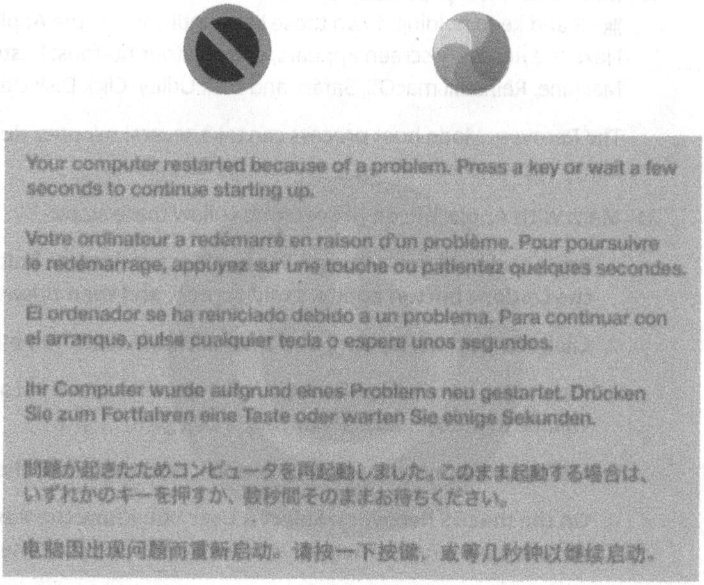

Your computer restarted because of a problem. Press a key or wait a few seconds to continue starting up.

Votre ordinateur a redémarré en raison d'un problème. Pour poursuivre le redémarrage, appuyez sur une touche ou patientez quelques secondes.

El ordenador se ha reiniciado debido a un problema. Para continuar con el arranque, pulse cualquier tecla o espere unos segundos.

Ihr Computer wurde aufgrund eines Problems neu gestartet. Drücken Sie zum Fortfahren eine Taste oder warten Sie einige Sekunden.

問題が起きたためコンピュータを再起動しました。このまま起動する場合は、いずれかのキーを押すか、数秒間そのままお待ちください。

電腦因出現問題而重新啟動。请按一下按键，或等几秒钟以继续启动。

FIGURE 22-1:
Any of these warnings means that it's trouble-shooting time.

Recovering with Recovery HD

If you see a prohibitory sign (top left in Figure 22-1), a spinning beach ball of death (top right), or a kernel-panic alert (the text in various languages that appears below the other two images) that doesn't go away when you start your Mac, first try to repair hidden damage to your hard drive with Disk Utility's First Aid feature.

Step 1: Run First Aid

In most cases, the first logical troubleshooting step is to use the First Aid option in Disk Utility.

Every drive has several strangely named components, such as B-trees, extent files, catalog files, and other creatively named invisible files. They're all involved in managing the data on your drives. Disk Utility's First Aid feature checks all those files and repairs the damaged ones.

Because your Mac isn't able to finish the boot process, you'll need to boot from the Recovery partition to perform this repair. The steps for rebooting your Mac into Recovery mode vary depending on its processor type:

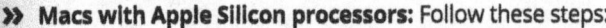

>> **Macs with Intel processors:** Restart the Mac. At the start-up chime, press ⌘+R and keep holding down these keys until you see the Apple logo appear. Next, the Recovery screen appears, offering four buttons: Restore from Time Machine, Reinstall macOS, Safari, and Disk Utility. Click Disk Utility to launch it.

The Recovery Mode boot process can take several minutes, during which time it may appear that nothing is happening. Be patient.

>> **Macs with Apple Silicon processors:** Follow these steps:

1. **Press and hold down the power button; continue to hold it down until the Options button appears mid-screen, and then release it.**

2. **Click the Options button, and then click the Continue button.**

   If your Mac has multiple bootable volumes, the macOS Recovery: Select a Volume to Recover screen appears. If not, go to Step 4.

3. **Click the volume you want to recover, and then click the Next button.**

4. **On the macOS Recovery: Select a User You Know the Password For screen, click a user (such as yourself), and then click the Next button.**

5. **In the Enter the Password dialog, type the password, and then click the Continue button.**

   The Recovery screen appears.

6. **Click Disk Utility, and then click the Continue button.**

Once you've launched Disk Utility, run First Aid like this:

1. **Click the icon for your Mac's boot hard drive in the left pane.**

   Your boot drive is the one with macOS and your Home folder on it. It's normally called Macintosh HD unless you've renamed it.

2. **Click the First Aid button in the toolbar.**

   A dialog opens, asking whether you'd like to run First Aid on that disk.

3. **Click the Run button.**

The Disk First Aid routine runs. It takes anywhere from a few minutes to an hour or more for First Aid to check and repair your disk.

4. **(Optional) Click Show Details in the dialog if you want to see (mostly unintelligible) details.**

When the routine is finished, the Done button is enabled.

If First Aid finds damage that it can't fix, a commercial disk-recovery tool such as Prosoft's Drive Genius *may* be able to repair the damage.

TIP

5. **Click the Done button.**

6. **Quit Disk Utility by choosing Disk Utility ⇨ Quit Disk Utility. Alternatively, press ⌘+Q or simply click the red Close gumdrop button.**

The Recovery screen appears again.

7. **Choose ⬤ ⇨ Restart to exit Recovery mode and restart your Mac.**

Make sure you're running a current version of any disk utilities you try; older versions may not be compatible with macOS Sequoia (or APFS) and could make things worse.

WARNING

If everything checks out with First Aid, but you still get the prohibitory sign after your Mac restarts, proceed to the next section to try booting into Safe mode.

Step 2: Boot into Safe mode

Booting your Mac in Safe mode may help you resolve your start-up issue by not loading nonessential (and non-macOS) software at boot time. Again, the way you invoke Safe mode depends on your Mac's processor type:

>> **Macs with Intel processors:** Press and hold down the Shift key during start-up.

>> **Macs with Apple M processors:** Shut down your Mac, wait 10 seconds, and then press and hold the power button on your Mac until the Startup Options window appears. Select your Mac's start-up disk. Then press and hold down the Shift key, click Continue in Safe Mode, and release the Shift key.

When the login screen appears, you'll see Safe Boot in red in the upper-right corner.

If your Mac is set up so that you don't have to log in, keep pressing the Shift key during start-up until Finder loads completely. If you do log in to your Mac, type your password as usual — but before clicking the Log In button, press the Shift key again and hold it down until Finder loads completely.

You'll know that you held the Shift key long enough if your login items don't load — assuming that you *have* login items. You can designate them in the Login Items pane in the System Settings app (choose System Settings ➪ General ➪ Login Items), but you may also find that some apps create them without consulting you.

To confirm that a Mac is in Safe mode, click to open the Apple menu, then hold down Option and click System Information. In the System Information window, click the Software heading in the sidebar on the left, and then verify that the Boot Mode readout in the right pane says Safe.

Booting in Safe mode does three things to help you with troubleshooting:

» It forces a directory check of the start-up (boot) volume.

» It loads only required kernel extensions (some of the items in /System/Library/Extensions).

» It runs only Apple-installed essential start-up items (some of the items in /Library/StartupItems and /System/Library/StartupItems). The Startup Items in the Library folders are different from the Login Items in the Login pane in System Preferences. Startup items run at boot time before the login window even appears; login items run only after you log into your user account.

Taken together, these changes often work around issues caused by software or directory damage on the start-up volume.

Some features don't work in Safe mode. Among them are DVD Player, capturing video (in iMovie or other video-editing software), and using FaceTime or certain audio input or output devices. Use Safe mode only when you need to troubleshoot a start-up issue, and reboot in normal mode as soon as possible.

Step 3: Zap the PRAM/NVRAM

If your Mac has an Apple Silicon processor, ignore this step. It doesn't apply to your Mac.

Sometimes, your Mac's parameter RAM (PRAM) or nonvolatile RAM (NVRAM) becomes scrambled and needs to be reset. Both of these small pieces of memory aren't erased or forgotten when you shut down your Mac. They keep track of things such as the following:

» Time-zone setting

» Startup-volume choice

- » Speaker volume
- » Any recent kernel-panic information
- » DVD region setting

To reset (a process often called *zapping*) your PRAM/NVRAM, restart your Mac and press ⌘+Option+P+R until your Mac restarts itself. It's kind of like a hiccup. You might see the spinning-disc pointer for a minute or two while your Mac thinks about it. Then the icon disappears, and your Mac chimes again (unless your Mac is a chimeless model) and restarts. Some power users believe that you should zap more than once, letting the Mac chime two, three, or even four times before releasing the keys and allowing the start-up process to proceed.

Now restart your Mac without holding down any keys. If the PRAM/NVRAM zap didn't fix your Mac, move on to "Step 4: Reinstall macOS."

REMEMBER

Your chosen start-up disk, time zone, and sound volume may be reset to their default values when you zap your PRAM. So after zapping, open the System Settings app to reselect your usual start-up disk and time zone, and set the sound volume the way you like it if necessary.

Step 4: Reinstall macOS

Reinstalling macOS is a second-to-last resort when your Mac won't boot correctly because it takes the longest and is the biggest hassle. Apple has a technical note on reinstallation at `https://support.apple.com/en-us/HT204904`.

Follow the instructions, taking care *not* to erase your disk before you reinstall macOS. As long as you don't erase the disk before you reinstall, you won't lose any data. This procedure simply installs a fresh copy of Sequoia; it doesn't affect your files, settings, or anything else.

Step 5: Things to try before taking your Mac in for repair

TIP

To get your Mac up and running again, you can try one of the following:

- » **Call the tech-support hotline.** Before you drag your Mac down to the shop, try calling 1-800-SOS-APPL, the Apple Tech Support hotline. The service representatives there may be able to suggest something else that you can try. If your Mac is still under warranty, it's even free.

>> **Ask a local user group for help.** Another thing you might consider is contacting your local Mac user group. You can find a group of Mac users near you by visiting Apple's User Group webpages at www.apple.com/usergroups.

If neither suggestion works for you, and you're still seeing something you shouldn't when you start up your Mac, you have big trouble. You could have any one of the following problems:

>> Your Mac's hard drive is dead.

>> Your Mac has some other type of hardware failure.

>> All your Mac's start-up disks are defective (unlikely).

The bottom line: If you still can't start up normally after trying all the cures explained in this chapter, you almost certainly need to have your Mac serviced by a qualified technician.

If Your Mac Crashes at Start-Up

Start-up crashes are other bad things that can happen to your Mac. These crashes can be more of a hassle to resolve than prohibitory-sign problems, but they're rarely fatal.

You know that a *crash* has happened when you see a Quit Unexpectedly dialog, a frozen cursor, a frozen screen, or any other disabling event. A *start-up crash* happens when your system shows a crash symptom any time between the moment you flick the power key or switch (or restarting) and the moment you have full use of the desktop.

Try all the steps in the preceding sections before you panic. In most cases, the easiest way to fix start-up crashes is to reinstall macOS from the Recovery partition. Again, Apple details this procedure online at https://support.apple.com/en-us/HT204904.

If you're still unsuccessful after that point, read "Step 5: Things to try before taking your Mac in for repair."

Managing Storage with the Storage Feature

macOS's Storage feature provides assistance if your Mac's start-up disk gets close to being full.

Here's why it's in the troubleshooting chapter: Your Mac will slow to a crawl as its start-up disk gets close to full. If the disk is more than 90 percent filled, you'll begin to experience slowness and jerkiness. And as the drive approaches 100 percent fullness, things grow even slower and jerkier.

The Storage feature aims to help you out as your disk fills up by scanning for duplicates, old email attachments, and downloads so you can delete them or move them to the cloud. But you should read what follows even if your disk isn't approaching fullness right now, because Storage offers several options that may keep your disk from ever getting too full.

To check it out, choose ⇨ System Settings, click the General button to display the General pane, and then click the Storage button to display the Storage pane (see Figure 22-2). The Recommendations section provides suggestions, such as the following, for fixing your Mac's storage woes:

WARNING

>> **Store in iCloud.** Store all your files in iCloud to save space, keeping only recently opened files on your Mac when storage space is needed.

Storing files in iCloud could be convenient, but it's going to chew through your 5GB of free iCloud storage in no time. With additional iCloud storage currently selling for 99 cents a month (50GB), $3.99 a month (200GB), $9.99 a month (2TB), $29.99 a month (6TB), or $59.99 a month (12TB), it could be costly as well as convenient.

>> **Optimize Storage.** Remove from your Mac any movies and TV shows you've already watched.

>> **Empty Trash automatically.** Automatically empty files that have been in the Trash for 30 days.

>> **Recommendations for individual apps and categories.** This section lists categories, such as Applications and Documents, and individual apps, such as Mail and Messages, where you might be able to save some space. Click the Info icon (the *i*-in-a-circle) to open a dialog that explains the possibilities for that category or app.

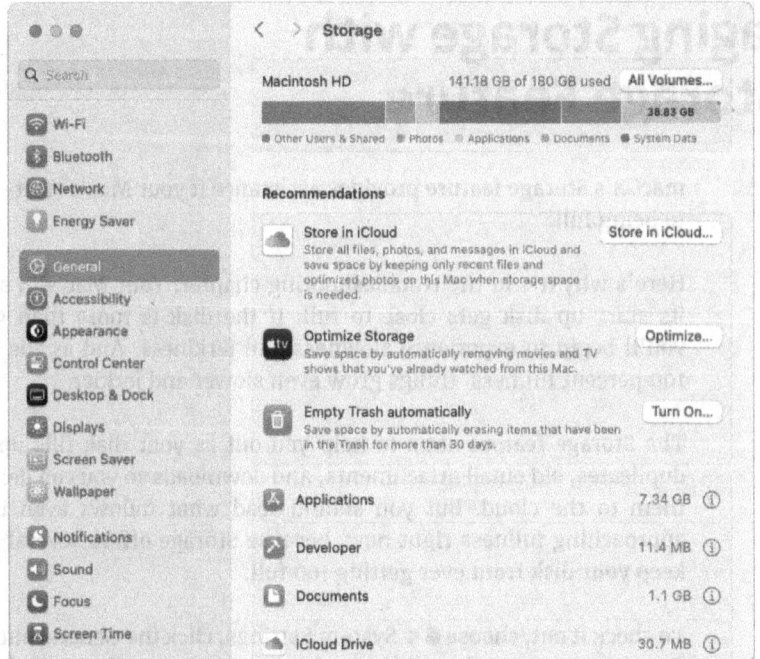

FIGURE 22-2:
If your disk is
getting full, use
the Storage
recommenda-
tions to
free up space.

When your Mac's disk runs low on space, work your way through the recommendations on the Storage screen to make sure that the shortage never becomes critical.

5

The Part of Tens

Learn ten ways to improve your Mac experience.

Put ten essential tools to use.

Chapter **23**

Ten Ways to Improve Your Mac Experience

Have you ever wished your Mac were faster? Join the club! It happens to us all sooner or later, even if you bought your Mac only last year and paid a pretty penny to max out its memory.

This chapter shows you ten ways to improve your Mac experience. Some of the tips make your Mac feel faster, or more responsive, or easier to use (or all three). Other tips actually make your Mac run faster.

Use Those Keyboard Shortcuts

Keyboard shortcuts (see Table 23-1 for the most useful ones) can make navigating your Mac a much faster experience compared with constantly using the mouse or trackpad. Keyboard shortcuts offer these benefits:

>> Your hands stay on the keyboard, reducing the amount of time that you remove your hand from the keyboard to fiddle with the mouse or trackpad.

>> When you memorize keyboard shortcuts with your head, your fingers will memorize them, too.

>> The more keyboard shortcuts you use, the faster you can do what you're doing.

TABLE 23-1   **Great Keyboard Shortcuts**

Keyboard Shortcut	Name	What It Does
⌘+O	Open	Opens the selected item.
⌘+. (period)	Cancel	Cancels the current operation in many apps, including Finder. The Esc key often does the same thing as Cancel.
⌘+P	Print	Brings up a dialog that enables you to print the active window's contents. (See Chapter 19 for info on printing.)
⌘+X	Cut	Cuts the current selection and places it on the Clipboard. (Chapter 9 covers the Clipboard.)
⌘+C	Copy	Copies the current selection and places it on the Clipboard.
⌘+V	Paste	Pastes the contents of the Clipboard at the insertion point's location.
⌘+F	Find	Displays a Searching window or tab in Finder; displays a Find dialog in most other apps.
⌘+A	Select All	Selects the entire contents of the active window in many apps, including Finder.
⌘+Z	Undo	Undoes the last thing you did in many apps, including Finder.
⌘+Shift+Z	Redo	Redoes the last thing you undid in many apps, including Finder.
⌘+Shift+?	Help	Displays the Mac Help window in Finder; usually the shortcut to summon Help in other apps.

Keyboard Shortcut	Name	What It Does
⌘+Q	Quit	Perhaps the most useful keyboard shortcut of all. Quits the current app (but not Finder because it's always running).
⌘+Shift+Q	Log Out	Logs out the current user. The login window appears on-screen until a user logs in.
⌘+Delete	Move to Trash	Moves the selected item to the Trash.
⌘+Shift+Delete	Empty Trash	Empties the Trash.

Using the keyboard shortcuts for commands you use often will save you a ton of effort and hours upon hours of time.

Improve Your Typing Skills

One way to make your Mac get things done sooner is to move your fingers faster. The quicker you finish a task, the quicker you're on to something else. Keyboard shortcuts are nifty tools, but improving your typing speed and accuracy *will* save you even more time. As a bonus, the more your typing skills improve, the less time you'll spend correcting errors. So you'll finish everything even faster!

The speed and accuracy that you gain have another bonus: When you're a touch typist, your fingers fly even faster on keyboard shortcuts, speeding them up even further.

The fastest way to improve your keyboarding skills is a typing training app for your Mac such as Ten Thumbs Typing Tutor ($25.99 at www.tenthumbstyping tutor.com), any of the myriad typing-instruction apps in the Mac App Store (search for *typing*), or a free typing-instruction website such as TypingTest (www.typingtest.com), which also offers free typing speed tests if you're curious. TypeRacer (https://play.typeracer.com) lets you work on your typing speed while racing against others.

Make sure your keyboard is up to the job. If your Mac is a MacBook, you're likely stuck with the built-in keyboard while you're out and about; but when you dock your MacBook at home to use your external displays (more on this shortly), you can connect most any keyboard you like — a 40 percent keyboard, a 60 percent keyboard, a full-size keyboard, an ergonomic keyboard, or even a split keyboard. The keyboard can be wired or wireless — whichever works better for you. If you have a desktop Mac, you can use your preferred keyboard all the time.

Use Text Replacements and Automatic Correction

No matter how fast and how accurately you type, you can enter text even faster by taking advantage of the Text Replacement feature built into macOS and similar automatic-correction features, such as the AutoCorrect feature in the Microsoft Office apps. With these features, you define each term you want to have replaced automatically, such as having *eavpsm* replaced with *Executive Assistant to the Vice-President of Sales & Marketing*. Then, when you type that term, the feature automatically inserts the replacement term in its place. You need never type your job title fully again.

To set up your terms in the Text Replacement feature, click System Settings on the Dock, click Keyboard near the bottom of the sidebar in the System Settings window, click Text Replacements in the Keyboard pane, and then work in the dialog that opens.

Change Your Resolution

A setting that you can change to potentially improve your Mac's performance is the resolution of your display. Most modern displays and video hardware can display multiple degrees of screen resolution. You change the resolution your display uses in the Displays pane in System Settings. Click the Displays item in the sidebar, set the Show All Resolutions switch to On, and then select a resolution to try from the list that appears. If the Show All Resolutions switch doesn't appear in the Displays pane, click Advanced at the bottom of the Displays pane to display the Advanced dialog. Set the Show Resolutions as List switch to On (blue), and then click Done.

Each LCD or LED screen has a "native resolution" specified by the number of pixels in its width and its height. The MacBook Air 15-inch M3's LED screen, for example, is 2,880 pixels wide by 1,864 pixels high. macOS normally uses the native resolution, as it gives the best image in theory, because the pixels sent to the screen map exactly to the physical pixels in the screen. But that doesn't mean that the native resolution will suit you best. You see many more items on the screen at native resolution, but you can make everything bigger by switching to a lower resolution, or make everything smaller (and see more of it) at a higher resolution.

How will this speed up your Mac? Well, if you lower the resolution, your Mac's graphics performance may improve. But the main thing is that the resolution should suit your eyes. If you can't discern icons on toolbars and other app components, switching to a lower resolution may enhance your work speed. Or if you can read more lines of smaller text comfortably at a higher resolution, that might save you time, too.

REMEMBER

Choose a resolution based on what looks best and works best for you. If things on the screen are too big or too small at your current resolution, try a higher or lower resolution until you find one that feels just right.

Finally, click Accessibility in the sidebar of the System Settings window to display the Accessibility pane, and then click Zoom in the Vision list to display the Zoom pane. Here, you can enable keyboard shortcuts and trackpad gestures to zoom in and out instantly.

Buy a Faster Mac

Apple keeps putting out faster and faster Macs at lower and lower prices, and all current Macs now ship with at least 8GB of RAM. This is the absolute minimum amount of RAM to run macOS Sequoia — but it's not enough to run Sequoia at its best, especially if you keep multiple apps running. If you're buying a Mac, consider 16GB of RAM to be the practical minimum.

Check out the latest Macs with Apple's M-series processors — they're speedy and powerful. Apple has now brought the M-series processors to the full range, from the thin-and-light MacBook Air all the way to the hefty and heavy Mac Pro. Alternatively, if you've been using an old Mac, you might get a bargain on a used Intel-based Mac that's still faster than yours. Keep in mind that the Intel-based Macs are getting long in the tooth, and Apple likely won't support them for much longer. In fact, some Apple software now requires M-series processors and won't run on Intel processors at all.

TIP

Another excellent option is to visit the Apple Store website's refurbished and clearance section. You can frequently save hundreds of dollars by purchasing a slightly used Mac that has been refurbished to factory specifications by Apple. Another advantage to Apple refurbs is that they come with an Apple warranty. If you're on a tight budget, definitely check it out (www.apple.com/shop/refurbished).

Add RAM

Your Mac can never have too much RAM, and it will run better, smoother, and faster with at least 16GB of RAM. If you have an older Mac, you may be able to add RAM at a reasonable price. You can find instructions in your User Guide booklet or on the Apple Technical Support pages (https://support.apple.com/; search for *RAM upgrade* and your Mac model).

These days, most Macs are no longer user-upgradeable. These models are sometimes difficult to open, and Apple frowns upon users opening some models at all. Plus, many Macs have the RAM soldered to the motherboard or integrated with the processor, which means they can never be upgraded. If your Mac is upgradeable and you're uncomfortable with upgrading RAM yourself, opt for the services of an authorized, certified Mac cracker-opener.

TIP

The bottom line is that it's best to order your Mac with as much RAM as you can afford in the first place. It will cost you more up front, but it's worth it in the long run.

Add a Second Display

For almost as long as I've been using a Mac, I've used one with two or more displays. All Macs today support a second display, and many support a third and fourth display. I find four displays great, but I have to admit I'm tempted by the Mac Pro, which supports a full dozen displays. In my opinion, screen real estate is among the biggest productivity enhancers you can add — right up there with typing faster.

Screen real estate is the holy grail when working in multi-windowed or multi-paletted apps such as Photoshop, Final Cut Pro, and Logic Pro X. Multiple displays are also great when you're working with two or more apps at the same time. With sufficient screen space, you can arrange all the windows and palettes for all apps in the way that best helps you work.

You don't need an expensive 4K, 5K, 6K, or 8K display, great though these can be. For one or two hundred bucks, you can find a second display that will double your screen real estate. Or if you have an iPad of recent vintage, read the next section.

Use Your iPad as an Extra Display

The Sidecar feature allows you to use a late-model iPad as an extra screen for your late-model Mac. You'll find the official list of supported hardware and tips for using Sidecar at https://support.apple.com/en-us/HT210380. Or just connect your iPad to your Mac with a USB cable, open System Settings, and then click Displays in the sidebar. In the Displays pane, click the Add (+) pop-up menu to the right of the thumbnails for your current displays, and then click the iPad in the Mirror or Extend To list. Your iPad appears as a thumbnail along with your other displays, and you can click the thumbnail to display the controls for configuring the iPad's display settings.

If the Add (+) pop-up menu doesn't appear, or if it does appear but the iPad doesn't appear on the Mirror or Extend To list, make sure that the iPad and your Mac are both signed in to the same iCloud account.

When you've chosen settings for the iPad as a display, click the Arrange button at the top of the Displays pane to open the Arrange Displays dialog. Here, drag the thumbnails for the iPad and the other displays into an arrangement that reflects their physical positioning. Then you'll be able to move the pointer off a display and straight onto the iPad for easy navigation.

Upgrade to a Solid-State Drive (SSD)

The latest and greatest storage device to appear is the solid-state drive (SSD). It uses flash memory in place of a mechanical hard drive's spinning platters, which means, among other things, that it has no moving parts. Another benefit is that an SSD performs most operations at up to twice the speed of mechanical drives.

The bad news is that an SSD is more expensive — three or more times the price per gigabyte — than a mechanical hard drive or a hybrid drive with the same capacity. That said, most users report that it's the best money they ever spent on an upgrade. So if your Mac has a hard drive, and that hard drive dies, look to replace it with an SSD.

If your Mac is a model that requires pro skills and tools to open it, plus an oxy-acetylene torch (okay, a soldering kit) to replace the drive, you can even use an external SSD as a temporary fix.

After switching to an SSD start-up drive — internal or external — your old Mac will feel almost new again.

Get More Storage

Your Mac will run slower and slower as its start-up disk gets fuller and fuller. If you can't afford to replace your start-up disk with a bigger SSD or purchase a bigger external SSD to use as a boot disk, another option is to get a big external hard disk (much less expensive per megabyte than an SSD) and move some of your data off your start-up disk and onto the external disk.

You can connect external hard disks (or SSDs) via USB or Thunderbolt. All Mac models that can run macOS Sequoia have either USB 3 and Thunderbolt 2 or USB 4 and Thunderbolt 3. Usually, a single USB-C port provides both the USB and Thunderbolt connectivity.

To check which versions of USB and Thunderbolt your Mac has, follow these steps:

1. **Click to open the Apple menu.**

2. **Press Option to display the System Information command in place of the About This Mac command.**

3. **Click System Information to open the System Information app.**

4. **In the sidebar, expand the Hardware category if it's collapsed.**

5. **Toward the bottom of the Hardware category, look at the Thunderbolt/ USB4 item and the USB item.**

TECHNICAL STUFF

Thunderbolt is faster than USB 3 and USB 4, but relatively few Thunderbolt devices are available, and most of them are more expensive than their USB 3 and USB 4 counterparts. This means a USB 3 or USB 4 device is usually a better choice than a Thunderbolt device. Unless the disk is preformatted for a PC and requires reformatting, there's nothing more you have to do.

Whether you get a USB device or a Thunderbolt device, you can usually just plug it in to your Mac's USB-C/Thunderbolt port and start using it. Depending on the cable the drive has, you may need a USB-C adapter, or a USB-C hub or dock, to make the connection.

Once you've connected your external disk, you can move data to it from your Mac's start-up disk. So copy the files or folders (your large files and folders are likely contained in your Pictures, Music, Movies, and Documents folders) to the new external disk; confirm that the files have been copied properly; make sure you have a backup, just in case; and then delete the files from your start-up disk.

IN THIS CHAPTER

» **Crunching numbers with Calculator**

» **Using Activity Monitor**

» **Getting a handle on your computer with Disk Utility**

» **Managing passwords with the Passwords app**

» **Transferring information with Migration Assistant**

» **Getting the lowdown on your Mac's hardware and software with System Information**

» **Taking your Mac to the next level with Terminal**

» **Scanning documents with Image Capture**

» **Applying virtual sticky notes to your screen with Stickies**

» **Using AirPort Utility**

Chapter **24**

Ten Tools That Make Your Life Easier

acOS Sequoia comes with a plethora of useful apps and utilities that make using your Mac more pleasant, or make you more productive when you use your Mac, or both. This chapter makes sure you're familiar with ten tools that you're likely to find useful.

macOS classes some of these tools, such as Calculator and Password, as "apps" and stores them in the Applications folder, which you can click in the Finder sidebar or display by choosing Go⇨ Applications or pressing ⌘+Shift+A. macOS classes other tools as "utilities" and stores them in the Utilities folder, which is a subfolder of the Applications folder. You can reach the Utilities folder quickly in Finder by choosing Go⇨ Utilities or pressing ⌘+Shift+U. You don't need to worry about the distinction between apps and utilities or where the tools live, because you can run all the tools from Launchpad. Open Launchpad, start typing the tool's name, and then click the appropriate result.

Calculator

 Need to do some quick math? The Calculator app gives you a simple calculator with all the basic number-crunching functions of a pocket calculator. To use it, you can either click the keys with the mouse or type numbers and operators (math symbols such as +, −, and =) using the number keys on your keyboard (or numeric keypad, if you have one). Calculator also offers a History feature (View⇨ Show History) to track your computations, as you can see on the left in Figure 24-1.

FIGURE 24-1:
Calculator with
the History pane
(left) and the
Convert
pane (right).

Calculator can also perform many types of conversion, including angles, area, and force (great when you need to convert poundals to newtons or whatever). Choose View⇨ Convert to switch to Convert view, enter the input in the top box, and then click the upper pop-up menu and select the input unit in the window that appears (see the right screen in Figure 24-1). Next, click the lower pop-up menu and select the output unit. The killer feature is live currency conversion — Calculator grabs the current exchange rate off the Internet before returning the result.

Beyond that, Calculator has three modes: Basic, Scientific, and Programmer. Basic is the default, and you access the other two modes as follows:

>> Pressing ⌘+2 (View ⇨ Scientific) turns the formerly anemic calculator into a powerful scientific calculator.

>> If you prefer Reverse Polish Notation (RPN), press ⌘+R or choose View ⇨ RPN Mode.

>> Choosing View ⇨ Programmer (⌘+3) turns Calculator into the programmer's friend, letting you display your data in binary, octal, hexadecimal, ASCII, and Unicode. It also performs programming operations, such as shifts and byte swaps. (If you're a programmer, you know what all that means; if you aren't, it really doesn't matter.)

TECHNICAL STUFF

One more thing: Spotlight (and Siri) can perform many basic math calculations and conversions faster than you can launch the Calculator app.

TIP

Activity Monitor

In Unix, which is the underlying operating system that powers macOS, the apps and other things going on behind the scenes are called *processes*. Each app and the operating system itself can run several processes at the same time. In Figure 24-2, you see 644 processes running, most of them behind the scenes. When this screen-shot was taken, the Mac had only a few apps running — the insuppressible Finder, Safari, System Settings, and Activity Monitor (its icon is shown in the margin).

To display the two CPU monitor windows on the right side of the Activity Monitor window, as shown in Figure 24-2, choose Window ⇨ CPU Usage (⌘+2) and Window ⇨ CPU History (⌘+3).

You also select what appears on the Activity Monitor's Dock icon — CPU Usage (shown in Figure 24-2), CPU History, Network Usage, Disk Activity, or the Activity Monitor — by choosing View ⇨ Dock Icon and then clicking the item you want on the continuation menu. All but the Activity Monitor icon appear *live*, meaning that they update every few seconds to reflect the current state of affairs. You can't display CPU Usage or CPU History in a window and on the Dock icon at the same time. Those two items can be displayed on the Dock or a window, but not both.

To choose how often these updates occur, choose View ⇨ Update Frequency, and then click Very Often (1 Sec), Often (2 Sec), or Normally (5 Sec).

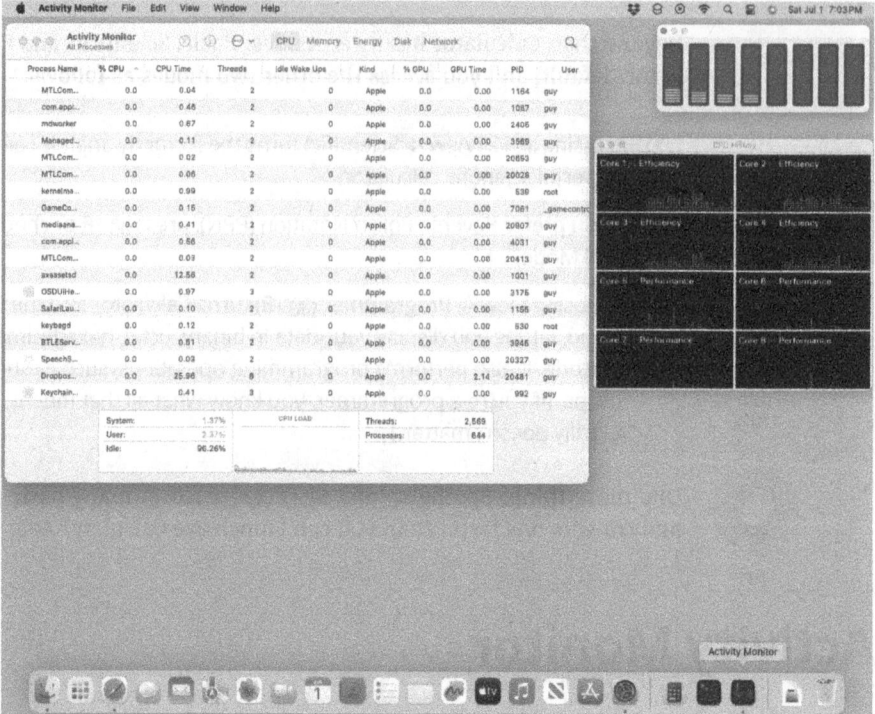

FIGURE 24-2:
The Activity
Monitor window,
two little CPU
monitors, and the
Activity Monitor
Dock icon.

WARNING

Setting Activity Monitor to update more frequently causes it to use more CPU cycles, which can decrease your Mac's overall performance slightly.

Finally, the bottom portion of the Activity Monitor window displays information for the active tab. Select the CPU, Memory, Energy, Disk, or Network tab at the top of the window, and the middle and bottom portions of the Activity Monitor window change to reflect that selection.

TECHNICAL STUFF

Because all Macs that can run Sequoia have at least a dual-core processor, you'll see at least two, and possibly four or more, CPUs displayed in Activity Monitor, one for each core.

Geeks and troubleshooters (and even you) can use Activity Monitor to identify what processes are running, which user owns the process, and how much CPU capacity and memory the process is using. You can even use this feature to quit or force-quit a process that you think might be causing problems for you.

WARNING

Messing around in Activity Monitor isn't a good idea for most users. If you're having problems with an app or with macOS, try quitting open apps, force-quitting apps (press ⌘+Option+Esc), logging out and then logging back in again, or restarting your Mac before you start mucking around with killing processes.

Disk Utility

 If you're having problems with your hard drive or need to make changes to it, Disk Utility is a good place to start. Start by clicking a disk or volume in the column on the left and then click one of the buttons on the toolbar as described in the following sections.

APFS VERSUS HFS+

In the old days, the term *partitioning* described creating multiple virtual disks out of a single hard or solid-state drive. But with macOS High Sierra, Apple introduced a new filesystem called APFS (Apple File System). The old scheme (prior to High Sierra) is HFS+ (Hierarchical File System +). In other words, APFS is the modern replacement for HFS+, though HFS+ is still available in Disk Utility.

According to Apple, when you install macOS High Sierra, Mojave, Catalina, Big Sur, Monterey, Ventura, Sonoma, or Sequoia on a solid-state drive (SSD) or other all-flash storage device, the volume will *automatically* be converted to APFS. If, however, the drive is *not* solid-state or flash — a Fusion drive or a traditional hard disk — it will *not* be converted to APFS.

Disk Utility in Sequoia can format most storage devices using either filesystem. If you need to reformat a device manually, consider these points made in a helpful Apple Support article:

- APFS requires macOS High Sierra or later. Earlier versions of the Mac operating system don't mount APFS-formatted volumes.

- APFS is optimized for SSDs and other all-flash storage devices.

- Disk Utility tries to detect the type of storage you're formatting and then shows the appropriate format in the Format menu. If it can't detect the type of storage, it defaults to Mac OS Extended (aka HFS+), which works with all versions of macOS.

Long story short, if you have to format an SSD, use APFS; for all other internal drive types, use HFS+. To find out which format (filesystem) a device is currently using, Control-click or right-click the device in Finder, and choose Get Info from the contextual menu. In the info window that opens, look at the Format readout in the General section. *Format: APFS* means that the device is using APFS, *Format: Mac OS Extended* means the device is using HFS+.

Although APFS will allow you to create partitions instead of volumes, volumes are almost always the better choice.

Volume +/–

The Volume + and Volume – buttons make it easier than ever to subdivide your hard or solid-state disk into virtual volumes, which look and act like separate disks but are volumes on a single disk. If you think this sounds a lot like what we used to call *partitioning*, it is. But to understand the difference between a volume and a partition, you first have to understand the difference between APFS and HFS+ by reading the nearby sidebar.

Partition button

Speaking of partitions, you can use the Partition button to create disk *partitions* (multiple volumes on a single disk) on disks formatted as HFS+. macOS treats each partition as a separate disk. The Partition button is enabled only when an eligible item is selected in the column on the left.

Partitioning a drive lets you create multiple volumes. A *volume* is a storage space that (from the Mac's point of view) looks and acts just like a hard drive. A *partition* is simply a designated volume on a drive, separate from all other partitions (volumes). You can create any number of partitions, but it's a good idea to limit yourself to no more than a small handful.

By the same token, it's absolutely not necessary to use partitions unless you're running Boot Camp (a feature that enables dual-booting macOS and Windows) on an Intel-powered Mac. Many users never partition a hard drive and get along just fine. If you do choose to partition, you probably should limit the number of partitions you create. An iMac with a 1TB drive will do just fine as shipped (with a single partition); there's no need to create more.

WARNING

Be careful here. Although some adjustments can be made to partitions without loss of data, not all adjustments can. Disk Utility will warn you if what you're about to do will permanently erase your data, so make sure you read all warnings that pop up. And, of course, you should always have a backup (see Chapter 21) before making changes to your Mac's disk.

Finally, if you click the Partition button with an APFS disk selected in the sidebar, you'll see an explanation that suggests you might be happier with a volume than with a partition.

First Aid button

If you suspect that something's not quite right with your Mac's start-up disk (or any other disk connected to your Mac), try using Disk Utility's First Aid feature to verify and (if necessary) repair the disk. Select the ailing disk in the sidebar and then click the First Aid button on the Disk Utility toolbar. In the dialog that asks if you'd like to run First Aid on the selected disk, click the Run button.

If the disk you're trying to repair is your Mac's start-up disk, Disk Utility will warn you that it needs to temporarily lock the boot volume and that other apps will be unresponsive until the operation has completed. Go have a cup of coffee or something; the process takes 15–30 minutes for most disks.

When First Aid is finished, you'll get information about any problems that the software finds. If First Aid doesn't find any problems, you can go on your merry way, secure in the knowledge that that disk is A-OK. If First Aid turns up a problem that it can't fix, it will advise you what to do next. In most cases, that advice is to boot your Mac to Recovery mode and run First Aid again.

Here's how to boot to Recovery mode: On Macs with Intel processors, restart the Mac and hold down ⌘+R. On Macs with Apple Silicon processors, press and hold down the power button until the Recovery Options screen appears, and then click Continue.

TIP

You can't use Disk Utility First Aid to fix a CD or DVD; neither can you use it to fix most disk image (DMG) files. These types of disks are read-only and can't be altered.

Erase button

Use Erase to format (erase) any disk except the current start-up disk.

WARNING

When you format a disk, you erase all information on it permanently. Formatting can't be undone — so unless you're *absolutely sure* this is what you want, don't do it. Unless you have no use for whatever's currently on the disk, make a complete backup of the disk before you format it. If the data is critical, you should have at least two known-to-be-valid backup copies of that disk before you reformat.

After you click the Erase button, a dialog opens, prompting you to name the disk you're about to erase and specify the post-erasure format in the drop-down Format menu.

REMEMBER

Use Mac OS Extended (Journaled) for rotational and hybrid disks. Use APFS for SSDs.

WARNING

Don't try any of the other options (case-sensitive, encrypted, and other variations) unless you know what you're doing and have a good reason. Formatting a disk using many of these options can cause Mac software to misbehave. Don't do it. Choose only Mac OS Extended (Journaled) or APFS — unless you're prepared to spend time troubleshooting when your Mac doesn't work as expected.

This warning applies only to bootable disks with macOS installed on them. If the disk isn't going to be used as a boot disk, you can format it any way you care to.

Mount/Unmount button

A drive can be connected but not available to your Mac. When you eject a hard drive or SSD, for example, it's still connected to the computer but doesn't appear in Finder. This drive is called an *unmounted disk.*

The Mount/Unmount button lets you dismount (eject) or mount a connected disk or partition on a disk. For reasons that should be obvious, you can't eject the disk from which your Mac booted.

Info button

Click the Info button to see myriad technical details about the selected disk, including its size, capacity, and free and used space. You find out more about Disk Utility (mostly how to use it for troubleshooting) in Chapter 22.

Passwords App

NEW

Sequoia introduces a new password-management app, called simply Passwords, which replaces the Keychain Access utility that managed passwords in earlier versions of macOS. Passwords keeps your passwords encrypted; enables you to sync your passwords seamlessly across your Apple devices, plus your Windows PC (if it runs Apple's iCloud for Windows software); and lets you look up and change passwords. Passwords even warns you about any of your passwords that may be weak, compromised, or otherwise problematic.

To get started, launch Passwords by clicking Launchpad on the Dock and clicking the Passwords icon on the Launchpad screen. Enter your Sequoia login password to authenticate yourself as being on the side of the angels, and the Passwords interface appears (see Figure 24-3).

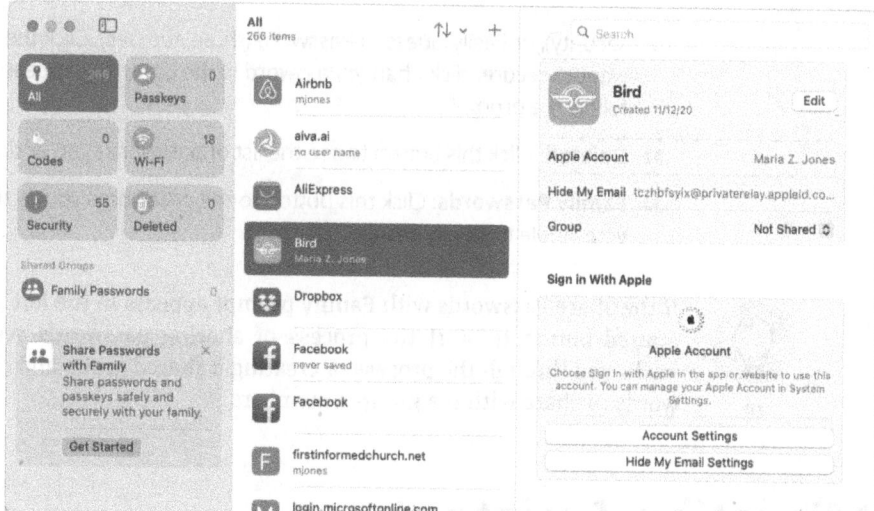

FIGURE 24-3:
The Passwords app gives you quick access to your passwords and warns you about weak or compromised passwords.

TIP If you have passwords, verification codes, and notes stored in another password manager, you can import them into Passwords. Export the passwords or other information from that password manager in comma-separated values (CSV) format, and then import them into Passwords by choosing File ⇨ Import Passwords and following the prompts.

Passwords is straightforward to use. Normally, you'll want to start by clicking one of the buttons in the left pane:

>> **All:** Click this button to see all the passwords that Passwords is storing.

>> **Passkeys:** Click this button to see only passkeys. You may not have any.

>> **Codes:** Click this button to see authentication codes (such as those for accessing websites on which you have accounts).

>> **Wi-Fi:** Click this button to see your stored Wi-Fi passwords. Click the network for which you want to see or manipulate the password. You can then copy the password by clicking it and clicking Copy Password in the bubble that appears; share the password by clicking the Share icon, and then choosing the means of sharing on the pop-up menu; or display a QR code for the network by clicking Show Network QR Code. If you've tired of this network, click the Forget This Network button, and then click the Forget button in the Are You Sure You Want to Forget This Wi-Fi Network? dialog.

>> **Security:** Click this button to see the list of passwords with which Passwords has identified a security problem. Each password shows Passwords' objection, such as Compromised Password (meaning it has appeared in a data breach), Reused Password (you shouldn't reuse passwords, as doing so reduces your

security), or Easily Guessed Password (three guesses). Click the password you want to secure, click Change Password in the pane that appears, and then follow the prompts.

>> **Deleted:** Click this button to see the list of passwords you've deleted.

>> **Family Passwords:** Click this button to see passwords you've shared with your Apple ID family group.

TIP

If the Share Passwords with Family prompt appears in the left pane, click the Get Started button to start the process of sharing passwords securely. Passwords walks you through the process of creating a shared group and choosing the passwords to share with the group's members.

Migration Assistant

Migration Assistant enables you to transfer your account and other user information from another Mac, another volume on the current Mac, a Windows PC, or a Time Machine backup. You need to authenticate as an administrator to use it, but it's a pretty handy way to transfer an entire account without having to re-create your preferences and other settings. When you first installed Sequoia (or when you booted your nice, new Sequoia-based Mac for the first time), the setup utility asked you whether you wanted to transfer your information from another Mac. If you answered in the affirmative, it ran Migration Assistant.

TIP

Migration Assistant isn't just for new Sequoia installs. You can launch Migration Assistant anytime to transfer all or some user accounts, apps, settings, and files from another Mac, PC, or Time Machine backup to this one. You can also use it after replacing a hard drive or reinstalling macOS. Last but not least, Migration Assistant can import user accounts, apps, settings, and files from Windows PCs as well as from Macs.

System Information

System Information is a little utility you can launch by clicking , holding down Option to make the System Information menu item replace the About This Mac menu item, and then clicking System Information. You can also launch System Information from Launchpad or by clicking the System Report button at the bottom of the About pane in System Settings, which you reach by clicking the About button in the General pane.

System Information provides in-depth information about your Mac's hardware and software. If you're curious about arcane questions such as what processor your Mac has or what devices are stashed inside it or are connected to it, open System Information, and start digging. Click various items in the Contents list on the left side of the window, and information about the item appears on the right side of the window. System Information is read-only: The utility lets you view information but not change it, so you can't mangle your Mac's settings here. (If you need to mangle settings, use the System Settings app — or Terminal, which you'll meet next.)

If you ever have occasion to call for technical support for your Mac, software, or peripherals, you may be asked to provide information from System Information.

TIP

Terminal

macOS is based on Unix. If you need proof — or if you want to operate your Mac as the Unix machine that it is — Terminal is the place to start.

Because Unix is a command-line-based operating system, you use Terminal to type your commands. You can issue commands that show a directory listing, copy and move files, search for filenames or contents, or establish or change passwords. In short, if you know what you're doing, you can do everything on the command line that you can do in macOS. For most folks, that's not a desirable alternative to the windows and icons of the Finder window. But rest assured that true geeks who are also Mac lovers get all misty-eyed about the combination of a command line *and* a graphical user interface.

You can wreak havoc upon your poor operating system with Terminal. You can harm your macOS installation in many ways that just aren't possible using mere windows and icons and clicks. *Before you type a single command in Terminal, think seriously about that warning.* And if you're not 100 percent certain about the command you just typed, don't even think about pressing Return.

WARNING

Image Capture

The Image Capture app enables you to scan documents using a scanner. Plug in your scanner (usually via USB), and Image Capture may spring into life like a spaniel detecting the prospect of a walk; if not, click the Launchpad icon on the Dock, and then click Image Capture. In the Image Capture window, select your scanner in the Devices list in the sidebar. Load your first document into the scanner, and then scan it either by pressing the scanner's hardware button or by clicking the Scan button in Image Capture.

TIP

If you have an older scanner, macOS Sequoia may not have a driver for it. This is infuriating, especially if the scanner is only a few years old, and particularly if earlier versions of macOS *did* include a driver for it. In this case, look for a third-party app that supports the scanner. I use VueScan (https://www.hamrick.com), which keeps my old scanner working. It's not cheap — $49.95 to buy the Standard Edition outright; alternatively, you can choose monthly payments if you need only scan in the short term — but it's much less than a new scanner. You can download a trial edition to make sure VueScan works with your scanner. (Before you ask — the trial edition watermarks each scanned image.)

Stickies

The Stickies applet enables you to apply virtual sticky notes to your screen. Stickies is great for jotting down brief notes, reminders, or other snippets of information that you need to keep to hand either temporarily or until you find a better long-term place for it. For example, you might use a sticky note to store a delivery reference number until the delivery company finally shows up; or you might capture a name and phone number in a sticky note, and then later go to the Contacts app and create a full contact record for the person.

To launch Stickies, click the Launchpad icon on the Dock, type **st**, and then click the Stickies icon. Stickies opens a couple of explanatory sticky notes to get you started. You can then create a new note by pressing ⌘+N and change its color by pressing ⌘+1 for yellow, ⌘+2 for blue, ⌘+3 for green, ⌘+4 for pink, ⌘+5 for purple, or ⌘+6 for gray.

You can type or paste in text, or paste in other data, such as an image. Resize the sticky note as needed by dragging its borders or corners, and drag it to a convenient position on the screen. Double-click the title bar, or click the icon at its right end, to collapse the sticky note to its title bar; repeat either move to expand the note again.

You can apply formatting to text if you want — but generally, if you find yourself using complex formatting in a sticky note, it's a sign that you should transfer the information to a better form of long-term storage. To do so, copy and paste is often the best bet, but you can also use the File ⇨ Export Text command to export a note's text to an unformatted text file (in .txt format) or a rich-text format text file (in either RTF or RTFD format).

To delete a sticky note, click the Close button (the square icon) in the upper-left corner, and then click the Delete Note button in the confirmation dialog that opens.

AirPort Utility

 Earlier this millennium, Apple built and sold a line of wireless access points called AirPort, including the AirPort Express (a home model including features for streaming music), the AirPort Extreme (a more powerful model aimed at the home-office and corporate markets), and the AirPort Time Capsule (essentially an AirPort Extreme with a built-in hard drive for easy backup).

Apple stopped selling the AirPort models in 2018, but many of them are still in use today — which is why macOS still includes AirPort Utility, a tool for configuring and managing them. Figure 24-4 shows AirPort Utility running on a network that has one AirPort Express and one AirPort Extreme connected.

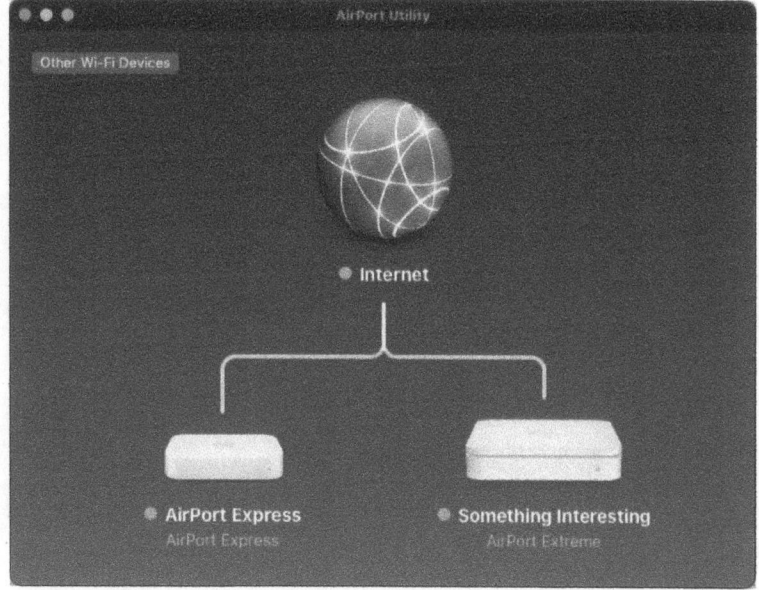

FIGURE 24-4: If you have an AirPort wireless access point, you can use AirPort Utility to configure and manage it.

Index

C

Calculator app, 442–443
Calendar app
  creating calendars, 191
  deleting calendars, 192–193
  events, 193–195
  lists, 191
  overview, 189
  sharing and publishing calendars, 192
  views, 190
Clean Up By command, Finder views, 76–77
Clean Up command, Finder views, 76
clicking
  control-click, 17
  double-click, 16–17
  right-click, 17
  single-click, 16
Clipboard
  copying, 164–166
  overview, 163–164
  pasting, 166
  Universal Clipboard, 166–167
Clock, 16
close button, 15
Column Browser, Radio, 343–345
Column view, Finder, 71–72
Command key, 44
commercial backup software, 410–411
compressing files, 157
Computer folder, 130–131
Contacts app
  adding contacts, 268–270
  importing contacts into, 270–271
  lists, 271–273
  Mail app and, 286–287
  Maps app and, 217–218
  overview, 267–268
  smart lists, 272–273
  syncing contacts across devices, 273–274
contextual menus, 40–41
Continuity Camera, 382–384
Control Center, 16, 186–187
control-click, 17

copying, 164–166
crashes, 428
Create PDF Quick Action, 99–100
Crop tool, 97
Current Location, Maps app, 213–214
custom routes, Maps app, 223–224
cycling directions, Maps app, 223

D

Dark mode, 379–381
default icons, Dock, 46–47
desktop, Finder, 61–64
Desktop & Dock pane
  Desktop section, 112–113
  Widgets section, 113
  Windows section, 113–114
dialogs, 34–36
Dictation feature, 385–386
disabled commands, 41–42
Disk Utility
  APFS, 445
  Erase button, 447–448
  First Aid feature, 423–425, 446–447
  Info button, 448
  Mount/Unmount button, 448
  Partition button, 446
  volume buttons, 446
displays
  adding second, 438–439
  resolution, 436–437
Dock
  customizing
    adding icons, 53–55
    configuring settings, 55–59
    removing icons, 55
    resizing, 55
  default icons, 46–47
  defined, 16
  global Dock settings, 56–58
  icon body language, 52
  opening app menus on, 50–52
  opening files from, 52–53
  overview, 45–46

S

About the Author

Guy Hart-Davis is the author of more than 180 computer books, including Teach Yourself VISUALLY iPhone 16; iPhone For Dummies, 2025 Edition; Teach Yourself VISUALLY MacBook Pro and MacBook Air; Killer ChatGPT Prompts: Harness the Power of AI for Success and Profit; macOS Sonoma For Dummies; Teach Yourself VISUALLY HTML and CSS, 2nd Edition; Teach Yourself VISUALLY Google Workspace; Teach Yourself VISUALLY Chromebook; Teach Yourself VISUALLY Word 2019; Teach Yourself VISUALLY iPad; and Teach Yourself VISUALLY Android Phones and Tablets, 2nd Edition.

Author's Acknowledgments

Many thanks to Steve Hayes for asking me to write this book, Hanna Sytsma for handling the administration, Lynn Northrup for editing the book skillfully, Doug Holland for reviewing the contents for technical accuracy and contributing helpful suggestions, Evelyn Wellborn for proofreading the pages closely.

Publisher's Acknowledgments

Executive Editor: Steven Hayes

Senior Editorial Assistant: Hanna Sytsma

Project Editor: Lynn Northrup

Copy Editor: Lynn Northrup

Technical Editor: Doug Holland

Production Editor: Tamilmani Varadharaj

Cover Image: © Gerald Corsi/Getty Images